A NETWORKED SELF AND LOVE

We fall in love every day, with others, with ideas, with ourselves. Stories of love excite us and baffle us. This volume is about love and the networked self. It focuses on how love forms, grows, or dissolves. Chapters address how relationships of love develop, are sustained or broken up through technologies of expression and connection. Authors explore how technologies reproduce, reorganize, or reimagine our dominant rituals of love. Contributors also address what our experiences with love teach us about ourselves, others, and the art of living. Every love story has a beginning and an end. Technology does not give love the kiss of eternity; but it can afford love new meaning.

Zizi Papacharissi is Professor and Head of the Communication Department and Professor of Political Science at the University of Illinois-Chicago, and University Scholar at the University of Illinois System. Her work focuses on the social and political consequences of online media. She has published nine books, including *Affective Publics, A Private Sphere, A Networked Self: Identity, Community, and Culture on Social Network Sites* (Routledge, 2010) and over 60 journal articles, book chapters and reviews. She is the founding and current editor of the open access journal *Social Media and Society*.

A Networked Self

Each volume in this series develops and pursues a distinct theme focused on the concept of the Networked Self. The five volumes cover the broad range of sociocultural, political, economic, and sociotechnical issues that shape and are shaped by the (networked) self in late modernity—what we have come to describe as the anthropocene.

A Networked Self: Identity, Community and Culture on Social Network Sites
A Networked Self and Platforms, Stories, Connections
A Networked Self and Love
A Networked Self and Birth, Life, Death
A Networked Self and Human Augmentics, Artificial Intelligence, Sentience

Growing upon the initial volume, *A Networked Self: Identity, Community and Culture on Social Network Sites*, published in 2010, the five volumes will form a picture of the way digital media shape contemporary notions of identity.

A NETWORKED SELF AND LOVE

Edited by Zizi Papacharissi

NEW YORK AND LONDON

First published 2018
by Routledge
711 Third Avenue, New York, NY 10017

and by Routledge
2 Park Square, Milton Park, Abingdon, Oxon OX14 4RN

Routledge is an imprint of the Taylor & Francis Group, an informa business

© 2018 Taylor & Francis

The right of the editor to be identified as the author of the editorial material, and of the authors for their individual chapters, has been asserted in accordance with sections 77 and 78 of the Copyright, Designs and Patents Act 1988.

All rights reserved. No part of this book may be reprinted or reproduced or utilized in any form or by any electronic, mechanical, or other means, now known or hereafter invented, including photocopying and recording, or in any information storage or retrieval system, without permission in writing from the publishers.

Trademark notice: Product or corporate names may be trademarks or registered trademarks, and are used only for identification and explanation without intent to infringe.

Library of Congress Cataloging-in-Publication Data
Names: Papacharissi, Zizi, editor.
Title: A networked self and love/edited by Zizi Papacharissi.
Description: New York, NY : Routledge, 2018. | Series: A networked self
Identifiers: LCCN 2017053662 | ISBN 9781138722538 (hardback) |
    ISBN 9781138722552 (pbk.)
Subjects: LCSH: Online social networks. | Information technology—Social
    aspects. | Love. | Interpersonal communication. | Identity (Psychology)
Classification: LCC HM742 .N487 2018 | DDC 302.30285—dc23
LC record available at https://lccn.loc.gov/2017053662

ISBN: 978-1-138-72253-8 (hbk)
ISBN: 978-1-138-72255-2 (pbk)
ISBN: 978-1-315-19347-2 (ebk)

Typeset in Bembo
by Apex CoVantage, LLC

Printed and bound in Great Britain by
TJ International Ltd, Padstow, Cornwall

To Si, who showed me love

CONTENTS

List of Figures		ix
List of Contributors		x
Acknowledgments		xv
1	Introduction *Zizi Papacharissi*	1
2	Calling the Irrational Unmanageable Neoliberal Self *Ilana Gershon*	12
3	Channel Navigation in Interpersonal Communication: Contemporary Practices and Proposed Future Research Directions *Penny Trieu and Nicole B. Ellison*	31
4	Interpersonal Dynamics in Online Dating: Profiles, Matching, and Discovery *David M. Markowitz, Jeffrey T. Hancock, and Stephanie Tom Tong*	50
5	Connection, Conflict, and Communication Technologies: How Romantic Couples Use the Media for Relationship Management *Catalina L. Toma*	62

6 Social Media and Subjective Well-Being:
   A Relational Perspective   86
   Samuel Hardman Taylor and Natalya N. Bazarova

7 Break-Ups and the Limits of Encoding Love   113
   Bernie Hogan

8 Technologically Enhanced Dating: Augmented Human
   Relationships, Robots, and Fantasy   129
   Brittany Davidson, Adam Joinson, and Simon Jones

9 Mobilizing the Biopolitical Category: Problems, Devices, and
   Designs in the Construction of the Gay Sexual Marketplace   156
   Kane Race

10 "How Angels are Made": Ashley Madison and the
   Social Bot Affair   173
   Tero Karppi

11 Disruptive Joy: #BlackOutDay's Affirmative Resonances   189
   Alexander Cho

12 Am I Why I Can't Have Nice Things? A Reflection on
   Personal Trauma, Networked Play, and Ethical Sight   202
   Whitney Phillips

13 On Love and Touch: The Radical Haptics of
   Gestational Surrogacy   213
   Margaret Schwartz

14 What's Love Got to Do With It?   230
   Shaka McGlotten

Index   *253*

FIGURES

6.1	A relational perspective on social media and well-being	91
8.1	Social Penetration Theory	130
8.2	Knapp's Relational Development Model	132
14.1	Love as a black box	231
14.2	All the feels	238
14.3	Blue heart emoji symbolizes a deep and stable love	239
14.4	Distributed network	240
14.5	The indebtedness of notifications	243
14.6	Me please!	246
14.7	Not very good Shibari	247

CONTRIBUTORS

Natalya (Natalie) Bazarova is Associate Professor of Communication and Technology at the Department of Communication and Director of the Social Media Lab at Cornell University. Her research examines the use and effects of communication technologies on social interactions, personal relationships, and well-being. Her research efforts have been supported with funding from the National Science Foundation, the National Institutes of Health, the U.S. Department of Agriculture, Cornell Institute for the Social Sciences, and Cornell Bronfenbrenner Center for Translational Research. She serves on the editorial boards of *Human Communication Research*, *Journal of Communication*, *Journal of Computer-Mediated Communication*, and *Social Media+Society*.

Alexander Cho is a postdoctoral scholar at the University of California Humanities Research Institute at UC Irvine. He is a digital media anthropologist who studies youth social media use with a focus on issues of race, gender, and sexuality. His work has appeared in *New Media & Society*, *Cinema Journal*, *GLQ: A Journal of Lesbian and Gay Studies*, and the volumes *Networked Affect* (MIT Press), and *Inequity in the Technopolis* (University of Texas Press). He is currently co-editing an anthology about Tumblr for the University of Iowa Press and drafting a monograph about queer youth of color social media practices.

Brittany Davidson is a PhD student at the University of Bath in the Information, Decisions, and Operations Division within the School of Management. Brittany is also associated with the Centre for Research and Evidence on Security Threats. Her PhD concerns identity, and how this changes over time and within different environments and systems. Brittany has previously written a book chapter on the challenges of Big Data analytics. She is currently writing about identity stability across various social media platforms and how collections of users change over time within forums.

Nicole B. Ellison is a professor in the School of Information at the University of Michigan. Her research addresses issues of social capital, relationship development, self-presentation, and identity in social media environments. Recent work has focused on the self-presentational strategies used by online dating participants, the role of social media in reshaping college access patterns for low-income and first-generation college students, and the ways in which users employ the communication affordances of Facebook to access social and informational support. Her work has been published in the *Journal of Computer-Mediated Communication*, *New Media & Society*, *Communication Research*, and the *Personality and Social Psychology Bulletin*. Nicole received her PhD in Communication Theory and Research from the University of Southern California's Annenberg School for Communication.

Ilana Gershon is a professor of anthropology at Indiana University. She studies how people in the United States use media for complicated social tasks, such as breaking up or hiring. She is the author of *The Breakup 2.0: Disconnecting over New Media* as well as *Down and Out in the New Economy: How People Find (or Don't Find) Work Today*. She also edits collections of imagined manuals written by anthropologists about different jobs around the world (*A World of Work*) or how humans live alongside non-human animals around the world (*Living with Animals*).

Jeffrey T. Hancock is a professor in the Department of Communication at Stanford University. He works on understanding psychological and interpersonal processes in social media. His specialism is in using computational linguistics and experiments to understand how the words we use can reveal psychological and social dynamics, such as deception and trust, emotional dynamics, intimacy and relationships, and social support. Recently he has begun work on understanding the mental models people have about algorithms in social media, as well as working on the ethical issues associated with computational social science.

Bernie Hogan is a senior research fellow at the Oxford Internet Institute at the University of Oxford. His work focuses on how individuals come to understand their identity in a networked world, particularly through the use of computer visualizations. He is part of the complex data collective, currently developing Network Canvas for social network data capture in interviews. His work on networks and identity spans the gamut from the journals *Field Methods* to *Energy Policy*, *Annals of the Association of American Geographers* to *Social Networks* and *New Media & Society* as well as within social computing venues such as CHI, CSCW, and ICWSM. His current theoretical focus is the role of names and naming in the regulation of identity on social media.

Adam Joinson holds the post of Professor of Information Systems at the University of Bath, School of Management. His research focuses on the interaction between psychology and technology, with a particular focus on how technology can be used to shape behavior, social relations, and attitudes. Recently this work has taken in privacy attitudes and behaviors, the social impact of monitoring technology, computer-mediated communication and communication behaviors, and the human aspects of cyber-security and security compliance. The EPSRC, ESRC, EU, British Academy, and UK government have funded this work, and he has published over eighty articles in the field, as well as editing the *Oxford Handbook of Internet Psychology* (OUP, 2007), and authoring two books on psychology and technology. He is principal investigator for the Cyber-Security Across the LifeSpan (www.cSALSA.uk) project, and co-investigator for the Centre for Research and Evidence on Security Threats (www.crestresearch.ac.uk). His personal website is: www.joinson.com

Simon L. Jones is a lecturer in Human-Computer Interaction at the University of Bath, UK. He is a co-investigator on the Cyber Security Across the Lifespan (cSALSA) and Language of Collaborative Manufacturing (LOCM) EPSRC-funded research projects. He conducts research in areas related to privacy, security, communication analysis, personal informatics, and data visualization. He is particularly interested in the analysis and visualization of large bodies of data for healthcare applications, and data mining techniques for studying computer-mediated communication.

Tero Karppi is Assistant Professor in the Institute of Communication, Culture, Information and Technology at the University of Toronto Mississauga. His research uses critical and non-human based approaches to examine social media sites and the modes of connectivity these platforms establish. His work has been published in journals such as *Theory, Culture, & Society*, *International Journal of Cultural Studies*, and *Fibreculture*. He is a co-editor of the Affective Capitalism special issue for the *Ephemera Journal* (2016).

David M. Markowitz is a PhD student in the Department of Communication at Stanford University, and will start as an assistant professor at the University of Oregon in Fall 2018. His research uses computational methods to analyze how language is affected by psychological dynamics (e.g. deception, persuasion, status), and evaluates how communication media (e.g. the mobile phone, immersive Virtual Reality) modify social and psychological experiences.

Shaka McGlotten is a social anthropologist with a background in the fine arts. Their work brings together the theoretical insights of queer studies with the methodological toolkit of anthropology to consider new media technologies in relation to queer cultures. Their first book, *Virtual Intimacies: Media, Affect, and*

Queer Sociality, was published by SUNY Press in 2013. They are the co-editor of two edited collections, *Black Genders and Sexualities* (with Dana-ain Davis) and *Zombie Sexuality* (with Steve Jones). Currently they are at work on two book projects: *The Political Aesthetics of Drag* and *Black Data: Queer of Color Critique Meets Network Culture Studies*. In 2014 they were the recipient of the Alexander von Humboldt Foundation Award for Experienced Researchers and in 2017–2018 they are a fellow at the Akademie Schloss Solitude. They are also a recipient of a 2018 Creative Capital | Andy Warhol Foundation Arts Writers Grant.

Whitney Phillips is Assistant Professor of Communication, Culture, and Digital Technologies in the Communication and Rhetorical Studies Department at Syracuse University, and holds a PhD in English with a folklore structured emphasis (digital culture focus). She is the author of *This is Why We Can't Have Nice Things: Mapping the Relationship between Online Trolling and Mainstream Culture*, and the co-author of *The Ambivalent Internet: Mischief, Oddity, and Antagonism Online* with Ryan M. Milner. Across her books, numerous journal articles and book chapters, and popular press pieces in outlets like *New York Times*, *The Atlantic*, and *Slate*, her work explores antagonism and identity-based harassment; the reciprocal relationship between public expression, corporate and state institutions, and technological affordances; political memes and other forms of ambivalent civic participation; and digital ethics, including journalistic ethics and the ethics of everyday social media use.

Kane Race is Associate Professor of Gender and Cultural Studies at the University of Sydney. He is the author of *The Gay Science: Intimate Experiments with the Problem of HIV* (Routledge, 2018); *Plastic Water: The Social and Material Life of Bottled Water* (with Gay Hawkins and Emily Potter, MIT Press, 2015), and *Pleasure Consuming Medicine: The Queer Politics of Drugs* (2009, Duke University Press). He serves on the editorial board of several journals in critical drug studies, sexualities, health and cultural studies including *Sexualities*, *International Journal of Drug Policy*, and *International Journal of Cultural Studies*.

Margaret Schwartz is Associate Professor of Communication and Media Studies at Fordham University and a feminist media theorist working primarily with questions of embodiment and materiality in the context of archival and containment media. Her book *Dead Matter: The Meaning of Iconic Corpses* was published in 2015 by the University of Minnesota Press. She is currently working on a project that theorizes an ethics of care in the context of gestational surrogacy and other gendered forms of social reproduction.

Samuel Hardman Taylor is a PhD candidate in the Department of Communication at Cornell University. He is a member of the Cornell Social Media Lab. His work on digital media and interpersonal communication has appeared in

New Media & Society, Journal of Computer-Mediated Communication, Communication Research, Cyberpsychology, Social Networking, and Behavior, Computers in Human Behavior, and the ACM Conference on Human Factors in Computing Systems.

Catalina L. Toma is an associate professor of Communication Science in the Department of Communication Arts at the University of Wisconsin-Madison. Her research is concerned with how people understand and relate to one another when interacting via new communication technologies (e.g. online dating, social network sites, texting). She examines how relational processes such as self-presentation, impression formation, deception, trust, and emotional well-being are shaped by the affordances and limitations of computer-mediated environments. Catalina's research has appeared in publication venues in Communication (e.g. *Communication Research, Journal of Communication, New Media & Society*), Psychology (e.g. *Personality and Social Psychology Bulletin, Cyberpsychology, Behavior, and Social Networking*), and Human-Computer Interaction (e.g. *Computer-Supported Cooperative Work*).

Stephanie Tom Tong is an associate professor of communication at Wayne State University. Her research examines how people use technology to initiate, maintain, and terminate close relationships with family, friends, and partners. Stephanie's work has appeared in a variety of top academic journals (*Personal Relationships, Journal of Computer-Mediated Communication, Media Psychology, Communication Research*) and in the popular press (*Cosmopolitan, Gawker, Allure*). Her forthcoming book (Peter Lang) explores the influence of popular online and mobile technologies on people's romantic relationships.

Penny Trieu is a PhD candidate in the School of Information at the University of Michigan. Her research concerns how people can use communication technologies, particularly social media, to better support their interpersonal relationships. She also looks at identity processes, notably self-presentation and impression management, on social media. Her research has appeared in venues such as *Information, Communication, & Society, Social Media + Society*, and the *International Communication Association* conference.

ACKNOWLEDGMENTS

Let me use this space to acknowledge the support of Jamie Foster, my whiz of a research assistant and presently working toward her PhD on something that will undoubtedly be thoughtful, fun, and provocative. Erica Wetter, here's to your guts and foresight, and not thinking I'm crazy when you asked for a single sequel to the first *A Networked Self*, and I said how about four sequel volumes instead? Mia Moran, I know you will bring many more inspired projects to fruition with your insight.

The rest of you rascals, you know who you are. You are in my heart. I have thanked you personally, many times. I will probably continue to do so. Cheers.

1
INTRODUCTION

Zizi Papacharissi

Networks can only be as lively as the information and sentiments that flow through them. Without this flow, networks subsist as places where individual nodes of egos co-exist, but do not connect. They are dead spaces where distinct selves pass through but never bond, forever remaining strangers. Such a notion of a non-network is describable, but not possible. Humans are social beings, and survive through forming relationships. Relationships are what happen when information and sentiment blend and evolve over time.

Networks evolve as webs of relationships (e.g. Wellman & Rainie, 2012), but truly flourish when the relationships that populate them are driven by a balance of information and sentiment. A predominantly affective network, for instance, may be driven by an abundance of emotive communication but also stalled in a state of engaged passivity in the absence of informational sustenance. By contrast, a network characterized by the exchange of information may be functional, but lacks the pathos of affectively driven attunement. Balance between sentiment and information sharing renders networks, and the relationships that sustain them, lively, but also lovable.

Love is what happens as we process information and develop sentiments about others and as we experience sentiments and direct them to others using information. We learn about others and develop sentiments for them; we reconsider these sentiments or amplify them the more we learn about others and ourselves; and we allow these sentiments to positively influence our sense of being the more we learn how to live. I separate these processes in order to describe them, but it is not my intention to suggest that they are distinct. These processes are co-occurring, interrelated, and overlapping. I do not mean to be clinical or dry about an emotion that makes our lives more interesting. On the contrary, with this volume I ponder, and invite others to think along with me, why and how love happens in a contemporary age and in the networked spaces that we inhabit.

Thus, this volume is about love and the networked self. It focuses on realms across which love forms, grows, or dissolves. I am influenced by Bauman's understanding of liquid love as the quest for human bonds that offer security without threatening individual autonomy. We aspire to evolve through our interaction with others. Social media amplify such interaction and saturate our social environment with opportunities for both frail and more lasting bonds (Bauman, 2003; Gergen, 1991). What is central here is the need to connect, yet not define ourselves through others.

The Networked Self and Displaced Persons

In formulating the construct of the networked self, I sought to describe how people navigate a world saturated with opportunities for social connection and expression without losing sight of who they are. My intention was to focus on autonomy, not as independence but rather as the ability to attain self-fulfillment. I am influenced by Castoriadis (1987), who did not see autonomy as disregard for the needs of others but rather viewed positive autonomy as a way to reconcile the needs of others with the self. He envisioned the path to autonomy as one paved with the practice of self-limitation. One's path to independence must not impinge upon the freedom of others. It rests on a form of creativity that does not disrespect the needs of others. Autonomy "can be more than and different from mere exhortation if it is embodied in the creation of free and responsible individuals" (Castoriadis, 1997, p. 405). Out of this undoubtedly difficult and soft balance, a sense of self-knowing, self-fulfillment, and self-actualization may be attained. It is this sense that might most resemble a feeling of freedom, emancipation, and liberty.

I believe that technologies can help us attain this affective equilibrium. Ultimately, autonomy is this soft, light, evanescent sense of balance that leads to the ability to love selflessly. But I also find that it is easy for technologies to overwhelm us, first by saturating our worlds with opportunities for social connection that are often devoid of meaning, and second by reproducing relational cul-de-sacs instead of helping us reinvent how we relate to others. By using the word "technology," of course, I do not refer to the contemporary tendency to use the term to describe tools, platforms, and processes. The Greek root of the word (*techne* or τέχνη) does not divorce technology from its maker or user, thus avoiding deterministic assertions of what technology may or may not do to us. Technology is human and humans are technology. We emancipate, we confine, or we create standstills for ourselves through our technologies of being.

Early on, in the seminal *The Saturated Self: Dilemmas of Identity in Contemporary Life*, Gergen (1991) had anticipated some of these developments. He was concerned about technologies of social saturation: media that connect but also overpopulate the self with potential for expression and connection. The work described how post-modern individuals connect to others through a vortex of self-referential and reflexive media narratives. It also foresaw the opportunities and challenges for publicity, sociality, and privacy that would emerge at the next iteration of net-supported, interconnected online media. Gergen used the term "technologies of social saturation" to describe media that provoke a form of performative incoherence, by populating the self with multiple, disparate, and even competing potentials for being. These potentials reflexively support a form of *pastiche* personality, as each self contains an ever-increasing multiplicity of others, or voices, which do not inherently harmonize, presented in contexts that frequently lack situational definition (see also Meyrowitz, 1985). Understanding these multiple potentials requires constant and intense self-reflection. Self-monitoring thus becomes a preferred strategy for the *mutable* self that emerges; a self that evolves beyond the fixity of the self as object to the liquidity of self as process. This line of thinking aligns with Giddens's (1991) theorization of the ongoing project of the self, or Bauman's (2000) interpretations on the conditions of liquid modernity. The constant self-reflection, however, potentially leaves the self in postmodernity slightly more narcissistic and styled as a result (Gergen, 1991; Lasch, 1979).

Self-reflection, self-awareness, and reflexivity are amplified by the affordances of online media. Gergen (1991) had suggested that, confronted with the multiple potentials for being, self-presentation frequently evolves from play into the foray of carnival. Carnival permits the individual to strive for an authentic and coherent narrative of the self that will support multiple potentials. However, carnival also permits the individual to acknowledge and poke fun at the incredulity inherent in trying to align so many discordant potentialities for identity. Consequently, self-reflexivity, irony, and play become core strategies in performing the self across realities that are relational. These observations attain new gravitas in the context of networked media, which frequently collapse and converge public and private boundaries. As individuals make decisions about how to traverse the converged context of social media, they find themselves weighing opportunity against risk associated with the multiple selves that these media afford. Conditions that Castells has described as *timeless time* and the *space of flows*, amplify *ersatz being*, affording the possibility to both reconcile multiple potentials for identity and connect them to yet further mutations of those potentials, advancing a form of networked individualism (Castells, 2001; Wellman, 2001). Alternatively, we might interpret these tendencies as supportive of a networked sense of self, sustained through sociality performed to a network of relations, via a network of relations. These performances of sociality are driven by a polysemy that serves multiple selves and multiple audiences, without (ideally) losing narrative coherence.[1] This is where the idea of the networked self becomes relevant, as it provides foundational structure for studying and theorizing how the storytelling project of the self can lead to autonomy, rather than entrapment or compromise.

Gergen's (2009) follow-up work, on relational being, explicates how people may find their way out of a web of media saturation. He highlights the balance necessary between narratives of the self and narratives of belonging, so that these narratives support relations as organic, and not as constructed. Popular discourses frequently present relationships as artifice that must be worked on, developed, or fall apart as a result of actions of the self. Gergen (2009) emphasizes that relations happen and are primary, not artifacts. The self stands as the connecting point of a myriad of relationships, or as "the whole that is equal to the sum of relations" (Gergen, 2009, p. 55). Individual autonomy then implies being at ease with, but not dependent on the sum of relations embedded within one's own sense(s) of self. It is this form of love that this volume attempts to explore. Turkle (2011), in response to the social saturation online media infuse everyday life with, frequently suggests that in order to be with others we must learn to be alone, and if we do not learn to be alone, we can only be lonely. I would add that in order to learn how to love, we must first learn how to be alone.

A Networked Self, Love, and Connection

Any understanding of how technology can lead to love must be founded on the premise of restoring autonomy. And yet so many platforms that promise to deliver love are built upon tired, tried, and often failed rituals of introduction and courtship. They cater to the needs of a world described by Hannah Arendt as filling up with "displaced persons." We exist in late modernity and we live liquid lives, precarious and always changing (Bauman, 2005). Our social worlds have been reorganized and are constantly in flux, but if this is a problem, then it cannot be fixed by using technology to get rid of the elements that dissatisfy us and instill order to the parts that are unpredictable.

Turning over to love, tools cannot restore bonds that are lost, cannot invent bonds that do not already exist, nor can they restore bonds that are frail. Tinder does not deliver bonds. Match.com does not construct relationships. Facebook does not cure loneliness. Instagram does not make one authentic. We must learn to live with the frailty and insecurity of human existence first, in order to figure out how technology can help us. Love is unpredictable, as it should be, otherwise, where is the charm? Technology cannot predict love, algorithms cannot render it out of databased profiles, and platforms cannot fix love that is broken. *All love stories have a beginning and an end, and technology does not grant them the kiss of eternity.*

Platforms cannot restore calm in the parts of our life that feel vulnerable or liquid. That is on us. Organizing one's personal chaos is not the same as independence. Compromise does not soothe the heart. Efficient relationship management is not self-fulfillment. Yes, we can put technology to use as we strive toward autonomy in a world that becomes increasingly reflexive. And, we can use technology to adjust to unpredictability; the unpredictability of liquid love and liquid life, but also the unpredictability of life in general. But technology cannot help us until we know what we want from love, and life. And once we know what that is, I believe technology can help us reimagine and reinvent how we understand love and life, over and over again. Following this cue, contributors to this volume challenge our traditions of academic thinking and writing, and our traditions of thinking and researching "love."

Several authors address how relationships of love develop, are sustained, or broken up through technologies of expression and connection. Others take on how technologies of connection and expression reproduce, reorganize, or reimagine our dominant dogmas and rituals for meeting people, falling in love with them, and deciding what our relationships of love will look like. Finally, all of them ponder what our experiences of love teach us about ourselves, about others, and about the art of living. The emphasis here is on technologies of expression and connection, and the ways in which these technologies bring us closer to self-actualization and fulfillment through love.

Gershon, in search of love in the space of networked flows, pages the irrational, unmanageable neoliberal self. The networked, neoliberal self is "one in which the self possesses itself as though it was a business, collection of skills, assets, qualities, experiences, and alliances that must be constantly maintained and enhanced." Still, these actions lend the self shape and meaning, within historically specific and socioculturally nuanced media ecologies. Through conducting a set of interviews, Gershon excavates and organizes evolving rituals of adapting the self to the neoliberal web of networked, mobile, and digital technologies. Each platform is unique, and offers distinct ways of managing the relationships that form the foundation upon which the storytelling project of the self is mediated, remediated, and reinvented. If networked love is to be defined as a sense of balance that leads to moments of fleeting happiness, then that involves, among other things, an artful composition of the digital artifacts that saturate the self with the potential for social contact.

Within a shared media ecology, channel repertoires and habitual patterns are individualized and collaborative in nature. Trieu and Ellison offer an examination of channel navigation patterns as a new way of interpreting the complex paths through which our interpersonal relations evolve into love, suggest selfhood, and provide the basis for living. This holistic view of interactions across multiple platforms, digital and non-, permits a comprehensive theorization of networked life. Balance of networked being derives from relational media literacy and enhanced ability for channel coordination. Recalling the work of early medium theorists, such as McLuhan and Ong, the two authors suggest that we are at the cusp of a monumental shift in how we communicate, one that requires us to develop unique skills for remembering and importing information across media multiplexes in ways that support authentic engagement. Advancing toward what I have described as a digital orality (see Papacharissi, 2015) rests upon this very ability to reconcile our interpersonal conventions for expression and connection with the multiple vernaculars for such connection and expression that the digital offers. We may think of this as a new relational vocabulary for the networked self.

Romantic love is a game of revealing and discovering information, and flirting rituals are often based on this premise. Markowitz, Hancock, and Tong remind us that modern romantic relationships often begin with a profile, mediated in a variety of ways. The authors trace how these rituals are adapted to online dating. Digital platforms seek to organize compatibility in ways that assist but also confuse potential romantic partners. The logic of algorithms supplants the serendipity of acquaintance. The affordances of online platforms invite people to be more calculating, and often deceitful, in how they present themselves online. Deceit, as a form of concealment or lying, is not uncommon in romantic relationships, but it does take on a different texture online. Decision making is both rationally and affectively enabled, as people engage in selective self-presentation and strategies for uncertainty reduction, without sacrificing playfulness.

Connection or conflict, asks Toma as she sets out to examine how couples use media for relationship management. She offers a playful yet methodical examination of the great adventure of romantic love, as it is supported, thwarted, or reinvented through media. It is a broad question, because the presence of media in our everyday lives permeates our rituals and impulses in ways that we frequently recognize, but often also (choose to) ignore. Yet, the author fearlessly tackles all of these aspects, and cleverly synthesizes what we know, to ask how we can use it to find a place of meaning for technology in our lives. Media offer a constantly evolving vocabulary, landscape, and network within which our experiences are defined, challenged, and attain multiple meanings. Technology redefines connection, yes, but perhaps it can help us understand conflict as yet another iteration of connection and closeness.

Perceptions of closeness and relational satisfaction interact with social experiences on social media as we assess subjective well-being. Hardman Taylor and Bazarova explore the extent to which online technologies enhance relationships and subjective well-being. Research offers mixed results; primarily due to the tendency to emphasize short-term and direct effects over long-term relational processes that develop throughout the life course and as people learn to integrate technology into their lives in a meaningful manner. The two authors shift through this puzzle of findings to suggest a focus on subjective well-being. They emphasize the indirect effects of social media on relational closeness. As a result, they understand technological affordances and media multiplexity as the primary avenues of unpacking the consequences of social media on relational development and subjective well-being. It is through this lens that we can properly contextualize the ways in which processes of attachment form, and modalities of connection further develop. Ultimately, the path to balance, and eventually happiness, as it is objectively experienced, may be attained as people become better able to utilize their social experiences online as a way of regulating subjective well-being.

What is the place of the network self then, in experiences of happiness attained through relationships? Hogan draws our attention to the distinction between the exhibited self and the exhibited relation. He explains that online, performances of the self are curated to the point where they are better understood as complex and networked exhibits of the self. Similarly, exhibits of relationships are steered to convey particular impressions. All relationships involve rituals of performance, but the construct of the exhibit helps Hogan, and us, understand how love, a deeply private experience, may be transformed into a public act of being that is exhibited, encoded with meaning, and subsequently decoded in a variety of ways. Through a careful analysis of contemporary stories about love, Hogan explains that if we design platforms for connection, then we must also design for disconnection. I would add that if we socialize people to connect and perform rituals of connection, then we must also socialize people to disconnect and provide conventions that give comfort in doing so.

Davidson, Joinson, and Jones consider how online dating reproduces conventions of romantic courtship while also permitting these traditions to evolve within the nexus of networked love. Central to their conceptualization are aspects that frequently elude traditional forays into online dating, including the unpredictability of love; a questioning of whether we really should be searching for "the One"; and human playfulness vs. algorithmically organized interaction. They suggest that technologies be designed to improve rather than replicate existing patterns of courtship. With this in mind, technology may help us evolve our attitudes toward monogamy and human-to-human relations.

At the same time, platforms exist within marketplaces, and the relational infrastructures they afford embed potential for sexual objectification. Race invites us to think along with him, as he mobilizes the biopolitical category to think beyond the "critical impasse of sexual commodification." Sex, intimacy, community, friendship, and romance all intertwine in a marketplace of networked relations wherein market actors are able to reflexively identify and renegotiate what Race understands as, following Foucault, activities of "problematization." Biopolitical devices are vested with performative potential that permits market actors to repurpose and reimagine *relations-as-problems*, and in so doing, to present biopolitical artifacts that are polysemically open. Through a theoretically rich analysis of gay sexual networking apps as significant new biopolitical players, Race is able to trace how objects reified within a market "stage the categories according to which members are required to present themselves online as provisional, historically situated," yet at the same time "available to experimentation, contestation and critical transformation."

The manufactured marketplace of love is of concern also to Karppi, who takes on love, deceit, and longing in a sphere populated with potential romantic partners that include social bots. In the aftermath of the Ashley Madison affair, he examines how our networked selves connect and are potentially exposed within social media platforms. In this context, he argues, "relations are not only interactions between humans and social bots, but also intra-actions"; that is, "inseparable assemblages" of bots and humans, as well as "infra-actions," wherein given socialite patterns are suggested "before and beyond rational inputs." In these synthetic, yet human-centric situations, the notion of an "angel" as the ideal romantic partner fetishizes human-to-human relationship prototypes even though what is ultimately on sale is "an affair with the platform." Karppi turns to Raymond Williams's structures of feeling to help conceptually suggest synthetic structure of being, wherein "the human perspective is only one among many."

Cho centers on the concept of disruptive joy to redefine and propose a new understanding of networked love. He situates joy in the spirit of the moment; in the rejection of dutiful "happiness"; and in the visceral value that arises out of impromptu and collaborative acts of expression and connection. Using #BlackOutDay as a case study and selfies as a medium for such connection and expression, he proposes a new vocabulary for interpreting love as the fluidification of typically static ways of dissecting and organizing experiences. In this liquidly defined manner of feeling solvent experiences in the making, we may achieve a state of disruptive and technologically facilitated joy. Such experiences of joy both permit the celebration of who we are but also pave, through the potentiality of disruption, the way to redefining who we are. A sense of love for the self is after all inseparable from appreciation of both its current state and the potential to evolve beyond it.

Phillips contributes a deeply personal and intensely theoretical chapter about self-knowing and the intimacy, yet fleeting ambivalence of connection. Networks bare the capacity for connection, and relationships sustained via networks further nurture, nullify, or sever these connections. Love is fulfilling and deceitful; shaped by how we see ourselves through the eyes of others as much as our own. There are many ways of seeing things, and it is perhaps not until we arrive at our own, unique way of seeing the world and who we are, that we are able to identify intimacy and claim it as our own. Phillips asks a question that so many looking for love ask, and in responding to that question, reveals her very own way of seeing.

Love is inextricably tied to the senses, of course. In a deeply original essay, Schwartz writes about the possibilities of touch. She explores touch not only as a practice of love, but also as a demonstration of caring. Touch mediates and remediates intimacy and immediacy in ways that redefine the relationship between media and corporeality. Ranging from caring and soothing to a variety of acts of sexual love, touch is crucial to sustaining connections and relationships. In a broader sense, touch can be understood as extending beyond the body to further connect or network human to non-human agents. Schwartz reminds us that media are ordering technologies, which contain by creating and maintaining space. "Yet this technology is not merely a matter of machines," she argues, in the same way that "touch is not only a matter of skin to skin contact." As a result, a distributed network of love is about connecting and transcending boundaries between self and other, human and non-human, material and digital. In the words of Schwartz, these "radically material yet technologically imbricated practices of care . . . are the literal condition of possibility for our being."

In a cornucopia of digital artifacts that connect but also separate, what do we think of when we think of love, McGlotten asks. They aptly point out that in network culture studies and queer studies, love tends to be perceived either as the effect of something, or as a structure of its own. In the evocative chapter, "What's Love Got to Do with It?" they ponder all the questions that we have been afraid to ask, in terms that we have hesitated to phrase them in. And they answer them, by offering deep, intellectual, and often unexpected insights of what intimacy, virtual or not, really means in the context of that connection and fragmentation digitally mediated life produces. Confronting this reality requires evolving beyond contemporary structures and conventions of what it means to love. It necessitates reinventing, and perhaps forgetting, habits we have learned and roles that have been imposed so as to advance to an understanding of love that is poor, authentic, and personal. This is, as the author pens in closing, a love letter to the Self.

I had urged contributors to think about conventional understandings of love and how we might evolve out of them in inviting them to contribute to this volume. I also encouraged them to feel free to be creative with their thinking processes, their writing styles, and their overall approach. I did not want this volume to be about how we use technologies to date. I am not suggesting that type of work is irrelevant; it is simply not within the scope of this volume. I have argued here, and elsewhere, that many conventions of romantic love are contractually bound in ways that are historically specific, yet no longer personally relevant to us. It is only a matter of time till we evolve out of these conventions. Same-sex marriages, civil unions, ascending divorce rates accompanied by ascending marriage rates at a younger age all characterize societies that are uneasy with prescribed formulas for romantic union. To this end, it is important to explore how technology may help us evolve out of the discomfort traditional conventions associated with love impose upon us. This is a core theme for all contributing authors. All chapters in this volume used advanced, interdisciplinary, and state-of-the-art theories and methods to explicate how we may use technologies to cross and redefine boundaries we encounter in seeking love.

I also invited contributors to think beyond romantic interpretations of love to include a broader understanding of how love for one's self might pave the way to wellness, healthy relationships, and happiness. Happiness is, of course, subjectively defined, but I have always internalized it as a sense of balance that derives from feeling at peace with who you are, however fleeting that sense may be. And it is always fleeting. No one walks around being balanced all the time. With this in mind, I really looked forward to what the contributors to this volume—all original thinkers whose work I have admired for some time—would offer. Indeed, these scientists extended their findings beyond romantic love, to explicate how feelings of love and affection develop and spread across networks driven by sentiment. A second theme thus emerged as all authors, in their unique ways, reinforced the idea that people use technology, knowingly or in passing, to renegotiate boundaries, and to evolve out of them, by veering sometimes to new boundaries, and sometimes to hybridity, always in search of connection that may be ambivalent (in Whitney Phillips's words) and a sense of balance that may well be elusive.

A final, third theme evolved out of what our own stories, the stories of our contributors and the afterthoughts I hope they generate, tell us about what love means. Someone had asked me once if I had ever been in love with another person. I said yes, and then quickly added, whatever being in love may mean. I am not sure it is something that we fully understand, or if it is one of those things that we have words to describe. But I like to think I fall in love every day, every time I see something that moves me as a person and helps me both affirm and reimagine who I am. It is these evanescent moments that constitute love for others, for the self, and for the world we live in. I am thankful that all contributors to this volume pointed to this direction and potentiality. They all acknowledged that evolving out of conventional boundaries means reimagining how, who, and where we love. While love is communal in nature, it is self-based in its origin. Being alone is different from being lonely. Being with others does not negate loneliness. Being alone does not mean being without love. The object of one's affection can take on many forms. And love toward others cannot flourish unless first directed at yours truly, yourself. So, in paraphrasing Shaka McGlotten, this is a love letter to you, a networked self.

Note

1 These last two paragraphs based on thought previously published in reviewing Kenneth Gergen's work for iJOC (Papacharissi, 2012).

References

Bauman, Z. (2000). *Liquid modernity*. Cambridge: Polity Press.
Bauman, Z. (2003). *Liquid love*. Cambridge: Polity Press.
Bauman, Z. (2005). *Identity*. Cambridge: Polity Press.
Castells, M. (2001). *The Internet galaxy: Reflections on the Internet, business, and society*. Oxford: Oxford University Press.
Castoriadis, C. (1987). *The imaginary institution of society*. Trans. K. Blamey. Cambridge, MA: MIT Press.
Castoriadis, C. (1997) *The Castoriadis reader*. Trans. and ed. D. Ames Curtis. New York: Blackwell.
Gergen, K. J. (1991). *The saturated self: Dilemmas of identity in contemporary life*. New York: Basic Books.
Gergen, K. J. (2009). *Relational being*. New York: Oxford University Press.

Giddens, A. (1991). *Modernity and self-identity.* Cambridge: Polity Press.
Lasch, C. L. (1979). *The culture of narcissism.* New York: Norton.
Meyrowitz, J. (1985). *No sense of place: The impact of electronic media on social behavior.* New York: Oxford University Press.
Papacharissi, Z. (2012). Review of *Relational Being: Beyond Self and Community* by Kenneth Gergen. *International Journal of Communication,* 6, 834–837. ijoc.org/ojs/index.php/ijoc/article/viewFile/1611/734
Papacharissi, Z. (2015). The unbearable lightness of information and the impossible gravitas of knowledge: Big Data and the makings of a Digital Orality. *Media, Culture and Society,* 37(7), 1–6. doi: 10.1177/0163443715594103
Turkle, S. (2011). *Alone together: Why we expect more from technology and less from each other.* New York: Basic Books.
Wellman, B. (2001). Physical place and cyberplace: The rise of personalized networking. *International Journal of Urban and Regional Research,* 25(2), 227–252. doi: 10.1111/1468-2427.00309
Wellman, B., & Rainie, L. (2012). *Networked.* Cambridge, MA: MIT Press.

2

CALLING THE IRRATIONAL UNMANAGEABLE NEOLIBERAL SELF

Ilana Gershon

When I was interviewing undergraduates at my home institution in 2007 and 2008 about how they were using new media as they ended friendships and romantic relationships, many people told me about the ways they struggled with being unmanageable selves. This was a narrative that they told all too frequently about themselves—sometimes they were unmanageable in the midst of heartbreak, but all too often, they told stories in which their impulses to use technologies were unruly impulses, regardless of the relationships they were creating or untangling through these technologies. Cell phones and Facebook stand out in my research as two technologies that collected the most anxiety, that were seen to transform people into being selves they did not want to be or encouraging them to stay in contact with others in ways they would prefer not to do. They would tell me about how they could not stop searching for more and more information about others on Facebook, they were constantly Facebook stalking. Or conversely, some women reported to me that when they deactivated from Facebook, their friends all commented on how strong they were to be able to abstain from this temptation. By contrast, when my interviewees told me about their experiences as unmanageable selves using cell phones, the stories focused on different types of practices. They talked about how difficult it was to resist texting back once they were caught in a text message fight. Or they talked about giving their friends their cell phones when they went to bars to prevent the risk of drunk dialing. The technologies seemed to make visible how one might be uncontrollable to oneself in different ways. Facebook was seen as transforming people into selves that they did not want to be, while cell phones were seen as creating social connections and communication that become excessive and inappropriate. This contrast, as other chapters in this volume point out, is occurring through technologies that allow people to mix affect and information, and mix them according to notions of what information is and can do that are deeply informed by neoliberal logics. In this chapter, I discuss what the contrasting dilemmas these technologies present to users reveal about the complications neoliberal logic offers to people when they try to live as selves shaped by neoliberal principles.

In what ways is the unmanageable self that these American undergraduates were describing to me a specifically neoliberal self? Selves have been unruly and chaotic in many different historical moments and cultural contexts. The ways in which one may be chaotic, however, are always defined in relationship to what counts as orderly. The particular kind of uncontrollability undergraduates described to me occurs against the backdrop of the rational choice actor, the person who has to navigate various marketplaces, and encourage certain types of putatively instrumental alliances. I was interviewing young adults who were going to college and for the most part hoped to get middle-class jobs. What they did in college was supposed to prepare them for these job markets. At the same time that they were learning to be romantically involved or friends with others, they were also wrestling with how to become an employable self in a neoliberal economy. Their concerns about being a manageable or unmanageable self took place in a context in which selves are supposed to act according to business principles.

The neoliberal self is one in which the self possesses itself as though it was a business, a collection of skills, assets, qualities, experiences, and alliances that must be constantly maintained and enhanced, as well as urges that must be constantly monitored (see Gershon, 2011b, 2017; Martin, 2000). The neoliberal self's particular configuration hinges in part on this notion of manageability, of being a self that can be controlled. This self is thus conceptually split between the self one brings to the marketplace and that which animates the marketable self, the hopefully employable self (visible as information) and the putatively authentic actor (visible through affect) (Gershon, 2016). With the idealized neoliberal self, the self is always manageable, always able to be improved to further enhance how the person negotiates various marketplaces. When people I interviewed would use different media to reflect on the ways they were bundles of impulses instead of bundles of enhanceable skills, they were speaking to how this tension between the managed self and the potentially unmanageable self points to the ways being neoliberal is an idealized social theory that often produces its own paradoxes and impossibilities when put into practice.

My argument is strongly influenced by Frederick Kittler, a German media theorist who argued that every new technology transforms people's experiences of the self. Indeed, Kittler goes further than I would in suggesting that people are ontologically different selves with each new technology, largely because people are fundamentally discourse machines. In what sense is the person who lived before Facebook was invented a radically different person than the people living post-Facebook? For Kittler, when the medium through which knowledge flows in and out of people changes, then they too are transformed. These new communicative materialities are historically altering people's consciousness, people's bodily sense of themselves, as well as their ways of being relational. In short, the media through which people express themselves transform their being-in-the-world. Thus, every substantive innovation in communication technology transforms people's ontological being. Humans were different beings before the printing press, then different again before the gramophone, before the typewriter and again, before the computer. This is a strong ontological claim that I am reluctant to make, but those I interviewed might not be so hesitant. As I will explain at more length later in this article, several women told me that Facebook changed who they were, transforming them into suspicious jealous selves. When they quit Facebook, they quit being that self, and returned to a self that they were more comfortable being (see also Gershon, 2011a).

I am influenced by Kittler's efforts to analyze each medium as existing in historically and culturally specific media ecologies that shape how people understand what it means to be a self. For example, Kittler argues that in nineteenth-century Germany, typewriters introduce a new notion of an author, a new type of self became possible with the invention of the typewriter.[1] Yet, typewriters only transform German relationships to letters because of an earlier pedagogical effort in German schools to teach literacy practices that connect the voice to handwriting. Kittler examines a moment in German educational history when scholars were re-fashioning the education system to teach phonetics that would produce a uniform (and thus national) German pronunciation, as well as uniform and aesthetic writing that would ideally produce bourgeois individuals. What counts as pleasingly uniform is a cultural construction—at this German moment, the ideal was continuous writing in which the letters flowed into each other to create a whole word (Kittler, 1990, pp. 82–83). The aim was to create words that were all legible in similar ways, yet each expressed a distinctive connection between the inner self of the writer and his representations. Fluid and interconnected letters stood for fluid and interconnected engagement between the inner self of the bourgeois individual and the world. The German eighteenth-century vision of the inner self was a self that was both unconscious and natural, writing was inscribing and re-shaping pre-linguistic impulses into a coded and transmittable account. Thus writing was always an act of translation, but an act of translation in which the author was discovering himself (since the author at that time was also assumed to be masculine) while reading the letters his pen forms at the same time that he is writing.

Only after handwriting has been established as an act of translation, transforming the inner inchoate and creative self into legible unities, can typing be understood as separating the self from inscription. The authorial function that Foucault describes in "What is an author?" becomes available for analysis precisely because of the ways in which typing makes apparent that the author can be a construct (Foucault, 1984). Typewriters are storage machines, sorting not the embodied thoughts of a specific individual but transforming writing into a mechanical, and thus unmotivated, process. Kittler discusses one of the first fictional reflections on how typewriters obscure authorship, a Sherlock Holmes mystery, "A case of identity," in which a criminal stepfather types letters supposedly written by his stepdaughter. Holmes, whose methods are based on making intelligible the traces people leave as they pass through the world, discovers that the typewriter can be used to obscure these traces, although, for Holmes, they can reveal as much as handwriting. It is no accident that typewriters inspired stories of a troop of typing monkeys eventually typing out one of Shakespeare's plays—typewriters divorce inspiration or thought from the act of placing legible words on paper.

With this perspective, Kittler clears a path for ethnographers of media to explore how people's media ideologies about particular technologies are moments in which people articulate the paradoxes of being a self in a given historical period. Kittler is articulating three aspects that are useful for my argument. He establishes that the material structures of technologies significantly shape communication, and yet in underdetermined ways. The typewriter is structured so that anyone could be typing without apparently leaving an imprint of their personality, not so handwriting. Yet, the question of imprint is a culturally specific aspect. For people without a concept of the Romanticist creative inner self, whether or not a technology enabled what one could interpret as the imprint of an inner personality might be irrelevant.[2] Second, Kittler points to the importance of interpreting media and media ideologies in relation to each other—Facebook's supposed effect on American selves is also always partially in contrast to cell phones' supposed effect. Third, Kittler in his analysis of new technologies and their transformations puts the question of the self front and center. And in this chapter, I want to explore people's ambivalent appreciations of and concerns with Facebook and cell phones as symptomatic of the problems of having a self in contexts where the neoliberal self is frequently taken as an ideal one strives for.

I interviewed people at Indiana University, primarily undergraduates, during 2007–2008. In those years, Facebook had been around for three to four years and most college students had a Facebook profile. If they did not have one, they often would have to explain why to new acquaintances—becoming Facebook friends was already part of the ritual of becoming friends for many college students. Facebook only allowed high school students to have accounts in 2006, so many of my interviewees talked about how their Facebook account marked their new status as college students. Adults were slower to have Facebook accounts, and students talked about being taken aback when they had to decide whether to friend their parents or their friends' parents. MySpace was still a viable option in those days, and some students saw MySpace as marking their high school period and Facebook as marking their college years.[3] I was surprised by the number of times I would discuss with students their puzzlement over what social media to switch to next. Many wanted a new social media platform to mark their new stage of life as working adults. Anne mentioned: "I do not want to be someone who is Facebooking at 45." Ten years later, I would be as surprised to hear the converse, and I do not expect anyone to tell me that they do not think Facebook is for adults, or that they want to find a new social media platform to mark their graduation from college. In fact, these days I am often told that Snapchat is for teenagers and college students, and that Facebook is for adults.

To continue describing the media ecology of those I interviewed, all students used email; many used Skype, especially those who spent a college year abroad; none used Twitter, and perhaps two had avatars on virtual worlds (Second Life and World of Warcraft were the only two mentioned). While most had used instant messaging, my sense was that many had begun to see it as a medium for high school students or freshmen. Everyone had a cell phone among those I interviewed, and some commented when their friends did not have the capability of texting because it was so unusual. Some of my older interviewees talked about learning how to text recently, in part because new dating possibilities after their divorce seemed to require it. Not many students had smartphones, I only remember seeing a handful in my interviews. This meant that most students were very conscious of how many characters texting allowed, and came up with imaginative strategies around these limitations.

In part, my focus on my interviewees' media ecologies and their media ideologies about multiple media emerges from the emphasis of my fieldwork. I was interviewing people about how they used media, any media, to accomplish a social task—breaking up with someone else. Focusing on a task instead of a medium affected my interviews in a number of ways. I invariably heard about the many different media they turned to as they ended relationships. Few relationships ended in a single conversation, or over a single medium. Despite my interviewees' common understanding that there had been one break-up conversation, in practice it turns out that it takes many conversations with one's soon to be ex-lover as well as with one's friends and family to disentangle a relationship. People's break-up stories involved accounts of the many different media used, and detailed analysis of the implications behind the media-switching (see Gershon, 2010b). Through these stories, it became clear that people's ideas and uses of one medium were informed by their ideas and uses of all other media in their media ecologies, including ones that they never used. To understand people's texting ideologies and practices, one also has to understand the media they were choosing not to use.

When I remember Olivia's interview, I tend to think of it as an interview about why someone would de-activate from Facebook. Olivia was one of a number of undergraduates I spoke to in February and March of 2008, all of whom had vivid stories about choosing to deactivate from Facebook, and the social consequences of that decision. But when I re-read the transcript of her interview in anticipation of writing this article, I realized that this is only half the story. When Olivia starts telling me about how new media are affecting her relationships, she begins by talking about her strategies for texting her current boyfriend, Jeff. She tells me that she has an "alternative personality" when she texts. She is ruefully self-aware, she knows that she will sometimes text him messages that are passive-aggressive and double-edged when he is out late. She does not like this aspect of herself, but she also finds it very convenient that texting carries no intonation. She uses this to her advantage, texting him messages which can be read as sarcastic or nagging, an interpretation she can later deny when they are chatting in-person.

OLIVIA: I was thinking a lot about it last night, and with my recent boyfriend, there have been, and we spend a lot of time together, so it's not a long distance relationship in which we talk about important things necessarily over text message or email but I have noticed that I have this tendency to, uh, I have like this alternate uh texting personality. I become extremely passive-aggressive, like um, and there have been times when he has misconstrued what I said to him in a text message to me breaking up with him actually. And I never really had that intention.

ILANA: Right.

OLIVIA: Its mainly we spend a lot of time together, and then, you know I am twenty-one years old, but I have to say that sometimes, if he is spending the night with his guys, and my friends are busy, and I end up alone, and it's like, I call it like going for the bottle, I will go for my cell phone, and it's like I send these messages like "oh, what are you doing now?" Or, I don't know, something that can make him feel guilty, like "maybe you will plan on coming over later to stay with me?" And I will say "just text me, I am on my way to bed." And I feel like it kind of becomes that way because you can always just say "oh, I didn't mean it that way." I can't remember exactly what happened when he thought I broke up with him, but it can always be said "well, that wasn't my tone." And it is so easy that way. And sometimes, you know, the next day he will call me out on it, and he will say something like: "Why were you being like that? You were being kind of crazy." And sometimes he won't say anything at all. So really, he will take these texts a lot of different ways.

ILANA: So you are texting him. Do you have an intonation in your head as you are texting him then you then know you can deny if you need to?

OLIVIA: Actually, yeah, it's funny, because, um, I do know how it is in my head, and it's sarcastic or it's whatever it is.

ILANA: Right.

OLIVIA: And I do kind of go through a lot of metacognition. I know what I want it to sound like, I know what it could sound like, and I know what my defense will sound like.

Olivia opens her musings about how she uses different technologies by talking about the ways in which texting allows her to structure ambiguous exchanges with her boyfriend in which she can send double messages, and claim responsibility for only some of the message's interpretations, not all.

While Olivia shared with others a belief that texting presented temptations to contact, and shared strategies for resisting this impulse, not everyone shared her media ideology about texting. Olivia believed that texting was less intrusive than other ways of contacting someone, and so tended to text her boyfriends when they were with friends.

ILANA: So how do you decide between calling and texting?

OLIVIA: That's a good question. Well obviously there is my initial anecdote [this is 50 minutes after she told me the previous story], if you are feeling insecure and you don't want to be held accountable for. So in those cases you are kind of being, if you know that maybe you are not doing the right thing, you text.

ILANA: So kind of checking up on things? That you will do by text.

OLIVIA: Checking up on the relationship? Or checking up on the person in general?

ILANA: Yeah, I think I mean checking up on the person in general. Like you talked about where they are, and who they are with. You could call and say "who are you with right now?" and you would hear people in the background. So, you might possibly get more information that way.

OLIVIA: It's true.

ILANA: But people tend to seem to text now.

OLIVIA: To check up. Yes, I would say that, I mean, I am trying to think what it is right now with my current boyfriend and it is like he had this thing he had to finish today before class and he was feeling bad about it, so I texted him, how did it go? . . . Or with my bad ex, it was the kind of thing: oh I don't want to be that annoying girlfriend who calls all the time. And if I say "who are you with?" and he answers verbally people can hear him, and they know what's going on . . . People don't know what you are texting.

While everyone else agreed with her that texting was informal, people held a variety of opinions about the kind of informal contact texting entailed. Rose explained to me that she felt texting required immediate response, indeed she preferred texting to in-person conversations when fighting with her boyfriend because it helped him focus his attention on her words. But there are downsides as well, since there is a record of the conversation. Rose explained that in-person fights allowed for boyfriends to be too inattentive.

ROSE: I feel like for the most part in fights [i.e. face-to-face fights], women, like I said, scream at men, and the men nod like this [demonstrates how the men stare off a bit into space] and nod like this, and [the woman says] "oh, you said this" and you scream at them more for saying it and they nod.

ILANA: And they make sure not to make eye contact.

ROSE: And by the end of the fight you feel better, a little bit, and they just let it go and everything is okay. Usually, if you get it through . . .

Versus text-messaging, where you remember him saying "well, you are stupid for thinking that."
ILANA: Because you save that.
ROSE: Yeah, and you look at that, and you never forget "you called me stupid. I can't believe you." And women, I feel like we hold grudges.

For Rose, unlike Olivia, the fact that texts were written instead of spoken, and cell phones were seemingly always available, ensured speed and even careful attention to one's texted replies. But it also assured traces of arguments that could last long past the moment of the actual argument.

As my interview with Olivia unfolded, it became clear that cell phones and Facebook were becoming even more complex tools for crafting relationships for her. Olivia is the first person who made me wonder if my informants were channeling Kittler. After telling me about her current texting strategies and how she has a different personality when texting, she admitted that she was no longer on Facebook because she turned into a self she did not want to be whenever she used Facebook. Kittler echoes indeed, both texting and Facebook transform her into a different self, although the different technologies create selves that pose different problems for her. In her previous relationship, being on Facebook had turned her into a "jealous girlfriend," one she stopped being, in her own mind, as soon as she quit Facebook. Olivia had been dating a very social man, one who went to bars and met up with lots of female friends most evenings. Olivia could not accompany him because she was not old enough to legally drink, and she refused to get a fake ID. Her friendly boyfriend did not have a cell phone with a camera. So, his many female friends would take pictures of him and other friends at the various college bars, and then post them on Facebook the next day, often writing flirtatious comments on his Facebook wall as well.

Olivia started to find herself in an unwelcome pattern of behavior. She would text him while he was out on the town, asking him questions about how his night was going, and who he was chatting with. She texted instead of calling because of her previously mentioned media ideology that texting was less intrusive. The next day she would check Facebook, corroborating the information he had texted to her. Was he really only with the girls he mentioned? Was he in fact doing only what he had claimed by text the night before? She would text and check, text and check. Olivia describes this pattern as partially encouraged by how Facebook profiles circulate information—the profiles are so underdetermined she often must expend quite a bit of effort interpreting Facebook traces. She explains: that "you fill in the blanks yourself" when confronted with information gaps on Facebook. Meanwhile her friends too were involved in this task of filling in the blanks as they looked at the Facebook traces of her boyfriend's social life, and kept asking Olivia if she was sure that he was being faithful. Both the creation of her ex-boyfriend's Facebook profile and its interpretation were deeply social activities. Finally, sick of this cycle and the fights she started so often after texting and checking, Olivia quit Facebook. In part, this helped her leave this cycle. Not entirely, however, even after quitting, she asked for a friend's Facebook password and would use her friend's profile to examine her then boyfriend's profile.

Deactivating Facebook also helped her as she anticipated a break-up that she suspected was likely. Quitting allowed her to avoid the awkwardness of changing her Facebook status to single. By deactivating, she was able to avoid the phone calls and Facebook wallposts that seemed so inevitable after one makes one's break-up "Facebook official."

After the break-up, she began to flirt with Jeff, her current boyfriend. In describing this moment, Olivia tells me another story about ambivalent interactions with communicative technology, this time with her cell phone. She has Jeff's number in her cell phone, but she does not want to contact him too often. So, she deletes it. When she and Jeff finally become a couple, he admits to her that he did exactly the same thing—he deleted her phone number from his phone to control his impulses to contact her. Of course, she had also deleted her ex-boyfriend's number from her phone, and then would inevitably enter the phone number into her phone's address book again. Olivia likens the impulse to call to an addiction, commenting that people's phone numbers end up in all sorts of nooks and crannies in one's history of contacts with them:

> You have to delete it from your message inbox. You have to delete it from the call log. You have to delete it from . . . it shows up in all these different places, because I tried. You have to think about all these places that the number is. It could be in your Facebook inbox because maybe it's the first time he gave you his number, like, you still have it. . . . It's almost like, hiding a bottle of liquor from an alcoholic.

As she describes the difficulty she experiences controlling her impulses to contact someone using her cell phone, she describes how the phone appears to have "a mind of its own, you take it out and there you go [texting someone after telling yourself you absolutely would not text him]." Olivia in explaining the problems she experiences regulating her self begins to describe the technologies surrounding her as having their own agency, an agency that manifests itself as offering temptations, as undermining her control.

Olivia talks about many of the dilemmas that occur when one is engaging imperfectly with the trappings of being a neoliberal self (see Gershon, 2011a, 2011b; Rose, 1990, 1996). She is concerned about how to control herself, she experiences herself not only as a bundle of skills and alliances but also as a bundle of ill-conceived impulses that might not help her fashion the type of alliances she wants. Technologies intermittently both help her and hinder her in her efforts to manage herself. Her story is one among many I heard that year about self management dilemmas as people used new media. In analyzing her story, I want to locate it within my larger interview set, discussing what themes she discusses that others told me about over and over again, and what seems specific to Olivia's own experiences.

Olivia, like others, describes Facebook and cell phones as presenting different types of dilemmas in terms of managing the impulsive self. She talks about the urge to "Facebook stalk," the colloquial term for searching unnoticed through other people's Facebook profiles for information. People see this as a slightly inappropriate activity, everyone might stalk, but admitting it is either admitting to a guilty pleasure, or sometimes, admitting to inappropriate curiosity or worse. This, I want to stress is seeking information, not interacting with the subject of your curiosity. This is not to say that Facebook stalking is asocial. It is sometimes an activity done with friends, most typically friends helping you through their own access to certain Facebook profiles to find information about a specific other person. Facebook stalking, in short, was an activity about knowing, about mapping one's social network, but while what one knows could be revealed, how one knows it should not be. Let me return to Rose, who explained to me:

> Women are much better Facebook stalkers than men. I wish I had it so I could show you how you can get into it. Men don't sit there and think "So Rose was with Megan last night, and Megan hangs out with Joseph last night, so I should check Joseph's pictures to see if Rose was there last night." Men don't think like that, where we do. So-and-so was hanging out with So-and-so, so if I go to their page, I can see the pictures that they always put up. But men don't do that, at all, ever. I have never known a guy to sit there and search through Facebook to see if his girlfriend was there or not.[4] But women do all the time. It's embarrassing when you found something and you have to explain how you found it too. "I found this picture going through your cousin's friend's sister's pictures." And they think, "why were you doing that?"

Rose proceeded to tell me about strategies for hiding Facebook stalking, her friends and others I spoke to would often go to considerable lengths to conceal how they know what they happen to know. The unseemly curiosity that led to Facebook stalking in the first place reveals too much about one's own impulses to others. Acting on the knowledge one gained through determined Facebook stalking could reveal that one had done such Facebook stalking. That could turn into a dilemma that might lead to people choosing not to act at all on the information, because they felt it was more important to conceal their Facebook stalking.

Many people talked to me about being Facebook addicts, or labeled other people as Facebook addicts. Facebook stalking was the only practice that people consistently described as addictive. When they talked about other Facebook practices, they did not stress how hard it was to manage the self they became on Facebook. Facebook stalking was particularly compelling, according to the people I interviewed, because Facebook reveals the traces of social interactions without providing enough context. So they would get hints that something might be going on, but not enough details to know with certainty that what they suspected was actually occurring. Facebook, as I discuss elsewhere in more detail, brings people into a system of partial information, in which people view just enough information to want more details about ex-lovers or current lovers, but not enough information to be satisfied (see Gershon, 2018).

Facebook stalking was often described as too absorbing and too time-consuming; people tried various techniques to control themselves. Felicity was worried that she was becoming a Facebook addict. So, she decided to control herself by using a timer whenever she logged on. She knew that she might not notice how much time she was spending searching for information while she was Facebook stalking, but maybe an external device might help startle her out of her Facebook stalking fugue state. She was using technology to regulate the problems that she saw other technology as creating by turning her into a self that might be uncontrollably seeking information. Other people might try to keep their Facebook stalking impulses in check by deactivating entirely from Facebook for similar reasons to Olivia's. Yet just like Olivia, they still continued to use their friend's Facebook profiles occasionally when there was information they wanted to know, and felt Facebook was the best medium for discovering this information. People who deactivated from Facebook often continued relying on their friends to gather the information for them, or used their friends' passwords and profiles to search for the information more directly.

Cell phones led to other dilemmas in part because cell phones putatively triggered a different kind of impulse—the urge to contact. While Facebook was seen as encouraging people to play detective, cell phones were seen as encouraging contact, often too much contact. Many talked about their strategies for controlling their urges to text. Some people gave their phones to their friends when they went to bars to try to avoid drunk texting, or when they felt the impulse too strongly to contact someone they should not, they simply asked their friends to keep their phones overnight. Some people altered the names stored in their phones so that they could not find someone's phone number easily. Trill explained her strategies in response to one of my questions.

ILANA: Have you taken any one's number out of your phone?
TRILL: Yes, but, sometimes I save text messages and like um they'll be there. I'll go and if I am really really desperate to call him or text him, I know I can look at my saved messages and they are right there. Or sometimes I actually like, this is so weird, but I close my eyes, I'll not pay attention to my phone, I'll just change the name really quickly and then I won't know what name it is so I can't look for it.

For Trill and others, the problem was the temptation to contact. While Facebook offered the temptations of gathering information without the person of interest knowing, cell phones seemed to offer the temptations of contact that was too easily initiated.

Judging Others

My interviewees were not only describing themselves as frustratingly unmanageable, they were also evaluating other people in terms of their ability to manage these impulses. That is, people were using the neoliberal rubric of an ideal relationship as one that balances risk and responsibility for all participants as guidelines for judging others and deciding who they wanted to be in a relationship with in the first place. I heard the most explicit accounts of this type of evaluation when people talked about deactivating from Facebook to stop being unwelcome selves. I often asked how this affected their social lives, and how others around them reacted to their decision to deactivate from Facebook. Women reported to me that their friends and acquaintances often commented on how strong they were to stay off Facebook, and would admit sheepishly that they were not that strong themselves. In these conversations, Facebook was figured as an addictive technology and women had to have strong will power to withstand its siren calls.

There were more tacit moments in which American undergraduates implied that they evaluated others in terms of the self-control apparently exhibited in relation to both cell phones and Facebook. I would often chat with people about how they decided not to become involved with someone, that is, when did they end a budding flirtation before it became serious? In my book (Gershon, 2010a), I discuss how women often paid attention to the degree of contact someone initiated when they were first flirting, seeing this as indicative of how much attention and communication a potential lover would demand once they were in a relationship. Women in college far more than men were understood, however erroneously, as longing to be in a relationship. Yet, relationships were often very time-consuming, forcing women to add another obligation as they already juggled spending time with their friends, studying, and working part time. Not everyone was equally eager to add this new obligation, and some were understandably cautious about entering into certain relationships. In weighing the pros and cons of a potential lover, women evaluated all the ways this person contacted them, not just focusing on one medium. In the following story, Sassie explains why she has lost any interest in an interested neighbor, largely because she finds his forms of communication unappealing and even frustrating:

ILANA: How do you know he is checking your Facebook?
SASSIE: By subtle comments that he makes. And sometimes when a guy will comment on my wall, he will comment right after, such as, for example, one of my guy friends, who is really attractive and I wouldn't mind talking

to him, I took him home from a gathering that we had, and he fell on the ice. It was really funny, and so I was laughing at him. And I wrote on his wall: "I hope your butt isn't too sore, blah-blah-blah." Totally trying to give him a hard time about it. . . . And then Harry comments on my wall about something, he changed my oil in my car, and he commented about how when I get home, I need to come get him and he will check to see if my oil level is still good enough for the car to run properly. . . . So I don't know, sometimes I used to be so fanatic about my phone. Because I could never let it go unanswered, or let a text message go unanswered. And now, I don't even want to look at my phone because I am afraid it is him. I try to avoid it. . . . If I could set his text messages to a different ring, that would be a good idea. Text messages I see as a simple "Hey, I'm here" or "I saw something funny today, I thought of you"; or just little like, notes, I guess; not a way to try and have a conversation. Because if I want to talk to someone, I will call them. Or I will try to say "hey, can you meet me somewhere so we can have a talk?" or something like that.

For a complex set of reasons (see Gershon, 2010b) that are only partially due to the wide range of options of communicative channels, as Sassie implies in her increasing discomfort with texting someone back she does not fancy, love now means being constantly accessible to one's lover. While people can ignore communication from parents and friends, although this is increasingly becoming less acceptable according to my students these days, ignoring a missive from one's lover may be a much more fraught decision, often seen as signaling an increasing lack of interest from one's lover.[5] When someone could not control their impulses to contact someone during a flirtation, this served as a warning for the women I interviewed that these men might behave in similarly impulsive ways once they were in a relationship. And the women wanted to have nothing to do with that.

People were also concerned when others could not manage their curiosity when they had access to their lover's "backstage" interactions on Facebook or on their cell phones. Undergraduates frequently told me about sharing passwords with their lovers, so that their lovers had access to all their communication by Facebook or email. Yet granting this access was not understood as a free pass. Those who shared passwords expected their lovers to respect their privacy according to their own personal expectations. These expectations, I want to note, were specific to that person, and were not always even discussed between the two lovers. When lovers violated their expectations, this often contributed significantly to a break-up. Lynn told me about the consequences of sharing email passwords in a recently ended relationship:

> I was abroad last semester, and he snooped onto my email account and claimed that he was deleting an email that he had sent me, but he had seen an email that I had received from another mutual friend of ours, and he decided

to take it upon himself to read it and, um, then he told my two best friends here at school that he had read this email and they of course came and told me. And then I confronted him on it. And then he said "Yeah, I did look at it." And I was like, okay, you shouldn't have. It is one thing to know my password, but it is another thing to be looking through my email.

For Lynn, sharing passwords was not allowing her boyfriend to read any email he wanted, he was supposed to understand and respect boundaries. People seemed to assume that those who had their passwords would behave appropriately, however they defined what was appropriate behavior (and this varied from person to person). Sharing Facebook and email passwords was a gesture of trust. This was not the case for similar stories about cell phones and curious lovers.

My interviewees would tell me that their lovers and their friends would, given the opportunity, look through their lovers' cell phones, reading their texting histories and checking who was in the phone's list of contacts.

COURTNEY: I don't know anyone's boyfriend who does not read their girlfriend's saved texts. The inbox, the outbox, all of them. I know that my boyfriend right now does, as soon as I leave. He won't do this in front of me, he has too much pride. I know that as soon as I walk out the room, he picks up my phone and goes through it.
ILANA: Do girls do this also?
COURTNEY: Yeah, they do. I guess it goes both ways. But that causes a ton of problems. Things are taken the wrong way. . . .
ILANA: So do people say "no, I won't give you my password?"
COURTNEY: Some people do. My friend from back home, who I was saying knows his girlfriend's passwords, he knows her instant messenger password, her Facebook password, he knows all of that but he will not give her his. He has a lock on his phone where he has to enter the password before you can get on his phone.
ILANA: Wait, so he thinks it is okay for him to have all his girlfriend's passwords, but
COURTNEY: He doesn't give her his.
ILANA: Does she say anything about this?
COURTNEY: No, she doesn't. And me and my boyfriend will always talk about that, because we are all a group of friends, and she won't say anything to him. He'll be like: "give me your phone." And she will just hand it over. If she is texting, he will come right over and say "who are you texting? Why are you texting them?" And he'll get real mad about it. She will say "well, let me see your phone." And he will be like: "no!"

As Courtney explained, this could be a fraught practice. She viewed the friends' romantic relationship as an imbalanced one, and was uncomfortable that the man could access his girlfriend's phone whenever he wanted, but he kept her from ever checking his. Courtney also explained that while she would never openly look at her own boyfriend's cell phone, if he left it lying around while he left the room (say, to go to the bathroom), she would not be able to resist checking. While people were supposed to show restraint with passwords, no one seemed to expect this when cell phones were involved.

Facebook and cell phones together not only allow people to experiment with new media-dependent expressions of intimacy, but also compel people to explicitly engage with the indeterminacy of messages' meanings. There is a widespread media ideology that text messages are easily misunderstood. People mainly focus on the lack of intonation or the brevity of the messages when describing why text messages are so commonly misunderstood. Some people would tell me about turning to emoticons to help guide potential readers in their interpretations of authorial intention when reading texts. Indeed Zee, a woman who used what I personally viewed as a surprisingly large number of emoticons when she sent me emails, explained about her media ideology about texting and email:

ZEE: You can never tell the tone of someone's voice. You can be joking around about something, and someone will get really upset and you will think "should have added 'haha' at the end of that."
ILANA: Ah, those emoticons!
ZEE: I feel stupid typing it, but if I don't, someone could take it totally the wrong way. It is the same with emails. I have to put a smiley face at the ends of my work emails to like my boss because otherwise he will like think I am saying something really rude.
ILANA: Zee, I have to say, you use more emoticons in emailing me than anybody else.
ZEE: I have to! That's because I have had so many misunderstandings with people.

While Zee and others tend to focus on text messages or emails, people also would mention to me that phone calls were easily misinterpreted as well. One group of three women explained to me that they preferred to text or talk in person to avoid disagreements—texting because everyone knew it could be so easily misinterpreted so people tried to text only the most general and easily interpreted messages. In their eyes, face-to-face conversations provided the most conversational cues. But phone calls could too easily lead to fights, because it took a while to familiarize oneself with another person's phone manner—intonations over the phone, from their perspective, could all too easily be misinterpreted if one did not know one's conversational partner well. Facebook too was widely understood as too underdetermined a medium; it was too easy to misinterpret what one saw in photographs or on wallpostings. As Alan explained:

> What I don't like about a picture is that it is physically shot, and you see what you see. But you don't know any of the background of what was going on at the time. You only see whatever you see in the picture. So you don't see if maybe this person didn't want to be in the picture, but they were forced to. You don't know if this person was maybe just walking by and someone said "hey, come get in this picture." All you see is that they were in the picture.

In Alan's case, photographs are an older medium that in the context of a Facebook profile's temporality become newly described as underdetermined.

Conclusion

I have argued elsewhere that these media's indeterminacy has much more to do with how Americans are currently (in 2017) experiencing the "newness" of new media under neoliberal capitalism. Under Fordist capitalism, companies, schools, and various government agencies were all very involved in creating standardized and homogenous experiences of new media. For example, when stereographs were introduced, companies also circulated manuals about how one should sit vis-à-vis the stereograph, and, when introduced to schools, the instructions on how students should hold their bodies while looking at stereographs eerily resemble Taylorist factory manuals on how workers should best move in the name of increasing efficiency. New communicative technologies always pose social quandaries to their users. When phones were first introduced, people had to determine how to answer the phone. Edison and his company recommended "hello," Graham Bell and his company advocated "ahoy." In the long run, Edison's company's pedagogical efforts were more successful. Yet companies are no longer as concerned with these pedagogical efforts.

In part, neoliberal companies no longer care about homogenizing users' behavior because their focus has shifted to turning information into a commodity, a focus that has led to far greater attention being paid to privacy rights and issues surrounding intellectual property. At the same time, companies have started to encourage users to develop their own practices in relationship to these technologies in their attempts to generate what they perceive as greater product loyalty as well as promoting a diversity of markets.

This, however, leaves users to devise their own social norms for these technologies, which they do by observing and discussing with their families and friends how best to use these technologies. As a consequence, figuring out how to use these technologies is reorganizing the ways in which people break up with each other. After all, what one group of friends decides might be the way to use Facebook is not how another group of friends decide to use it. One must learn how to interpret the messages of every new acquaintance, in part because of the lack of companies' or governments' pedagogical projects aimed at creating widespread standardization. Courtney discussed this problem as she was explaining to me how challenging she found it to effectively interpret people's texts initially:

> You know what I find is hard is when you meet a new friend. Because you don't know how they text. And I know when I came to school I found that was weird because you'll be talking to someone, and like I said, I know how my roommate texts, and I know when she puts 2 y's ["heyy"] and when she puts one ["hey"], and when you meet a new friend you don't know. So then you don't know—you can't read their texting, which is frustrating because with your actual friends you can read it, like you know exactly how they're feeling through it. Like through a text, which is weird but . . .

Courtney is addressing a common experience, that part of getting to know people in the contemporary American college media ecology involves learning people's media ideologies and media practices. This process of learning is always also revealing how underdetermined the messages on these technologies can be—how many pockets of media practice there are among one's acquaintances. All too often, people these days learn that they have been dating someone who has very different ideas about how one should use media to communicate, a realization that comes in the moment of ending a relationship and reorganizes how break-ups unfold these days.

In this chapter, I have followed Kittler's analytical insights by asking how different technologies both enable people to experience their selves in new ways, as well as exploring how these technologies can help orient people to the problems of being social in new ways. Unlike Kittler, I have posed this in terms of clashes between discursive formations and daily practices,[6] as a moment in which neoliberal logics of what it means to be a self are unevenly being adopted and often presenting concrete social problems to those trying to live by neoliberal assumptions. Each technology serves as a distinctive vehicle for people to explore the quandaries of being a neoliberal self. Facebook enables people to explore the dilemmas of managing one's social relationships using neoliberal views of information—always incomplete and yet one must decide future actions based on this information by imagining particular future scenarios (imaginatively filling in the gaps) that putatively allow one to manage risk. Cell phones, by contrast, allow people to explore the problems of managing one's alliances when too much contact (or too little) can unravel the alliances.

Notes

1 For brevity's sake, I am not discussing Kittler's larger argument about the typewriter, namely that the invention of the gramophone, film, and typewriter was simultaneously the creation of the Lacanian self (see Kittler, 1999).
2 Webb Keane's concept of semiotic ideologies is also apropos here. I am turning in part to Kittler instead because of Kittler's emphasis on the self. I think for most other analyses, Keane's concept is more flexible (Keane, 2003, 2007).
3 danah boyd argues that MySpace was a social media platform favored by high school students who were not oriented toward college and minorities. She found in her research that high school students who planned to go to college tended to be on Facebook (boyd, 2014).
4 I did interview men who did this. Rose's gendered assumptions about media practices were not borne out in my other interviews.
5 Indeed, several undergraduates described to me break-ups in which there was no "Break-up Conversation" but only a cessation of contact for a few weeks that was then interpreted retrospectively as a break-up. My interviewees did not yet use the term 'ghosting' for this practice.
6 This is similar to the moment in Michel Foucault's *Discipline and Punish* (1975, pp. 258–261) when he points out that new disciplinary regimes are unevenly adopted, that convicts may still travel in open carriages through towns on their ways to closed prisons as the traces of former disciplinary regimes continue to linger in some practices.

References

boyd, d. (2014). *It's complicated: The social lives of networked teens.* New Haven: Yale University Press.
Gershon, I. (2010a). *The break up 2.0: Disconnecting over new media.* Ithaca: Cornell University Press.
Gershon, I. (2010b). Breaking up is hard to do: Media ideologies and media switching. *Journal of Linguistic Anthropology*, 20(2), 389–405.
Gershon, I. (2011a). Un-friend my heart: Facebook, promiscuity, and heartbreak in a neoliberal age. *Anthropological Quarterly*, 84(4), 867–896.
Gershon, I. (2011b). Neoliberal agency. *Current Anthropology*, 52(4), 537–555.
Gershon, I. (2016). 'I'm not a businessman, I'm a business, man': Typing the neoliberal self into a branded existence. *HAU*, 6 (3). doi: 10.14318/hau6.3.017
Gershon, I. (2017). *Down and out in the new economy: How people find (or don't find) work today.* Chicago: University of Chicago Press.
Gershon, I. (2018, in press). Every click you make, I'll be watching you: Facebook stalking and neoliberal information. In Z. Papacharissi (Ed.), *A networked self and birth, life, death.* Abingdon: Taylor & Francis.
Foucault, M. (1975). *Discipline and punish: The birth of the prison.* New York: Vintage.
Foucault, M. (1984). What is an author? In J. Faubion (Ed.), *Aesthetics, method, and epistemology* (pp. 205–222). New York: New Press.
Keane, Webb. (2003). Semiotics and the social analysis of material things. *Language & Communication*, 23: 409–425.
Keane, Webb. (2007). *Christian moderns: Freedom and fetish in the mission encounter.* Berkeley, CA: University of California Press.

Kittler, Frederich. (1990). *Discourse networks 1800/1900*. Stanford: Stanford University Press.
Kittler, Frederich. (1999). *Gramophone, film, typewriter*. Stanford: Stanford University Press.
Martin, E. (2000). Mind-body problems. *American Ethnologist*, 27(3), 569–590.
Rose, N. (1990). *Governing the soul: The shaping of the private self*. London: Routledge.
Rose, N. (1996). *Inventing our selves: Psychology, power, and personhood*. Cambridge: Cambridge University Press.

3

CHANNEL NAVIGATION IN INTERPERSONAL COMMUNICATION

Contemporary Practices and Proposed Future Research Directions

Penny Trieu and Nicole B. Ellison

As individuals in today's networked society establish, maintain, and terminate relationships, they employ a web of intertwined modes of communication to accomplish their interpersonal goals. Because interpersonal communication and relationship maintenance processes increasingly involve the use of communication technologies, how people use these technologies has proven to be a fruitful area of research for technology scholars. This chapter thus focuses on questions around *channel navigation* in interpersonal communication contexts: individuals' use of multiple communication channels to maintain their relationships and the relational implications of such use.

In most developed societies today, individuals can choose among a wide range of communication channel options when interacting with others, including (if co-located) face-to-face interaction as well as phone calls, emails, and social media. Conversations can start in one channel, continue in another, and then hop to a third or fourth medium or back to the original. In many cases, these channel switches are seamless: interactants may not even notice. In other cases, the choice of channel may be the result of a careful and arduous decision-making process. Furthermore, the "receiver" may interpret the use of a particular channel as an intentional signal not just about the interaction, but perhaps a signal about the relationship itself. Scholarship on communication technologies often focuses on one particular channel, a choice no doubt informed by methodological considerations. However, this choice limits our understanding by focusing on only one source of interaction, when in actual practice interpersonal communication often takes place via several channels, with multiple streams of interactions feeding into and out of one another.

In this chapter, we first explicate why it is important for researchers to undertake a holistic view of interactions by considering multiple platforms—not just the subset of interactions that occur on one specific channel—when studying interpersonal interactions in online contexts. We argue that widening the scope of considered channels, while posing methodological challenges, will provide researchers with a more nuanced and comprehensive understanding of interpersonal communication in contemporary media environments. This understanding may offer opportunities to revisit existing theories of computer-mediated communication (CMC), specifically around relationship maintenance and technology use. We then identify salient factors that may influence which channel people gravitate toward or avoid in their navigation and synthesize them in a preliminary framework of channel navigation. Finally, as a way of prompting intellectual engagement with this topic, we describe three research areas that future scholarship could address.

Rationale for a Multi-Channel Approach

Focusing only on a single channel may pose both methodological and conceptual limitations in our understanding of how these channels support relationships. Although many interactions involve multiple individuals, we limit the scope of our discussion to dyadic interactions. As our framework suggests, there are many factors to consider when making decisions about channel navigation with even two communication partners; additional interactants add more complexity than can be addressed here.

Methodological Advantage of a Multi-Channel Approach

In studying how people communicate with each other via contemporary technologies, particularly mobile phones or social network sites (SNSs), behavioral trace data—digital footprints generated by user actions such as "likes" on Facebook or call logs on mobile phones—represent an exciting trend for technology scholars. The granularity of these data, which enables researchers to access information such as precisely how long a user spent on a particular page or even how long they spent composing a message, is understandably compelling to researchers: in addition to precision, this type of data bypasses issues such as low survey participation rates, faulty or biased self-reports of behaviors, and sampling concerns.

However, these datasets only capture activities that result in visible traces on the platform, such as comments or messages, and are often limited to a single platform given the difficulty in linking users across multiple profiles on different platforms. Actions that do not leave persistent traces, such as reading status updates on Facebook, may thus be "invisible" to both other users and researchers using these server logs. As we explain below, these invisible behaviors, sometimes considered "passive SNS behavior" by researchers, can have important implications for relational maintenance when people use or inject information obtained from one channel into other interactions or move conversations from one platform to another. Consider, for instance, a user who shares a piece of information on Facebook about the passing of a loved one, and then receives a phone call, presumably a more effortful action than clicking a "sad" emoticon. Moreover, the phone call is from a close friend who has not acknowledged the status on the platform itself. Behavioral trace data from Facebook would not capture this interaction, a relational maintenance behavior arguably as significant—and perhaps more so as we argue later—as leaving a "like" or commenting on the platform itself. The increasing popularity of data-driven approaches highlights the significance of the work we propose here: users might be engaging with others and their content in meaningful ways that are not visible either within the SNS platform or in the trace data they produce. As data-driven scholarship becomes more common, a better understanding of what this type of data may not capture—namely how streams of communication across disparate channels are related to one another in the context of a relationship—becomes more necessary. An additional benefit of this multi-platform approach is that it offers researchers without access to server-level data an approach that is superior for addressing some kinds of research questions.

The Relevance of the Multi-Channel Approach to Interpersonal Dynamics

CMC scholars have long advocated for the necessity of looking at multi-channel interaction, particularly to understand relationships (Baym et al., 2004). These hidden cross-channel interactions, if hidden from researchers, can stymie attempts at fully understanding the link between online interaction patterns and their social and psychological implications. For example, a pattern of diminishing text messages may not be evidence of relationship dissolution, as would appear at first glance, but rather the result of the couple "upgrading" to video-conferencing or voice calls. Alternatively, a cohabitating married couple may have the same Facebook relationship patterns as a pair of disinterested acquaintances—little to no communication on the platform—because they use many other channels, including face-to-face interaction, to communicate. In the rest of the chapter, we present a framework to understand how people navigate their multi-channel ecology. We then advance three research directions stemming from the components of this framework that highlight the complex and vibrant opportunities for theory development.

A Framework of Channel Navigation in Dyadic Communication

What kinds of factors influence decisions about channel navigation? In the next section, we explicate a framework of the factors at play in channel navigation decisions within dyadic communication. As researchers enlarge the scope of their focus to include multi-channel communication, this framework can hopefully help guide them to the factors we see as relevant for channel navigation decisions and stimulate future scholarship and discussion.

Our framework considers three major kinds of factors at play in channel navigation decisions: (1) the self, (2) the communication partner, and (3) the interaction itself. After outlining the framework briefly, we discuss the framework as a whole and proceed to delve into a more in-depth discussion of several factors most relevant to researchers interested in interpersonal communication. These are not intended to be exhaustive but represent major themes in the general CMC literature. Moreover, while we categorize certain factors as more self-related or partner-related, many of these factors may cross the self–other spectrum and do not fall entirely within any particular category.

Our Approach to Understanding Multi-Channel Communication

CMC theorists have from the onset acknowledged that many relationships are enacted across a wide set of interaction channels. Walther and Parks (2002) describe "mixed mode relationships," noting that "these new social arrangements not only pose challenges for existing theories, they also afford new opportunities for theory" (p. 550). Similarly, work by Ramirez and colleagues (2015) considers relational outcomes associated with the transition from mediated to face-to-face interaction among online daters. In contrast to these projects and others that consider the introduction of a new medium into a dyad's communication patterns, here our focus is not the number of channels a dyad may use or when a new one is introduced. Rather, we consider the movement across channels, with an emphasis on relationship maintenance as enacted via these multi-channel interactions.

Furthermore, during each interaction, users can draw from multiple channels simultaneously, and use of one particular channel is often not clear-cut or independent of other channels (Isaacs et al., 2012). From recordings of social interactions, Isaacs and colleagues (2012) described how daily conversations may happen via a combination of simultaneous interactions on multiple channels, and not any single one channel. In a particularly telling example, one roommate was listening on another roommate's video call conversation (with mutual friends) and participated intermittently by shouting over to the next room (Isaacs et al., 2012). Separate platforms are thus brought together to form a coherent conversation (Isaacs et al., 2012).

Individuals select communication channels based on many factors, stemming from qualities of the platform but also the relational and interpersonal context of the interaction. Moreover, in a media environment where multiple channels are readily available, a user's decision to use one channel over another carries emotional, social, and moral meaning in themselves (Madianou & Miller, 2013). For example, in studying how couples switch between channels during a conflict,

Scissors and Gergle (2013) emphasized interpersonally motivated reasons for switching channels during the conflict episode. Interestingly, while Scissors and Gergle (2013) identified a set of motivations for channel switching, their findings suggest that, within each motivation, the patterns of channel switch differ across situations and users. For instance, for the same motivation of avoiding conflict escalation, for example, some participants found CMC to be appropriate in mitigating a conflict, but others felt that CMC would actually escalate the conflict. This highlights that a variety of factors can be at play during channel navigation, ranging from the purpose of the interaction, the affordances perceived in the technologies, to individualistic perceptions of such technologies. It is these factors that we try to acknowledge in our framework of multi-channel communication.

The Framework of Multi-channel Communication

Coming back to our framework, although it seems obvious to state, communication partners are limited by the set of platforms available to—and used by—both parties: their *shared media ecology*. While non-use of a channel definitely excludes the possibility of using it, use can vary along a spectrum, as surfaced by Baumer and colleagues (2013) in their research into non-use of Facebook. Especially in the early stages of a relationship, before technology patterns have congealed, misunderstandings may result in communication failures (e.g. a message sent to a platform that is never checked or a defunct email address).

Other than voluntary choices to include or not include a channel in one's media ecology, a range of factors, such as *media literacy* or *monetary cost*, can present obstacles to using a channel. In fact, 33% of Americans do not have broadband internet at home, and the cost of either the broadband connection or a computer is frequently cited as a key reason for not getting broadband Internet (Horrigan & Duggan, 2015). While a substantial proportion of this population can rely on their smartphones and mobile data to accomplish many tasks (Horrigan & Duggan, 2015), the cost can still impose certain restrictions. For example, smartphone-only Internet users with restrictions on their data usage may be more hesitant to use video calls because of the greater amount of data they consume.

People have *idiosyncratic perceptions* about how they want to use certain communication channels, including whether the channel is appropriate for relational development or self-disclosure (Ledbetter & Mazer, 2014), which channels they enjoy using (Ledbetter et al., 2016), or how they feel about connectedness as enabled by contemporary technologies in general (Gonzales & Wu, 2016). Naturally, these preferences and perceptions influence which technology they gravitate toward or how they perceive interactions involving these technologies.

Moreover, these cognitive processes can have further implications for how people interpret their everyday interactions (Gonzales & Wu, 2016) and relationships (Ledbetter & Mazer, 2014; Ledbetter et al., 2016)—consequently shaping the effects of these interactions. For example, Ledbetter and Mazer (2014) found that frequency of Facebook communication was predictive of relational closeness *only* when the communicator holds favorable attitudes about online self-disclosure and online communication. Similarly, when a physically co-present person uses their phone instead of talking to their co-located partner, only participants who express high frustration with technology use see this action as ostracizing (Gonzales & Wu, 2016).

In addition, *habits* can be a powerful predictor of media use (LaRose, 2015). Indeed, desires to use media—including browsing the Web, checking email, and using SNS—are particularly resistant to self-control (Hofmann et al., 2012). Notably, LaRose (2015) views the ubiquity of media devices and their use by others, as well as our reliable access to them, as a constant trigger for media use and reinforcing media habits. Habits become more ingrained over time through structural considerations as well. For instance, platforms like Facebook make change of address announcements unnecessary, because the platform enables people to keep in touch even if they do not have access to a current address or phone number: long-time users may thus find it difficult to leave the platform and the interpersonal connections maintained there. Acknowledging the power of habit, our model suggests that dyads that are accustomed to communicating through a specific platform will also be more likely to choose that platform in the future.

The *interpersonal context* in which communication occurs can determine the patterns of channel navigation by making certain acts of communication more or less appropriate, thus shaping channel decisions. For example, the exchange of phone calls may not occur until two friends reach a certain level of closeness; however, it would not be odd for work colleagues to call one another for work-related tasks immediately after beginning to work together.

One's *closeness to the communication partner* and implications for media use understandably occupy a prominent place in this literature. Media multiplexity theory (MMT), proposed by Haythornthwaite (2005), posits that strong ties use more communication channels with each other, while weak ties can be largely dependent on a single channel. The theory also suggests that media use is unidimensional within a group (Haythornthwaite, 2005); that is, "those who use only one medium, use the same one medium; those who use two, tend to use the same second medium" (p. 130). Work extending MMT has consistently supported the theory's conclusion that closer pairs use more channels to communicate with each other (Baym & Ledbetter, 2009; Caughlin & Sharabi, 2013).

Existing literature shows that, especially with repeated interactions, people develop *an understanding of the preferences and practices of their communication partner.* Scissors and Gergle (2013) identified "adjusting to partner preferences" as a motivation for channel switching during romantic couple conflict. For instance, one participant compromised by replacing emails with calls or face-to-face meetings when arguing with her partner to adapt to his preferences. Cramer and Jacobs (2015) echo this observation in their investigation of communication channels use between romantic partners more generally: couples factor in their intimate knowledge of partner's habits and preferences in deciding which channel to use. Similarly, past interactions with someone can provide cues beyond stated preferences about which channel works and which does not. For example, after repeated, unsuccessful attempts to contact someone via text messaging, one participant interviewed by Wohn and Birnholtz (2015) eventually learned to avoid texting that particular person.

The choice to use a channel can be deliberate and sends its own message (Gershon, 2010; Madianou & Miller, 2013), which we refer to as *symbolic signaling*. Sometimes one can opt for a channel seen as less intimate and more impersonal to keep an appropriate social distance between communication partners (Eden & Veksler, 2016). Conversely, people may switch to a more private channel to send a stronger signal of intimacy with the receiver. Bazarova (2012) found that the same disclosure sent via private message was perceived as more intimate than one shared via a public channel. Similarly, the platform itself is imbued with symbolic connotations due to a wide range of factors, including how the platform is marketed and how one's peer group views the platform. Presumably, one could send a lunch invitation to the same person from a professional email account or via Tinder (an online dating application), with very different interpretations.

The *goal of the interaction* influences what kind of communicative environment or affordances people will desire and thus influences the channel used. A common theme across previous work is that participants frequently attribute their decision regarding communication channel to properties of the channel and the utility of these properties for satisfying certain goals. Indeed, several prominent theories of media use, including media richness theory (Daft & Lengel, 1986), uses and gratifications theory (Katz et al., 1973), or the theory of the niche (Dimmick et al., 2000), all consider the gratification of some need or task as a primary determinant of what channel people will use or abandon. Similarly, the necessity of or desire for certain affordances—defined here as the perceived possible uses of an object or tool—to satisfy interaction goals emerges as a major influence of channel navigation.

For instance, in the case of Snapchat, which allows users to send non-persistent messages and pictures, people may capitalize on the ephemerality affordance to share playful snippets of everyday life (Bayer et al., 2016). Accordingly, people mostly use Snapchat with close ties, with whom they are more comfortable sharing everyday, less curated images (Bayer et al., 2016). Meanwhile, on anonymous channels such as the anonymous question and answer site Ask.fm, adolescents described using anonymity to circumvent social expectations and ask more sensitive questions about sexuality or to address rumors (Ellison et al., 2016).

Future Directions for Research

As we consider these factors, it becomes evident that the decision to use a particular platform in each situation can be highly idiosyncratic, although we can point to specific factors that are likely to influence this decision across multiple kinds of relationships and contexts. As our model reflects, the self, the other person, and the context of communication all exert a variety of influences in how we navigate our personal media ecology. This focus on multiple channel interactions represents a vital new area of research topic that will enable scholars to better understand how channel use practices allow individuals to meet their interpersonal goals within the networked modes of communication and interaction they are embedded within. Below we explicate three areas we believe are particularly compelling.

Relational Media Literacy and Channel Coordination

Above we outline some of the factors that may enter into the complex calculus involved in conversations that traverse different communication modes. As with any interaction, every individual may have their own unique set of goals, preferences, and practices—even different interpretations of the same exchange. Moreover, they may not be aware that not everyone shares their "media ideologies"—how they think a channel should be used (Gershon, 2010; Haimson et al., 2017). The increasing number of channels in contemporary communication environments complicates these decisions. What are the consequences of decisions around channel choice for individuals and their communication partners? Are some individuals better at making channel decisions? One potential area for future work is inspired by these questions.

Given the multiple channels to choose from, the appropriate use of channel and sensitivity to the preferences of communication partners can become more consequential, especially in relationships involving frequent and important communication (e.g. romantic partners, close friends, important colleagues). Early work on the use of technology in organizational communication contexts, such as the social information processing model (Fulk et al., 1987) or the social construction view of communication technology (Fulk, 1993), underscores the argument that perceptions about technology draw from not just objective assessments of the technologies but also the social context and one's past experiences (Fulk et al., 1987). The findings of Fulk (1993) support this proposal: social influence factors, operationalized here as one's work group's attitudes toward and use of a technology, predicted their own attitudes and use of the technology. More interestingly, the influence is stronger for those with high attraction to their work group, bolstering the importance of social influence (Fulk, 1993).

The same influences are potentially relevant for interpersonal communication outside the workplace. As Scissors and Gergle (2013) note, consideration of and adjustment to the media use patterns and preferences of one's partner can be important for achieving satisfactory communication, such as the resolution of conflict. Similarly, Wohn and Birnholtz (2015) found that, in some cases, not knowing the media use patterns of the other person can result in unsuccessful interaction attempts, as when users keep trying to contact another person on a channel they do not use. Finally, Caughlin and Sharabi (2013) advanced the communicative interdependence perspective in studying technology use in interpersonal contexts, which emphasizes the importance of how messages and interactions occurring via different modes of communication are interconnected to one another within close relationships. Empirically, their findings illustrate that the ease of integrating and transitioning exchanges occurring on mediated channels and face-to-face is predictive of relational closeness, and ease of transitioning also predicts relational satisfaction (Caughlin & Sharabi, 2013). Thus, the skillful navigation of the multi-channel ecology cannot be taken for granted in relationships but can have implications for relationship quality. Several questions thus arise from a focus on *relational media literacy*: How (if at all) does relational media literacy, or the lack thereof, influence relationship quality? What kind of behaviors do high-literacy individuals engage in? Are there individual personality traits associated with high relational media literacy?

Within close relationships, we have a variety of platforms at our disposal to connect with others. In this context, relational media literacy may manifest as effective and seamless coordination between channels, that is, knowing which channel to use when or which channel will best get the partner's attention.

Just as individuals can vary in their communication competence or media literacy, presumably there are also differences in how well they navigate the ecology of possible communication channels. For example, participants interviewed by Scissors and Gergle (2013) described paying attention to cues such as the partner's tone via text messages or their lack of response to email, which prompted these participants to switch to a more appropriate or effective channel, actions believed to help facilitate the resolution of conflicts. However, similar to the way people may differ in how attentive and adaptable their self-presentation can be depending on the situation, as is the case with the self-monitoring trait (Snyder, 1974), it is likely that sensitivity to these communicative issues will differ between individuals, but this has not been explored. Similarly, we do not know how the ability to effectively select channels affects others' perceptions of the user. For example, a job seeker may be seen in a more favorable light if they attempt to connect with a recruiter via LinkedIn, an SNS devoted to professional networking, rather than a more socially oriented platform such as Facebook or Snapchat.

Within friendships that are developing, the process through which people intensify their communication and how this intensification relates to the expansion of channels used between two people can be investigated further. Media multiplexity theory (Haythornthwaite, 2005) stated that closer pairs use more channels with each other. The question then becomes how people achieve this deepening of channel use. For example, if someone is already regularly meeting a school mate face-to-face (the first layer of channel use), when is the most appropriate opportunity to add this person on Facebook or to ask for their phone number? Coming back to the question of relational media competence, one's greater facility with channel navigation can thus have positive implications for success in cultivating and maintaining friendships.

Finally, we also have latent ties—"a tie for which a connection is available technically but that has not yet been activated by social interaction" (Haythornthwaite, 2002, p. 389), such as coworkers sharing the same email system or school mates connected on a school Facebook group. Although certain platforms can technically provide the means to convert latent ties to weak ties, not everyone employs these platforms successfully. For example, in researching how IBM employees used the company's enterprise social network site, DiMicco and colleagues (2008) offered an example of a particular employee who was able to amass a large group of followers to support her projects within the company. Although many people use the same platform, not all of them achieved such connections. What might be distinguishing characters or strategies that explain why some people succeed at establishing new relationships while others do not when equipped with the same platform?

Signals of Relational Investment in Online Contexts

A second area for future research considers the implications of platform switches for relational development and maintenance, including how interactants perceive such switches. What is the relational signal communicated by a platform switch which occurs, *not* in the middle of an interaction, but rather when information from one platform is imported into another? For example, after seeing a friend's birthday photos on Instagram (a picture sharing social media platform), I send her a text message to wish her a happy birthday, instead of using the platform's commenting or messaging features.

Posts shared on social media often serve as conversational openings, starting a thread of responses within the same channel. Accordingly, a substantial literature already exists about how users interpret responses to SNS updates that occur within the same platform (Grinberg et al., 2017; Hayes et al. 2016; Scissors et al., 2016). However, here we consider instances in which users do not respond in the same channel (e.g. a comment on a Facebook post) but instead use a separate channel (e.g. a phone call) when responding. In doing so, individuals implicitly signal that they have seen and attended to the information shared via SNS. We believe instances in which users respond at a later time or via another channel offer scholars a useful case to consider, in that these acts may have implications for relational development that are as significant as—if not more meaningful than—responses on the platform itself.

The social capital framework highlights an important dimension of durable social relationships: reciprocity. Building upon Lin's (2002) definition of social capital as "investments in social relations with expected returns in the marketplace" (p. 19), we propose the concept of "*attention capital*"—investment in attention (literally, "*paying* attention") and returns (receiving attention)—as a useful way to understand relationship maintenance in SNS contexts. Better understanding how individuals perceive these signals has the potential to extend existing theories about relationship development that reflect today's media environment, where choice of channel has the power to shape how interactions unfold and their implications for relationship development.

SNSs contain a set of affordances that shape how attention is communicated, directed, and obscured. As we describe above, the structure of many social media platforms is such that leaving a digital trace is the most obvious and straightforward way for users to register that they have attended to a piece of content. Platforms then use these accumulated clicks to manage future information flow patterns. In contrast to earlier forms of mass media, in which editors and experts made decisions about what content should receive more attention (i.e. which stories constituted "front page news"), contemporary media environments offer users a vast smorgasbord of unfiltered content. The term "attention economy" highlights the dynamics at play, wherein getting content on a user's screen is only the first barrier. Actually ensuring that they engage with it involves an entirely different set of challenges. This may be why commenters such as Rheingold and Weeks (2012), for instance, frame attention management as one of the five key skills necessary for digital literacy. Of course, interpersonal interactions via social media function differently than the sharing of news stories on social media: these interactions incorporate reciprocity. "Investing" in a Friend's post via a comment likely improves the chances that they will reciprocate in the future, due to both social (e.g. reciprocity norms) as well as technical factors (e.g. input into the algorithm that determines visibility of future posts).

SNSs thus reshape attention dynamics in key ways, and SNS users must contend with additional layers of uncertainty about how attention is configured in social media spaces. The first layer of uncertainty is *visibility*, which considers whether the post is visible or not. Content on SNSs is algorithmically manipulated in ways that individuals cannot calculate. If one does not comment on a story shared by a friend, "It didn't show up in my feed" is a reasonable excuse.

The second layer of uncertainty is *attention*. As argued by Ellison and Vitak (2015), attention in SNSs is not communicated by traditional, and easier to read, signals such as eye contact. Even if a particular post was displayed on a user's screen, she may not have actually read, or even noticed, it. In contemporary media environments, attention cannot be assessed unless individuals take specific action, such as liking a photo or responding to a status update with a comment (Ellison et al., 2014). Indeed, previous research indicates that people often underestimate how many people view their posts on Facebook, generally assuming it to be only 27% of its true size (Bernstein et al., 2013). Analysis of the rationales participants provided for their guesses suggested that friend count and feedback, such as likes and comments, provide the main mechanisms of audience estimation, again highlighting the role of visible responses (Bernstein et al., 2013). In the context of SNSs, visible actions—the only actions that can be seen, counted, and assessed in digital spaces—seem to be the only currency that matter, unless this information is brought into another channel, as examined here.

The third layer of uncertainty, and one that is more recently introduced and much less understood, is around *authentic engagement*. Due to changing user practices and platform affordances, attention signals can be manipulated more easily than in the past. Ellison and colleagues (2014, p. 858) argue, "On SNSs, social grooming occurs via interactions between connected members, with the content, frequency, and length of messages serving as signals of the strength and context of the relationship." In the last few years, however, these attention calculi have been reformulated through automation, either technical or human. Users may engage in gratuitous, mindless mass "liking" in an attempt to build up stores of reciprocated social support and meet social expectations. Technical innovations support these behaviors, such as tools that automate the delivery of some of these messages, such as "happy birthday" comments. Together, these dynamics mean that visible traces of attention constitute less reliable signals of authentic engagement than in the past. For example, Wee and Lee (2017) find that "likes" (either from or to Friends) were not associated with perceptions of intimacy, whereas comments from Friends were. Interestingly, and perhaps supporting a relational signals frame, chat initiated by others and comments from others were associated with intimacy feelings, but outbound comments and chat requests were not. As they note, "Since likes require the least effort to engage, participants may not necessarily relate the activity to the psychological closeness they feel towards their friends" (Wee & Lee, 2017, p. 11).

In comparison, when individuals import information from one platform into another, it is clear that they have engaged with it authentically. As we have argued, digital technologies typically lower the transaction costs associated with signaling interest. In contrast, seeing messages in one medium and then responding in another constitute stronger signals of engagement, because this gesture often requires individuals to actually remember and activate information. Thinking about the difference between assessment signals, signals that are inherently reliable, and conventional signals, signals that can easily be fabricated (Donath, 2007), it is clear that passing someone in the hall and mentioning their last Facebook post is undeniably an assessment signal of attention, whereas "liking" that same post is a much more easily fabricated (conventional) signal of attention. Given the multiple layers of uncertainty surrounding attention assessment via SNS, as well as the growing prominent role of SNS attention and reciprocity, the transfer of information obtained from SNS to other contexts might be an increasingly common phenomenon with unexplored research possibilities.

Social Information Seeking

A third possible research focus involves actively seeking information about others—as opposed to encountering it via social media or other means—and the ways in which this information is incorporated (or not) into future interactions. As described above, in some cases, encountering information in one platform (e.g. a SNS) and bringing it into another (e.g. a face-to-face interaction) may be seen as a true signal of interest, engagement, and attention. In other cases, however, finding information about someone online is framed as "stalking"—a shameful act which is best hidden from public audiences. The broad spectrum of information-seeking behaviors has been a focus of researchers since before the prevalence of social media (e.g. Uncertainty Reduction Theory considers the ways in which individuals learn information about others, such as asking mutual friends), but the opportunities for self-expression found in online fora, especially social media, change this process considerably. Writing in 2002 about "extractive" strategies that include using search engines to locate newsgroup postings by the target, Ramirez and colleagues (2002) note that

> [b]ecause these postings reflect statements enacted in social settings—in many cases made without the target suspecting that they would be stored for years and available for public consumption beyond the group for which they were originally intended—they may offer particularly valuable insights to information seekers, especially because the information can be collected covertly, and without the target's knowledge.
>
> (p. 220)

These points are not only still relevant for social media contexts, but also significantly more so, given the vast amounts of personal information individuals share over years of use.

Yet using social media sites to gain information about others is not always an activity freely admitted by information seekers. These social media investigations, sometimes called "stalking" or "creeping," enable individuals to gather information about someone without their knowledge, by reading their content but purposefully withholding explicit signals of attention such as likes and comments. In some instances, looking through a target's corpus of past social media posts, or "backstalking" (Schoenebeck et al., 2016), is considered to be a violation of social norms, as evidenced by popular press narratives where those who engage in this practice recount horror stories of a slipped finger. One writer expresses: "A 'deep like' is the worst thing that can happen when you're lurking on Instagram" and describes the feelings of "panic, profound regret, and infinite embarrassment" she experienced when accidentally liking a post "92 weeks deep in a stranger's Instagram account" (Thompson, 2017). However, research on this topic is thin. What factors dictate when information-gathering is something to be candidly shared and when it is a shameful practice, to be obscured at all costs? For the latter, are there strategies for using this information to ingratiate oneself without revealing the original of one's information? Similarly, what factors determine whether discovering this kind of detective work is seen as a compliment versus a "creepy" or undesirable practice?

We can speculate about what factors might determine the acceptability of social information seeking online and thus the chance that information will be used and its source described. The relationship itself is of course key: it is probably more acceptable to look for information about a close tie as opposed to a weak one. Backstalking—revisiting old SNS posts—was practiced discreetly with weak ties but openly with strong ties, such as romantic partners or best friends, among participants interviewed by Schoenebeck and colleagues (2016). Finally, the effort involved likely plays a role in the acceptability of the practice. We have described effort as being related to the strength of the signal, where low-effort clicks are less reliable signals of attention than a response in another channel. Similarly, opportunistically encountering information in one's feed is likely more acceptable than five hours of clicking Google links or paying a private investigator.[1]

A related set of questions considers the implications of such information seeking, for seeker and seekee. What are the effects of looking for information about others using SNSs on self-esteem and psychological well-being? When people look at content on SNS without acting on it in any way on the platform itself, this behavior is commonly conceptualized in SNS research as "passive" (Verduyn et al., 2015). Previous research has provided persuasive evidence of a link between behaviors appearing to be passive and declines in well-being (Verduyn et al., 2015) or increases in loneliness (Burke et al., 2010). But intentional information-seeking may have different outcomes than low-engagement scrolling, although they look similar in activity logs and survey responses.

As a result, outcomes associated with information-seeking are unclear, due in part to different definitions and understandings of this practice. In particular, when people use information gathered from SNS to springboard interactions, it can be positive. Ellison and colleagues (2011) consider a set of interaction practices dubbed "social information-seeking": asking participants about using Facebook for purposes such as to "check out someone [they] met socially," "to learn more about other people in [their] classes," and "to learn more about other people living near [them]." Ellison and colleagues (2011) find that this set of behaviors, wherein individuals use Facebook to learn information about people they have an offline connection with, is predictive of both bridging and bonding social capital. They speculate that the "identity information typically included in Facebook profiles may be used to trigger offline interactions. In this sense, Facebook use can act as a catalyst of, rather than a replacement for, offline interaction," in contrast to using the site to maintain existing relationships or using the site to try to meet new people (Ellison et al., 2011, p. 886). Additionally, Leonardi and Meyer (2015) identified browsing behaviors as helping to transfer knowledge between members of an organization, especially between organizational members who do not know each other well. When organizational members observe each other's activities on SNS, these activities can create conversational material and ease the transfer of knowledge (Leonardi & Meyer, 2015).

Overall, while research could distinguish more clearly what kinds of information-gathering activities are associated with positive psychological and social implications versus with depression and other negative outcomes, certain patterns emerge from the literature. As explicated above, when the individuals approach the information-seeking process with socialization motives, as in Ellison and colleagues (2011), outcomes appear to be positive. Meanwhile, Tandoc and colleagues (2015) measured surveillance behaviors on Facebook—operationalized as frequency of activities such as reading updates, *without* specifying a motivation— and identified a positive link between surveillance and envy. Facebook envy, in turn, is associated with depression, but, without accounting for the envy, the relationship between Facebook use and depression is actually negative (Tandoc et al., 2015). Nonetheless, there might be other important mediators of this relationship between browsing behaviors and declines in well-being or envy. For example, users possessing a more sophisticated understanding of the self-presentational pressures at play may take social media displays with a "grain of salt," understanding that people are more likely to post positive and socially desirable content on SNS, leaving out unflattering photos or mundane activities. Recognizing that social media portrayals are heavily filtered may ameliorate feelings of envy, regret, fear of missing out, and other negative emotions sometimes associated with SNS use.

Together, these studies demonstrate how browsing behaviors may have different implications for well-being contingent on how researchers operationalized browsing behaviors. Burke and colleagues (2010) and Tandoc and colleagues (2015) both demonstrated negative implications of browsing behaviors. Both studies also measured only frequency of browsing behaviors, that is, the frequency of looking at others' profiles, browsing the news feed, or reading updates, without considering the motivation behind the browsing. Meanwhile, Ellison and colleagues (2011) and Leonardi and Meyer (2015) gauged browsing behaviors associated with specific social information-seeking motivations. These two studies revealed favorable implications of browsing behaviors. Hence, a key distinction might be that users with clear social motives while browsing, which certain studies gauged while others did not, may be able to use the information productively, while those who do not may instead experience envy and loneliness from the same activities. Overall, the implications of browsing behaviors could benefit from further clarification, and investigating how information gained from browsing behaviors is used elsewhere can be a helpful direction for this line of research.

Conclusion

In a networked society, the use of multiple channels in relational maintenance practices and the navigation of these channels take on layers of significance and meanings, for both users and researchers. Relationships are increasingly being maintained via these technologies, adding additional resonance to the choice of one channel over another. Moreover, these technologies, particularly SNSs, also serve as substantial depositories of personal information, which can unconsciously seep into or be strategically leveraged in interactions via other media.

Recognizing the relevance of these phenomena in studies of networked selves, we have employed a multichannel approach to interpersonal communication in this chapter, articulated a framework for channel navigation scholarship, and proposed three research directions in this area. From monitoring communication partners' channel preferences to considering the appropriate response to signal one's investment in a relationship, we believe these new communication repertoires offer researchers a new avenue for exploring how relationship dynamics unfold across different platforms.

One of the key affordances of digitally inscribed information is its persistence. Early medium theorists such as McLuhan and Ong considered the effects of literacy and suggest that access to writing (expression of thought that is persistent and sharable in ways that oral communication is not) might have implications for humans' capacity for memory, the development of science, and the nature of human society (Ong, 2013). Now, we have become so familiar with—and reliant upon—the persistence of written information that we may be at the edge of another monumental shift: in a communicative environment where mindless clicking often serves little communicative value, the ability to remember and to import information from one context into another will take on increased importance as a signal of authentic engagement. How individuals and societies adjust to this communication environment by finding new ways to indicate interest and investment offers communication and technology scholars an exciting opportunity to better understand human nature and technological innovation.

Note

1 This may be in part why practices changed after the introduction of Facebook's current profile format. The Timeline format makes it much easier and more seamless to scroll back in time compared to the previous Facebook profile format—and some might argue that the Timeline format encourages this behavior.

References

Baumer, E. P., Adams, P., Khovanskaya, V. D., Liao, T. C., Smith, M. E., Schwanda Sosik, V., & Williams, K. (2013). Limiting, leaving, and (re) lapsing: An exploration of facebook non-use practices and experiences. *Proceedings of the SIGCHI conference on human factors in computing systems* (pp. 3257–3266). New York: ACM.

Bayer, J. B., Ellison, N. B., Schoenebeck, S. Y., & Falk, E. B. (2016). Sharing the small moments: Ephemeral social interaction on Snapchat. *Information, Communication & Society*, 19(7), 956–977.

Baym, N. K., & Ledbetter, A. (2009). Tunes that bind? Predicting friendship strength in a music-based social network. *Information, Communication & Society*, 12(3), 408–427.

Baym, N. K., Zhang, Y. B., & Lin, M.-C. (2004). Social interactions across media: Interpersonal communication on the internet, telephone and face-to-face. *New Media & Society*, 6(3), 299–318.

Bazarova, N. N. (2012). Public intimacy: Disclosure interpretation and social judgments on Facebook. *Journal of Communication,* 62(5), 815–832.

Bernstein, M. S., Bakshy, E., Burke, M., & Karrer, B. (2013). Quantifying the invisible audience in social networks. *Proceedings of the SIGCHI conference on human factors in computing systems* (pp. 21–30). New York: ACM.

Burke, M., Marlow, C., & Lento, T. (2010). Social network activity and social well-being. *Proceedings of the SIGCHI conference on human factors in computing systems* (pp. 1909–1912). New York: ACM.

Caughlin, J. P., & Sharabi, L. L. (2013). A communicative interdependence perspective of close relationships: The connections between mediated and unmediated interactions matter. *Journal of Communication,* 63(5), 873–893.

Cramer, H., & Jacobs, M. L. (2015). Couples' communication channels: What, when & why? *Proceedings of the 33rd annual ACM conference on human factors in computing systems* (pp. 1349–1354). New York: ACM.

Daft, R. L., & Lengel, R. H. (1986). Organizational information requirements, media richness and structural design. *Management Science,* 32(5), 554–571.

DiMicco, J., Millen, D. R., Geyer, W., Dugan, C., Brownholtz, B., & Muller, M. (2008). Motivations for social networking at work. *Proceedings of the 2008 ACM conference on computer supported cooperative work* (pp. 1545–1554). New York: ACM.

Dimmick, J., Kline, S., & Stafford, L. (2000). The gratification niches of personal e-mail and the telephone: Competition, displacement, and complementarity. *Communication Research,* 27(2), 227–248.

Donath, J. (2007). Signals in social supernets. *Journal of Computer-Mediated Communication,* 13(1), 231–251.

Eden, J., & Veksler, A. E. (2016). Relational maintenance in the digital age: Implicit rules and multiple modalities. *Communication Quarterly,* 64(2), 119–144.

Ellison, N. B., & Vitak, J. (2015). Social network site affordances and their relationship to social capital processes. *The handbook of the psychology of communication technology* (pp. 205–228). Chichester: Wiley Blackwell.

Ellison, N. B., Steinfield, C., & Lampe, C. (2011). Connection strategies: Social capital implications of Facebook-enabled communication practices. *New Media & Society,* 13(6), 873–892.

Ellison, N. B., Vitak, J., Gray, R., & Lampe, C. (2014). Cultivating social resources on social network sites: Facebook relationship maintenance behaviors and their role in social capital processes. *Journal of Computer-Mediated Communication,* 19(4), 855–870.

Ellison, N. B., Blackwell, L., Lampe, C., & Trieu, P. (2016). "The question exists, but you don't exist with it": Strategic anonymity in the social lives of adolescents. *Social Media+ Society,* 2(4). doi: 10.1177/2056305116670673

Fulk, J. (1993). Social construction of communication technology. *Academy of Management Journal,* 36(5), 921–950.

Fulk, J., Steinfield, C. W., Schmitz, J., & Power, J. G. (1987). A social information processing model of media use in organizations. *Communication Research,* 14(5), 529–552.

Gershon, I. (2010). Media ideologies: An introduction. *Journal of Linguistic Anthropology,* 20(2), 283–293.

Gonzales, A. L., & Wu, Y. (2016). Public cellphone use does not activate negative responses in others . . . Unless they hate cellphones. *Journal of Computer-Mediated Communication,* 21(5), 384–398.

Grinberg, N., Kalyanaraman, S., Adamic, L. A., & Naaman, M. (2017). Understanding feedback expectations on Facebook. *Proceedings of the 2017 ACM conference on computer supported cooperative work* (pp. 1726–1739). New York: ACM.

Haimson, O. L., Andalibi, N., De Choudhury, M., & Hayes, G. R. (2017). Relationship breakup disclosures and media ideologies on Facebook. *New Media & Society*. doi: 10.1177/1461444817711402.

Hayes, R. A., Carr, C. T., & Wohn, D. Y. (2016). One click, many meanings: Interpreting paralinguistic digital affordances in social media. *Journal of Broadcasting & Electronic Media*, 60(1), 171–187.

Haythornthwaite, C. (2002). Strong, weak, and latent ties and the impact of new media. *The Information Society*, 18(5), 385–401.

Haythornthwaite, C. (2005). Social networks and Internet connectivity effects. *Information, Community & Society*, 8(2), 125–147.

Hofmann, W., Vohs, K. D., & Baumeister, R. F. (2012). What people desire, feel conflicted about, and try to resist in everyday life. *Psychological Science*, 23(6), 582–588.

Horrigan, J. B., & Duggan, M. (2015). Home broadband 2015. *Pew Research Center*, December 21.

Isaacs, E., Szymanski, M., Yamauchi, Y., Glasnapp, J., & Iwamoto, K. (2012). Integrating local and remote worlds through channel blending. *Proceedings of the ACM 2012 conference on computer supported cooperative work* (pp. 617–626). New York: ACM.

Katz, E., Blumler, J. G., & Gurevitch, M. (1973). Uses and gratifications research. *The Public Opinion Quarterly*, 37(4), 509–523.

LaRose, R. (2015). The psychology of interactive media habits. *The handbook of the psychology of communication technology* (pp. 365–383). Chichester: Wiley Blackwell.

Ledbetter, A. M., & Mazer, J. P. (2014). Do online communication attitudes mitigate the association between Facebook use and relational interdependence? An extension of media multiplexity theory. *New Media & Society*, 16(5), 806–822.

Ledbetter, A. M., Taylor, S. H., & Mazer, J. P. (2016). Enjoyment fosters media use frequency and determines its relational outcomes: Toward a synthesis of uses and gratifications theory and media multiplexity theory. *Computers in Human Behavior*, 54, 149–157.

Leonardi, P. M., & Meyer, S. R. (2015). Social media as social lubricant: How ambient awareness eases knowledge transfer. *American Behavioral Scientist*, 59(1), 10–34.

Lin, N. (2002). *Social capital: A theory of social structure and action*. New York: Cambridge University Press.

Madianou, M., & Miller, D. (2013). Polymedia: Towards a new theory of digital media in interpersonal communication. *International Journal of Cultural Studies*, 16(2), 169–187.

Ong, W. J. (2013). *Orality and literacy*. New York, NY: Routledge.

Ramirez, A., Walther, J. B., Burgoon, J. K., & Sunnafrank, M. (2002). Information-seeking strategies, uncertainty, and computer-mediated communication. *Human Communication Research*, 28(2), 213–228.

Ramirez, A., Sumner, E. M. B., Fleuriet, C., & Cole, M. (2015). When online dating partners meet offline: The effect of modality switching on relational communication between online daters. *Journal of Computer-Mediated Communication*, 20(1), 99–114.

Rheingold, H. (2012). *Net smart: How to thrive online*. Cambridge, MA: MIT Press.

Schoenebeck, S., Ellison, N. B., Blackwell, L., Bayer, J. B., & Falk, E. B. (2016). Playful backstalking and serious impression management: How young adults reflect on their past identities on Facebook. *Proceedings of the 19th ACM conference on computer-supported cooperative work & social computing* (pp. 1475–1487). New York: ACM.

Scissors, L. E., & Gergle, D. (2013). Back and forth, back and forth: Channel switching in romantic couple conflict. *Proceedings of the 2013 conference on computer supported cooperative work* (pp. 237–248). New York: ACM.

Scissors, L. E., Burke, M., & Wengrovitz, S. (2016). What's in a Like?: Attitudes and behaviors around receiving Likes on Facebook. *Proceedings of the 19th ACM conference on computer-supported cooperative work & social computing* (pp. 1501–1510). New York: ACM.

Snyder, M. (1974). Self-monitoring of expressive behavior. *Journal of Personality and Social Psychology*, 30(4), 526–537.

Tandoc, E. C., Ferrucci, P., & Duffy, M. (2015). Facebook use, envy, and depression among college students: Is facebooking depressing? *Computers in Human Behavior*, 43, 139–146.

Thompson, R. (2017). A 'deep like' is the worst thing that can happen when you're lurking on Instagram. http://mashable.com/2017/05/31/deep-like-instagram/#P_PuHXXXKSqC

Verduyn, P., Lee, D. S., Park, J., Shablack, H., Orvell, A., Bayer, J., . . . Kross, E. (2015). Passive Facebook usage undermines affective well-being: Experimental and longitudinal evidence. *Journal of Experimental Psychology: General*, 144(2), 480.

Walther, J. B., & Parks, M. R. (2002). Cues filtered out, cues filtered in: Computer-mediated communication and relationships. In M. L. Knapp & J. A. Daly (Eds.), *Handbook of interpersonal communication*, 3rd ed. (pp. 529–563). Thousand Oaks: Sage.

Wee, J., & Lee, J. (2017). With whom do you feel most intimate?: Exploring the quality of Facebook friendships in relation to similarities and interaction behaviors. *PloS one*, 12(4), e0176319.

Wohn, D. Y., & Birnholtz, J. (2015). From ambient to adaptation: Interpersonal attention management among young adults. *Proceedings of the 17th international conference on human-computer interaction with mobile devices and services* (pp. 26–35). New York: ACM.

4

INTERPERSONAL DYNAMICS IN ONLINE DATING

Profiles, Matching, and Discovery

David M. Markowitz, Jeffrey T. Hancock, and Stephanie Tom Tong

Nearly one in six Americans now use online dating sites or mobile applications to meet romantic partners (Smith, 2016). The popularity of online and mobile dating has increased three-fold over the past five years and continues to grow for several reasons. First, online dating has become less stigmatized and more normative, especially for younger populations (Finkel et al., 2012). Early online daters were viewed as desperate people who had difficulty meeting someone face-to-face or were socially awkward and this perception has steadily dissolved (Fiore & Donath, 2004; Gibbs et al., 2011). Second, daters can carefully form a romantic identity online and manage what others see. People shape their dating profiles to reveal who they are, while also trying to appear attractive and interesting to potential partners (Ellison et al., 2006; Toma et al., 2008), a phenomenon consistent with the idea that people selectively self-present online to manage others' impressions (Walther, 1996). Therefore, online dating has become popular not only because of its scale and the number of dating options it provides, but also because it allows the user to control the image and identity that he or she wants to project in the dating environment (Toma & Hancock, 2010).

While most online dating research has evaluated the strategies that people use to selectively self-present with photos or text, less attention has focused on other periods of the relationship initiation process that determine if two people will like each other and eventually meet. In this chapter, we investigate the dynamics of online dating by looking at three benchmarks of the dating experience. We first investigate the *profile stage* and evaluate how people use photos and text to form an online identity and enhance their appearance. Second, we examine the *matching stage*, a decision-making period when daters indicate romantic interest in a partner based on profile information. We identify how the matching process occurs and whom daters tend to match with. Finally, we discuss the *discovery phase*, which occurs after profile matching but before a face-to-face interaction, when mediated conversation influences if people will meet in person. We identify relationship and psychological dynamics that occur during the discovery phase and examine how they affect the possibility of a face-to-face meeting.

"Online dating" is an umbrella term for using the Internet or technology to facilitate a romantic connection and interaction. The three benchmarks of online dating discussed in this chapter apply to both web-based dating (e.g. eHarmony, OkCupid) and mobile dating applications (e.g. Tinder, Hinge). Most web-based sites have mobile versions but few dating applications operate on the Web. For clarity, when we discuss online dating, we conceptualize both web-based and mobile technologies unless one medium is specified.

The Profile Stage

Online dating starts as an intrapersonal phenomenon. All users create an online identity in the form of a profile. A profile serves as one's romantic identity to others in the network, and its purpose is to attract others' attention in an effort to develop future interactions and conversation. The profile is the first impression that a dater can make of another person and, therefore, it is the catalyst for potential online and face-to-face interactions.

Most sites and applications allow daters to provide physical characteristics (e.g. height, body type) and other identification details (e.g. gender, orientation) that may be important to communicate to a prospective date. Photos are a major part of the profile stage because they offer clues about the person's appearance or interest in activities, and self-authored text allows users to provide information that could not be communicated in other parts of the profile. On some mobile dating applications, users can communicate more than physical and identification details in the profile. For example, Blackwell and colleagues (2015) describe how Grindr, a men-seeking-men dating application, allows users to identify romantic, relational, or sexual intentions. Grindr users can fill out a "looking for" section, although Blackwell and colleagues (2015) note that this indicator is not always effective because people often want to conceal their motivations for using the dating service or their identity.

Given that profiles are the first impression that partners receive, most daters strive to create an appealing and interesting representation of the self that will attract dates (Toma, 2015). An important question, however, is whether daters accurately represent their identity within the profile's contents. Prior work has found that, on average, most profiles are largely genuine because gross inconsistencies between the profile and offline version of the self will likely result in an unfavorable in-person meeting (Ellison et al., 2012). There are instances, however, when profiles contain false information for self-enhancement purposes. Hancock and colleagues (2007) observed that men often overstate their height (by less than one inch) and women tend to understate their weight (by approximately eight pounds) when comparing profile information to real-life measurements. Daters are also affected by the goal to appear interpersonally or physically attractive, with research revealing that women are more likely to alter their photographs than men (Toma & Hancock, 2010). Together, these data are consistent with gendered ideals; women often believe that being thin and appearing young is more attractive to men, and men believe that being tall is more attractive to women.

Why are dating profile deceptions subtle, but frequent? Considering that most daters want to meet a partner face-to-face (see Ellison et al., 2006), people may make small embellishments to meet societal standards of gender ideals. Profile fabrications cannot be egregious, however, because this would jeopardize the possibility of future in-person interactions. For example, if an online dater suggests that he is 6'0" on his profile, but is truly 5'11", this lie would likely go unnoticed and would not terminate the relationship. On the other hand, the dater who suggests that he is 6'4" on his profile when he is truly 5'9", would have created a discrepancy easily observed face-to-face. Obvious deceptions are likely intolerable, but smaller misrepresentations, distortions, or deceptions may be self-enhancing enough to make the person appear attractive and interesting over a dating pool that is potentially large (Ariely, 2012; Ellison et al., 2012; Finkel et al., 2012). Because people are mostly honest in their self-representations, the dating profile is conceptualized as a promise. That is, the fundamental characteristics of the offline individual (e.g. number of children) do not often differ from the person represented in the profile (Ellison et al., 2012), but other characteristics (e.g. height, weight) may differ slightly to nudge the positive impression of the partner.

Like physical characteristics, online daters may also enhance their self-presented identities in the text portions of the profile. A laboratory study by Toma and Hancock (2012) measured a dater's in-person height, weight, and age versus his or her profile height, weight, and age. Self-presentation discrepancies between offline and online attributes were then analyzed against the textual "about me" section of the profile. The data revealed that deceptions in the profile were associated with fewer self-references (e.g. *I, me, my*) and fewer negative emotion terms (e.g. *hate, dislike*). Self-references are markers of attention (Pennebaker, 2011) and suggest where the speaker is focusing the discourse (e.g. on the self or on the social world). Prior deception and language research has found that liars use fewer self-references than truth-tellers to psychologically distance the deception from the speaker (Newman et al., 2003), and a consistent effect was observed in the online dating environment.

Negative emotion terms, on the other hand, are often amplified in deceptive speech relative to truthful speech as liars may give off anxiety or distress cues in their language patterns (Ekman, 2001). Deceptions in the dating profile were associated with fewer negative emotion terms, a pattern inconsistent with most deception and language theory (see Hauch et al., 2015). Considering the goals of online daters, which are to appear attractive, interesting, and likeable, it is reasonable that daters want to attract a partner by appearing positive and encouraging, instead of negative and unfavorable. Any negativity in the profile may produce warning signs for potential partners and daters purposefully exclude traces of negativity to enhance their self-presentation.

Taken together, the profile stage represents a time when users can create an online self that they want to communicate to potential dates. The prior evidence suggests that profiles are crucial to the dating process and can affect how people are perceived (Toma, 2015). Most profiles are genuine because they represent the core attitudes and representations of the user (Ellison et al., 2012). Embellishments in photos and other content are for self-enhancement purposes, but they are not extreme because an in-person meeting would be problematic if physical characteristics were demonstrably false.

The Matching Stage

After online daters create a profile, they respond to a variety of selection criteria (e.g. age, race, religion) that will refine their list of prospective dates, called matches. For web-based online dating, most sites follow a few popular designs (Finkel et al., 2012; Tong et al., 2016). Some websites like PlentyofFish.com follow a *see-and-screen* format in which daters can scroll through thousands of available profiles. Many see-and-screen sites have filters that allow daters to narrow down the dating pool based on searchable criteria such as height, weight, or location. Others employ matching *algorithms*; the most popular example is eHarmony's patented "Compatibility Matching System." On this website, daters are required to answer a series of questions about personality, interests, and traits. Based on the answers to these questions and a dater's stated selection criteria, the site then algorithmically culls his or her list of partners and provides a smaller, more manageable list of potential matches. Some *blended* sites like OkCupid.com provide both see-and-screen profile searching with a matching or compatibility score between the dater and his or her potential matches. Almost all of these dating websites have curated matches located on a single landing page for the dater to view.

For see-and-screen sites, the process of trying to find a match through profile search can be difficult and is often compared to a shopping experience or a marketplace (e.g. *relationshopping*; Heino et al., 2010; Whitty & Carr, 2006). Daters must "sell" themselves in the profile to be perceived as attractive and interesting during the matching stage. At the same time, daters must determine who and what information they want to "buy" based on the others' profiles. Therefore, a person has a higher chance of being selected if he or she matches the initial selection criteria of another, and fits his or her image of a desirable partner. As Finkel et al. (2012) describe, "you can only procure a redhead from a dating site if she wants you in return" (p. 16). Although the shopping metaphor applies to offline dating as well, its effects are magnified online because this process now happens at scale and faster than ever before. In fact, recent research has indicated that "choice overload" effects that occur in shopping or consumer environments can also occur in online dating environments. When faced with too many potential partners, daters report feeling overloaded with options, which can lead to feelings of reduced satisfaction with their partner-selection decisions, greater likelihood to reverse their decisions, and greater regret with their selected partners (see D'Angelo & Toma, 2017; Lenton et al., 2008; Tong et al., 2016; Wu & Chiou, 2009).

For users of algorithmic dating websites, the matching process can be a "black box" because matching and sorting algorithms are often not transparent. Users can provide information about their likes, dislikes, interests, and intentions, but it is unclear why or how certain partners are prioritized or how matches are presented to the dater. The lack of transparency with the algorithmic matching process can make daters feel like they have less control over their romantic decision making. While this can be satisfying for some users (Tong et al., 2017), it can also create feelings of disappointment if daters perceive that the algorithm is not providing a satisfactory amount or quality of romantic connections (see, e.g., Single Steve, 2011).

Mobile dating applications also make use of daters' profiles during the matching stage, but information fields are usually less detailed in mobile platforms than in web-based platforms. Also, most mobile dating applications make use of daters' geolocation data. Just like in web-based dating, users might indicate desirable mate selection criteria such as age, sexual orientation, and height or body type; but the geographical distance feature of mobile dating applications leverages the accuracy of smartphone technology to connect two people within a specific distance (Blackwell et al., 2015). After a variety of selection criteria are submitted, the dating application will create a list of potential matches, presenting each partner's profile to the dater individually. Daters view each profile and must decide whether or not they like the potential partner. In Tinder, for example, when daters are presented with a profile, they indicate their choice through haptic feedback. If a dater "swipes left" on another's profile this indicates dislike, which rejects any opportunity to match with the person in the profile. A "swipe right" suggests mutual interest and that the dater would like to connect (Ward, 2016).

There are important differences between the matching and decision-making processes across platforms within web or mobile. For example, after daters complete their profiles, submit answers to survey questions, and indicate their own selection criteria, daters on most web-based platforms can then message anyone on the site that they find interesting or attractive. In sites like OkCupid and PlentyofFish, as long as users maintain an active dating account, there are no restrictions on whom they may contact through the website. Other platforms like Tinder and Bumble require a "reciprocal interest" mechanism for conversation to occur. That is, daters can only message each other if both partners indicate they are willing to communicate. As described, in Tinder when both mobile daters "swipe right," this signal of mutual interest opens communication channels for daters to exchange messages in the platform itself. The reciprocal interest feature is not unique to mobile platforms; in fact, eHarmony requires that daters begin with opening series of questions, and when both parties answer these questions, the matching process can continue.

With so many dating sites and applications on the market, it can be a difficult decision for daters to select which platform to use. Recent research indicates that certain personality characteristics affect daters' satisfaction with different designs and features. Tong and colleagues (2017) found that daters' need for cognition became an important factor that influenced people's willingness to use an algorithm for mate selection. When faced with a great amount of choice (e.g. approximately 800 profiles) that created overload, those daters with a low need for cognition were more likely to deploy the algorithmic agent to select partners on their behalf in an effort to reduce cognitive load. Daters high in need for cognition were also likely to use the algorithm to help sort potential partners, but not in response to feeling overloaded. Instead, high need for cognition daters used the algorithm as a form of adaptive decision making, adjusting their mate selection behavior by deploying technology according to the increasing amount of choice they encountered. Such findings indicate that aspects of one's personal identity are even reflected in how they use online dating technology to make connections.

Finally, after online daters craft their profile and browse their matches on the web or a mobile interface, whom do they decide to connect with? Prior research by Hitsch and colleagues (2010) observed that daters tend to match with those similar in age, race, and ratings of attractiveness. Significant, positive correlations were also observed for daters' height, income, and education level. These data demonstrate that for web-based online dating, people tend to match with those who are similar and attainable, rather than those who are exotic or "out of my league."

Once daters have gone through all of the decision making work of selecting a potential partner, whether based on profile information or matching algorithms, they then enter a new phase where the two daters determine if the relationship will progress to face-to-face. Below, we discuss research and open questions for this period of message exchange that often determines if two daters will meet.

The Discovery Phase

The time after people match on profiles and before daters meet face-to-face is a benchmark we call *the discovery phase*. We suggest that this a phase rather than a period or stage because a phase is typically flexible in nature. The discovery phase starts when daters begin to exchange messages via the dating platform (either mobile or web-based), but the end of mediated message exchange can occur through many different means. Perhaps, the messages ended gradually as the conversation dissolved, daters moved the conversation to another medium, or daters met face-to-face. While profile and matching stages are relatively short because daters make decisions quickly and express clear interest or disinterest in another person, the discovery phase is typically longer and represents a time when daters become familiar with one another through conversation.

Prior work has investigated social, psychological, and relationship dynamics during the discovery phase. In their analysis of web-based daters, Hitsch and colleagues (2010) observed that the probability of receiving an email response from a partner differs by gender. Male-initiated messages to a partner are responded to less than 30% of the time, while female-initiated messages receive a response rate close to 50%. If daters do receive a response, men and women exchange approximately twelve messages before providing their contact information to a partner and possibly meeting him or her face-to-face. As expected, the chance of receiving an email back from a prospective date increases with profile and photo attractiveness. These data suggest that the information exchanged during the discovery phase is essential when daters are deciding whether to invest in the relationship. It is important to be initially attractive and interesting in the profile, but conversations are crucial for determining whether two people will progress to a more intimate medium off the dating platform (e.g. text messaging, phone calls) or meet face-to-face.

Given that online dating profiles provide a limited amount of information about a prospective partner, people use a variety of strategies to learn more about their match in the discovery phase. These methods are typically *extractive* (e.g. searching the web for an online dater to obtain information), *active* (e.g. saving a record of exchanged messages), *passive* (e.g. looking for consistencies or inconsistencies in a dating profile), or *interactive* (e.g. communicating with the prospective date to learn more). Gibbs and colleagues (2011) outline how people typically use artifacts in the mobile dating infrastructure (e.g. date of last login) or in other social media outlets to assess the partner during conversation (e.g. examining mutual friends on Facebook). People also use extractive methods and Internet resources (e.g. Google) to verify the information that people discuss during the discovery phase. For instance, if a dater mentions that he or she is a musician, a partner may look for online videos or sound clips to learn more about the date or to substantiate this information. In this case, videos or sound clips are called warrants (Walther & Parks, 2002), or items that bridge the offline and online world and hold daters accountable for details that are communicated.

Gibbs and colleagues (2011) also observed that daters often use interactive methods to verify that the partner created a truthful profile and continues to provide genuine information in conversation. This suggests that profiles are not enough to alleviate relationship concerns and people need to communicate to understand if the relationship will progress, to relieve anxieties in a high-stakes setting such as online dating, and to verify that the information exchanged during the discovery phase is real. Therefore, daters gather additional data about their partner through message exchange with the hope of learning more about the individual (Whitty, 2008).

Interestingly daters' information-seeking behaviors also differ with respect to daters' romantic and relational goals. Corriero and Tong (2016) found that male users of Grindr varied in their amount of information seeking—daters seeking sexual encounters preferred greater amounts of interpersonal uncertainty and as a result, sought less interpersonal information about hookup partners. Those who were more relational-oriented in their goals were motivated to reduce uncertainty, and did so by searching for specific information that verified potential partners' self-presented profiles.

In a recent study, Markowitz and Hancock (2017) collected the conversations between mobile daters to understand how often people lie and the content of their deceptions. Daters rated the deceptiveness of each dating app message and on average, the majority of daters did not tell any lies, a finding consistent with prior work that suggests most people are honest with their everyday communication activities (Serota & Levine, 2015). Overall, slightly less than 10% of mobile dating messages were deceptive and participant lying rates were uncorrelated with attractiveness ratings of the partner, trust in the partner, or partner likeability. Instead, lying rates were positively correlated with dating motivations such as the need to find new sexual partners, to satisfy sexual curiosity, and to browse the pictures of others for entertainment.

Content analyses of the deceptive mobile dating messages revealed that over two-thirds of the participant lies were related to self-presentation (e.g. lies to appear attractive) and lies to manage availability. This suggests that impression management and identity formation is important for daters starting new romantic relationships on the mobile phone. Finally, Markowitz and Hancock (2017) observed a strong positive correlation between the number of lies from the dater and his or her partner. Called the *deception consensus effect*, this trend suggests that the more a dater lies, the more that he or she believes that the partner has lied as well. This effect is consistent with other research on false consensus biases, where people base the behavior of others on their own actions (Epley, 2015).

Trends and Future Directions

This chapter outlines the online dating experience through three benchmarks. The profile stage is a time when daters craft a profile, or an online identity for potential dates to evaluate and appraise. Daters spend a substantial amount of time creating an online dating profile because relationship success is largely dependent on the interest and attraction garnered in the profile stage. Next, the matching stage is a decision-making period of connecting with another person, based on his or her profile information. People tend to match with similar others, but the matching process can change depending on the features and designs of different web-based sites and mobile dating applications. Finally, the discovery phase is an exploratory period when messages are exchanged between two daters to learn more about each other and determine if they want to meet face-to-face. People use profile artifacts (e.g. mutual friends), interactive strategies (e.g. message exchange), and extractive strategies (e.g. Internet browsing) to learn more about another person who is romantically interesting.

The prior studies suggest that most online dating research has been concerned with the impression management strategies people use during different periods of the relationship. Future work should identify how these strategies relate to intentions and goals for dating. There are open questions about why people browse online sites when they have little intent to meet someone face-to-face, or why committed individuals (e.g. those in a relationship or married) explore online dating. Understanding the motivations for use among these unique populations would be interesting to explore, especially if these individuals display behavioral patterns that could be detected. For instance, online daters who are simply browsing may not be appropriate to match with daters who are looking for a long-term partner. Perhaps using behavioral traces, such as the dater's rapidity of swiping, time spent on a profile, or number of messages sent to partners in the network to proxy their dating intentions, could improve matching algorithms and sorting.

A second consideration for future work is to understand the portfolio of dating services that people use to find a partner. It is unclear how many sites or mobile applications people use at one time to acquire matches and why people choose to include or exclude dating services from their repertoire. Are online dating services associated with stigmas that prevent people from joining? Is web-based online dating viewed as more serious than mobile applications? Some work is beginning to uncover the influence of daters' personality traits on platform use (Tong et al., 2017), but deeper investigation of the social dynamics and reputations of online dating sites is needed. In an industry crowded with sites and apps, it would be useful to know how and when daters select certain platforms over others, and what factors motivate them to change, swap, or quit using online dating technology altogether.

Finally, as mentioned, a goal of online dating is to eventually meet another person face-to-face. Are there parts of the profile stage, matching stage, or discovery phase that facilitate the in-person meeting? Prior work on deception in mobile dating conversations during the discovery phase (Markowitz & Hancock, 2017) observed that lying rates also did not affect whether two people met, likely because deception is difficult to detect (Bond & DePaulo, 2006) and most lies are subtle (Toma & Hancock, 2010, 2012). Therefore, it may be important to inspect all three benchmarks of the mobile dating relationship and interview daters, to understand the point when a dater decided that he or she would be comfortable meeting the other person face-to-face. These data would indicate which benchmark (e.g. profile stage, matching stage, discovery phase) is crucial for sustaining or dissolving the relationship.

Conclusion

Online daters begin their search for love with a profile. This profile contains a portfolio of photos, likes, and interests that advertise the self and it serves as an overview of the person's individual and romantic identity. Information in the profile is then used in the decision-making phase, where daters must choose to connect with other daters. Once daters make it through this matching and decision-making phase, they then engage in a period of message exchange, called the discovery phase, to determine if they will meet face-to-face. Daters draw on a variety of communication strategies, such as selective self-presentation and uncertainty reduction, to manage each of these dating benchmarks. The early phases of an online dating experience are crucial because people must first distill their identity into a single, attractive, but predominantly honest representation of the self. The stages of an online dating relationship build on each other, however, suggesting that success in online dating (e.g. meeting face-to-face and sustaining the relationship) is likely dependent on favorable impressions, decisions, and interactions at each phase of the online dating experience.

References

Ariely, D. (2012). *The (honest) truth about dishonesty: How we lie to everyone – especially ourselves*. New York: HarperCollins.

Blackwell, C., Birnholtz, J., & Abbott, C. (2015). Seeing and being seen: Co-situation and impression formation using Grindr, a location-aware gay dating app. *New Media & Society*, 17, 1117–1136.

Bond, C. F., & DePaulo, B. M. (2006). Accuracy of deception judgments. *Personality and Social Psychology Review*, 10, 214–234.

Corriero, E. F., & Tong, S. T. (2016). Managing uncertainty in mobile dating applications: Goals, concerns of use, and information seeking in Grindr. *Mobile Media & Communication*, 4, 121–141.

D'Angelo, J. D., & Toma, C. L. (2017). There are plenty of fish in the sea: The effects of choice overload and reversibility on online daters' satisfaction with selected partners. *Media Psychology*, 20, 1–27.

Ekman, P. (2001). *Telling lies: Clues to deceit in the marketplace, politics, and marriage*. New York: W. W. Norton.

Ellison, N., Heino, R., & Gibbs, J. (2006). Managing impressions online: Self-presentation processes in the online dating environment. *Journal of Computer-Mediated Communication*, 11, 415–441.

Ellison, N. B., Hancock, J. T., & Toma, C. L. (2012). Profile as promise: A framework for conceptualizing veracity in online dating self-presentations. *New Media & Society*, 14, 45–62.

Epley, N. (2015). *Mindwise: Why we misunderstand what others think, believe, feel, and want*. New York: Vintage.

Finkel, E. J., Eastwick, P. W., Karney, B. R., Reis, H. T., & Sprecher, S. (2012). Online dating: A critical analysis from the perspective of psychological science. *Psychological Science in the Public Interest*, 13, 3–66.

Fiore, A. T., & Donath, J. S. (2004). Online personals: An overview. Paper presented at the CHI '04 Extended Abstracts on Human Factors in Computing Systems, Vienna, Austria.

Gibbs, J. L., Ellison, N. B., & Lai, C.-H. (2011). First comes love, then comes Google: An investigation of uncertainty reduction strategies and self-disclosure in online dating. *Communication Research*, 38, 70–100.

Hancock, J. T., Toma, C., & Ellison, N. (2007). The truth about lying in online dating profiles. Paper presented at the Proceedings of the SIGCHI Conference on Human Factors in Computing Systems, San Jose, California, USA.

Hauch, V., Blandón-Gitlin, I., Masip, J., & Sporer, S. L. (2015). Are computers effective lie detectors? A meta-analysis of linguistic cues to deception. *Personality and Social Psychology Review*, 19, 307–342.

Heino, R., Ellison, N., & Gibbs, J. (2010). Relationshopping: Investigating the market metaphor in online dating. *Journal of Social and Personal Relationships*, 27, 427–447.

Hitsch, G. J., Hortaçsu, A., & Ariely, D. (2010). Matching and sorting in online dating. *American Economic Review*, 100, 130–163.

Lenton, A., Fasolo, B., & Todd, P. (2008). "Shopping" for a mate: Expected versus experienced preferences in online mate choice. *IEEE Transactions on Professional Communication*, 51, 169–182.

Markowitz, D. M., & Hancock, J. T. (2017). Matchmaker, matchmaker, swipe me an (honest) match: Deception dynamics in mobile dating messages. Presentation at the 67th Annual Conference of the International Communication Association, San Diego.

Newman, M. L., Pennebaker, J. W., Berry, D. S., & Richards, J. M. (2003). Lying words: Predicting deception from linguistic styles. *Personality and Social Psychology Bulletin*, 29, 665–675.

Pennebaker, J. W. (2011). *The secret life of pronouns: What our words say about us*. London: Bloomsbury Press.

Serota, K. B. & Levine, T. R. (2015). A few prolific liars: Variation in the prevalence of lying. *Journal of Language and Social Psychology*, 34, 138–157.

Single Steve. (2011). "Dear eHarmony, fuck you." Blog post. www.singlesteve.com/2011/01/dear-eharmony-fuck-you

Smith, A. (2016). 15% of American adults have used online dating sites or mobile dating apps. www.pewinternet.org/2016/02/11/15-percent-of-american-adults-have-used-online-dating-sites-or-mobile-dating-apps/

Toma, C. L. (2015). Online dating. In C. Berger & M. Roloff (Eds.), *The international encyclopedia of interpersonal communication* (pp. 1–5). Chichester: John Wiley.

Toma, C. L., & Hancock, J. T. (2010). Looks and lies: The role of physical attractiveness in online dating self-presentation and deception. *Communication Research*, 37, 335–351.

Toma, C. L., & Hancock, J. T. (2012). What lies beneath: The linguistic traces of deception in online dating profiles. *Journal of Communication*, 62, 78–97.

Toma, C. L., Hancock, J. T., & Ellison, N. B. (2008). Separating fact from fiction: An examination of deceptive self-presentation in online dating profiles. *Personality and Social Psychology Bulletin*, 34, 1023–1036.

Tong, S. T., Hancock, J. T., & Slatcher, R. B. (2016). Online dating system design and relational decision-making: Choice, algorithms, and control. *Personal Relationships*, 23, 645–662.

Tong, S. T., Corriero, E. F., Hancock, J. T., Matheny, R., & Slatcher, R. B. (2017). (Assortment) size matters: Choice overload in online dating decision making. Paper presented at the annual conference of the International Communication Association. San Diego, CA.

Walther, J. B. (1996). Computer-mediated communication: Impersonal, interpersonal, and hyperpersonal interaction. *Communication Research*, 1, 3–43.

Walther, J. B., & Parks, M. R. (2002). Cues filtered out, cues filtered in: Computer-mediated communication and relationships. In M. L. Knapp & J. A. Daly (Eds.), *Handbook of interpersonal communication*, 3rd ed. (pp. 529–563). Thousand Oaks, CA: Sage.

Ward, J. R. (2016). Swiping, matching, chatting: Self-presentation and self-disclosure on mobile dating apps. *Human IT*, 13, 81–95.

Whitty, M. T. (2008). Revealing the "real" me, searching for the "actual" you: Presentations of self on an internet dating site. *Computers in Human Behavior*, 24, 1707–1723.

Whitty, M. T., & Carr, A. (2006). *Cyberspace romance: The psychology of online relationships*. New York: Palgrave Macmillan.

Wu, P., & Chiou, W. (2009). More options lead to more searching and worse choices in finding partners for romantic relationships online: An experimental study. *Cyberpsychology & Behavior: The Impact of the Internet, Multimedia and Virtual Reality on Behavior and Society*, 12, 315–318.

5

CONNECTION, CONFLICT, AND COMMUNICATION TECHNOLOGIES

How Romantic Couples Use the Media for Relationship Management

Catalina L. Toma

The experience of falling in love can be exhilarating and is much sought after by most people. Yet, romantic relationships, once formed, can be difficult to navigate. Two different people come together and must negotiate how to communicate effectively, how to resolve differences, and whether and how to steer their relationship into the future. In the twenty-first century, the process of relationship management is rendered even more complex by the widespread availability of communication technologies, such as texting, voice calling, instant messenger (IM), email, and social network sites (SNSs). These technologies present romantic partners with opportunities and challenges. Perpetual contact is made easy by texting and the phone, but couples must decide how much such contact is desirable. Sexting can offer the possibility of better sexual communication, but it may also thwart emotional intimacy. SNSs allow couples to broadcast their relationship to hundreds of followers, thus possibly cementing relational commitment, yet they also allow users to surreptitiously track romantic partners and these partners' previous partners, thus generating jealousy.

The purpose of this chapter is to provide a state-of-the-art review of the literature on the uses and effects of communication technologies during the maintenance phase of romantic relationships. Note that romantic relationships go through three distinct phases (Rubin, 1986). In the initiation stage, romantic couples come together and begin their relationship. In the maintenance stage, typically the longest one, they carry on their relationship and manage all afferent issues, such as spending time together, dealing with conflict, and sharing feelings. In the termination stage, couples break up, through unilateral or mutual decisions, or through the proverbial "death do us part." Communication technologies have profoundly affected romantic relationships at all three stages. For instance, online dating has revolutionized the relationship initiation process (e.g.

Finkel et al., 2012; Toma, 2015). Similarly, SNSs can add an extra layer of difficulty to romantic break-ups by enabling people to monitor their ex-partners (Marshall, 2012). This chapter will only focus on the role of communication technologies in the maintenance stage of romantic relationships. We will also focus exclusively on geographically collocated romantic relationships, since long-distance relationships rely on communication technologies in a different way. While we aimed our focus broadly, to include heterosexual and homosexual relationships along the continuum of commitment (from casual dating to marital relationships), the bulk of the literature has investigated heterosexual dating relationships, typically among college students. Our conclusions, then, are mostly applicable to this segment.

The chapter is structured into two overarching sections: connection and conflict. By connection we simply mean couples' everyday communication, interactions, and self-presentation. We then focus on conflict, a type of couple interaction that is prevalent in the relational maintenance stage and highly impactful on partners' well-being and the couple's stability. For both connection and conflict, we identify the opportunities and challenges presented by the use of communication technologies. To ease the summary of the many studies on this topic, we organize them by the extent to which they focus on *dyadic mediated communication* (i.e. communication technologies used for one-on-one contact between romantic partners; these include texting, the phone, email, and IM) and *broadcast mediated communication* (i.e. communication technologies used for one-to-many interaction; these include SNSs, group texting, and sometimes Snapchat). For connection, we first review the uses and effects of dyadic mediated communication on relational quality; then focus on sexting, a specific type of texting that involves sexually suggestive messages; and then discuss SNS presentations of coupledom, and how these presentations can both reflect and affect the status of romantic relationships. For conflict, we review the extent to which romantic partners use communication technologies for addressing conflict; then discuss the perceived advantages and disadvantages of these technologies, as well as the effects of technology use on conflict resolution; and finally we review the extent to which technologies can themselves be a source of romantic conflict, with special emphasis on romantic jealousy generated by partner surveillance on SNSs and the new phenomenon of phubbing (i.e. phone snubbing). Throughout, we offer a critical view of the literature by discussing the extent of theoretical development in these areas of inquiry, and pointing out avenues for future studies.

Connection

Today's romantic couples have an abundance of media options at their disposal. They can connect on an one-on-one basis using communication technologies such as the phone or texting (a process we defined as dyadic mediated communication) and they can also talk to each other on public technological platforms such as SNSs (a process we defined as broadcast mediated communication). We consider the relational dynamics of both of these types of communication.

Dyadic Mediated Communication

The uses and effects of dyadic media have been thoroughly investigated in the context of long-distance romantic relationships, where, during periods of geographic separation, the very possibility for contact between romantic partners rests upon these media (Dainton & Aylor, 2002). Predictably, long-distance couples use technology to a substantial extent (Billedo et al., 2015; Neustaedter & Greenberg, 2012), and this use not only keeps the relationship alive, but even enhances its intimacy (e.g. Jiang & Hancock, 2013). While geographically collocated couples have easy access to face-to-face (FtF) communication and therefore do not depend on dyadic media in the same way, they can still be expected to use it for maintaining everyday contact and for coordinating activities; in turn, this use is likely to affect the quality of their relationship.

Consider first collocated couples' frequency of media use. An early study (Baym et al., 2007) found that media use, especially online media, played a relatively small part in collocated couples' interactions: a sample of college students estimated that, of the total amount of time they spent with their romantic partner, more than 50% occurred FtF, 25% via the phone, and 12% via the Internet, broadly defined. However, subsequent studies paint a different picture, likely illustrating the increasing popularity of low-cost, low-effort media such as texting. A 2011 survey of over 1,000 participants in serious heterosexual relationships revealed that, on average, respondents used the phone to connect with their partners multiple times a day, texting on a weekly basis, and email on a monthly basis (Coyne et al., 2011). A couple of years later, over 80% of a sample of young adults reported using texting multiple times a day to connect with their partners, and only about 5% never texted with their partner (Schade et al., 2013). By 2016, texting had become the most prevalent medium for connecting with romantic partners, used by over 98% of young adults in dating relationships. The phone remained frequently used (by 84% of the respondents), but email was less so (by 16% of respondents). Participants in this study indicated that they spent about three hours a day in FtF interactions with their partners, and a full two hours texting, although this average was distorted by a few outliers; the median amount of time spent on texting daily was one hour. The phone was used, on average, about 20 minutes daily, and email a mere 5 minutes (Toma & Choi, 2016). In sum, this literature reveals that mobile media (texting and voice calling) has seen a surge in popularity in the past decade, now constituting a substantial means of communication for geographically collocated couples. Texting in particular is widespread, indicating that these couples maintain contact through brief messages throughout the day. The use of email is negligible.

Consider now the effects of dyadic media use on collocated couples' relational quality. Early studies found no such effects (Emmers-Sommer, 2004; Baym et al., 2007), likely because there was little media use at that time. Subsequent studies revealed a pattern of mostly positive associations between media use (phone, texting) and markers of relationship quality (love, commitment, intimacy, satisfaction) (Jin & Peña, 2010; Morey et al., 2013; Schade et al., 2013). These studies argued that media use benefits romantic relationships, although the reverse pattern of causality could not be ruled out (i.e. happier couples used more media), due to the studies' correlational designs.

Theoretically speaking, how does dyadic media use generate these positive relational outcomes? A recent study argues that one mechanism behind these effects is *hyperpersonal projections* (Toma & Choi, 2016). The Hyperpersonal model (Walther, 1996) proposes that mediated environments reduce the availability of information about a communication partner's whereabouts, behaviors, and feelings (as demonstrated through non-verbal behaviors) compared to FtF environments. Thus, individuals are left to mentally fill in the blanks for this information, which they do by projecting their pre-existing beliefs and impressions about their partner. When these pre-existing beliefs are positive, interactants perceive more positive undertones in mediated messages than they would in comparable FtF messages (where there is less space for imagination). Negative projections similarly happen for negative pre-existing beliefs. In the case of romantic couples, pre-existing beliefs tend to be positive—partners like and care for one another, which is why their projections should be positive. For example, a simple message from one's partner ("how are you doing?") can come across as especially sweet when sent via texting, as one can imagine it is delivered with a smile, a loving tone of voice, and open arms—even though these non-verbal cues may not have been present had the message been delivered FtF. Consistent with this reasoning, Toma and Choi (2016) found that the quality of texting and phone-based communication among dating couples predicted partner idealization, which in turn increased relational satisfaction. The reverse pattern, where relational satisfaction would have predicted, rather than been predicted by media use, was not supported by the data. To summarize, a handful of studies reveal relational benefits of dyadic media use for dating couples. Only one mechanism for these effects has been thoroughly described in the literature, although it is likely that dyadic media use affects couples through a multitude of routes, such as promoting a sense of connectedness during periods of the day when the couple is separated, increasing self-disclosure, and boosting the use of relational maintenance strategies. Future research is necessary to unpack these mechanisms.

A related pressing issue that remains to be addressed is the *content* of the mediated messages exchanged by collocated couples, especially those delivered through texting, which, as we have seen, has become the predominant form of mediated communication in this relational context. Based on previous research on long-distance relationships (Aylor, 2003) and friendships (Brody, 2013), it is likely that textual exchanges involve the coordination of everyday activities, such as meeting times and locations, and the enactment of relational maintenance behaviors, such as those delineated by Stafford and Canary's taxonomy (1991). These include positivity (i.e. being cheerful), openness (i.e. discussing the relationship directly), assurances (i.e. conveying love, commitment, and loyalty), sharing tasks (i.e. jointly contributing to chores and activities), and networks (i.e. spending time with or talking about common friends and acquaintances). Some of these strategies are thoughtful, consciously enacted, and tend to weigh heavily on the outcome of the relationship—for example, couples deciding to discuss the status of their relationships and their respective feelings (i.e. openness). Other strategies are more routinized (e.g. sharing tasks), playful (e.g. positivity), or seemingly trivial (e.g. talking about mutual friends), and hence often do not register as relational maintenance strategies. Yet these unremarkable behaviors, labeled "mundane sharing" or "everyday talk," have been shown to be vital in the maintenance of romantic relationships. Simply being in contact and sharing details of one's life provide a sense of closeness and comfort, and bring couples together (Jin & Peña, 2010). It is likely that texting serves this function in couples' lives, and thus can be understood through Hall and Baym's (2012) conceptualization of mobile maintenance, a framework originally developed to explain the role of mobile media in the maintenance of close friendships. Mobile maintenance refers to the media's ability to facilitate the enactment of frequent, simple, but psychologically potent behaviors that sustain personal relationships. We believe it is an apt framework to describe the role of dyadic media within the maintenance of geographically close romantic relationships as well.

Sexting

Sexting is a particular type of dyadic mediated communication within romantic relationships that has received a great deal of scholarly attention recently. Defined as the sending or receiving of sexually laden textual messages and sexually suggestive, nude, or partially nude photos or videos via a mobile phone (Weisskirch & Delevi, 2011), sexting has become quite prevalent, with approximately 10% of adolescents and 50% of adults having engaged in this practice, according to a recent review (Klettke et al., 2014). While sexting can take place in a variety of relational contexts, it is most frequent within committed romantic relationships, contrary to popular beliefs that sexting is the hallmark of hookups (e.g. Drouin et al., 2017; Drouin et al., 2013; Weisskirch & Delevi, 2011). Individuals sext in order to initiate sexual activity, gain attention from a partner, convey playfulness and flirtatiousness, or compensate for a lack of sex due to geographic separation (Drouin et al., 2013; Henderson & Morgan, 2011). For this reason, sexting can be conceptualized as a form of relational maintenance accomplished via dyadic media.

What form does sexting take? Descriptive research shows that, among college students and married couples, sexting involves textual (i.e. word-only) messages more frequently than photographic or video messages, and tends to be less (e.g. nearly nude photos) rather than more explicit (e.g. nude photos) (Drouin et al., 2013; McDaniel & Drouin, 2015). Who is more likely to engage in sexting? A systematic review (Klettke et al., 2014) shows that, in adult populations, most studies found that the likelihood to sext did not vary by gender, sexual orientation, or marital status. The lack of demographic differences in sexting, coupled with its high prevalence, suggests that sexting has become a run-of-the-mill relational management strategy for couples. Nonetheless, the likelihood of sexting appears to be predicted by individual differences in attachment style, which refers to people's enduring patterns of relating to intimate partners (Bartholomew & Horowitz, 1991). Securely attached individuals value intimacy, have good self-esteem, and are trusting toward their romantic partners. Insecurely attached individuals can be either avoidant, in which case they dislike intimacy and create distance from their partners, or anxious, in which case they fear rejection and engage in excessive clinginess on and reassurance-seeking from their partners (Brennan et al., 1998). Research has found that both avoidantly and anxiously attached individuals engage in more sexting than securely attached individuals, arguably in an attempt to manage their emotional needs—albeit in different ways. For avoidantly attached individuals, sexting can serve as a way to ward off emotional intimacy by focusing on the sexual aspect of the relationship, thus creating distance. For anxiously attached individuals, sexting may be a way to elicit attention from the partner and to maintain their interest, thus increasing closeness (Drouin & Landgraff, 2012; Weisskirch & Delevi, 2011).

But perhaps the most critical question in this area of research concerns the effect of sexting on relationship quality. Does sexting benefit or harm relationships? A recent study found that half of sexters reported positive relationship consequences, while only one in ten reported negative ones. These positive consequences materialized especially in committed relationships, where sexters reported more benefits and fewer regrets than sexters in casual relationships (Drouin et al., 2017). Other studies were more reserved on the benefits of sexting, finding either no association between sexting frequency and relationship satisfaction (Parker et al., 2013), or a positive association that held only for (a) individuals in casual relationships, but not committed ones (Stasko & Geller, 2015) and (b) avoidantly attached, but not anxiously or securely attached, individuals (McDaniel & Drouin, 2015). On balance, this incipient line of research suggests that there are more relational benefits than costs associated with sexting, although some groups may benefit more than others. Future research should theorize more deeply on the mechanism through which sexting affects relational satisfaction in various types of relationships—perhaps it is promoting sexual communication and comfort for new, less committed couples, promoting emotional intimacy for established couples, or promoting emotional distance for couples where an individual is avoidantly attached.

Broadcast Mediated Communication

One of the novel challenges faced by today's romantic couples is the public presentation of their relationship on SNSs. SNSs allow users to share personal information with large audiences of friends, family members, acquaintances, and even strangers, and are widely used by both younger and older adults (e.g. Brenner & Smith, 2013). SNSs that are geared toward the maintenance of personal relationships, such as Facebook, invite users to disclose their relationship status (e.g. "single," "in a relationship," "engaged," "married") and to share relationship-relevant information, such as dyadic photographs (i.e. photos depicting the user with their romantic partner) and conversations with romantic partners. In effect, SNSs allow users to publicly broadcast information about their romantic relationships, allowing hundreds of friends a glance into this highly intimate realm of their lives. At no other point in history was it possible to round up such large numbers of people and tell them about one's love life. How, then, do SNS users present their romantic relationships?

Little research has investigated this issue directly. Mod's (2010) interviews reveal that college students think of their relationship presentations on Facebook as the online equivalent of traditional public displays of affection (e.g. hand-holding, hugging, kissing). These Facebook displays of affection frequently involve the posting of dyadic photographs, publicly saying "I love you" and "I miss you" to the partner, and sharing inside jokes openly. As such, they serve two purposes: to convey the image of a happy, loving relationship and to ward off potential romantic interests by showing that one's partner is "taken." More evidence that romantic presentations on Facebook are of the saccharine variety comes from Emery and colleagues (2014a), who found that couples with high relationship visibility on Facebook (i.e. those who posted dyadic photographs and revealed their relational status) came across as more satisfied with their relationship, but also less likeable. This suggests that relationship presentations on Facebook were positive to the point of portraying the couple as smug.

The flattering nature of SNS relationship presentations is consistent with the *selective self-presentation* theoretical framework (Walther, 2007), which claims that online communicators are well-equipped to exercise control over their messages and to align them with their self-presentational goals. This control is facilitated by technological affordances that allow for careful message composition, such as asynchronicity, or having unlimited time to think through one's message, and editability, or having the option to revise and polish the message. Note that these affordances are unavailable to FtF communicators, who must compose messages extemporaneously and cannot edit them once uttered. Simply put, online communicators can craft highly strategic and flattering messages if they are motivated to do so. On SNSs, this motivation should be high, due to the simple fact that messages are available for scrutiny to unprecedentedly large audiences. While the selective self-presentation framework has not been explicitly applied to relationship presentations on SNSs, it has received much support when it comes to SNS self-presentations in general. For instance, research shows that Facebook users think they come across as funnier, more adventurous, and more outgoing in their profiles than they really are (Toma & Carlson, 2015); they actively curate their self-presentations to convey popularity and edit out negative traits, such as pessimism and anxiety (Zhao et al., 2008); and they experience a boost in self-esteem after viewing their own profiles (Toma, 2013). It stands to reason that relationship presentations on SNSs should follow the same general pattern, offering audiences glamorized glimpses into the users' love lives, rather than the full complexity of their feelings and relational issues.

When it comes to selective self-presentation, the most basic decision is to select whether to reveal a certain aspect about oneself at all. Perhaps this is the reason why much of the literature on romantic presentations on SNSs has focused on the issue of *who* is more likely to disclose relationship information on SNSs. Support has emerged for the hypothesis that it is the happier and more satisfied couples who are more likely to do so. Fox and colleagues' (2013) focus groups with college students reveal that listing oneself as "in a relationship" on Facebook (colloquially referred to as being "Facebook official") is a relational milestone that reflects the couple's attainment of a high degree of commitment. In other words, only when couples consider their relationship to be well-established do they disclose it on Facebook. Correlational studies with both married and dating couples show a positive link between relationship satisfaction and the tendency to post dyadic profile photographs (Saslow et al., 2012), to list oneself as "in a relationship" (Lane et al., 2016; Orosz et al., 2015), and to disclose relationship-relevant information (Saslow et al., 2012) on Facebook. Again, this fits into the logic of selective self-presentation: happy couples reveal their happiness on Facebook, whereas less happy ones refrain from discussing their relationships. Both strategies—highlighting positive information and obscuring negative information—service the goal of portraying a flattering image of self to the audience. Note, however, that the vast majority of this research has been conducted on college students, a demographic who use Facebook actively and abundantly. Thus, the findings do not apply to older adults who might not be on Facebook at all, or who might use it sparingly.

Only one study has considered individual differences as predictors of relationship disclosures on Facebook. Emery and colleagues (2014b) showed that it is anxiously attached individuals who desire and have greater relationship visibility (i.e., posting dyadic photographs and listing oneself as in a relationship) on Facebook, whereas avoidantly attached individuals desire and have less relationship visibility. As discussed, attachment anxiety refers to a tendency to be insecure and clingy in romantic relationships, and attachment avoidance refers to the tendency to be distant and independent-minded. By publicly linking people with their romantic partners, relationship disclosures on Facebook made anxious individuals feel better about themselves, but avoidant individuals feel worse about themselves. This points to the possibility that relationship disclosures on SNSs are not simple reflections of the status of the relationship, but that they might also be used to influence its trajectory—in this case, by serving disclosers' emotional regulation needs.

The ways in which relationship presentations on SNSs *affect* romantic relationships have been explicitly investigated by two studies. The only longitudinal study in this area has found that couples who engaged in public displays of affection on Facebook by listing themselves as in a relationship, posting more dyadic photographs, and writing on the partner's wall, experienced more commitment toward their partner and were more likely to stay together after six months (Toma & Choi, 2015). This pattern was explained through the lens of public commitment theory (Schlenker et al., 1994), which posits that discrepancies between public self-presentations and private beliefs are psychologically uncomfortable, and people resolve them by incorporating public claims into the self-concept, such that the gap between the two is reduced. Simply put, people who publicly declare to be committed to their romantic partner become, in fact, more committed, a pattern which was borne out by the data. While this study underscores potential benefits of Facebook on relational stability, Papp and colleagues (2012) illuminate the ways in which Facebook self-presentations can be a source of relational strife. Using couple-level data, they found that disagreements over listing oneself as "in a relationship" on Facebook, reported by both men and women, lowered women's, but not men's, relationship satisfaction. We discuss this study in more detail in the next section. For now, suffice it to say that this study highlights the ability of SNSs to affect romantic relationships: SNSs are significant enough to generate relational dissatisfaction when SNS-related behaviors are improperly negotiated.

To summarize, several important insights emerge from the literature on romantic relationships and broadcast mediated communication. The presentation of these relationships on SNSs tends to be positive and affirming, marking them as online public displays of affection. SNS self-presentations *reflect* the status of romantic relationships, with more satisfying relationships more likely to be visible on SNSs. But they also *affect* the status of romantic relationships, with highly visible relationships more likely to endure, and with relational dissatisfaction stemming from a failure to negotiate the visibility of these relationships. The literature is relatively small and exclusively focused on Facebook and on heterosexual relationships between young, unmarried couples. We recommend replications and extensions with a variety of relationship types and with other SNSs.

Conflict

Defined as "an expressed struggle between at least two independent parties who perceive incompatible goals, scarce resources, and interference from the other party in achieving their goals" (Hocker & Wilmot, 1995, p. 21), conflict refers to the friction that occurs when the differences between people rub against one another. While romantic partners often exhibit a great deal of similarity in terms of values, beliefs, education, physical attractiveness, and age (Buss, 1985; Vandenberg, 1972), they are nonetheless different people, and these differences are bound to surface and require negotiation. Romantic conflict is, therefore, neither good nor bad, but simply par for the course. In fact, the notion that "good relationships" should be free of conflict is often cited as a dysfunctional relationship belief (Eidelson & Epstein, 1982) because it can stifle the healthy negotiation of differences.

While conflict itself is value-free, the way it is managed can be either positive or negative. Poorly managed conflicts can be destructive to the relationship, while well-handled ones often enhance the quality of the relationship, bringing couples to heights of intimacy that would have been impossible to scale in the absence of the conflict (Pietromonaco et al., 2004). Yet appropriate conflict management can be difficult. Many people view conflict as inherently threatening, both to themselves and to the relationship, and thus have trouble broaching it directly. Conflict can also be accompanied by strong negative emotions, leading those who struggle with affect regulation to lash out at their partners or communicate in hurtful ways (Pietromonaco et al., 2004).

In sum, conflict is a commonplace aspect of romantic relationships, and conflict management is influential on the state and fate of relationships. At the same time, communication technologies have become widely used for interacting with romantic partners. Thus, romantic conflict and technology are bound to interface in interesting ways. Several important questions present themselves:

1. To what extent are dyadic media used in romantic conflict?
2. Why do couples use or avoid the media for conflict? What are the advantages and disadvantages of media use in this context?
3. What is the effect of media use on romantic conflict resolution and relationship satisfaction?
4. Can communication technology itself be a source of romantic conflict?

Despite the importance of this topic, the existing literature is scarce, counting only a handful of studies. Below, we review this literature and point out avenues for future research.

Extent of Dyadic Media Use in Romantic Conflict

As reviewed, the current media landscape is one of high choice, with an abundance of dyadic media facilitating one-on-one contact any time, any place. Given the availability and convenience of these media, to what extent do people resort to them when facing romantic conflict?

When asked if they had ever used the media to engage in romantic conflict, college students indicated that they did so to a substantial degree. Frisby and Westerman (2010) found that 61% of participants used a mediated channel for romantic conflict, specifically texting (51%), the phone (25%), instant messenger (13%), SNSs (8%), and email (4%). More recently, Scissors and colleagues (2014) found that 64% of their student sample used texting, followed by the phone (60%), IM (37%), SNSs (29%), video chat (22%), and email (21%) for romantic conflict. A different picture emerges for non-college students. A single study, to our knowledge, has examined a community sample (Coyne et al., 2011) and found that only 25% of couples used the media to broach serious relational topics, and a mere 10% did so by bringing up confrontational issues. Together, these studies indicate that younger adults rely on the media for broaching romantic conflict to a larger degree than older adults, a state of affairs which parallels cohort differences in media use in general. Thus, one reason why people resort to the media for romantic conflict may be habitual use. Along the same lines, college students demonstrated an upward trend in their use of media for conflict over time, with more college students using it in 2014 than in 2011. This again parallels young people's increasing adoption of technology (Lenhart, 2015) and points to the possibility that media use may be even higher today.

Despite these upward trends, FtF communication appears to remain the most widely used venue for addressing romantic conflict, even among college students, 82% of whom reported broaching romantic conflicts FtF (Scissors et al., 2014). This is perhaps an illustration of the fact that many conflicts emerge spontaneously FtF during routine couple interactions (e.g. "why haven't you done the dishes?"). Additionally, the measures used in the present studies only asked respondents if they had "ever" used FtF communication and specific media for conflict negotiation. This is not the same as ascertaining the extent to which the media is "usually" or "routinely" used for individual instances of conflict, nor does it account for the fact that conflict is a process that unfolds over time, and therefore may involve the use of several media as well as FtF communication. To better understand the space occupied by technology in romantic conflict, we recommend replication with more nuanced methods, such as daily diaries, where participants report on each conflict and all the media through which it was addressed, or surveys that measure time spent using each medium or the relative frequency of using each medium while engaged in romantic conflict.

Advantages and Disadvantages of Media Use in Romantic Conflict

Now we delve more deeply into the question of why romantic couples choose or eschew technology when addressing conflicts. Several interview studies (Caughlin et al., 2016; Perry & Werner-Wilson, 2011; Scissors & Gergle, 2013) had participants, mostly college students, reflect on the advantages and disadvantages of using the media for romantic conflict.

Consider the media's perceived advantages. First, asynchronicity, or unlimited composition time, and editability, or the opportunity to revise messages, were viewed as allowing couples to respond in a thoughtful manner, rather than merely react in the heat of the moment. Thus, composing a lengthy email detailing one's perspective could be a superior option to speaking off-the-cuff FtF or via the phone (Caughlin et al., 2016; Perry & Werner-Wilson, 2011). Relatedly, respondents noted that asynchronous technologies eliminate interruptions, and therefore can facilitate more equitable turn-taking. Indeed, over email, one partner can only respond once the other has finished saying their piece, unlike FtF communication (Caughlin et al., 2016; Perry & Werner-Wilson, 2011). Second, the reduction in non-verbal cues, a characteristic of text-based channels, was perceived as reducing flooding, or the experience of being overcome by intense negative emotion. Participants reported that their partners' embodied presence, often featuring angry voices and distressed facial expressions, can cause negative feelings to escalate; conversely, reduced-cue environments allow for more "breathing room" and an opportunity to cool off (Perry & Werner-Wilson, 2011; Scissors & Gergle, 2013). In the same vein, some participants reported being more comfortable voicing criticism or negative emotions in reduced-cue environments than FtF, where such expressions could be anxiety-producing (Caughlin et al., 2016; Scissors & Gergle, 2013).

To summarize, participants identified sizeable advantages to using technology for handling romantic conflict, including: 1) constructing more careful messages; 2) avoiding interruptions; 3) maintaining emotional control; and 4) expressing negative emotions and dissenting opinions more easily. To reap these advantages, participants reported engaging in strategies such as switching channels from FtF to dyadic media when the conflict became too heated (Scissors & Gergle, 2013) or engaging in incremental introduction, whereby they eased into FtF conflict by broaching it via the media first (Caughlin et al., 2016). This latter practice allowed participants to be more prepared in terms of message construction and more aware of, and guarded against, their own likelihood of emotional flooding. One final strategy was to compartmentalize conflictual situations away from FtF interaction, by delegating them to the media, such that the FtF relationship could be preserved as happy and conflict-free (Scissors & Gergle, 2013).

Nonetheless, communication technologies were also described as presenting disadvantages for romantic conflict. While asynchronicity enabled message construction, it also increased response latencies, or the interval of time participants waited for their partners to respond. This waiting time was fraught with anxiety and often escalating anger (Scissors & Gergle, 2013). Indeed, participants reported being 2.8 times more likely to purposefully delay responding, and 3.8 times more likely to ignore their partners in texting than FtF (Scissors et al., 2014). Reduced non-verbal cues enabled better emotional expression and control for some people, yet others felt it was harder to emotionally connect with their partners in the absence of embodied, FtF contact (Frisby & Westerman, 2010; Scissors & Gergle, 2013), or harder to ascertain how their partner was truly feeling (Frisby & Westerman, 2010). Finally, some participants reported dissatisfaction with resolving conflict via the media rather than FtF; such resolution did not feel "final," leaving unresolved feelings and increased uncertainty about the relationship (Scissors & Gergle, 2013).

Given that dyadic media appear to simultaneously offer advantages and disadvantages, how do couples make choices of whether to broach the conflict FtF or through the media? The studies reviewed above do not investigate the extent to which these reported benefits and drawbacks affected actual media choice. In other words, under what circumstances are people strategic about selecting the most appropriate medium for conflict resolution, carefully weighing advantages and disadvantages, and under what circumstances are they not so? This question is worthy of future research. We might expect moderating factors, such as the gravity of the conflict, and individual differences, such as personality traits, to play a part. For instance, serious conflicts, such as those regarding the future of the relationship, might provoke more careful deliberation about media choice than more trivial conflicts, such as those about household chores. By the same token, individuals high in impulsivity, neuroticism, or attachment anxiety might be more likely to react immediately to a conflictual issue, reaching out to their partner through whatever media are most convenient, rather than reflecting on the appropriateness of various media for positive conflict resolution. What constitutes "appropriate" media choice for conflict resolution may itself be subject to moderating variables, such as the type of conflict being addressed, the personalities and preferences of the people involved, and the nature of the relationships. Who has a better chance of solving various types of conflicts over the media or FtF? We discuss some of these issues in the next section.

Effects of Media Use on Conflict Resolution

Appropriate conflict resolution, or resolving the conflict in ways that enhance the quality of the romantic relationship and are satisfactory to both partners, is the most desirable outcome in conflict episodes. Is media use conducive to this outcome? This question was tackled in a series of studies, either surveys where participants recalled instances of romantic conflict across the media (Frisby &

Westerman, 2010; Scissors et al., 2014), or experiments where couples were brought to the lab and asked to discuss a conflictual issue using experimentally assigned media (Burge & Tatar, 2009; Scissors & Gergle, 2016).

By and large, results reveal negative effects of dyadic media use on conflict resolution. Burge and Tatar (2009) found that romantic partners who discussed a topic on which they disagreed registered sharper declines in mood if the discussion took place using the media (phone and IM) than FtF. Scissors and colleagues (2014) found that individuals engaged in more distancing behaviors (i.e., purposefully delaying responses and ignoring the partner) and perceived their partner as engaging in more distancing behaviors when the interaction took place online (texting, email, IM) compared to FtF. Importantly, conflicts where resolution was attempted online were associated with lower relational quality than conflicts where resolution was attempted FtF. In a replication and extension of this work, Scissors and Gergle (2016) found that couples who engaged in conflict FtF and through IM experienced equal levels of satisfaction with the interaction. However, this relationship was moderated by self-esteem, such that individuals with low self-esteem who communicated with their partners via IM reported a decline in satisfaction compared to their FtF counterparts; meanwhile, individuals with high self-esteem were unaffected by the communication channel. The authors theorize that low self-esteem causes individuals to perceive communication encounters in a biased, negative way, but that these biases only get activated in reduced-cue environments, such as instant messenger, where there is more room for imagination and interpretation than in FtF environments. Therefore, low self-esteem individuals should be cautioned against broaching romantic conflicts using the media. Only one study (Perry & Werner-Wilson, 2011) found no detriment of media use compared to FtF communication, as couples who used the media for problem-solving were equally satisfied with their communication as those who used FtF communication.

In conclusion, despite the numerous advantages of media use listed by participants in interview studies, the literature on conflict resolution is somewhat less encouraging vis-à-vis the use of media. However, these results need to be interpreted with caution. The literature is still limited, with only four studies investigating the effect of media use on conflict resolution. While providing tight experimental control, the studies where participants were randomly assigned to use the media or FtF did not account for the media that participants would have chosen in a naturalistic setting, nor for the use of multiple media during the process of conflict negotiation (see also Scissors & Gergle, 2013). Similarly, the literature is yet to offer a clear picture of what media features and affordances are detrimental to conflict resolution—perhaps it is the reduction of non-verbal cues, the lack of synchronicity, or recordability. Save for the argument that reduced-cue media activate self-esteem biases (Scissors & Gergle, 2016) and increase actual and perceived distancing behaviors (Scissors et al., 2014), there is little theorizing on the mechanism through which media use may harm conflict resolution. These are all rich avenues for future research.

Media Use as a Source of Romantic Conflict

Finally, it is important to recognize that the use of communication technologies is itself an issue that must be negotiated by romantic couples. While these technologies benefit couples by facilitating connection and communication, they also create opportunities for disconnection or reveal differences among partners that ultimately result in conflict. For instance, couples must now negotiate how frequently to text each other during the day, what is an acceptable time frame for responding to the partner's texts or calls, whether to disclose the relationship on Facebook (see our previous discussion), and how to engage with former partners or potential romantic interests using mediated communication, especially SNSs. Couples might disagree on these points, or might fail to live up to their promises, creating conflict.

The literature has begun to investigate the extent to which media practices create discord within romantic relationships. Much of this literature has focused on Facebook, which creates opportunities for romantic conflict via two primary routes. The first is enabling *public presentations of the relationship*, an issue addressed in the previous section. Research has identified conflict over the management of this joint self-presentation. For instance, Papp and colleagues (2012) found that disagreements about whether to become "Facebook official" occurred with some regularity, and importantly, they were associated with lower levels of relationship satisfaction for the female, but not male, partner in heterosexual relationships. Fox and colleagues (2014) also found that too much sharing about the couple's activities and thoughts in such a public venue could undermine partners' sense of autonomy within the relationship. Yet too little sharing could also be problematic, as individuals who imagined a situation in which their partner posted few or no couple photographs on Facebook felt more insecure about the relationship than individuals who imagined their partner posting copious photographs (Muscanell et al., 2013).

Second, Facebook creates opportunities for romantic conflict by enabling *partner surveillance*, or the ability to keep tabs on the partner's Facebook activity. This surveillance can reveal that the partner engages in jealousy-provoking behaviors, such as making and accepting friend requests from potential romantic interests (Drouin et al., 2014; Utz et al., 2015), keeping in touch with former partners, or being flirtatious with potential partners. This can be fuel for romantic discord. The literature has found robust support for the notion that partner surveillance on Facebook elicits romantic jealousy, arguably because it exposes individuals to information about their partners' jealousy-inducing activities. The first study on this topic found that Facebook use, broadly defined, increased romantic jealousy above and beyond trait jealousy, or individuals' propensity to be jealous in general (Muise et al., 2009). More granular investigations found that specific types of information gleaned from Facebook increased jealousy, such as noticing that the partner added or messaged a previous partner or an unknown person of the opposite sex (in the case of heterosexual relationships) (Utz et al., 2015), and that specific types of people were more prone to Facebook jealousy, such as those high in attachment anxiety (Marshall et al., 2013) and those in newer relationships (Clayton et al., 2013). This body of literature has not investigated couples' discussions and negotiations around the issue of Facebook jealousy, so it is unclear to what extent partner surveillance on Facebook produces explicit conflict among relational partners. However, it is likely that such conflict does occur, especially since research shows that Facebook jealousy is linked with poor relational outcomes (Clayton et al., 2013; Elphinston & Noller, 2011; Fox et al., 2014). Thus, individuals may address their issues directly with their partner, creating relational strife, or may simply decide to leave their partners. These possibilities need to be investigated by future research.

Mobile phones have also emerged as a source of relational conflict. Duran and colleagues (2011) found that mobile phone use produced autonomy–connection conflict for undergraduate students in romantic relationships. Some felt too tethered to their partner due to the partner's excessive bids for connection (calls, texts) and expectations of perpetual contact. Others felt that their partner was insufficiently available, this unavailability rendered stark by the fact that mobile phones offer low-effort means of connection (e.g. "why couldn't she take two seconds to answer my text?"). In response to these tensions, some conflictual couples developed rules for managing contact via mobile phones, such as not texting while in class or at work, expecting the partner to answer the phone if the phone is on, or calling each other before going to sleep. Similarly, interviews with Mexican-American teenagers revealed conflict around who the partner could or could not text with, and around flirtatious behaviors on social media (Rueda et al., 2015).

Are these rules effective, in the sense that they increase couples' relational satisfaction? Only one study has addressed this topic and found that rules prohibiting partners from arguing over the phone were positively linked with relational satisfaction, but rules prohibiting partners from (a) calling or texting repetitively when not receiving a response and (b) checking each other's call and texts logs were *negatively* associated with relational satisfaction (Miller-Ott et al., 2012). Since this is a correlational study, it is unclear whether these latter rules decreased relational satisfaction, or whether it was dissatisfied couples who were more likely to come up with such rules. Nonetheless, it will be important for future research to examine the effectiveness of rules regulating mobile phone use in romantic relationships.

Recently, the term "phubbing" was coined to describe instances where individuals feel ignored or interrupted by their romantic partner's use of a mobile phone. Phubbing is a portmanteau of phone and snubbing, thus signifying that one partner feels excluded by the other's mobile phone use (Roberts & David, 2016). Phubbing has been theorized to provoke conflict in romantic relationships because the partner being phubbed feels unimportant and deprioritized compared to the digital content delivered through their partner's mobile phone. This conflict appears to be consequential for the quality of the romantic relationship: two correlational studies found that phubbing provoked conflict, with the phubbed partner expressing discontent over being ignored in favor of the mobile phone, which, in turn, decreased relational satisfaction and increased depression for the phubbed partner (McDaniel & Coyne, 2016; Roberts & David, 2016). Similarly, Krasnova and colleagues (2016) found that phubbing increased negative emotions (sadness, worry, anger, feeling excluded, and offended), which decreased relational cohesion. It is unclear how prevalent phubbing is, although one study (McDaniel & Coyne, 2016) warns that it might be a big relational issue: over 70% of a sample of 143 women reported that their partner's phone use interfered with couple interactions "sometimes," "often," "very often," or "all the time."

In sum, the literature indicates that communication technologies offer several opportunities for romantic conflict when 1) partners are dissatisfied with their quantity of mediated contact; 2) partners disagree on their public self-presentation on SNSs; 3) jealousy is provoked by surveilling the partner's SNS activities; and 4) one partner feels phubbed, or ignored due to the other's mobile phone use. The findings on romantic jealousy are robust, but the other areas of research are still incipient. How frequently do these conflicts occur? How do couples address them? How does the negotiation of these conflicts affect relationship quality? Are there individual differences in the experience of these conflicts?

Concluding Remarks

The purpose of this chapter was to review the literature on the uses and effects of communication technologies in the maintenance phase of romantic relationships, for geographically collocated couples. The review reveals a rich array of issues being tackled in the literature: How prevalent is the use of dyadic media and how does it affect relational satisfaction? How do couples present themselves on SNSs and what are the effects of these presentations? To what extent do couples use dyadic media to engage in conflict and to what effects? Are communication technologies a source of discord in romantic relationships?

Some general patterns emerge. The use of communication technologies appears to be on the rise both in the sphere of everyday communication and for conflict management, despite the fact that collocated couples have easy access to FtF communication. In particular, texting has become a powerful tool for everyday communication, likely used when couples are separated by work, school, or hobbies, or because they are not cohabitating. As the use of communication technologies has grown, so have its relational consequences. While FtF contact is expected to be highly meaningful when it comes to the quality of romantic relationships, the media have an additional, also meaningful effect. Several studies show that the more mediated contact (including sexting), the better off the relationships are—with the exception of conflict. Despite identifying a range of benefits of dyadic media for managing conflict, couples appeared less satisfied with conflict resolution and with their relationship when the conflict was broached via the media. Broadcast mediated communication, enacted through SNSs, offered opportunities for relational enhancement, as when couples experienced more relational commitment and stability as a result of declaring themselves Facebook official, but also for relational strife, as when partners experienced jealousy due to Facebook surveillance.

Interestingly, these trends were generally not moderated by gender, indicating that the uses and effects of communication technologies are fairly uniform for women and men. Attachment style does appear to be a meaningful moderator of several effects, suggesting that it is an important variable for future research to consider. Anxiously attached individuals made their relationships more visible on Facebook, experienced more Facebook jealousy, and engaged in more sexting. Avoidantly attached individuals made their relationships less visible on Facebook, sexted more, and derived more relational benefits from sexting. Age might also be an important moderator but, as discussed, most studies focused on young adults, and there is insufficient data to generalize to older adults. It does appear, however, that younger people use more media in their romantic relationships and are more affected by it. A related variable that has received little attention is the commitment level of relationships. The evidence is clear that more committed partners sext more and experience more benefits from sexting, and that they make their relationships more visible on SNSs. But it is unclear if older, married adults disclose their relationships on SNSs to the same extent or whether they engage in conflict using technology.

Theoretically speaking, the literature is young and has room to grow. Many of these studies were pioneering in documenting effects of communication technologies in romantic relationships, although the mechanisms underlying the effects were yet to be specified. As the literature developed, several important theoretical frameworks were advanced. The Hyperpersonal model of communication usefully predicts the content of couples' SNS presentations (through its notion of selective self-presentation), the mechanism through which couples derive relational benefits from dyadic media communication (through its notion of hyperpersonal projections), and might predict the construction of careful online messages during conflict episodes (also through its notion of selective self-presentation), although this issue is yet to be investigated. The framework of mobile maintenance appears to have great utility in explaining both the patterns and the effects of casual, everyday couple interactions through dyadic media. Note that both the Hyperpersonal model and the mobile maintenance framework were designed specifically to explain technology effects in interpersonal relationships.

Yet classic theories in interpersonal communication and social psychology can also be useful in understanding couple dynamics in mediated environments, even though these theories were not originally meant to account for the influence of the medium of communication. In particular, multiple studies have successfully applied attachment theory, which is concerned with how interactions with primary caregivers during infancy and childhood shape individuals' behaviors in adult romantic relationships. As reviewed, attachment style appears to be a robust predictor of how people engage with their partners in mediated spaces. Public commitment theory also usefully explains relational dynamics stemming from broadcast mediated communication. Finally, relational dialectics theory (Baxter, 1988) explains the struggle romantic partners experience in handling the unbounded opportunities for connection offered by communication technologies with their own personal need for autonomy. Many issues remain in need of theoretical development. For example, what accounts for the negative consequences of using communication technologies in conflict management? What explains the benefits of sexting? Why do some individuals engage in phubbing and what perceptual mechanism explains why phubbing leads to a deterioration of the relationship?

On a methodological level, the literature to date has deployed mostly cross-sectional surveys, resulting in numerous descriptions of media use, and correlations between media use variables and relationship-level variables. While valuable, these are dubious on questions of causality. We recommend that future work uses experimental or longitudinal designs. The latter, which is currently almost completely absent from the literature, can provide stronger evidence of causality when it comes to variables that cannot be experimentally manipulated, such as attachment style or relationship commitment, and can also elucidate the longer-term consequences of communication technologies in romantic relationships. As previously noted, it will be important for future research to expand its focus from college students to more diverse community samples, including married couples, same-sex couples, and older couples.

To conclude, individuals in the twenty-first century are challenged to navigate the complexities of romantic relationships in an environment resplendent with media options. These media shape relational dynamics in important ways, sometimes facilitating closeness and intimacy, other times producing discord and dissatisfaction. Understanding these dynamics will undoubtedly constitute a rich and theoretically meaningful avenue for future scholarship.

References

Aylor, B. A. (2003). Maintaining long-distance relationships. In D. J. Canary & M. Dainton (Eds.), *Maintaining relationships through communication: Relational, contextual, and cultural variations* (pp. 127–139). Mahwah, NJ: Lawrence Erlbaum Associates.

Bartholomew, K., & Horowitz, L. M. (1991). Attachment styles among young adults: A test of a four-category model. *Journal of Personality and Social Psychology*, 61(2), 226–244.

Baxter, L. A. (1988). A dialectical perspective on communication strategies in relationship development. In S. Duck, D. F. Hay, S. E. Hobfoll, W. Ickes, & B. M. Montgomery (Eds.), *Handbook of personal relationships: Theory, research and interventions* (pp. 257–273). Oxford: John Wiley.

Baym, N. K., Zhang, Y. B., Kunkel, A., Ledbetter, A., & Lin, M. (2007). Relational quality and media use in interpersonal relationships. *New Media & Society*, 9(5), 735–752. doi: 10.1177/1461444807080339

Billedo, C. J., Kerkhof, P., & Finkenauer, C. (2015). The use of social networking sites for relationship maintenance in long-distance and geographically close romantic relationships. *Cyberpsychology, Behavior, and Social Networking*, 18(3), 152–157. doi:10.1089/cyber.2014.0469

Brennan, K. A., Clark, C. L., & Shaver, P. R. (1998). Self-report measurement of adult attachment: An integrative overview. In J. A. Simpson & W. S. Rholes (Eds.), *Attachment theory and close relationships*. New York: Guilford Press.

Brenner, J., & Smith, A. (2013). 72% of online adults are social networking site users. *Pew Research Center*, August 5. www.pewinternet.org/2013/08/05/72-of-online-adults-are-social-networking-site-users/

Brody, N. (2013). Absence—and mediated communication—makes the heart grow fonder: Clarifying the predictors of satisfaction and commitment in long-distance friendships. *Communication Research Reports*, 30(4), 323–332. doi: 10.1080/08824096.2013.837388

Burge, J. D., & Tatar, D. (2009). Affect and dyads: Conflict across different technological media. In S. Harrison (Ed.), *Media space 20+ years of mediated life*. London: Springer.

Buss, D. M. (1985). Human mate selection: Opposites are sometimes said to attract, but in fact we are likely to marry someone who is similar to us in almost every variable. *American Scientist*, 73(1), 47–51.

Caughlin, J. P., Basinger, E. D., & Sharabi, L. L. (2016). The connections between communication technologies and relational conflict: A multiple goals and communication interdependence perspective. In J. A. Samp (Ed.), *Communicating interpersonal conflict in close relationships: Contexts, challenges, and opportunities* (pp. 57–72). New York: Routledge.

Clayton, R. B., Nagurney, A., & Smith, J. R. (2013). Cheating, breakup, and divorce: Is Facebook use to blame? *Cyberpsychology, Behavior, and Social Networking*, 16, 717–720. doi:10.1089/cyber.2012.0424

Coyne, S. M., Stockdale, L., Busby, D., Iverson, B., & Grant, D. M. (2011). "I luv u :)!": A descriptive study of the media use of individuals in romantic relationships. *Family Relations*, 60, 150–162. doi:10.1111/j.1741-3729.2010.00639.x

Dainton, M., & Aylor, B. (2002). Patterns of communication channel use in the maintenance of long-distance relationships. *Communication Research Reports*, 19(2), 118–129. doi:10.1080/08824090209384839

Drouin, M., & Landgraff, C. (2012). Texting, sexting, and attachment in college students' romantic relationships. *Computers in Human Behavior*, 28(2), 444–449. doi:10.1016/j.chb.2011.10.015

Drouin, M., Vogel, K. N., Surbey, A., & Stills, J. R. (2013). Let's talk about sexting, baby: Computer-mediated sexual behaviors among young adults. *Computers in Human Behavior*, 29(5), A25–A30. doi:10.1016/j.chb.2012.12.030

Drouin, M., Miller, D. A., & Dibble, J. L. (2014). Ignore your partners' current Facebook friends; beware the ones they add! *Computers in Human Behavior*, 35, 483–488. doi:10.1016/j.chb.2014.02032

Drouin, M., Coupe, M., & Temple, J. (2017). Is sexting good for your relationship? It depends . . . *Computers in Human Behavior*, 75, 749–756. doi:10.1016/j.chb.2017.06.018

Duran, R. L., Kelly, L., & Rotaru, T. (2011). Mobile phones in romantic relationships and the dialectic of autonomy versus connection. *Communication Quarterly*, 59(1), 19–36. doi:10.1080/01463373.2011.541336

Eidelson, R. J., & Epstein, N. (1982). Cognition and relationship maladjustment: Development of a measure of dysfunctional relationship beliefs. *Journal of Consulting and Clinical Psychology*, 50(5), 715–720. doi:10.1037/0022-006X.50.5.715

Elphinston, R. A., & Noller, P. (2011). Time to face it! Facebook intrusion and the implication for romantic jealousy and relationship satisfaction. *Cyberpsychology, Behavior, and Social Networking*, 14(11), 631–635. doi:10.1089/cyber.2010.0318

Emery, L. F., Muise, A., Alpert, E., & Le, B. (2014a). Do we look happy? Perceptions of romantic relationship quality on Facebook. *Personal Relationships*, 22(1), 1–7. doi:10.1111/pere.12059

Emery, L. F., Muise, A., Dix, E. L., & Le, B. (2014b). Can you tell that I'm in a relationship? Attachment and relationship visibility on Facebook. *Personality and Social Psychology Bulletin*, 40(11), 1466–1479. doi:10.1177/0146167214549944

Emmers-Sommer, T. M. (2004). The effect of communication quality and quantity indicators on intimacy and relational satisfaction. *Journal of Social and Personal Relationships*, 21(3), 399–411. doi:10.1177/0265407504042839

Finkel, E. J., Eastwick, P. W., Karney, B. R., Reis, H. T., & Sprecher, S. (2012). Online dating: A critical analysis from the perspective of psychological science. *Psychological Science in the Public Interest*, 13(1), 3–66. doi:10.1177/1529100612436522

Fox, J., Warber, K. M., & Makstaller, D. C. (2013). The role of Facebook in romantic relationship development: An exploration of Knapp's relational stage model. *Journal of Social and Personal Relationships*, 30(6). doi:10.1177/0265407512468370

Fox, J., Osborn, J. L., & Warber, K. M. (2014). Relational dialectics and social networking sites: The role of Facebook in romantic relationship escalation, maintenance, conflict, and dissolution. *Computers in Human Behavior*, 35, 527–534. doi:10.1016/j.chb.2014.02.031

Frisby, B. N., & Westerman, D. (2010). Rational actors: Channel selection and rational choices in romantic conflict episodes. *Journal of Social and Personal Relationships*, 27(7), 970–981. doi:10.1177/0265407510378302

Hall, J. A., & Baym, N. K. (2012). Calling and texting (too much): Mobile maintenance expectations, (over) dependence, entrapment, and friendship satisfaction. *New Media & Society*, 14(2), 316–331. doi:10.1177/1461444811415047

Henderson, L., & Morgan, E. (2011). Sexting and sexual relationships among teens and young adults. *McNair Scholars Research Journal*, 7(1), 9.

Hocker, J. L., & Wilmot, W. E. (1995). *Interpersonal conflict*, 4th ed. Dubuque, IA: William C. Brown.

Jiang, L. C., & Hancock, J. T. (2013). Absence makes the communication grow fonder: Geographic separation, interpersonal media, and intimacy in dating relationships. *Journal of Communication*, 63(3), 556–577. doi:10.1111/jcom.12029

Jin, B., & Peña, J. F. (2010). Mobile communication in romantic relationships: Mobile phone use, relational uncertainty, love, commitment, and attachment styles. *Communication Reports*, 23(1), 39–51. doi:10.1080/08934211003598742

Klettke, B., Hallford, D. J., & Mellor, D. J. (2014). Sexting prevalence and correlates: A systematic literature review. *Clinical Psychology Review*, 34(1), 44–53. doi:10.1016/j.cpr.2013.10.007

Krasnova, H., Abramova, O., Notter, I., & Baumann, A. (2016). Why phubbing is toxic for your relationship: Understanding the role of smartphone jealousy among "generation y" users. *Proceeding of the European Conference on Information Systems*, Istanbul, Turkey.

Lane, B. L., Piercy, C. W., & Carr, C. T. (2016). Making it Facebook official: The warranting value of online relationship status disclosures on relational characteristics. *Computers in Human Behavior*, 56, 1–8. doi:10.1016/j.chb.2015.11.016

Lenhart, A. (2015). Teens, social media and technology overview 2015. *Pew Research Center*, April 9. www.pewinternet.org/2015/04/09/teens-social-media-technology-2015/

Marshall, T. C. (2012). Facebook surveillance of former romantic partners: Associations with postbreakup recovery and personal growth. *Cyberpsychology, Behavior, and Social Networking*, 15, 521–526.

Marshall, T. C., Bejanyan, K., Castro, G. D., & Lee, R. A. (2013). Attachment styles as predictors of Facebook-related jealousy and surveillance in romantic relationships. *Personal Relationships*, 20(1), 1–22. doi:10.1111/j.1475-6811.2011.01393.x

McDaniel, B. T., & Coyne, S. M. (2016). "Technoference": The interference of technology in couple relationships and implications for women's personal and relational well-being. *Psychology of Popular Media Culture*, 5(1), 85. doi:10.1037/ppm0000065

McDaniel, B. T., & Drouin, M. (2015). Sexting among married couples: Who is doing it, and are they more satisfied? *Cyberpsychology, Behavior, and Social Networking*, 18(11), 628–634. doi:10.1089/cyber.2015.0334

Miller-Ott, A. E., Kelly, L., & Duran, R. L. (2012). The effects of cell phone usage rules on satisfaction in romantic relationships. *Communication Quarterly*, 60(1), 17–34. doi: 10.1080/01463373.2012.642263

Mod, G. B. B. A. (2010). Reading romance: The impact Facebook rituals can have on a romantic relationship. *Journal of Comparative Research in Anthropology and Sociology*, 1(2), 61–77.

Morey, J. N., Gentzler, A. L., Creasy, B., Oberhauser, A. M., & Westerman, D. (2013). Young adults' use of communication technology within their romantic relationships and associations with attachment style. *Computers in Human Behavior*, 29(4), 1771–1778. doi:10.1016/j.chb.2013.02.019

Muise, A., Christofides, E., & Desmarais, S. (2009). More information than you ever wanted: Does Facebook bring out the green-eyed monster of jealousy? *CyberPsychology & Behavior*, 12(4), 441–444. doi:10.1089/cpb.2008.0263

Muscanell, N. L., Guadagno, R. E., Rice, L., & Murphy, S. (2013). Don't it make my brown eyes green? An analysis of Facebook use and romantic jealousy. *Cyberpsychology, Behavior, and Social Networking*, 16(4), 237–242. doi:10.1089/cyber.2012.0411

Neustaedter, C. & Greenberg, S. (2012). Intimacy in long-distance relationships over video chat. *Proceedings of the SIGCHI conference on human factors in computing systems* (pp. 753–762). New York: ACM.

Orosz, G., Szekeres, A., Kiss, Z. G., Farkas, P., & Roland-Levy, C. (2015). Elevated romantic love and jealousy if relationship is declared on Facebook. *Frontiers in Psychology*, 6. doi:10.3389/fpsyg.2015.00214

Papp, L. M., Danielewicz, J., & Cayemberg, C. (2012). "Are we Facebook official?" Implications of dating partners' Facebook use and profiles for intimate relationship satisfaction. *Cyberpsychology, Behavior, and Social Networking*, 15(2), 85–90. doi:10.1089/cyber.2011.0291

Parker, T. S., Blackburn, K. M., Perry, M. S., & Hawks, J. M. (2013). Sexting as an intervention: Relationship satisfaction and motivation considerations. *The American Journal of Family Therapy*, 41(1), 1–12. doi:10.2080/01926187.2011.635134

Perry, M. S. & Werner-Wilson, R. J. (2011). Couples and computer-mediated communication: A closer look at the affordances and use of the channel. *Family and Consumer Sciences Research Journal*, 40(2), 120–134. doi:10.1111/j.1552-3934.2011.02099.x

Pietromonaco, P. R., Greenwood, D., & Barrett, L. F. (2004). Conflict in adult close relationships: An attachment perspective. In W. S. Rholes and J. A. Simpson (Eds.), *Adult attachment: Theory, research, and clinical implications* (pp. 267–299). New York: Guilford Press.

Roberts, J. A., & David, M. E. (2016). My life has become a major distraction from my cell phone: Partner phubbing and relationship satisfaction among romantic partners. *Computers in Human Behavior*, 54, 134–141. doi:10.1016/j.chb.2015.07.058

Rubin, R. B. (1986). *Relationship Development*. Chichester: John Wiley & Sons.

Rueda, H. A., Lindsay, M., & Williams, L. R. (2015). "She posted it on Facebook": Mexican American adolescents' experiences with technology and romantic relationship conflict. *Journal of Adolescent Research*, 30(4), 419–445. doi:10.1177/0743558414566236

Saslow, L. R., Muise, A., Impett, E. A., & Dubin, M. (2012). Can you see how happy we are? Facebook images and relationship satisfaction. *Social Psychological and Personality Science*, 4(4). doi:10.1177/1948550612460059

Schade, L. C., Sandberg, J., Bean, R., Busby, D., & Coyne, S. (2013). Using technology to connect in romantic relationships: Effects on attachment, relationship satisfaction, and stability in emerging adults. *Journal of Couple & Relationship Therapy*, 12(4), 314–338. doi:10.1080/15332691.2013.836051

Schlenker, B. R., Dlugolecki, D. W., & Doherty, K. (1994). The impact of self-presentations of self-appraisals and behavior: The power of public commitment. *Personality and Social Psychology Bulletin*, 20(1), 20–33. doi:10.1177/0146167294201002

Scissors, L. E., & Gergle, D. (2013). "Back and forth, back and forth": Channel switching in romantic couple conflict. *Proceedings of the 2013 conference on computer supported cooperative work—CSCW* 13. doi:10.1145/2441776.2441804

Scissors, L., & Gergle, D. (2016). On the bias: Self-esteem biases across communication channels during romantic couple conflict. *Proceedings of the 19th ACM conference on computer-supported cooperative work & social computing—CSCW* 16. doi:10.1145/2818048.2820080

Scissors, L. E., Roloff, M. E., & Gergle, D. (2014). Room for interpretation: The role of self-esteem and CMC in romantic couple conflict. *Proceedings of the 32nd annual ACM conference on human factors in computing systems—CHI* 14. doi:10.1145/2556288.2557177

Stafford, L., & Canary, D. J. (1991). Maintenance strategies and romantic relationship type, gender, and relational characteristics. *Journal of Social and Personal Relationships*, 8, 217–242.

Stasko, E. C., & Geller, P. A. (2015). Reframing sexting as a positive relationship behavior. *American Psychological Association*, 6–9.

Toma, C. L. (2013). Feeling better but doing worse: Effects of Facebook self-presentation on implicit self-esteem and cognitive task performance. *Media Psychology*, 16(2), 199–220. doi:10.1080/15213269.762189

Toma, C. L. (2015). Online dating. In C. R. Berger & M. E. Roloff (Eds.), *International encyclopedia of interpersonal communication*. Chichester: Wiley-Blackwell.

Toma, C. L., & Carlson, C. L. (2015). How do Facebook users believe they come across in their profiles? A meta-perception approach to investigating Facebook self-presentation. *Communication Research Reports*, 32(1), 93–101. doi:10.1080/08824096.2014.990557

Toma, C. L., & Choi, M. (2015). The couple who Facebooks together, stays together: Facebook self-presentation and relationship longevity among college-aged dating couples. *Cyberpsychology, Behavior, and Social Networking*, 18(7), 367–372. doi:10.1089/cyber.2015.0060

Toma, C. L., & Choi, M. (2016). Mobile media matters: Media use and relationship satisfaction among geographically close dating couples. *Proceedings of the 19th ACM conference on computer-supported cooperative work & social computing* (pp. 394–404). New York: ACM.

Utz, S., Muscanell, N., & Khalid, C. (2015). Snapchat elicits more jealousy than Facebook: A comparison of Snapchat and Facebook use. *Cyberpsychology, Behavior, and Social Networking*, 18(3), 141–146. doi:10.1089/cyber.2014.0479

Vandenberg, S. G. (1972). Assortative mating, or who marries whom? *Behavior Genetics*, 2(3), 127–155.

Walther, J. B. (1996). Computer-mediated communication: Impersonal, interpersonal, and hyperpersonal interaction. *Communication Research*, 23(1), 3–43.

Walther, J. B. (2007). Selective self-presentation in computer-mediated communication: Hyperpersonal dimensions of technology, language, and cognition. *Computers in Human Behavior*, 23(5), 2538–2557. doi:10.1016/j.chb.05.002

Weisskirch, R. S., & Delevi, R. (2011). "Sexting" and adult romantic attachment. *Computers in Human Behavior*, 27(5), 1697–1701. doi:10.1016/j.chb.2011.02.008

Zhao, S., Grasmuck, S., & Martin, J. (2008). Identity construction on Facebook: Digital empowerment in anchored relationships. *Computers in Human Behavior*, 24(5), 1816–1836. doi:10.1016/j.chb.2008.02.012

6

SOCIAL MEDIA AND SUBJECTIVE WELL-BEING

A Relational Perspective

Samuel Hardman Taylor and Natalya N. Bazarova

The pervasiveness of social media has raised considerable concern among health professionals, educators, parents, and researchers about how living a networked life impacts subjective well-being (e.g. Jelenchick et al., 2013). The American Academy of Pediatrics suggests limiting the amount of time children and adolescents spend on social media and other communication technologies because of potential deleterious mental health outcomes. There is even the term "Facebook depression" to refer to a possible link between time spent on Facebook and users' depression (O'Keeffe & Clarke-Pearson, 2011). These worries derive from perspectives that time spent online does not constitute quality connection with others and potentially displaces the health benefits of socializing with family and friends offline.

Although time spent on social media is at the center of public concerns and the focus of many research studies, the evidence for the effect of time spent on social media on well-being is mixed. Some articles conclude that social media use can improve well-being and reduce depression and loneliness (Burke & Kraut, 2016; Burke et al., 2010; Gonzales, 2014). On the other hand, using social media has been shown to have a net-negative impact on well-being (Kross et al., 2013; Steers et al., 2014; Shakya & Christakis, 2017; Verduyn et al., 2015). Whereas concerns about the effects of social media on wellness are high, research to date has been inconclusive and produced limited guidance on what should be encouraged as healthy social media use.

This puzzle of inconclusive and mixed research findings may be partly due to the predominant interest in direct effects of social media use on well-being, instead of processes and mechanisms that underlie these effects (Valkenburg & Peter, 2008). In this chapter, we attempt to explicate some of these processes and mechanisms through the lens of close relationship research. This lens is warranted because of the importance of close relationships in social media (Burke & Kraut, 2016; Kraut et al., 2002; Joinson, 2008), and the unique effect of communicating with close relations (as opposed to weak ties or other networked audiences) on well-being in social media (Feeney & Collins, 2015). This lens is also consistent with long-standing evidence in relationship science about how quality close relationships are necessary for subjective well-being (Diener & McGavran, 2008), and critical for determining health outcomes across the lifespan (Pietromonaco et al., 2013; Robles et al., 2014).

A close relationships perspective on the networked self and well-being differs from perceived social support or access to network resources because it focuses on a fundamental human biopsychological need to form intimate relationships in order to maintain positive well-being (Hazan & Campa, 2013). Humans need intimate relationships for their psychological and physical health, and a lack of quality close relationships is as predictive of mortality as major public health concerns, such as smoking (Holt-Lunstad et al., 2015). People living in the networked age communicate their identity and relationships on social network sites, text messaging, face-to-face (FtF), telephone calls, and many other media (Papacharissi, 2010). Consequently, how people connect with the loved ones that are fundamental to their happiness and health has shifted to a multimedia experience.

In this chapter, we explore what effect networked social connections have on subjective well-being. We advocate a close relational perspective toward understanding the tangled question of social media and subjective well-being. To accomplish this objective, we first conduct a brief review of subjective well-being and social media research on well-being. Second, we develop two pathways through which social media can influence well-being: one in which social media communication strengthens relational closeness and the other one grounded in the functions of existing close relationships. In these two pathways, we pull from interpersonal communication and relationship science research to establish relational mechanisms for how social media influence the way that close relationships regulate subjective well-being. For each pathway, a research agenda and emerging questions for scholars studying the effects of social media and subjective well-being are articulated.

Subjective Well-Being

There are numerous conceptualizations of personal well-being (e.g. psychological flourishing), but in this review, we limit our scope to subjective well-being (SWB). SWB refers to the affective experiences and evaluations about life quality (Diener, 1984). Colloquially, SWB is a synonym for happiness. Across cultures, striving for high levels of SWB is perhaps the most important goal humans pursue (Tay et al., 2015). There is increasing public policy attention toward SWB because high SWB predicts physical health and longevity (Diener & Chan, 2011).

Subjective well-being is a multi-dimensional construct with three components: positive affect, negative affect, and life satisfaction. It focuses on both the absence of negative emotions (e.g. anger) and the presence of pleasant emotions (e.g. enjoyment). Life satisfaction is the global evaluation individuals make of their personal life. Empirical studies of subjective well-being find that positive affect, negative affect, and life satisfaction contribute uniquely to subjective well-being (Diener, 2013). The components of SWB are predicted by different processes: 1) life satisfaction is predicted by fulfillment of basic needs; 2) positive affect is associated with love and social support; 3) negative affect is negatively correlated with autonomy, respect, and mastery (Tay & Diener, 2011). Thus, SWB is not a single entity, and establishing how the use of social media contributes separately to life satisfaction, positive affect, and negative affect is critical for informing interventions and public policy around social media (Verduyn et al., 2015).

Importantly, SWB is a malleable aspect of people's lives. Although genetics determine a part of SWB, life experiences can substantially change perceived quality of life (Tay et al., 2015). What contributes to SWB depends on the timeframe, which can range from one's entire life to daily experiences down to moment-to-moment fluctuations (Diener, 2009). Generalized communication patterns are likely to influence overall affect or life satisfaction, whereas specific communication instances may create variance from day to day in SWB (Dienlin et al., 2017; Reis et al., 2000). Investigations of SWB on multiple levels of analysis within social media research will provide the most robust picture of how SWB changes in connection to social media use.

Social Media and Well-Being

There is an emerging line of inquiry investigating how the use of social media impacts well-being. Defining social media is a moving target, but in general the term refers to "a set of [online] features and tools that enable peer-to-peer communication in ways not supported by mass media which use 'one-to-many' broadcast models" (Ellison & Vitak, 2015, p. 205). Thus, our approach to social media is general, including public newsfeed content as well as one-to-one instant messenger conversations, on desktop or mobile devices. Initial studies of social media use and SWB focused on the amount of time people spent using various social media tools and applications. The results are mixed, at best. Whereas a negative relationship between time spent online and SWB, that is, affect and life satisfaction, has been well-documented (Huang, 2010; Kross et al., 2013; Lin et al., 2016; Tromholt, 2016), some other studies found that time spent on social media can improve SWB (Dienlin et al., 2017; Gonzales, 2014). There is also evidence that too little and too much time spent on social media is equally bad for well-being, in support of the goldilocks effect which states that moderate use of social media is the most optimal for well-being (Przybylski & Weinstein, 2017). These mixed findings suggest the relationship between frequency of social media use and SWB calls for a more nuanced understanding of communication happening on social media as well as the structure of SWB.

Indeed, the many affordances of social media provide numerous communication opportunities for users (Treem & Leonardi, 2012) that argue against the monolithic approach to social media as a single, uniform activity (Burke et al., 2010). Three general types of communication are often discussed in social media research: directed, broadcast, and passive. Directed communication refers to one-to-one interactions between two users of a social media platform (e.g. private messaging or comments on photographs). Broadcast communication consists of messages that are shared to the entire social network with no targeted recipient, such as status updates or tweets. Passive consumption is defined as the surveillance of information shared on social media without interacting with the post or profile. Examples of passive consumption include scrolling through the Facebook newsfeed or browsing another user's photographs (Burke et al., 2010).

The distinct types of communication enabled by social media have unique effects on SWB. Directed communication between users is positively associated with measures of well-being (Frison & Eggermont, 2015; Kim & Lee, 2011). College students who were randomly assigned to post more status updates on Facebook reported higher well-being after one week than students who did not change their use of Facebook (Deters & Mehl, 2012). Yet, numerous studies have found that SWB decreases with passive consumption on Facebook (Krasnova et al., 2015; Shaw et al., 2015; Tandoc et al., 2015). However, a longitudinal study measuring passive consumption from Facebook log data found no association between passive consumption and well-being (Burke & Kraut, 2016). Together these findings suggest that active communication (i.e. directed and broadcast) is potentially more beneficial for SWB than passive consumption, although these findings need more replication on social media platforms other than Facebook.

The accumulated evidence about different, sometimes opposite, effects of social media engagement on well-being begs the question about the process and mechanisms responsible for these differences. Social capital, which refers to gains in social resources through access to weak and strong ties in a network, is often evoked as the mechanism explaining positive effects of social media (see for review, Trepte & Scharkow, 2017). In contrast, envy is viewed as a negative force behind passive use of social media that decreases SWB because passive consumption often involves engaging in social comparisons (Krasnova et al., 2015; Verduyn et al., 2015). Thus, increased access to communication and information resources in social media networks can activate both positive (e.g. social bonding) and negative (e.g. envy) processes, partly depending on the type of communication in which people engage, that is, passive browsing vs. active posting. However, it is important to note that people typically engage in both passive and active activities on social media, and future research will need to understand how these activities work together rather than in isolation from one another to impact well-being.

Equally important is whom people communicate with on social media, with one recent study showing that beneficial well-being effects of receiving Facebook communication were limited exclusively to strong ties or close relationships (Burke & Kraut, 2016). Only when people received composed and targeted communication from their strong ties did they report improvements in well-being. This comes as no surprise given the long-standing findings from relationship science about the importance of close relationships for SWB (Robles et al., 2014), but the new questions arise about how the complex business of personal relationships transpires in social media, and what role, if any, emerging technologies play in their functioning and impact on well-being. We now lay out a brief overview of research on close relationships and subjective well-being that provides guidance on how to explore some of these questions.

A Relational Perspective on Social Media and Well-Being: Two Pathways to Subjective Well-Being

Social relationships predict better SWB across most socioeconomic statuses, cultures, and personalities (Diener, 2009). Although the quantity of social relationships is slightly correlated with SWB, quality of close relationships is a much better predictor than quantity (Saphire-Bernstein & Taylor, 2013). In fact, many studies find that quality of social relationships is the strongest predictor of SWB, which holds true across the lifespan for various family relationships, such as parent–child or marriage (Diener, 2009; Diener & McGavran, 2008). As a fundamentally social species, humans have an innate need for intimate interpersonal relationships (Bowlby, 1969), and the fulfillment of this need is key to SWB. For example, a study of SWB in 155 countries found that social relationships were most closely tied to positive affect, and global evaluations of marital bonds predict life satisfaction in numerous studies (Tay & Diener, 2011; Saphire-Bernstein & Taylor, 2013).

Close relationships are clearly important to people's lives, but what is unknown is the effect of social media on the link between close relationships and well-being. Given the evidence that the importance of close relationships holds on social media (e.g. Chan, 2015), we argue that social media research must start to programmatically address social media and SWB from a close relational perspective. In the following section, we explicate two pathways through which social media, SWB, and close relationships are connected to one another. The first pathway connects social media use and SWB through the effect that social media have on the development of relational closeness and satisfaction. As such, social media use has an indirect effect on SWB in so far as it assists in improving relational closeness and satisfaction. The second pathway positions social media communication in established close relationships as directly consequential for SWB. This position takes a close relationship approach and examines communication in established relationships from the attachment theory

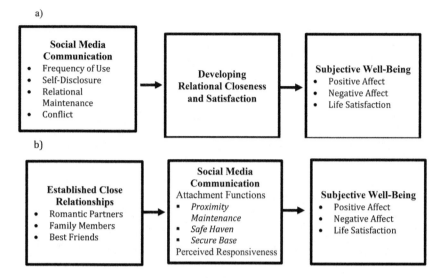

FIGURE 6.1 A relational perspective on social media and well-being: a) first pathway: indirect effect of social media on SWB through relational closeness; b) second pathway: SWB developed through communication in established close relationships.

(Bowlby, 1969) and perceived partner responsiveness (Reis, 2013) perspectives. Figure 6.1 offers an overview of both pathways.

First Pathway: Indirect Effect of Social Media on SWB through Relational Closeness

In this section, we first describe how social media can affect SWB through relational closeness, and then outline opportunities to move research forward in this area. First, social media can impact SWB through the development of close relationships. Having close, supportive relationships is essential for SWB (Diener & McGavran, 2008). Although some are skeptical of the quality of relationships developed on social media (Turkle, 2015), the overwhelming majority of research suggests that people can grow closer together through their use of social media and other communication technologies (Walther et al., 2015). Social information processing theory (SIPT) provides an account of how people can develop and maintain close bonds outside of FtF interactions (Walther, 1992). SIPT argues that people are driven to develop relationships, regardless of the medium used for communication. The development of close relationships in mediated environments requires more time than offline, and partners adapt non-verbal information into verbal expressions (Walther & Burgoon, 1992; Walther et al., 2005).

The frequency of social media use is related to whether people draw closer together. Numerous surveys of college students in dating relationships found that frequency and quality of mediated communication are positively associated with relational closeness and satisfaction (Caughlin & Sharabi, 2013; Toma & Choi, 2016). The positive association between relational closeness and social media frequency has been found across numerous types of social relationships, including romantic, friendships, and family relationships (Ledbetter et al., 2011; Ledbetter et al., 2016). Following the trend of Facebook SWB research, the effects of frequency of Facebook communication on relational closeness have been broken down into directed, broadcast, and passive consumption. Directed and passive communication on Facebook is associated with increases in relational closeness among non-family bonds (Burke & Kraut, 2014).

Because most connections on social media are known offline as well (Ellison & boyd, 2013), an important question is whether social media communication contributes to the development of relational closeness above and beyond other channels. Controlling for FtF interaction, frequency of Facebook communication was found to be positively associated with relational closeness, if people believe that the internet is an appropriate way to achieve social connection (Ledbetter et al., 2011). In fact, each additional channel of communication explains increases in friendship closeness (Baym & Ledbetter, 2009), and the more channels people use, the closer they are (Ruppel et al., 2017), consistent with the media multiplexity theory assertion about the positive association between the use of multiple communication channels and relational closeness (Haythornthwaite, 2005).

Communication processes

How does social media communication bridge to SWB through the pathway of relational closeness? To date, the internet-enhanced self-disclosure hypothesis offers the most complete answer to this question (Valkenburg & Peter, 2009a). This hypothesis argues that the direct effect of online communication on SWB is mediated by the communication process of self-disclosure. Spending time interacting with others in directed communication channels promotes intimate self-disclosure (Bazarova & Choi, 2014; Bazarova et al., 2015; Valkenburg & Peter, 2008; Taylor et al., 2017), and intimate self-disclosure, in turn, facilitates the development of quality relationships (Valkenburg & Peter, 2009b). Quality close relationships promote higher SWB (Valkenburg & Peter, 2009a). In summary, the hypothesis suggests the effect of social media use on SWB is mediated by self-disclosure and quality relationship building. Support for the internet-enhanced self-disclosure hypothesis exists for offline-established friendship relationships and college dating relationships, but not online-only contacts (Boyle & O'Sullivan, 2016; Valkenburg & Peter, 2007). Although the internet-enhanced self-disclosure hypothesis focuses on the mechanism of intimate self-disclosure, there is potential to expand this hypothesis to other communication variables, such as relational maintenance behaviors, that are important for relational intimacy, commitment, or liking to understand the role of social media in SWB.

Relational maintenance behaviors help keep relationships happy and healthy (Stafford & Canary, 1991). People who are connected on social media usually know one another, and this means that a large portion of social media communication is relational maintenance. Some researchers even argue that relationship maintenance is the primary relational function that happens on social media (Tong & Walther, 2011). There are two categories of relational maintenance: strategic and mundane communication. Both types of relational maintenance are vital to the health of a relationship. Following the model set forth by the internet-enhanced self-disclosure hypothesis, the use of social media for relational maintenance should indirectly positively impact SWB because it gives dyads opportunities to maintain relational closeness and satisfaction while physically apart from one another.

Stafford and Canary (1991) developed the relational maintenance strategies typology to explain the deliberate actions people take to preserve their relationship. Relational maintenance strategies include 1) positive, cheerful communication, 2) open conversations about the relationship, 3) assurances of love and commitment, 4) sharing tasks together, and 5) spending time with mutual friends. When couples engage in strategic relational maintenance, this tends to promote many positive relational outcomes, including relational commitment and satisfaction (see for review, Ogolsky & Bowers, 2013). Evidence suggests that relational maintenance strategies employed offline transfer over to some online environments with similar effects (Dainton & Aylor, 2002; Ramirez & Broneck, 2009). The use of social network sites for strategic relational maintenance is more common among couples who are geographically separated from one another (Billedo et al., 2015). Some research has found new types of maintenance behaviors happening on social media that are enabled by the affordances of communication technologies, such as partner surveillance and response-seeking (McEwan et al., 2014). Although some online strategies are different than offline, social media relational maintenance strategies are also positively associated with relationship closeness and satisfaction (McEwan, 2013).

Sharing mundane moments is another critical element required to keep close relationships together (Duck et al., 1991). Tong and Walther (2011) suggest that mundane interactions between close partners, such as answering the question "what is happening now?," are especially common over computer-mediated communication because the system encourages users to share mundane, routine information. Thus, we consider how mundane interactions encouraged by social media may facilitate positive SWB through relational closeness. For example, studies of Snapchat and Facebook find that people use social media to share mundane, everyday experiences with their close friends, significant others, and family members (Burke & Kraut, 2014; Xu et al., 2016). Because content shared on Snapchat is ephemeral, people tend to share more ordinary moments on that medium, compared to other social media (Bayer et al., 2016). Consistent with strategic relational maintenance, routine communication on social media is more frequent for long-distance romantic couples than geographically proximal couples (Billedo et al., 2015). Sosik and Bazarova (2014) used a custom-built application that downloaded Facebook communication between Facebook friends to determine what types of Facebook communication predicted relationship escalation. Temporal patterns of Facebook interactions, such as frequency of Facebook contact and more recent Facebook interactions, and the number of ways people contacted each other via Facebook, escalated relational closeness. The content of communication on Facebook was not associated, however, with relational escalation in that study. This result suggests that staying in touch via frequent check-ins and partaking in one another's lives may be more important symbolic gestures in Facebook relational maintenance than the types of content people share.

Although many of these communication behaviors can drive relationships closer together, Valkenburg and Peter (2009a) argue that the logic of the internet-enhanced self-disclosure hypothesis can be extended to explain negative consequences as well. Therefore, research that establishes a negative relationship between communication on social media and relational quality fits into this framework for understanding effects of SWB. One such mechanism is conflict. Conflict generated from the use of social network sites can lead to negative relational outcomes for romantic partners (Clayton, 2014; Clayton et al., 2013; McDaniel & Coyne, 2016; Ridgway & Clayton, 2016). Although many relational maintenance behaviors are positive, certain behaviors on Facebook, such as photo impression management, oversharing, and relationship broadcasting, are negatively correlated with relational closeness (Brody et al., 2016; McEwan, 2013). Thus, thinking about the indirect effect of close relationships provides for the possibilities of harmful well-being outcomes. If communication that happens over social media reduces the connection between friends, romantic partners, or family members, this will negatively impact SWB.

Gaps in Indirect Effect Research

The challenges of understanding the social media-SWB pathway via relational development are compounded by an almost daily changing landscape of social media that gives users new ways to build and maintain relationships. Furthermore, there is a theoretical vacuum with the internet-enhanced self-disclosure hypothesis being the only comprehensive model of how close relationships fit into the picture of social media and SWB research (Valkenburg & Peter, 2009b). The lack of studies explicating mechanisms through which social media communication affects both relationships and well-being leaves many questions about contributions of relationships developed through social media to affective or cognitive well-being. Below we suggest potential opportunities for developing scholarship in this area.

First of all, only recently have studies begun separating quantity and quality of mediated communication in close relationships (e.g. Gonzales, 2014; Toma & Choi, 2016). Second, directed, broadcast, and passive communication conceptualized as channels with distinct effects on SWB (Burke et al., 2010) are general categories defined by target directedness and passive/active engagement without specific information about the communication happening in each of them. For example, only receiving, but not sending, messages in Facebook-targeted channels was associated with better SWB (Burke & Kraut, 2016), suggesting that types of communication happening on those channels are also important. Furthermore, people tend to communicate in both passive and active, broadcasting and receiver-targeted (directed) ways on the same platform. For example, a typical Facebook user spends time passively browsing through the newsfeed, occasionally broadcasting status updates and photos, and commenting on friends' news publicly or messaging them privately. How do these activities add up to influence SWB, and how can we measure quality and not only quantity of communication on social media? There are promising developments with recent measures of types of behaviors adapted to social media, such as the Facebook relational maintenance measure (McEwan et al., 2014) and the measure of relational behaviors on SNS (Brody et al., 2016). Understanding communication and relational behavior types, not only their amount or quantity, may help to resolve the perplexing mixed findings of social media and SWB discussed above.

In terms of theoretical developments on social media, the two ways forward for understanding social media communication and SWB through relational closeness are 1) technological affordances and 2) media multiplexity. An affordances approach acknowledges both the materiality of the technology and the agency of the user (Evans et al., 2017). Rather than technology causing certain behaviors, affordances encourage several types of communication based on their design (Bazarova, 2012). Treem and Leonardi (2012) suggested that the affordances of persistence, visibility, editability, and association in social media have changed the functioning of organizations. Several studies have adopted Treem and Leonardi's framework for understanding relational communication (e.g. Bayer et al., 2016; Bazarova & Choi, 2014), but it is uncertain if these same affordances matter in the context of close relationships. One indication for their relevance is that they have an effect on relational communication and relational effects, such as intimacy of communication (Bazarova et al., 2015). Investigations of specific affordances will help to provide a clearer picture of what is new in relationships developed in social media and what is an extension of the same relational dynamics as FtF.

The other approach is based on media multiplexity theory (Haythornthwaite, 2005), which underscores the importance of how close partners use many media to communicate with one another (see for recent review, Taylor & Ledbetter, 2017). Rather than doing inter-media comparisons based on the affordance approach, media multiplexity studies contextualize social media within the many other media used in a relationship. Since people use many different channels to interact, studying one medium in isolation or even in comparison with other media cannot yield a full picture of the effects of social media communication on SWB. The consistent finding in the media multiplexity research is that relational closeness predicts both the number of media used for communication (Haythornthwaite, 2005) and the frequency of social media use (Ledbetter et al., 2011). However, there is little advancement of knowledge about the connections between media since Haythornthwaite's original conceptualization (Baym, 2009; Walther et al., 2015). Toward addressing this theoretical dearth, Caughlin and Sharabi (2013) developed the communicative interdependence perspective on communication technologies. According to this approach, the ability to integrate communication across FtF and technologically mediated communication is positively associated with relational closeness; nevertheless, segmenting some conversations to only FtF is positive for relational closeness. The conversational interdependence across media channels and the media multiplexity link to relational closeness show the promise of the holistic approach to studying complicated interconnections of media, their integration in people's lives, and a joint shaping of multimedia use and relationship dynamics in order to advance knowledge on social media and SWB.

Second Pathway: SWB Developed through Communication in Established Close Relationships

The second pathway to SWB lies through communication within established close relationships. Rather than how social media communication can strengthen relational closeness, we here examine how already existing close relationships (e.g. romantic partners, family members, or best friends) use social media to stay connected, and how their communication on social media directly impacts SWB. Since the early days of the internet, online connections with existing close relationships have been recognized as having beneficial effects on SWB. Whereas online interactions with strangers can be problematic for SWB, staying in touch with close relations is helpful, whether it is through email (Kraut et al., 1998; Kraut et al., 2002), Facebook (Burke & Kraut, 2016), or mobile phone (Chan, 2015). Even when social media use does not promote relational growth—for example, with family members (Burke & Kraut, 2014)—social media use within personal relationships can influence SWB for reasons outside of growing closer together. This is well-known in offline research, with numerous studies linking communication with close relational partners to affective, cognitive, and physical health (Feeney & Collins, 2015; Reis & Collins, 2004; Thoits, 2011). Among the theoretical perspectives explaining the functions of close relationships in promoting well-being are attachment theory (Hazan & Shaver, 1987; Pietromonaco et al., 2013) and perceived partner responsiveness (Reis, 2013). We believe attachment and responsiveness can elucidate mechanisms and processes through which social media communication can impact SWB, and below we explore each theory and its application to social media.

Attachment Theory

Originally developed by Bowlby (1969), attachment theory explains parent–infant bonding, but the processes of attachment are expected to last for a person's entire life (Hazan & Shaver, 1987). In adult relationships, romantic partners are often considered an attachment figure, but various other types of relationships may develop into an attachment bond (Mikulincer & Shaver, 2013). A full literature review of attachment theory is beyond the scope of this chapter (see Mikulincer & Shaver, 2016), but we draw upon Bowlby's constructs and recent empirical evidence to understand why social media communication can aid or hinder attachment strategies that promote SWB.

According to this theory, humans have an inborn, biological attachment behavior system that regulates their propinquity to attachment figures to keep them safe from threats (Bowlby, 1969). *Proximity maintenance* is the primary attachment strategy encouraged by the system to keep people safe. Seeking proximity to an attachment figure is a useful strategy for finding support or care, regardless of age (Mikulincer & Shaver, 2003). The system is activated during threatening experiences, such as stress, physical pain, or illness. Thus, people maintain proximity to attachment figures because having an attachment figure offers security in times of stress, often referred to as a *safe haven*, and, thus, is a key element to their affective well-being (Collins & Feeney, 2000; Pietromonaco & Powers, 2015). During times with no immediate threat, attachment bonds also operate as a *secure base* for individuals that promotes exploration and growth. People can explore the world around them because they know they can fall back to their attachment figure, if necessary (Feeney, 2004; Feeney & Thrush, 2010).

Although Bowlby (1969) predicts that all humans are equipped with the attachment system, there are systematic differences in how people cope with stressors and seek proximity to their attachment figure. Ainsworth and colleagues first discovered individual differences among infants (Ainsworth et al., 1978), and these differences in *attachment style* have extended into adulthood (Hazan & Shaver, 1987). Attachment styles are the expectations, emotions, and behavior a person anticipates from interactions with attachment figures, and these mental representations of attachment figures are grounded in previous interactions (Mikulincer & Shaver, 2013). Attachment styles are conceptualized along two orthogonal dimensions: anxiety and avoidance (Mikulincer & Shaver, 2016). Anxious attachment refers to the extent to which a person worries about the availability of an attachment figure during times of distress, and is influenced by their own feelings of worthiness. Avoidant attachment is the degree to which someone distrusts relationships for providing support and seeks to establish independence from attachment figures.

Attachment theory has been applied to several studies of social media. Anxious attachment is predictive of frequent texting to romantic partners and the use of social network sites to develop intimacy (Gentzler et al., 2011; Morey et al., 2013; Oldmeadow et al., 2013; Weisskirch, 2012). Avoidance is negatively related to frequency of texting and voice telephone calls (Jin & Peña, 2010). Securely attached individuals appear to use texting and voice telephone calls often (Drouin & Ladgraff, 2012; Morey et al., 2013). There are several studies on the dark side of communication technology that find that attachment anxiety is associated with more intimate partner surveillance, sexting, Facebook jealousy, and use of communication technology to break up (Drouin & Tobin, 2014; Fox & Tokunaga, 2015; Fox & Warber, 2014; McDaniel & Drouin, 2015; Weisskirch & Delevi, 2012). Whereas avoidance is associated with less Facebook surveillance and jealousy post break-up, but positively associated with sexting (Drouin & Ladgraff, 2012; Marshall et al., 2013; McDaniel & Drouin, 2015).

Attachment and social media research tends to focus on the individual differences in attachment style but not the normative processes of attachment. To our knowledge, no research has addressed how the attachment behavioral system works online. A focus on attachment styles follows the trends of attachment research (Hazan & Selcuk, 2015), but the normative processes of attachment are likely to explain the process that links social media communication in close relationships to SWB with attachment styles moderating those associations (e.g. Selcuk et al., 2012). Furthermore, many communication studies do not establish the connection between attachment processes and SWB, rather focusing on the outcome of relational satisfaction or intimacy (Guerrero, 2015). Understanding how communication technologies aid or hinder attachment strategies of proximity maintenance, safe haven, and secure base can help to understand why social media researchers consistently find that interactions online with close, intimate bonds relate to higher SWB. Knowing how the system operates to regulate affect can provide an organizing frame to understand why some interactions on social media are more impactful on SWB than others.

There are many ways in which researchers can draw from attachment theory to understand why social media within close relationships influence SWB. For instance, proximity maintenance through social media is an open door for scholars to test attachment theory. Tong and Walther (2011) theorized that one of the main relational maintenance functions of mediated communication was establishing a sense of presence when physical presence is not available. The development of social media technologies, especially smartphones, provides pseudo-proximity by creating an ability to contact an attachment figure at nearly any moment of the day. Research has established that physical presence is not necessary to receive the felt security associated with attachment figures. Experiments find that imagining the face of an attachment figure or viewing a photograph of them can aid in coping with stress or pain (Master et al., 2009; Selcuk et al., 2012). Thus, maintaining attachment figure availability and proximity during times of physical separation may explain why sharing mundane moments with close relational partners online can foster positive SWB (e.g. Bayer et al., 2016).

The safe haven function of attachment on social media may also be useful to explain why communicating with weak ties online does not necessary translate into positive SWB (Burke & Kraut, 2016; Chan, 2015; Kim & Lee, 2011). Perceived support from social relationships is conceptualized as a primary mechanism explaining the positive effects of social media on SWB (Verduyn et al., 2015). Perceived support is the generalization people make about their available social resources to cope with a life stressor (Thoits, 2011). Many studies of social support on social media focus on the large quantities of potential support available through networked social ties, given that social media provide unprecedented amounts of social capital (Lu & Hampton, 2017). One limitation attachment theory suggests is that a handful of social media connections influence feelings of SWB more than others. Support from close partners is more consequential to health outcomes than that of non-close partners because of the qualitatively unique bond shared in close relationships (Feeney & Collins, 2015). Attachment bonds should not correlate with the number of ties on social media (Hazan & Zeifman, 1999). The number of Facebook friends, comments on a post, likes on an Instagram picture, and so on likely provide less perceived support than contact with an attachment figure. Despite the large number of potential social resources available, there is evidence that the individuals who are most likely to respond to distressing posts on social media are close relational partners (Brody & Vangelisti, 2016; Chang et al., in press). An attachment perspective on support may suggest that scholars focus less on the amount of support and more on who is providing support.

To summarize, this section offers only a brief introduction to attachment theory and the associated research, but the opportunities for social media research within this framework are plentiful. Importantly, attachment theory provides a basis for researchers to deduce hypotheses about how the use of social media in close relationships can influence SWB. In the following discussion, we highlight implications for a related construct that has emerged from attachment and relationship intimacy research: perceived partner responsiveness. Perceived partner responsiveness (PPR) has been conceptualized as the central theme that explains why social relationships influence SWB (Reis, 2013). Thus, PPR may have much to add to the conversation on how close relationships on social media predict SWB.

Perceived Partner Responsiveness

PPR is defined as "a process by which individuals come to believe that relationship partners both attend to and react supportively to central, core defining features of the self" (Reis et al., 2004, p. 203). PPR is achieved when a partner feels 1) understood, 2) validated, and 3) cared for by the other partner. Numerous studies have associated PPR to relational outcomes, such as intimacy, commitment, and satisfaction (see for review, Reis & Clark, 2013). Daily fluctuations in relatedness needs are fulfilled by feeling understood and appreciated during social interactions (Reis et al., 2000). Partner's responsiveness predicts short-term affect improvements after seeking support from a partner (Collins & Feeney, 2000). PPR is negatively associated with anxiety and depression symptoms (Selcuk et al., 2017). In heterosexual married dyads facing a long-term health problem, the association between emotional support and depressive symptoms is mediated by PPR (Fekete et al., 2007). A longitudinal study of marital dyads found a negative association between PPR and physiological signals of stress (i.e. salivary cortisol levels), across a ten-year time span (Slatcher et al., 2015). Reis (2013) also reasoned the PPR was related to SWB because people engage in less self-handicapping during stressful tasks when PPR is high.

Although PPR is often studied in the context of stressful situations, PPR facilitates the capitalization of positive life events as well. Capitalization happens when a person shares positive experience with others, and this sharing increases their benefit of the experience (Gable et al., 2006). PPR generates capitalization through enthusiastic responses to a partners' good news. In a series of experiments, Reis and colleagues (2010) demonstrated high PPR improved participants' evaluation of positive events. High PPR from a spouse predicted more personal goal achievement and problem solving (Feeney & Thrush, 2010). Feeney and Collins (2015) posit that PPR in the absence of stress or adversity helps individuals take advantage of life opportunities and obtain personal goals. Capitalization research suggests that having responsive partners can increase positive affect as well as evaluation of life quality.

Despite the predictive power of PPR on SWB, PPR is a relatively unexplored construct for social media. One exception is a daily diary study among geographically close and long-distant romantic couples conducted by Jiang and Hancock (2013). Long-distance couples reported greater PPR than geographically close couples, and this difference was explained by the increased intimacy of self-disclosure that happened during mediated interactions in long-distance relationships compared to geographically close couples. Another study of responsiveness found that the number of words used in comments on Facebook status updates was the strongest predictor of PPR (Freeman & Brinkley, 2014). PPR can be operationalized as the degree to which messages acknowledge, legitimize, and contextualize the support seeker's perspective, this type of communication is referred to as person-centered messaging (Burleson, 2003; Reis & Clark, 2013). An experiment comparing person-centered messages in FtF versus instant messaging revealed that high person-centered messages from men were considered more sensitive when offered via instant messaging than FtF, but low person-centered messages from women were rated more negatively in instant messenger than FtF (High & Solomon, 2014). In terms of capitalization, messages shared publicly on social media are usually more positively valenced than in private channels, and people derive capitalization from sharing positive emotions in social media (Bazarova et al., 2015). Because of the skew toward positive emotions shared on public social media, responsiveness in public social interactions on Facebook is likely to follow capitalization rather than elevating stress or negative emotions.

Applications of PPR on social media are still in the initial stages of development, and there are many opportunities for scholars to advance PPR. Investigations into PPR on social media may start by asking fundamental questions about PPR on social media, such as the role of relationship type and media affordances. Expected levels of PPR depend upon the type of relationship partners share (Reis et al., 2004). Strangers have the lowest expectations of PPR, and family members, romantic partners, and children have high levels of expected PPR. However, those expectations are also likely to depend upon affordances of the medium. Expectations of responsiveness to undirected posts (e.g. status updates) are likely to be lower than in directed messages (e.g. private chat) because the message is targeted at one specific person in directed interactions rather than an imagined audience (Bazarova & Choi, 2014). Another area of potential research is how affordances alter the perceptions of responsiveness. Reis and Clark (2013) argued that perceived responsiveness is more important for SWB than enacted responsiveness, but the two are correlated with one another. The limited cues available in mediated channels lead people to make more extreme judgments of their partner's behaviors (Walther, 1996), and so it is possible that a communication channel may moderate the association between enacted responsiveness and perceived responsiveness.

To conclude this section on the second pathway, understanding how social media interactions influence SWB in the context of close relationships is a promising area for future research. Here we covered attachment and PPR as two possible mechanisms that can account for the consistent findings about strong tie interactions promoting SWB that have emerged from a decade of research on the internet (Kraut et al., 2002; Burke & Kraut, 2016). Insights from relationship science can inform how researchers of social media should think about the social interactions that happen on various communication platforms. On the other hand, we believe that social media research can reveal new understanding on the nature and function of close relationships in regulating SWB.

Moving Forward: Interdependence of Personal Relationships

In the previous sections, we have discussed the effects of social media use on SWB from a psychological perspective, but this perspective only considers the experience of a single person in the relationship and does not capture the complexity of close relationships. A defining characteristic of personal relationships is interdependence between partners (Finkel et al., 2017). Interdependence in relationships argues that a person's outcome (e.g. SWB) is dependent upon the behavior of his/her partner (e.g. frequency of Instagram posting). Scholars are yet to conceptualize a relational perspective on the impact of social media on SWB as an interdependent process, although both attachment theory and perceived responsiveness account for interdependence (Reis & Clark, 2013). For example, attachment theory predicts that the attachment behavioral system is complemented by a caregiving system built into attachment figures (Collins & Feeney, 2000). Advances in statistical techniques have assisted in the rapid growth of studies looking at interdependence in personal relationships (e.g. Knobloch & Theiss, 2010), especially the Actor–Partner Interdependence Model (Kenny et al., 2006). Social media research lacks theory about interdependence between users, but the adoption of interdependence effects in social media is starting to emerge (Scissors et al., 2014). McEwan (2013) found that relationship satisfaction is predicted by a partner's displays of caring on Facebook, but partner's Facebook surveillance was not associated with relational satisfaction. Ledbetter (2014) investigated interdependence in media choice behavior based on the media attitudes of romantic partners. Another study discovered that problematic internet use among teens positively correlates with negative conflict communication behaviors in their parents (Ko et al., 2015).

The potential for interdependence influencing SWB in the area of personal relationships and technology is great for both of the relational pathways to SWB we have identified in this chapter. Numerous studies have established the one partner's SWB is dependent upon the behavior of his/her partner in FtF contexts. For instance, in college dating couples, self-reports of relational uncertainty predicted the experience of negative emotions in the other partner (Knobloch & Theiss, 2010). The SWB of married women is predicted by the physical health of their husband (Carr et al., 2014). SWB's cultivation through close relationships is a dyadic, interdependent process. An important research agenda moving forward on the area of close relationships and social media is to think about how the needs, goals, behaviors, and so on of one partner depend upon his or her partner.

Conclusion

This chapter advocates for a close relational perspective on understanding the effects of social media on SWB as an answer that may unify several of the contradictory findings on the subject. We conceptualized two ways of explaining why interactions with close others on social media can influence people's happiness. First, communication that happens in social media can have an indirect effect on SWB through changes in perceptions of relational closeness and satisfaction (Tay & Diener, 2011; Valkenburg & Peter, 2009a). Second, we argue that social media can impact how close relationships regulate SWB (Feeney & Collins, 2015). Attachment and perceived partner responsiveness were advanced as processes within close relationships that may be altered in social media communication.

When people engage in networked social life across the many communication technologies of today, investigating the role of close relationships in overall well-being can shed light on how people find happiness and overall health through social media.

As concern over effects of social media on well-being grows, it is important that scholars focus on theoretically grounded research that can persist beyond the latest social media trends. This type of research will provide a toolkit for understanding the networked self of today and in the future. Established research on SWB serves as an anchor to understand why communication technologies, such as social media, can influence affective and cognitive well-being (Diener, 2009). Hazan and Shaver (1994) suggested that one of the fundamental questions of studying social relationships and romantic love is articulating the function of these relationships in personal well-being, and we believe that social media research will provide innovative insights into these functions, once thought to be an offline-only phenomenon. Social media influence people's well-being because of the close relationships that inhabit them.

References

Ainsworth, M. D. S., Blehar, M. C., Waters, E., & Wall, S. N. (1978). *Patterns of attachment: A psychological study of the strange situation*. New York: Psychology Press.

Bayer, J. B., Ellison, N. B., Schoenebeck, S. Y., & Falk, E. B. (2016). Sharing the small moments: Ephemeral social interaction on Snapchat. *Information, Communication & Society*, 19, 956–977. doi: 10.1080/1369118X.2015.1084349

Baym, N. K. (2009). A call for grounding in the face of blurred boundaries. *Journal of Computer-Mediated Communication*, 14, 720–723. doi: 10.1111/j.1083-6101.2009.01461.x

Baym, N. K., & Ledbetter, A. (2009). Tunes that bind? Predicting friendship strength in a music-based social network. *Information, Communication & Society*, 12, 408–427. doi: 10.1080/13691180802635430

Bazarova, N. N. (2012). Public intimacy: Disclosure interpretation and social judgments on Facebook. *Journal of Communication*, 62, 815–832. doi: 10.1111/j.1460-2466.2012.01664.x

Bazarova, N. N., & Choi, Y. H. (2014). Self-disclosure in social media: Extending the functional approach to disclosure motivations and characteristics on social network sites. *Journal of Communication*, 64, 635–657. doi 10.1111/jcom.12106

Bazarova, N. N., Choi, Y. H., Sosik, V. S., Cosley, D., & Whitlock, J. L. (2015). Social sharing of emotions on Facebook: Channel differences, satisfaction, and replies. *Proceedings of the 18th ACM Conference on Computer-Supported Cooperative Work and Social Computing* (pp. 154–164). Vancouver, Canada.

Billedo, C. J., Kerkhof, P., & Finkenauer, C. (2015). The use of social networking sites for relationship maintenance in long-distance and geographically close romantic relationships. *Cyberpsychology, Behavior, and Social Networking*, 18, 152–157. doi: 10.1089/cyber.2014.0469

Bowlby, J. (1969). *Attachment and loss. Vol. 1: Attachment*. New York: Basic Books.

Boyle, A. M., & O'Sullivan, L. F. (2016). Staying connected: Computer-mediated and face-to-face communication in college students' dating relationships. *Cyberpsychology, Behavior, and Social Networking*, 19, 299–307. doi: 0.1089/cyber.2015.0293

Brody, N., & Vangelisti, A. L. (2016). Bystander intervention in cyberbullying. *Communication Monographs*, 83, 94–119. doi: 10.1080/03637751.2015.1044256

Brody, N., LeFebvre, L. E., & Blackburn, K. G. (2016). Social networking site behaviors across the relational lifespan: Measurement and association with relationship escalation and de-escalation. *Social Media + Society*, 2, 1–16. doi: 1177/2056305116680004.

Burke, M., & Kraut, R. E. (2014). Growing closer on Facebook: Changes in tie strength through social network site use. *Proceedings of the 32nd annual ACM conference on Human factors in computing systems* (pp. 4187–4196). Toronto, ON.

Burke, M., & Kraut, R. E. (2016). The relationship between Facebook use and well-being depends on communication type and tie strength. *Journal of Computer-Mediated Communication*, 21, 265–281. doi: 10.1111/jcc4.12162

Burke, M., Marlow, C., & Lento, T. (2010). Social network activity and social well-being. *Proceedings of the SIGCHI conference on human factors in computing systems* (pp. 1909–1912). Atlanta, GA.

Burleson, B. (2003). The experience and effects of emotional support: What the study of cultural and gender differences can tell us about close relationships, emotion, and interpersonal communication. *Personal Relationships*, 10, 1–23. doi: 10.1111/1475-6811.00033

Carr, D., Freedman, V. A., Cornman, J. C., & Schwarz, N. (2014). Happy marriage, happy life? Marital quality and subjective well-being in later life. *Journal of Marriage and Family*, 76, 930–948. doi: 10.1111/jomf.12133

Caughlin, J. P., & Sharabi, L. L. (2013). A communicative interdependence perspective of close relationships: The connections between mediated and unmediated interactions matter. *Journal of Communication*, 63, 873–893. doi: 10.1111/jcom.12046

Chan, M. (2015). Multimodal connectedness and quality of life: Examining the influences of technology adoption and interpersonal communication on well-being across the life-span. *Journal of Computer-Mediated Communication*, 20, 3–18. doi: 10.1111/jcc4.12089

Chang, P. F., Bazarova, N. N., & Whitlock, J. (in press). "To respond or not to respond, that is the question": Examining the decision-making process of providing social support to distressed posters. *Society Media + Society*.

Clayton, R. B. (2014). The third wheel: The impact of Twitter use on relationship infidelity and divorce. *Cyberpsychology, Behavior, and Social Networking*, 17, 425–430. doi: 10.1089/cyber.2013.0570

Clayton, R. B., Nagurney, A., & Smith, J. R. (2013). Cheating, breakup, and divorce: Is Facebook use to blame? *Cyberpsychology, Behavior, and Social Networking*, 16, 717–720. doi: 10.1089/cyber.2012.0424

Collins, N. L., & Feeney, B. C. (2000). A safe haven: An attachment theory perspective on support seeking and caregiving in intimate relationships. *Journal of Personality and Social Psychology*, 78, 1053–1073. doi: 10.1037/0022-3514.78.6.1053

Dainton, M., & Aylor, B. (2002). Patterns of communication channel use in the maintenance of long-distance relationships. *Communication Research Reports*, 19, 118–129. doi: 10.1080/08824090209384839

Deters, F., & Mehl, M. R. (2012). Does posting Facebook status updates increase or decrease loneliness? An online social networking experiment. *Social Psychological and Personality Science*, 4, 579–586. doi: 10.1177/1948550612469233

Diener, E. (1984). Subjective well-being. *Psychological Bulletin*, 95, 542–575.

Diener, E. (2009). Subjective well-being. In E. Diener (Ed.), *The science of well-being: The collected works of Ed Diener* (pp. 11–58). New York: Springer.

Diener, E. (2013). The remarkable changes in the science of subjective well-being. *Perspectives in Psychological Science*, 8, 663–66. doi: 10.1177/1745691613507583

Diener, E., & Chan, M. Y. (2011). Happy people live longer: Subjective well-being contributes to health and longevity. *Applied Psychology: Health and Well-Being*, 3, 1–43. doi: 10.1111/j.1758-0854.2010.01045.x

Diener, M. L., & McGavran, M. B. (2008). What makes people happy? A developmental approach to the literature on family relationships and well-being. In M. Eid & R. J. Larsen (Eds.), *The science of subjective well-being* (pp. 347–375). New York: Guilford Press.

Dienlin, T., Masur, P. K., & Trepte, S. (2017). Reinforcement or displacement? The reciprocity of FtF, IM, and SNS communication and their effects on loneliness and life satisfaction. *Journal of Computer-Mediated Communication*, 22, 71–87. doi: 10.1111/jcc4.12183

Drouin, M., & Ladgraff, C. (2012). Texting, sexting, and attachment in college students' romantic relationships. *Computers in Human Behavior*, 28, 444–449. doi: 10.1016/j.chb.2011.10.015

Drouin, M., & Tobin, E. (2014). Unwanted and consensual sexting among young adults: Relations with attachment and sexual motivations. *Computers in Human Behavior*, 31, 412–418. doi: 10.1016/j.chb.2013.11.001

Duck, S., Rutt, D. J., Hoy, M., & Strejc, H. H. (1991). Some evident truths about conversations in everyday relationships: All communications are not created equal. *Human Communication Research*, 18, 228–267. doi: 10.1111/j.1468-2958.1991.tb00545.x

Ellison, N. B., & boyd, d. (2013). Sociality through social network sites. In W. H. Dutton (Ed.), *The Oxford handbook of internet studies* (pp. 151–172). Oxford: Oxford University Press.

Ellison, N. B., & Vitak, J. (2015). Social network site affordances and their relationship to social capital processes. In S. Sundar (Ed.), *The handbook of the psychology of communication technology* (pp. 205–228). Chichester: Wiley Blackwell.

Evans, S. K., Pearce, K. E., Vitak, J., & Treem, J. W. (2017). Explicating affordances: A conceptual framework for understanding affordances in communication research. *Journal of Computer-Mediated Communication*, 22, 35–52. doi: 10.1111/jcc4.12180

Feeney, B. C. (2004). A secure base: Responsive support of goal strivings and exploration in adult intimate relationships. *Journal of Personality and Social Psychology*, 87, 631–648. doi: 10.1037/0022-3514.87.5.631

Feeney, B. C., & Collins, N. L. (2015). A new look at social support: A theoretical perspective on thriving through relationships. *Personality and Social Psychology Review*, 19, 113–147. doi: 10.1177/1088868314544222

Feeney, B. C., & Thrush, R. L. (2010). Relationship influences on exploration in adulthood: The characteristics and function of a secure base. *Journal of Personality and Social Psychology*, 98, 57–76. doi: 10.1037/a0016961

Fekete, E. M., Stephens, M. A. P., Mickelson, K. D., & Druley, J. A. (2007). Couples' support provision during illness: The role of perceived emotional responsiveness. *Families, Systems, & Health*, 25, 204–217. doi: 10.1037/1091-7527.25.2.204

Finkel, E. J., Simpson, J. A., & Eastwick, P. W. (2017). The psychology of close relationships: Fourteen core principles. *Annual Review of Psychology*, 68, 383–411. doi: 10.1146/annurev-psych-010416-044038

Fox, J., & Tokunaga, R. S. (2015). Romantic partner monitoring after breakups: Attachment, dependence, distress, and post-dissolution online surveillance via social networking sites. *Cyberpsychology, Behavior, and Social Networking*, 18, 491–498. doi: 10.1089/cyber.2015.0123

Fox, J., & Warber, K. M. (2014). Social networking sites in romantic relationships: Attachment, uncertainty, and partner surveillance on Facebook. *Cyberpsychology, Behavior, and Social Networking*, 17, 3–7. doi: 10.1089/cyber.2012.0667

Freeman, L. K., & Brinkley, J. (2014). Length matters: Message metrics that result in higher levels of perceived partner responsiveness and changes in intimacy as friends communicate through social network sites. *The Journal of Social Media in Society*, 3, 64–86.

Frison, E., & Eggermont, S. (2015). Toward an integrated and differential approach to the relationships between loneliness, different types of Facebook use, and adolescents' depressed mood. *Communication Research*, 6, 1–28. doi: 10.1177/0093650215617506

Gable, S. L., Gonzaga, G. C., & Strachman, A. (2006). Will you be there for me when things go right? Supportive responses to positive event disclosures. *Journal of Personality and Social Psychology*, 91, 904–917. doi: 10.1037/0022-3514.91.5.904

Gentzler, A. L., Oberhauser, A. M., Westerman, D., & Nadroff, D. K. (2011). College students' use of electronic communication with parents: Links to loneliness, attachment and relationship quality. *Cyberpsychology, Behavior, and Social Networking*, 14, 71–74. doi: 10.1089/cyber.2009.0409

Gonzales, A. L. (2014). Text-based communication influences self-esteem more than face-to-face or cellphone communication. *Computers in Human Behavior*, 39, 197–203. doi: 10.1016/j.chb.2014.07.026

Guerrero, L. K. (2015). Attachment theory. In L. A. Baxter & D. O. Braithwaite (Eds.), *Engaging theories in interpersonal communication: Multiple perspectives* (pp. 295–208). Los Angeles, CA: Sage.

Haythornthwaite, C. (2005). Social networks and Internet connectivity effects. *Information, Community & Society*, 8, 125–147. doi: 10.1080/13691180500146185

Hazan, C., & Campa, M. I. (Eds.). (2013). *Human bonding: The science of affectional ties*. New York: Guilford Press.

Hazan, C., & Selcuk, E. (2015). Normative processes in romantic attachment: Introduction and overview. In V. Zayas & C. Hazan (Eds.), *Bases of adult attachment: Linking brain, mind, and behavior* (pp. 3–8). New York: Springer.

Hazan, C., & Shaver, P. (1987). Romantic love conceptualized as an attachment process. *Journal of Personality and Social Psychology*, 52, 511–524. doi: 10.1037/0022-3514.52.3.511

Hazan, C., & Shaver, P. (1994). Attachment as an organizational framework for research on close relationships. *Psychological Inquiry*, 5, 1–22. doi: 10.1207/s15327965pli0501_1

Hazan, C., & Zeifman, D. (1999). Pair bonds as attachments. In J. Cassidy & P. R. Shaver (Eds.), *Handbook of attachment: Theory, research, and clinical applications* (pp. 336–354). New York: Guilford Press.

High, A. C., & Solomon, D. H. (2014). Communication channel, sex, and the immediate and longitudinal outcomes of verbal person-centered support. *Communication Monographs*, 81, 439–468. doi: 10.1080/03637751.2014.933245

Holt-Lunstad, J., Smith, T. B., Baker, M., Harris, T., & Stephenson, D. (2015). Loneliness and social isolation as risk factors for mortality: A meta-analytic review. *Perspectives on Psychological Science*, 10, 227–237. doi: 10.1177/1745691614568352

Huang, C. (2010). Internet use and psychological well-being: A meta-analysis. *Cyberpsychology, Behavior, and Social Networking*, 13, 241–249. doi: 10.1089/cyber.2009.0217

Jiang, L. C., & Hancock, J. T. (2013). Absence makes the communication grow fonder: Geographic separation, interpersonal media, and intimacy in dating relationships. *Journal of Communication*, 63, 556–577. doi: 10.1111/jcom.12029

Jin, B., & Peña, J. F. (2010). Mobile communication in romantic relationships: Mobile phone use, relational uncertainty, love, commitment, and attachment styles. *Communication Reports*, 23, 39–51. doi: 10.1080/08934211003598742

Jelenchick, L. A., Eickhoff, J. C., & Moreno, M. A. (2013). "Facebook depression?" Social networking site use and depression in older adolescents. *Journal of Adolescent Health*, 52, 128–130. doi: 10.1016/j.jadohealth.2012.05.008

Joinson, A. N. (2008). Looking at, looking up or keeping up with people? Motives and use of Facebook. *Proceedings of the SIGCHI conference on Human Factors in Computing Systems* (pp. 1027–1036). Florence, Italy.

Kenny, D. A., Kashy, D. A., & Cook, W. L. (2006). *The analysis of dyadic data*. New York: Guilford Press.

Kim, J., & Lee. J. R. (2011). The Facebook paths to happiness: Effects of the number of Facebook friends on self-presentation and subjective well-being. *Cyberpsychology, Behavior, and Social Networking*, 14, 359–364. doi: 10.1089/cyber.2010.0374

Knobloch, L. K., & Theiss, J. A. (2010). An actor–partner interdependence model of relational turbulence: Cognitions and emotions. *Journal of Social and Personal Relationships*, 27, 595–619. doi: 10.1177/0265407510368967

Ko, C. H., Wang, P. W., Liu, T. L., Yen, C. F., Chen, C. S., & Yen, J. Y. (2015). Bi-directional associations between family factors and internet addiction among adolescents in a prospective investigation. *Psychiatry and Clinical Neurosciences*, 69, 192–200. doi: 10.1111/pcn.12204

Krasnova, H., Widjaja, T., Buxmann, P., Wenninger, H., & Benbasat, I. (2015). Why following friends can hurt you: An exploratory investigation of the effects of envy on social networking sites among college-age users. *Information Systems Research*, 26, 585–605. doi: 0.1287/isre.2015.0588

Kraut, R., Patterson, M., Lundmark, V., Kiesler, S., Mukophadhyay, T., & Scherlis, W. (1998). Internet paradox: A social technology that reduces social involvement and psychological well-being? *American Psychologist*, 53, 1017–1031. doi: 10.1037/0003-066X.53.9.1017

Kraut, R., Kiesler, S., Boneva, B., Cummings, J., Helgeson, V., & Crawford, A. (2002). Internet paradox revisited. *Journal of Social Issues*, 58, 49–74. doi: 10.1111/1540-4560.00248

Kross, E., Verduyn, P., Demiralp, E., Park, J., Lee, D. S., Lin, N., ... Ybarra, O. (2013). Facebook use predicts declines in subjective well-being in young adults. *PloS one*, 8, e69841. doi: 10.1371/journal.pone.0069841

Ledbetter, A. M. (2014). Online communication attitude similarity in romantic dyads: Predicting couples' frequency of e-mail, instant messaging, and social networking site communication. *Communication Quarterly*, 62, 233–252. doi: 10.1080/01463373.2014.890120

Ledbetter, A. M., Mazer, J. P., DeGroot, J. M., Meyer, K. R., Mao, Y., & Swafford, B. (2011). Attitudes toward online social connection and self-disclosure as predictors of Facebook communication and relational closeness. *Communication Research*, 38, 27–53. doi: 10.1177/0093650210365537

Ledbetter, A. M., Taylor, S. H., & Mazer, J. P. (2016). Enjoyment fosters media use frequency and determines its relational outcomes: Toward a synthesis of uses and gratifications theory and media multiplexity theory. *Computers in Human Behavior*, 54, 149–157. doi: 10.1016/j.chb.2015.07.053

Lin, L., Sidani, J. E., Shensa, A., Radvoic, A., Miller, E., Colditz, J. B., . . . Primack, B. A. (2016). Association between social media use and depression among U.S. young adults. *Depression and Anxiety*, 33, 323–331. doi: 10.100/da.22466

Lu, W. & Hampton, K. N. (2017). Beyond the power of networks: Differentiating network structure from social media affordances for perceived social support. *New Media & Society*, 19, 861–879. doi: 10.1177/1461444815621514

Marshall, T. C., Bejanyan, K., Castro, G. D., & Lee, R. A. (2013). Attachment styles as predictors of Facebook-related jealousy and surveillance in romantic relationships. *Personal Relationships*, 20, 1–22. doi: 10.1111/j.1475–6811.2011.01393.x

Master, S. L., Eisenberger, N. I., Taylor, S. E., Naliboff, B. D., Shirinyan, D., & Lieberman, M. D. (2009). A picture's worth: Partner photographs reduce experimentally induced pain. *Psychological Science*, 20, 1316–1318. doi: 10.1111/j.1467–9280.2009.02444.x

McDaniel, B. T., & Coyne, S. M. (2016). "Technoference": The interference of technology in couple relationships and implications for women's personal and relational well-being. *Psychology of Popular Media Culture*, 5, 85–98. doi: 10.1037/ppm0000065

McDaniel, B. T., & Drouin, M. (2015). Sexting among married couples: Who is doing it, and are they more satisfied? *Cyberpsychology, Behavior, and Social Networking*, 18, 628–634. doi: 10.1089/cyber.2015.0334

McEwan, B. (2013). Sharing, caring, and surveilling: An actor–partner interdependence model examination of Facebook relational maintenance strategies. *Cyberpsychology, Behavior, and Social Networking*, 16, 863–869. doi: 10.1089/cyber.2012.0717

McEwan, B., Fletcher, J., Eden, J., & Sumner, E. (2014). Development and validation of a Facebook relational maintenance measure. *Communication Methods and Measures*, 8, 244–263. doi: 10.1080/19312458.2014.967844

Mikulincer, M., & Shaver, P. R. (2003). The attachment behavioral system in adulthood: Activation, psychodynamics, and interpersonal processes. *Advances in Experimental Social Psychology*, 35, 53–152. doi: 10.1016/S0065-2601(03)01002-5

Mikulincer, M., & Shaver, P. R. (2013). The role of attachment security in adolescent and adult close relationships. In J. A. Simpson & L. Campbell (Eds.), *The Oxford handbook of close relationships* (pp. 66–89). Oxford: Oxford University Press.

Mikulincer, M., & Shaver. P. R. (2016). *Attachment in adulthood*, 2nd ed. New York: Guilford Press.

Morey, J. M., Gentzler, A. L., Creasy, B., Oberhauser, A. M., & Westerman, D. (2013). Young adults' use of communication within their romantic relationships and associations with attachment style. *Computers in Human Behavior*, 29, 1771–1778. doi: 10.1016/j.chb.2013.02.019

Ogolsky, B. G., & Bowers, J. R. (2013). A meta-analytic review of relationship maintenance and its correlates. *Journal of Social and Personal Relationships*, 30, 343–367. doi: 10.1177/0265407512463338

O'Keeffe, G. S., & Clarke-Pearson, K. (2011). The impact of social media on children, adolescents, and families. *Pediatrics*, 127, 800–804. doi: 10.1542/peds.2011-0054

Oldmeadow, J. A., Quinn, S., & Kowert, R. (2013). Attachment style, social skills, and Facebook use amongst adults. *Computers in Human Behavior*, 29, 1142–1149. doi: 10.1016/j.chb.2012.10.006

Papacharissi, Z. (Ed.). (2010). *A networked self: Identity, community and culture on social network sites*. New York: Routledge.

Pietromonaco, P. R., & Powers, S. I. (2015). Attachment and health-related physiological stress processes. *Current Opinion in Psychology*, 1, 34–39. doi: 10.1016/j.copsyc.2014.12.001

Pietromonaco, P. R., Uchino, B., & Schetter, C. D. (2013). Close relationship processes and health: Implications of attachment theory for health and disease. *Health Psychology*, 32, 499–513. doi: 10.1037/a0029349

Przybylski, A. K., & Weinstein, N. (2017). A large-scale test of the goldilocks hypothesis: Quantifying the relations between digital-screen use and the mental well-being of adolescents. *Psychological Science*, 28, 204–215. doi: 10.1177/0956797616678438

Ramirez Jr, A., & Broneck, K. (2009). "IM me": Instant messaging as relational maintenance and everyday communication. *Journal of Social and Personal Relationships*, 26, 291–314. doi: 10.1177/0265407509106719

Reis, H. T. (2013). Perceived partner responsiveness as an organizing theme for the study of relationships and well-being. In L. Campbell & T. J. Loving (Eds.), *Interdisciplinary research on close relationships: The case for integration* (pp. 27–52). Washington, DC: APA.

Reis, H. T., & Clark, M. S. (2013). Responsiveness. In J. A. Simpson & L. Campbell (Eds.), *The Oxford handbook of close relationships* (pp. 66–89). Oxford: Oxford University Press.

Reis, H. T., & Collins, W. A. (2004). Relationships, human behavior, and psychological science. *Current Directions in Psychological Science*, 13, 233–237. doi: 10.1111/j.0963-7214.2004.00315.x

Reis, H. T., Sheldon, K. M., Gable, S. L., Roscoe, J., & Ryan, R. M. (2000). Daily well-being: The role of autonomy, competence, and relatedness. *Personality and Social Psychology Bulletin*, 26, 419–435. doi: 10.1177/0146167200266002

Reis, H. T., Clark, M. S., & Holmes, J. G. (2004). Perceived partner responsiveness as an organizing construct in the study of intimacy and closeness. In D. J. Mashek & A. Aron (Eds.), *Handbook of closeness and intimacy* (pp. 201–225). Mahwah, NJ: Lawrence Erlbaum.

Reis, H. T., Smith, S. M., Carmichael, C. L., Caprariello, P. A., Tsai, F.-F., Rodrigues, A., & Maniaci, M. R. (2010). Are you happy for me? How sharing positive events with others provides personal and interpersonal benefits. *Journal of Personality and Social Psychology*, 99, 311–329. doi: 10.1037/a0018344

Ridgway, J. L., & Clayton, R. B. (2016). Instagram unfiltered: Exploring associations of body image satisfaction, Instagram selfie posting, and negative romantic relationship outcomes. *Cyberpsychology, Behavior, and Social Networking*, 19, 2–7. doi: 10.1089/cyber.2015.0433

Robles, T. F., Slatcher, R. B., Trombello, J. M., & McGinn, M. M. (2014). Marital quality and health: A meta-analytic review. *Psychological Bulletin*, 140, 140–187. doi: 10.1037/a0031859

Ruppel, E. K., Burke, T. J., & Cherney, M. R. (2017). Channel complementarity and multiplexity in long-distance friends' patterns of communication technology use. *New Media & Society*. doi: 10.1177/1461444817699995

Saphire-Bernstein, S., & Taylor, S. E. (2013). Close relationships and happiness. In I. Boniwell, S. A. David, & A. C. Ayers (Eds.), *Oxford handbook of happiness*. London: Oxford University Press.

Scissors, L. E., Roloff, M. E., & Gergle, D. (2014). Room for interpretation: The role of self-esteem and CMC in romantic couple conflict. *Proceedings of the SIGCHI conference on human factors in computing systems* (pp. 3953–3962). Toronto, ON.

Selcuk, E., Zayas, V., Günaydin, G., Hazan, C., & Kross, E. (2012). Mental representations of attachment figures facilitate recovery following upsetting autobiographical memory recall. *Journal of Personality and Social Psychology*, 103, 362–378. doi: 10.1037/a0028125

Selcuk, E., Stanton, S. C., Slatcher, R. B., & Ong, A. D. (2017). Perceived partner responsiveness predicts better sleep quality through lower anxiety. *Social Psychological and Personality Science*, 8, 83–92. doi: 10.1177/1948550616662128

Shakya, H. B., & Christakis, N. A. (2017). Association of Facebook use with compromised well-being: A longitudinal study. *American Journal of Epidemiology*, 185, 203–211. doi: 10.1093/aje/kww189

Shaw, A. M., Timpano, K. R., Tran, T. B., & Joormann, J. (2015). Correlates of Facebook usage patterns: The relationship between passive Facebook use, social anxiety symptoms, and brooding. *Computers in Human Behavior*, 48, 575–580. doi: 10.1016/j.chb.2015.02.003

Slatcher, R. B., Selcuk, E., & Ong, A. D. (2015). Perceived partner responsiveness predicts diurnal cortisol profiles 10 years later. *Psychological Science*, 26, 972–982. doi: 10.1177/0956797615575022

Sosik, V. S., & Bazarova, N. N. (2014). Relational maintenance on social network sites: How Facebook communication predicts relational escalation. *Computers in Human Behavior*, 35, 124–131. doi: 10.1016/j.chb.2014.02.044

Stafford, L., & Canary, D. J. (1991). Maintenance strategies and romantic relationship type, gender and relational characteristics. *Journal of Social and Personal Relationships*, 8, 217–242. doi: 10.1177/0265407591082004

Steers, M. L. N., Wickham, R. E., & Acitelli, L. K. (2014). Seeing everyone else's highlight reels: How Facebook usage is linked to depressive symptoms. *Journal of Social and Clinical Psychology*, 33, 701–731. doi: 10.1521/jscp.2014.33.8.701

Tandoc, E. C., Ferrucci, P., & Duffy, M. (2015). Facebook use, envy, and depression among college students: Is facebooking depressing? *Computers in Human Behavior*, 43, 139–146. doi: 10.1016/j.chb.2014.10.053

Tay, L., & Diener, E. (2011). Needs and subjective well-being around the world. *Journal of Personality and Social Psychology*, 101, 354. doi: 10.1037/a0023779

Tay, L., Kuykendall, L., & Diener, E. (2015). Satisfaction and happiness: The bright side of quality of life. In W. Glatzer (Ed.), *Global handbook of quality of life*. New York: Springer.

Taylor, S. H., & Ledbetter, A. M. (2017). Extending media multiplexity theory to the extended family: Communication satisfaction and tie strength as moderators of violations of media use expectations. *New Media & Society*, 19, 1369–1387. doi: 10.1177/1461444816638458

Taylor, S. H., Hutson, J., & Alicea, T. R. (2017). Social consequences of Grindr use: Extending the Internet-enhanced self-disclosure hypothesis. *Proceedings ACM conference on human factors in computing systems* (pp. 6645–6657). Denver, CO.

Thoits, P. A. (2011). Mechanisms linking social ties and support to physical and mental health. *Journal of Health and Social Behavior*, 52, 145–161. doi: 10.1177/0022146510395592

Toma, C. L., & Choi, M. (2016). Mobile media matters: Media use and relationship satisfaction among geographically close dating couples. *Proceedings of the 19th ACM conference on computer-supported cooperative work & social computing* (pp. 394–404), San Francisco, CA.

Tong, S. T., & Walther, J. B. (2011). Relational maintenance and CMC. In K. B. Wright & L. M. Webb (Eds.), *Computer-mediated communication and personal relationships* (pp. 98–118). New York: Peter Lang.

Treem, J. W. & Leonardi, P. M. (2012). Social media use in organizations: Exploring the affordances of visibility, editability, persistence, and association. *Annals of the International Communication Association*, 36, 143–189. doi: 10.1080/23808985.2013.11679130

Trepte, S., & Scharkow, M. (2017). Friends and lifesavers: How social capital and social support received in media environments contribute to well-being. In L. Reinecke & M. B. Oliver (Eds.), *The Routledge handbook of media use and well-being* (pp. 304–316). New York: Routledge.

Tromholt, M. (2016). The Facebook experiment: Quitting Facebook leads to higher levels of well-being. *Cyberpsychology, Behavior, and Social Networking*, 19, 661–666. doi: 10.1089/cyber.2016.0259

Turkle, S. (2015). *Reclaiming conversation: The power of talk in a digital age*. New York: Penguin Random House.

Valkenburg, P. M., & Peter, J. (2007). Online communication and adolescent well-being: Testing the stimulation versus the displacement hypothesis. *Journal of Computer-Mediated Communication*, 12, 1169–1182. doi: 10.1111/j.1083–6101.2007.00368.x

Valkenburg, P. M., & Peter, J. (2008). Adolescents' identity experiments on the Internet: Consequences for social competence and self-concept unity. *Communication Research*, 35, 208–231. doi: 10.1177/0093650207313164

Valkenburg, P. M., & Peter, J. (2009a). The effects of instant messaging on the quality of adolescents' existing friendships: A longitudinal study. *Journal of Communication*, 59, 79–97. doi: 10.1111/j.1460–2466.2008.01405.x

Valkenburg, P. M., & Peter, J. (2009b). Social consequences of the Internet for adolescents: A decade of research. *Current Directions in Psychological Science*, 18, 1–5. doi: 10.1111/j.1467–8721.2009.01595.x

Verduyn, P., Lee, D. S., Park, J., Shablack, H., Orvell, A., Bayer, J., . . . Kross, E. (2015). Passive Facebook usage undermines affective well-being: Experimental and longitudinal evidence. *Journal of Experimental Psychology: General*, 144, 480. doi: 10.1037/xge0000057

Walther, J. B. (1992). Interpersonal effects in computer-mediated interaction: A relational perspective. *Communication Research*, 19, 52–90. doi: 10.1177/009365092019001003

Walther, J. B. (1996). Computer-mediated communication: Impersonal, interpersonal, and hyperpersonal interaction. *Communication Research*, 23, 3–43. doi: 10.1177/009365096023001001

Walther, J. B., & Burgoon, J. K. (1992). Relational communication in computer-mediated interaction. *Human Communication Research*, 19, 50–88. doi: 10.1111/j.1468–2958.1992.tb00295.x

Walther, J. B., Loh, T., & Granka, L. (2005). Let me count the ways: The interchange of verbal and non-verbal cues in computer-mediated and face-to-face affinity. *Journal of Language and Social Psychology*, 24, 36–65. doi: 10.1177/0261927X04273036

Walther, J. B., Van Der Heide, B., Ramirez, A., Burgoon, J. K., & Peña, J. (2015). Interpersonal and hyperpersonal dimensions of computer-mediated communication. In S. Sundar (Ed.), *The handbook of the psychology of communication technology* (pp. 3–22). New York: Wiley.

Weisskirch, R. S. (2012). Women's adult romantic attachment style and communication by cell phone with romantic partners. *Psychological Reports: Relationships & Communications*, 111, 281–288. doi: 10.2466/21.02.20.PR0.111.4.281-288

Weisskirch, R. S., & Delevi, R. (2012). Its over b/n u n me: Technology use, attachment styles, and gender roles in relationship dissolution. *Cyberpsychology, Behavior, and Social Networking*, 15, 486–490. doi: 10.1089/cyber.2012.0169

Xu, B., Chang, P. F., Welker, C., Bazarova, N. N., & Cosley, D. (2016). Automatic archiving vs. default deletion: What Snapchat tells us about ephemerality in design. *Proceedings of the 19th ACM conference on computer-supported cooperative work* (pp. 1662–1675), San Francisco, CA.

7
BREAK-UPS AND THE LIMITS OF ENCODING LOVE

Bernie Hogan

> We say, "The wind is blowing," as if the wind were actually a thing at rest which, at a given point in time, begins to move and blow . . . This reduction of processes to static conditions, which we shall call "process-reduction" for short, appears self-explanatory to people who have grown up with such languages.
>
> *(Norbert Elias; as quoted in Emirbayer, 1997)*

A relationship as experienced by people is a process. In order for it to be leveraged by computers, however, it must be turned into a static thing that signifies the state of that relationship. While we might suggest that such a conversion is a harmless and trivial matter, there are multiple instances when this conversion can create tension, unease, subversion or confusion. One clear example of this is in the case of the "break-up" whereby one or both parties wishes to cease their relationship or to alter it so that both people no longer interact with each other as if they are doing so jointly.

Break-ups are a compelling topic for thinking about the networked society as they are both very common and run counter to the logic of connectivity that powers much of network society. The logic of connectivity is that connections between individuals or individuals and entities that are real should be accounted for. It is thought that the more such connections are accounted for, the more effectively any algorithm can facilitate future connections (Hogan 2015), particularly for advertising purposes and enhanced user experience. A break-up signifies a dissolution of a link as two people change status from in a relationship to no longer in a relationship. While the ability to change a status, defriend another and even block someone is included within most social network sites, these choices are often implemented with little clarity. As will be shown below, the difficulty with breaking up online is that by their very nature, online profiles and the links between them do not cleanly map on to the lived experience of a relationship.

As Gershon noted in *The Breakup 2.0* (2010), young adults face a dizzying array of strategies when breaking up, from blocking, to changing statuses, to "ghosting" (offering no-response). These are in addition to the shifting norms on what is the appropriate medium within which to send the message. Beyond the evolving social norms of whether to Snapchat a break-up message or send by post is a far deeper matter of how network societies structure and control relations. Network societies thrive on connectivity as well as operationalization. The break-up is a "breaching moment" (Garfinkel, 1967) for the networked self. Breaching experiments occur when individuals intentionally violate expected norms or conventions in order to understand how such norms are enacted in everyday life. When two individuals undermine the codified norms of connectivity on a social network site, they can lay bare the ideologies of connectivity that are otherwise latent. One key insight in such a breaching is that a relationship is not a static codified object, nor will it ever be.

The Exhibited Self and the Exhibited Relation

In past work I have written of the exhibited self as distinct from the performative self (Hogan, 2010). The performative self is how the individual behaves for a specific audience. It is Goffman's idea that we can think of everyday life as a performance, like a stage play. The idea of the performative self has taken on a rich and varied life. Perhaps the biggest turning point is via Butler's notion of performativity. Situated between the linguistic use of performance (e.g. "I pronounce you husband and wife") and Goffman's notion of performance, Butler notes that we reproduce conventions and identities continuously as we enact them. We do not merely have a gender, but continuously perform it with gestures that signify our masculinity or femininity, our sexuality, our class, and so forth.

This notion of the self as a performance has been disrupted by social media. These media, and particularly social network sites are the quintessential form of media for the networked society. On these sites, performances happen every time we click to like a status update, upload a photo or write a post. We signify elements of ourselves that reveal and reinforce norms and identities. However, these performances are not presented as is to our audiences. Instead, they are filtered through a complex series of transformations, many of which are typically hidden from the person doing the performing. For example, when someone posts a status update on Twitter (i.e. a "tweet"), Twitter acts as a mediator. It adds "metadata" such as the time the tweet was sent, the device, and the location of the device (inferred or precise; Twitter, 2017). The tweet is not merely a performance, it is an artifact that is curated by Twitter. The platform decides whether to promote this tweet, whether to remove it, who to send it to in email updates or "since you've been gone" lists of tweets. What was once a simple performative gesture (saying something in under 140 characters) has now become part of a networked exhibit.

The notion of an exhibit reinforces the idea that current performances are mediated. Twitter, Facebook, Snapchat, Tumblr, and so forth host this data. In the past decade, it has become clear that there is too much socially relevant information for any individual to consume in any given sitting. Consequently, mediators have become *curators*. They do not simply intervene between two parties but exert agency. The most direct form of agency is in how they determine the sort order for a series of posts. They also insert advertisements in lists in order to extract some of the user's attention. Curators hide unpleasant posts (with varying degrees of accuracy). This newfound centrality of platforms in social life helps to reinforce the notion of life as networked life and individuals as networked individuals (Rainie & Wellman, 2012).

For platforms to work as curators between people requires more than an exhibited self, it requires an exhibited relation. Unlike exhibited relations, exhibited selves have now been extensively explored in the literature. For example, Zhao and colleagues (2013) describe how individuals enact a lowest-common denominator self of exhibited artifacts even though what constitutes the lowest common denominator shifts over time. People often delete old statuses or clean up their online personae. Vivienne and Burgess (2012) show how trans persons and their families carefully negotiate expected audiences for this exhibited self when making self-representing documentaries. Both Vitak and Kim (2014) and Marwick and boyd (2011) highlight how individuals consider potential "nightmare friends" or other potential threats when deciding whether to post a potentially controversial status. This is to say, not only is there an exhibited self, but that this self is something individuals understand as a part of networked life.

Despite the extensive work in computer-mediated communication on the exhibited self, there is much less work on the exhibited relation. Boyd was an early entrant in this space whereby she critiqued the stable notion of a friend. A 'friend' on MySpace could have meant any number of possible relations, from a true friend to a status symbol, a peer-pressure based acquaintance and more (boyd, 2006). This destabilization of the friendship implies that what is signified online as a relation does not adequately capture the notions of relations understood in everyday life. But why? I assert that it is not because the label stands for many things. This would imply that we could just use more labels. They might be unwieldy from a user-interface perspective but they would be sufficient. Instead, I assert that it is because relationships are processes and labels are things which, at most, represent states.

In past work, I noted that death is the ultimate arbiter between the exhibited self and the performed self (Hogan, 2010). When individuals die, their exhibited selves live on. The body does not contain a "kill switch" for the variety of media accounts held by third parties. Accounts go dormant, or in the case of the most sophisticated platforms, such as Facebook, a third party can notify Facebook that the person has passed and that their profile should be memorialized (Facebook, 2017). Whereas death is the ultimate arbiter of the distinction between the performed and exhibited self, the break-up (between friends or lovers) can be seen as an arbiter of the distinction between the performed relation as a dynamic process and the exhibited relation as a static object. Break-ups are typically initiated by one person in the relationship and continue until both parties understand that the break-up has occurred. Typically, one person will speak or write to the other person and signify that the relationship has ended or that they wish to end it. This is a performative gesture. To note, sometimes one of the parties will not agree that the relationship is over, which can complicate the process of breaking up but it does not nullify the break-up process.

While the break-up has then occurred in the minds (and hearts) of the two in the relationship, the online signifiers of that relationship persist. This includes labels, tagged photos, and past statuses. One must consider what to do with a publicly declared online status, whether to unfriend or block the other person on any variety of media and whether to engage in some form of impression management. That is, the inadequate mapping between the lived relation that is performed and the networked relation that is exhibited needs to be resolved somehow.

What is a World of Networks?

A world of networks is a world of particulars and relationships between them. The particulars might be people, accounts, photos, or pieces of text. If we can define a boundary we can say that everything inside this boundary is a particular. In social network analysis, everything contained by a particular boundary is a node. These nodes link to each other in some fashion. The set of nodes and relations define a network. We can observe the networks of people tagging each other in Facebook photos (Lewis et al., 2008), of HAM radio operators signaling each other (Bernard et al., 1982), of countries trading (Wallerstein, 1974) and indeed in many other ways.

We can distinguish between network societies and network analysis. In social network analysis, this linking was done by the analyst who would suggest some sufficient criteria. For example, a researcher might indicate links between two people if they have sent any direct communication in the last six months. This is obviously an artificial boundary, but often a workable one. With these links in place, we can build up a social network and analyze it as such, describe its overall features and make claims about how the structure of relationships has some sort of consequence to the people who make up the network. This, however, is not a network society. This is a network analysis.

In a network analysis, we turn phenomena into particulars (i.e. nodes) and create sufficient conditions for linking *at the point of analysis*. This might be in the lab or in a software program. In a network society, we turn phenomena into particulars *at the point of practice*. This is to say, we *enact* networks rather than merely analyze them. Healy (2015) has referred to this as the performativity of networks. This distinction is immensely important, for what is critical in a network society is to interrogate *how* objects are turned into nodes and processes turned into links.

This transformation to nodes and links makes the world a more calculable place. This is the general product of modernity. It is where we turn danger into risk (Beck, 1992; Luhmann, 1993). Gods, ghosts, and goblins as abstract dangers recede from view. In their place are the calculable risks we embed in futures markets, logistics, and insurance brokers. When these objects of calculation represent social phenomena, they are done by platforms that make expectations about what sort of profile and what sort of relating can be accomplished by people on that platform.

The problem with the transition to a world of particulars comes when we try to codify processes as static objects, and worse, feed these objects back into the system. Processes are hard to identify as they are dynamic in nature. We cannot capture wind. We can capture wind-energy through turbines and air that is blowing through pressurized tanks, but we cannot capture the movement of air for it is a process, not a thing.

To consider the relationship, it is useful to contrast it with a role and a status. For this I lean on Merton's (1996) notion of the "role set." In Merton's parlance, a status is an ascribed label, such as teacher or mother. A role is a particular configuration of social structure to accomplish some end. Roles never exist in isolation but as parts of role sets. Mothers have children, teachers have pupils. It is the structural arrangement of relationships that defines the role set. One can play a role, such as a nurse, by being nurse-like in their interactions with doctors and patients. If one is not supposed to play this role (i.e. they do not have the status of a nurse), then trouble might ensue for they do not have the status that signifies or legitimates that role.

A relationship is a specific process of interaction between two people. When a specific nurse deals with a specific patient this is a relationship. The patient has their own needs for care, their own history with the nurse. The two have a rapport shared among two mutually acknowledging persons. Unlike a role, a relationship is a dynamic process of continuously negotiated entrainment. Friendships come and go (Suitor and Keeton, 1997; Antonucci, 1986). Our respect and affection for our family members waxes and wanes, often in concert with family drama (Wellman and Wortley, 1989) and differences in political opinions. The specific structuring of statuses within the family unit is proscribed by culture, such as "first cousin once removed." Such a status does not necessitate a specific *relationship* that would happen between cousins. They may be friends, enemies or strangers, and still be cousins.

The problem for network society herein is that relationships cannot be easily codified except when filtered through the roles that set up social structure and the statuses that are used to codify roles. We think of marriage as a relationship, yet it is not, at least not directly. In Mertonian terms, a marriage is a role set. Speak to many couples and it is clear that between them, there are differing levels of engagement, marital satisfaction, and feelings of attachment (Norton et al., 2017). The couples, by necessity, have different lives and experiences and thus different relationships between them. Consider this distinction in the subtleties in the definition of marriage: "the legally or formally recognized union of a man and a woman (or, in some jurisdictions, two people of the same sex) as partners in a relationship" ("Marriage," n.d.). This definition asserts that the relationship is pre-existing and presumably ongoing. Marriage is not how the relationship starts. Rather, marriage is a formal recognition as a union. The term "husband" is a status. The way a husband relates to his partner, to the courts, and to family members is a role. The actual way the person behaves toward and feels about his husband or wife is his part of the relationship.

Love and Social Media

One of the most powerful and yet ambiguous processes in the world is love. A break-up neither eliminates love nor happens because we fall out of love, yet the two are inextricably linked. As Appignanesi notes:

> Love is deeply private and particularly in its passionate form oft-ungovernable, while marriage is an institution, championed by regulatory states in the name of an ordered society. The contradiction between the two can produce a deep malaise—from which long-term and public cohabitation, that intermediate arrangement, is hardly free.
>
> *(2011, p. 111)*

Love is not a static condition. It is a dynamic process whose qualities are known to many yet remain elusive to study. It is related to attachment, to fidelity, to rituals, and to the life course. Some societies privilege love in relationships and some try to contain love in favor of more pragmatic relationships. No society denies there is love between a mother and child and few societies deny that courtship involves affection, even if it is accomplished within politically or culturally arranged marriages (Shorter, 1977).

Instead of exploring the relationship between love and the network society directly, we can create boundary conditions around the codification of love by considering how relationships are handled in social network sites, as exemplars of this networking logic. Herein, it is important to note that people are not the particulars, accounts are. People can have multiple accounts and use pseudonyms. But each account has a set of profile data and a set of links to others. In this sense, the relations that people have with each other are not links in the way Facebook encodes them, or the way an analyst encodes them. Our lived experience only partially matches the technological encoding of our lived experience.

The mission of social networks, enacted through coders, designers, user experience researchers, security professionals, and the bureaucracy that props up and facilitates their activities, is to encompass ever more of lived experience in the coded world. Consider Facebook's two most recent mission statements. Up until 2017 their motto was "To give people the power to share and make the world more open and connected." This has recently changed to "Give people the power to build community and bring the world closer together" (Newton, 2017).

The first motto noted that openness and connectivity were self-evident goods. They were ends in themselves and Facebook was to *make the world* more open. With upwards of two billion users, this ambition is hardly an overreach. While openness has been excised from the recent mission statement, what remains is the conception of Facebook as mediating "the world" and in doing so, aspiring to create some positive outcome. In this case, both *community* and bringing *the world closer together* are seen as self-evident virtues. Yet, in bringing the world closer, it must first encode the world in the eyes of Facebook as well as appeal to the shareholders, employees, and advertisers who pay for this closeness.

Some things are more easily encoded than others. We can think of lossless coding for audio and photos, or screen resolutions so high that the human eye cannot distinguish distinct pixels. But what about encoding more abstract concepts like love or friendship? Most people would positively acknowledge the ontological status of both friendship and love. Most people believe love is, indeed, real. Nevertheless, love represents a considerable challenge for encoding. This is for at least three reasons:

1. *Love is ambiguous.* Does love represent infatuation? Affection? Care? A theory from antiquity proposed six distinct love styles (Eros, Storge, Pragma, Ludus, Agape, and Mania). These styles apply to many kinds of love beyond pair-bonding, yet all are plausibly seen within couples. Recent work has shown that differing styles have differing relationship outcomes (Vedes et al., 2016).
2. *Love is asymmetric.* Early love has been termed "limerence," an intense phase of infatuation that can border on obsession. Tennov (1999) has explored the life cycle of limerence, showing that it is temporary and often leads to stable romantic love, but that it does so to a different extent in different people. Limerence, when unreciprocated, can produce intense feelings of heartache bordering on illness. The unrequited lover would not doubt the strength of their affection, only its feasibility.
3. *Love is dynamic.* In some of the oldest living couples, love persists in a variety of forms. Yet, feelings recognizable as love do wax and wane in both enduring couples and those who eventually break up (McNulty et al., 2016). While we might say that being out of love predicts relationship dissolution, it does not guarantee it. The love shared between even the happiest couples varies in its intensity over time.

Ambiguity, asymmetry, and dynamism suggest that love is more like a process than an entity. *Love is not a thing, it is a mode of relating.* A network society cannot therefore encode love any more than it can code a relationship; it can only signify it and code the signification process. This signification tends to be done through a mix of categorical statuses and signals about the relationships between users—do the users click on each other's statuses on Facebook, thereby contributing to their increased prioritization in the newsfeed? Do they send each other the most snaps on Snapchat, thereby prompting Snapchat to show little emojis next to the other person's name?

Broadly speaking, these signals are meant to stand in for love. Platforms substitute in the signals we can measure (such as promptness) for more abstract, contextual, or relational signals that are more difficult to measure. With every action, every click, like, or tag, the individual is sending signals about their relationships that can then be used to update some strength of connections. Often this is done as part of a feedback loop where new relationships quickly entrain. Algorithms do not represent love, but steer it. Suddenly one lover is all over the other's feeds and limerence is not merely about repeatedly thinking of the other lover, but seeing them as well. Notably, this virtuous cycle of paying attention and then seeing one's lover appear at the top of a feed also applies for suggested purchases. When one purchases something on an online retailer, related purchases seem to follow the user around the web. With curated feeds and advertisements, a feedback loop of presentation and interest ensnares the user, steering attention toward both loved ones and products for sale.

Encoded data from platforms can steer a relationship to become more intense. This data can also predict the dissolution of a relationship. Backstrom and Kleinberg (2014) have noted a significant relationship between the social networks of individuals on Facebook and their likelihood of breaking up. Other members of the Facebook data team have noted that when someone changes their relationship status to single from being in a relationship, Facebook activity from the other party in the relationship spikes, presumably as they solicit social support and engage in impression management (Friggeri, 2014).

On social media platforms such as Facebook and Twitter, the network does not emerge from interaction so much as presupposes the interaction. In this sense, platforms do more than steer relationships, they act as gatekeepers of access for these relationships as well. We add friends and then we see their content. Thus, media come to define the parameters for what is possible and what is available in terms of social connections. For example, on Facebook, one cannot tag a person in a photo who is not their friend. On Twitter, one typically cannot send a direct message to an account if that account does not follow the user (though this is now configurable). These rules are set up to filter unwanted access as well as encourage people to denote specific links between individuals. A networked logic does not simply emerge from the interaction on a platform, but from the design of the platform itself.

To suggest that the world is networked does not merely mean that there are connections, but also that there are forms and protocols that permit specific kinds of connections. These protocols are currently set up and enacted by third parties who steer attention while they curate social signals. As these protocols cover more forms of social life, they require new kinds of behaviors and spark new anxieties. As stated above, the distinction between the lived relation and the static code can frustrate some dimensions of human behavior. This has been felt in popular culture as much as in academic work. In fact, free from the demands of empirical work, popular culture can exaggerate these anxieties in ways that highlight some of the present challenges for the network society. In the case of handling the distinction between the exhibited status and the relation as process, the TV show *Black Mirror* raises important and compelling questions.

Black Mirror and the Fragmented Digital

The near future dystopian show *Black Mirror* offers myriad cases of break-ups gone awry. Two in particular stand out for their poignancy. The first is a season two episode called *The Entire History of You* (Armstrong & Welsh, 2011), which is a meditation on how to deal with loss when everything can be remembered. The second, *White Christmas* (Brooker & Tibbetts, 2014), is a meditation on how to deal with loss when everything is mediated. Since *Black Mirror* is a show about near-future dystopias, the show tends to include some novel technological features. In both break-up episodes, this centers around the use of digitally enhanced eyes. In *The Entire History of You*, the eyes act as a sort of camera that can record and store everything using a small technology called "The Grain." It shows up in security checks and people converse while replaying old clips. In *White Christmas*, we observe a world where the eyes serve as a sort of augmented reality, but the user does not have dominion. People can literally "block" each other. A blocked person is viewed as a static silhouette whose voice cannot be heard. The person doing the blocking becomes a ghost to those blocked. When a person in the show is revealed (and convicted) as a sex offender, their punishment is not prison but the total blocking of all people, who now exist as a sea of static figures. The sex offender is reciprocally shown as a red silhouette to everyone else.

Both shows use visual technology as a narrative device that "virtualizes" the physical world; everything is now encoded and mediated. This sounds futuristic, but if we move beyond the need for digitally enhanced eyes that capture what we see, both stories are squarely embedded in the present.

The Entire History of You is perhaps the episode that is the closest to our current epoch. We can already set up cameras and record most of our daily lives. Some individuals already wear such cameras, most notably cyborg pioneer Steve Mann (Mann & Niedzviecki, 2001) and "eyeborg" Rob Spence who lost one eye years ago and replaced it with a camera (*Time*, 2009). As Google Glass has shown, the norms around such recording are still unclear (Hong, 2013).

In *The Entire History of You*, the protagonist is concerned that his wife is having an affair. Checking the recordings from his wife, these suspicions become increasingly plausible. Further, she has deleted a key sequence of memories that occurred roughly nine months before their son is born. The audience is aware by this time that the protagonist is probably not the father. The episode then watches as the drama unfolds between these two characters.

The technologies for such a narrative almost exist today. By default, most texting applications store communication indefinitely. In some cases, we can turn on some sort of erasing on one end (e.g. Apple iMessage can be set to delete messages older than thirty days). Yet, if it is not built into the platform, there is no guarantee that both parties will delete the message. Snapchat is premised on the idea of self-destructing data. In fact, the Snapchat's creators went further in suggesting that sending pictures to a new romantic interest was what motivated the creation of the app in the first place (Crook & Escher, 2015). Other programs such as Telegram and Whatsapp now include the ability to send photos that disappear after thirty days.

What happens to the artifacts of the other person after the break-up? They are currently linked to an account, not a person. The account is where deletion occurs and deletion is an active process that requires the user to actively remove content. That is to say, social network sites are typically not designed with a notion of decay in mind. Once a friend, always a friend. As a personal note, I can only recall Tumblr and LiveJournal as indicating that my account would expire due to a lack of activity. Facebook, Twitter, and LinkedIn provide no such feature. There are no affordances for how long it has been since last contact, or how to play "catch up" on an account's activities since the last time the person viewed their friend. Here we can see how the technology in *The Entire History of You* that stores one's communications and senses is a mere extension of the digitization of interactions experienced in everyday life today.

In the case of both *Black Mirror* episodes, the ocular technology has become domesticated and institutionalized. Domesticated because we are shown everyday practices that include such technologies as well as the subversion of norms. In *White Christmas* the protagonist sets up a shady business to help an awkward man on a date (watching through the awkward man's eyes). When the protagonist ends up witnessing a murder, this is seen as the subversion of acceptable norms. The ocular technology is institutionalized because when the protagonist is punished it is through the eye and ear pieces, by law. Similarly, in *The Entire History of You* the protagonist goes through customs only to have everything he saw on his trip played back by the customs officer. The drama from the show comes not from the technology of the eyes, but what is encoded, who gets to see it and when.

Part of the terror that emerges from these shows is not the ubiquity of the technology. It is dramatic tension set up via the uncanny valley in which the technology settles. Relationships are not absolute and binary. The line between taking interest in an ex-lover out of general welfare, appealing to an unhappy lover who is disinterested in talking, and cyberstalking as an offense can be unclear for some. For those who are in aggressive pursuit of a disinterested lover, cyberstalking "does not fundamentally differ from traditional, proximal stalking" (Sheridan & Grant, 2007, p. 627). Yet, what has frustrated efforts to provide accurate estimates for cyberstalking is that the asymmetric gaze of viewing others' online presences is an encouraged behavior for most social media (Reyns et al., 2011). This is evident even in the first definition of Social Network Sites by boyd and Ellison (2007). Their third criterion to define social network sites is that the user may traverse profiles. One here is not applying a symmetric gaze, where the viewer looks and the viewed can now perceive the viewer. Instead, it is an asymmetric gaze where the viewer looks at the profile and the viewed profile owner is not informed, or not told specifically. To note, within the current literature it is established that the lack of a victim's awareness of a specific event of cyberstalking does not legitimize or excuse the behavior.

Gershon (2010) among others notes how students wrestle with the temptations to view these old photos and living profiles as a routine part of the break-up experience. While jilted lovers might have always pined over old photos, what is novel is that they can now pine over an endlessly new stream of content. It is not a far step to think of them pining over high-fidelity life streams, endlessly negotiating the virtues of deleting and forgetting alongside the temptation to relive old memories, trapped as viewers of their own exhibitions.

The notion that one either has a memory, locked in and replayable, or does not, is foreign and upsetting. Our memories are fragile. Yet, the superimposition of digital technologies on top of everyday relationships requires us to encode our representations and associate them with profiles so that we may link to others. This is the central dilemma of the protagonist in *The Entire History of You*: remove The Grain and everything that comes with it, but finally excise the painful memories, or keep The Grain and live with the temptation to constantly revisit video clips that show his life to be a lie. There is no therapy, no new relationship, and no trajectory that appears to be able to resolve this dilemma. It is instead as binary as the bits used to encode this data.

Benjamin (1967) noted that with the advent of the camera, for the first time we come to sympathize with a fixed view. There is much absent on stage left that we never see and must infer, regardless of the fidelity of what is there in front of the screen. This, Walther notes (2007) is part of the experience of the online world as "hyper personal." In a retort to earlier thinkers who besmirched the Internet as cold and impersonal, Walther noted that we tend to want to engage with full realized personas. We want to understand motivations and desires. Where these cues of history and emotion are absent, our brain will fill in the details. No amount of life streaming will undermine this cold fact. When we encode our relations as exhibitions, we necessarily give something up.

In a telling experiment in a completely perpendicular field, wine tasting, we learn something that we can bring back to this chapter. In a between-subjects experiment, half the wine tasters were asked to describe the wine in words and the other half were told to remember the taste as is. In a return visit to the lab, those who had described the wine (with the traditional adjectives like floral and chocolate) were actually worse at re-identifying the wine. Melcher and Schooler (1996) described this phenomenon as verbal overshadowing. They offer the caveat that it was only untrained wine drinkers who were worse at reidentifying the wines. To note, the trained wine drinkers were no better. The same phenomenon can happen with visual memories as well (Schooler and Engstler-Schooler, 1990). Our attempts to encode our experiences can interfere with our understanding of them, for we are bodies of lived experience and our memories encode as such. Our attempts to digitize, verbalize, and otherwise capture the moment in order to make it networked and available can also interfere with the original memory. In seeking to capture and, in some respects, simplify our relationships to specific labels available on social network sites, we can make verbal overshadowing part of everyday life.

While some break-ups are definitive and absolute, many more are tumultuous and uncertain. The relationship may wither, people may become withdrawn, conflict may be resolved—for a time. In this context, there is something especially insidious about the notion that we can simply "change our status." It creates the illusion that our minds work as aggregators of static objects like computers do. It suggests that we are capable of such binarism. Yet, as was indicated here, our selves and our relationships are dynamic processes. We are co-constituted by our various entrainments with others. The performative gesture of breaking up is meant to reconfigure the status between two individuals. By saying "I'm breaking up with you" we are really saying, we cannot use the statuses we used before. But as noted above, statuses are labels, not relationships.

Slotter and colleagues (2010) show that clarity about one's self-concept has a significant effect on post-break-up distress. In this research, those who were less sure of themselves after a break-up felt more distressed. The markers online that persist in reminding someone of their links to another person can bring back notions of the relationship and thus again destabilize the self as one transitions to this newer sense of self after the break-up. This is reinforced by Lewandowski and colleagues (2006), who demonstrated that the remembrance of a past relationship was associated with a smaller self-concept than a control group. In both cases, we observe how the self itself ebbs and flows with signifiers of the external world. One's identity markers, such as a name or face, may remain relatively stable. Yet the phenomenon they represent (the self) is fragile and subject to variation based on external stimuli. By extension, networked selves are cultivated by interactions with particular other identities. The relationships that are signified by these identities are in flux and only ever approximately signified by status such as "is friend" or "in a relationship."

These studies suggest that the technologies designed to keep us "open and connected" (as was Facebook's recent mission statement), do little to manage what happens when we want to close off and disconnect from others. Instead of acting as coherent gatekeepers, the technologies typically work in an all or nothing fashion. We know that online activity spikes after an individual is broken up with (Friggeri, 2014), but we also know that there is no pleasant way to deal with the persistent and enmeshed markers of a past life. No one will expect to see a room full of photos of a wife and her ex-husband, yet, Facebook will still insensitively bring up old memories, even "friendaversaries."

What does this portend for life and love in the networked world? Is love even possible anymore? Surveys and interviews asking if people can find love will still inevitably return in the affirmative. Love is one of the strongest and most important dimensions of the human experience, regardless (or perhaps because) of its ineffable qualities. Yet, in contrast to this mysterious force, the networked world is one of operationalization and calculability. The networked world operates on its own "big data" logic (boyd and Crawford, 2012). Part of this logic is to encourage individuals to put as much online as possible in order to optimize online algorithms (Hogan, 2015). With increased information comes increased calculability. Advertisements get more relevant, lists are ranked in a more personalized order, media become more adept at circumscribing the self. Yet, as noted above, this ideology necessarily involves the alchemy of turning processes into things, and things into encoded things. Love, like the wind, is a process and not a thing. The networked world can facilitate it for the lonely or provide cruel and partial reminders when it leaves. But the networked world cannot contain love any more than a windmill's fins can contain the wind.

By circumscribing these limits, it is not my intention to undermine the networked world. Such a task would be as foolhardy as it was unrealistic. It is instead to provide a reminder of limits of encoding, regardless of the media. In doing so, it should enable individuals to step back from a triumphant discourse of digital connectivity. If we design for connection, we must also design for disconnection, and understand that both will only approximate the experience. As a fortuitous example of this hubris in action, while writing this conclusion Tumblr alerted my phone that "You'll never know love until you see this post." No doubt, the post and likely the timing of the alert, were selected algorithmically. If social media cannot contain love, at least it can trivialize it. Yet, by appreciating the difference between processes and things, exhibitions and performances, we may be more humble in the face of one of humanity's most painful and frustrating experiences, the break-up. We might also be humbled to the reason we risk such a tumultuous experience in the first place: to engage in the ineffably joyous process of love.

References

Antonucci, T. (1986). Measuring social support networks: Hierarchical mapping technique. *Generations*, 10, 10–12.

Appignanesi, L. (2011). *All about love: Anatomy of an unruly emotion*. New York: W. W. Norton.
Armstrong, J. (Writer), & Welsh, B. (Director). (2011). The entire history of you (Season 1, episode 3). In C. Brooker & A. Jones (Executive Producers), *Black Mirror*. London: Channel 4.
Backstrom, L., & Kleinberg, J. (2014). Romantic partnerships and the dispersion of social ties: A Network analysis of relationship status on Facebook. *Proceedings of the 17th ACM conference on computer supported cooperative work*. Baltimore, MD.
Beck, U. (1992). *Risk society: Towards a new modernity*. Thousand Oaks, CA: Sage.
Benjamin, W. (1967). The work of art in the age of mechanical reproduction. In *Illuminations* (pp. 217–251). New York: Schocken Books.
Bernard, H. R., Killworth, P. D., & Sailer, L. (1982). Informant accuracy in social-network data V: An experimental attempt to predict actual communication from recall data. *Social Science Research*, 11(1), 30–66.
boyd, d. (2006). Friends, friendsters and top 8: Writing community into being on social network sites. *First Monday*, 11(12).
boyd, d., & Crawford, K. (2012). Critical questions for big data. *Information, Communication & Society*, 15(5), 662–679.
boyd, d., & Ellison, N. (2007). Social network sites: Definition, history, and scholarship. *Journal of Computer Mediated Communication*, 13(1), 210–230.
Brooker, C. (Writer), & Tibbetts, C. (Director). (2014). White Christmas (Season 2, episode 4). In C. Brooker & A. Jones (Executive Producers), *Black Mirror*. London: Channel 4.
Crook, J., & Escher, A. (2015, October 15). A brief history of Snapchat. *TechCrunch*. https://techcrunch.com/gallery/a-brief-history-of-snapchat/
Emirbayer, M. (1997). Manifesto for a relational sociology. *American Journal of Sociology*, 103(2), 281–317.
Facebook. (2017). Memorialized accounts. www.facebook.com/help/1506822589577997/
Friggeri, A. (2014) When love goes awry. Facebook Data Science. www.facebook.com/notes/facebook-data-science/when-love-goes-awry/10152066701893859/
Garfinkel, H. (1967). *Studies in ethnomethodology*. Englewood Cliffs, NJ: Prentice-Hall.
Gershon, I. (2010). *The breakup 2.0: Disconnecting over new media*. Ithaca, NY: Cornell University Press.
Healy, K. (2015). The performativity of networks. *European Journal of Sociology*, 56(2), 175–205.
Hogan, B. (2010). The presentation of self in the age of social media: Distinguishing performances and exhibitions online. *Bulletin of Science, Technology & Society*, 30(6), 377–386.
Hogan, B. (2015). From invisible algorithms to interactive affordances: Data after the ideology of machine learning. In E. Bertino & S. A. Matei (Eds.), *Roles, trust, and reputation in social media knowledge markets* (pp. 103–117). Cham, Switzerland: Springer.
Hong, J. (2013). Considering privacy issues in the context of Google Glass. *Communications of the ACM*, 56(11), 10–11.
Lewandowski, G. W., Aron, A., Bassis, S., & Kunak, J. (2006). Losing a self-expanding relationship: Implications for the self-concept. *Personal Relationships*, 13(3), 317–331. doi: 10.1111/j.1475-6811.2006.00120.x
Lewis, K., Kaufman, J., Gonzalez, M., Wimmer, A., & Christakis, N. (2008). Tastes, ties, and time: A new social network dataset using Facebook.com. *Social Networks*, 30(4), 330–342.

Luhmann, N. (1993). *Risk: A sociological theory.* New York: Walter de Gruyter.
Mann, S. & Niedzviecki, H. (2001). *Cyborg: Digital destiny and human possibility in the age of the wearable computer.* Toronto: Doubleday Canada.
Marriage. (n.d.). In *Oxford English dictionary.* https://en.oxforddictionaries.com/definition/marriage
Marwick, A. E., & boyd, d. (2011). I tweet honestly, I tweet passionately: Twitter users, context collapse, and the imagined audience. *New Media & Society,* 13(1), 114–133. doi: 10.1177/1461444810365313
McNulty, J. K., Wenner, C. A., & Fisher, T. D. (2016). Longitudinal associations among relationship satisfaction, sexual satisfaction, and frequency of sex in early marriage. *Archives of Sexual Behavior,* 45(1), 85–97.
Melcher, J. M., & Schooler, J. W. (1996). The misremembrance of wines past: Verbal and perceptual expertise differentially mediate verbal overshadowing of taste memory. *Journal of Memory and Language,* 35(2), 231–245.
Merton, R. K. (1996). The role-set. In P. Sztompka (Ed.), *On social structure and science* (pp. 113–122). Chicago: University of Chicago Press.
Newton (2017). Facebook just changed its mission, because the old one was broken. *The Verge,* February 16. www.theverge.com/2017/2/16/14642164/facebook-mark-zuckerberg-letter-mission-statement
Norton, A. M., Baptist, J., & Hogan, B. (2017). Computer-mediated communication in intimate relationships: Associations of boundary crossing, intrusion, relationship satisfaction, and partner responsiveness. *Journal of Marital and Family Therapy,* 44(1), 165–182.
Rainie, L., & Wellman, B. (2012). *Networked: The new social operating system.* Cambridge, MA: MIT Press.
Reyns, B. W., Henson, B., & Fisher, B. S. (2011). Being pursued online: Applying cyberlifestyle–routine activities theory to cyberstalking victimization. *Criminal Justice and Behavior,* 38(11), 1149–1169.
Schooler, J. W., & Engstler-Schooler, T. Y. (1990). Verbal overshadowing of visual memories: Some things are better left unsaid. *Cognitive Psychology,* 22(1), 36–71.
Sheridan, L. P., & Grant, T. (2007). Is cyberstalking different? *Psychology, Crime & Law,* 13(6), 627–640.
Shorter, E. (1977). *The making of the modern family.* New York: Basic Books.
Slotter, E. B., Gardner, W. L., & Finkel, E. J. (2010). Who am I without you? The influence of romantic breakup on the self-concept. *Personality and Social Psychology Bulletin,* 36(2), 147–160. doi: 10.1177/0146167209352250
Suitor, J., & Keeton, S. (1997). Once a friend, always a friend? Effects of homophily on women's support networks across a decade. *Social Networks,* 19, 51–62.
Tennov, D. (1999). *Love and limerence.* London: Scarborough House.
Time. (2009) The Eyeborg. *The best 50 inventions of 2009.* http://content.time.com/time/specials/packages/article/0,28804,1934027_1934003_1933989,00.html
Twitter (2017). Tweet data dictionaries. https://developer.twitter.com/en/docs/tweets/data-dictionary/overview/tweet-object
Vedes, A., Hilpert, P., Nussbeck, F. W., Randall, A. K., Bodenmann, G., & Lind, W. R. (2016). Love styles, coping, and relationship satisfaction: A dyadic approach. *Personal Relationships,* 23(1), 84–97.
Vitak, J., & Kim, J. (2014). You can't block people offline: Examining how Facebook's affordances shape the disclosure process. *Proceedings of the 17th ACM conference on computer supported cooperative work* (pp. 461–474). New York: ACM.

Vivienne, S., & Burgess, J. (2012). The digital storyteller's stage: Queer everyday activists negotiating privacy and publicness. *Journal of Broadcasting & Electronic Media*, 56(3), 362–377. doi: 10.1080/08838151.2012.705194

Wallerstein, I. (1974). *The modern world system: Capitalist agriculture and the origins of the European world economy in the sixteenth century*. New York: Academic Press.

Walther, J. B. (2007). Selective self-presentation in computer-mediated communication: Hyperpersonal dimensions of technology, language, and cognition. *Computers in Human Behavior*, 23, 2538–2557.

Wellman, B., & Wortley, S. (1989). Brothers' keepers: Situating kinship relations in broader networks of social support. *Sociological Perspectives*, 32(3), 273–306.

Zhao, X., Salehi, N., & Naranjit, S. (2013). The many faces of Facebook: Experiencing social media as performance, exhibition, and personal archive. *Proceedings of the SIGCHI conference on human factors in computing systems (CHI '13)*. Paris, France.

8

TECHNOLOGICALLY ENHANCED DATING

Augmented Human Relationships, Robots, and Fantasy

Brittany Davidson, Adam Joinson, and Simon Jones

How do relationships develop? Social and behavioral scientists propose several theoretical frameworks in order to understand the development of offline relationships (e.g. Knapp, 1978; Altman & Taylor, 1973). Stage models are one class of theories that seek:

1. To identify archetypal phases that occur across the trajectory of relationship.
2. To describe the defining attributes of each phase.

Within stage models, relationship development occurs as a succession of discrete, delineated phases. Partners experience a unique collection of behaviors, thoughts, and emotions in each phase (Knobloch, 2009). A traditional trajectory within heterosexual relationships involves a gradual increase in intimate self-disclosures, emotional closeness, and sexual intimacy across the stages, preceded by an initial physical attraction (Christopher & Cate, 1985). While this scenario represents only one way that a relationship may evolve, such linear trajectories are common in stage theories of relationship development. Acknowledging the variance in relationships, stage models often are flexible regarding the number of stages and the direction of movement between them. Additionally, relationships possess unique characteristics, which makes them largely unpredictable.

Relationship Models and Theories

Social Penetration Theory (SPT; The Onion Model)

Altman and Taylor (1973) proposed one of the first process models of relationship progression: Social Penetration Theory, which suggested that relationships

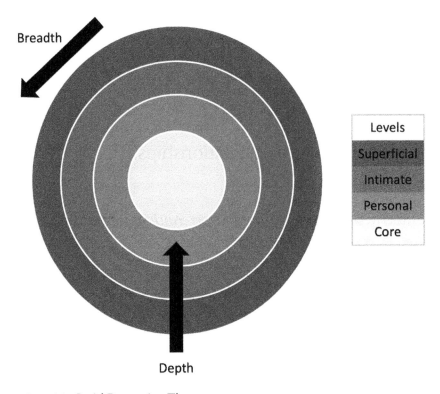

FIGURE 8.1 Social Penetration Theory

often follow a linear path, moving through four stages that represent increasing intimacy-orientation, exploratory affective exchange, affective exchange and stable-exchange between partners. Their theory is well known for its multi-layered onion analogy, where the outer layers represent one's public self, and the inner core represents one's private self (Figure 8.1).

The four stages of relationship growth are explained as follows:

1. *Orientation Stage*—engagement in shallow and superficial small talk, with the intention of feeling more comfortable with one another.
2. *Exploratory Affective Stage*—sharing more intimate thoughts and feelings, but still withholding one's most personal thoughts within this friendship stage.
3. *Affective Stage*—engagement in more physically intimate activities and revealing more personal information with one another.
4. *Stable Stage*—knowing one another to a deep and intimate level, which allows partners to accurately predict each other's emotional reactions.

In addition to the four stages of relationship growth, there may be a possible fifth stage, known as the "Penetration Stage," where relationships begin to break down, which can ultimately lead to the dissolution of the relationship.

A key issue with SPT is its over simplicity and lack of universal applicability to all relationships. Therefore, several theorists have developed and expanded it by considering partner responses (e.g. Intimacy Theory) and reward to cost ratios (Hatfield et al., 1979; Walster et al., 1978).

Filter and Stimulus-Value-Role Theory

According to Filter Theory (Kerckhoff & Davis, 1962), different filters come into play at different stages of romantic relationships. Successful progression is dependent on clearing these filter "hurdles" representing the shifting needs and priorities of individuals as relationships progress. The stages of filtering are as follows:

1. Screening for *social attributes* (e.g. religion, education).
2. Assessment of similarity of *attitudes and values*.
3. Assessment of *complementary/compatible traits/behaviors*.

While filter theory is theoretically interesting, subsequent research has not provided much support for this model of relationship development. It provides a general idea of people narrowing down potential relationship partners via principles of compatibility and complementarity, however, the model is simplistic and reductionist. Murstein (1977) subsequently introduced the Stimulus-Value-Role (SVR) theory, which is more widely used (e.g. Sprecher & Metts, 1999; Regan, 2008). SVR is a three-stage model, detailed as follows (Murstein, 1970):

1. *Stimulus*—focuses on external characteristics (e.g. physical attraction and behavior).
2. *Value*—analyses of similarity of attitudes, interests, beliefs, and needs.
3. *Role*—assessment of roles, which are expectations about how each partner will function within the relationship.

Both Kerckhoff and Davis's (1962) and Murstein's (1977) models align with early similarity theories, which suggest potential partners are determined by external characteristics such as age, socioeconomic status, race, religion, or physical attraction. Further, they suggest internal characteristics (e.g. values and attitudes) are also important. However, they differ in the third stage; Kerckhoff and Davis (1962) focus on need complementarity and Murstein (1977) discusses role fit, namely, what roles partners will assume in the relationship.

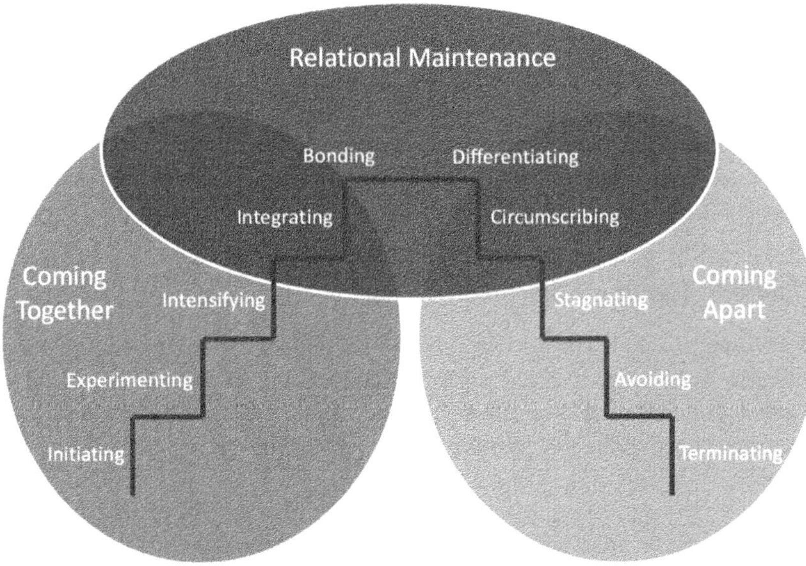

FIGURE 8.2 Knapp's Relational Development Model

Knapp's Relational Development Model (RDM) and Levinger's ABC Model

Knapp contended that romantic couples typically go through five stages of relationship development (Knapp & Vangelisti, 2005): initiation, experimentation, intensifying, integration, and bonding, referred to collectively as the 'Coming Together' phase. Potentially followed by the five phases of relationship dissolution: differentiating, circumscribing, stagnation, avoidance, and termination, known collectively as the 'Coming Apart' phase (Figure 8.2). Levinger (1983) offered a similar, but less refined model, with five stages covering both the growth and decline of a relationship: acquaintance, buildup, continuation, deterioration, and ending.

Stages of RDM and ABC models are as follows:

1. *Initiating stage*—aligns with Levinger's "acquaintance" stage and "orientation" stage of Altman's social penetration model. People exchange superficial information and develop an awareness of the potential partner. Physical appearance and external attributes are important at this stage of pursuing a romantic relationship.
2. *Experimenting stage*—aligns with Levinger's "build-up" stage and Altman's "exploratory affect" stage. Partners engage in small talk to discover commonalities, aiming to reduce uncertainty about one another.
3. *Intensifying stage*—aligns with Levinger's "continuation" stage. Partners build on common ground and begin to share more private information. Partners

may also engage in "secret tests" (Baxter & Wilmot, 1984) to test their potential partner's behavior and personality in certain situations and contexts.
4. *Integration stage*—partners begin to merge aspects of their lives (e.g. introducing friends to partners). The status of "couple" is confirmed by using the "we/us" pronoun, which creates an interdependent relational identity (Knapp & Vangelisti, 2009; Shea & Pearson, 1986). Often, a sexual relationship and disclosure of deeper secrets is involved here. Levinger's model does not distinguish this from the "continuation" stage.
5. *Bonding stage*—partners will achieve a unitary status (e.g. marriage, having children, etc.). Levinger's ABC model does not distinguish this from the "continuation" stage.

Knapp's model also has a series of five "Coming Apart" stages: differentiating, circumscribing, stagnating, avoiding, and finally terminating. Interestingly, Levinger does not provide specific distinctions; the first four stages from Knapp in Levinger's model are simply referred to as the "deterioration" stage. Further, one must appreciate that stage models cannot accurately describe all relationships. These models act as a guide, as each will progress uniquely due to the variance in the partner, personality, and communication.

Online Dating vs Offline Dating: Should We be Searching for "The One"?

Over the last decade, online dating has become a normal and accepted method for relationship initiation. While initially online dating was seen as taboo and was associated with several stigmas (Sritharan et al., 2010), more recently, it has seen a significant decrease in the stigma historically associated with finding a partner online (Sritharan et al., 2010) and become a part of mainstream culture. According to Pew Internet (2016), 15% of U.S. adults have used an online dating site or mobile app, with the largest growth (and demographic) being those aged 18–24 years (27% of whom have tried online dating, compared to only 10% two years earlier). According to eHarmony (2017), 20% of committed relationships began online.

The notion of finding "the one," or that one should be seeking a marital relationship has largely been fantasized across media: from books to film, and of course, online dating website mission statements (e.g. Match.com, "to help people find love"; or eHarmony.com, "We at eHarmony want you to find love and romance and to make it last"). While this has a positive sentiment, there is an argument for questioning this concept of finding "the one," whom in theory we spend the rest of our lives with. Perhaps the question of "why must we only be with one person?" could be asked to question this assumption, as online dating provides the ideal environment for meeting large amounts of people across the world instantly. Within previous generations, it was usual to marry and have children early. However, there is scope for the argument that due to the longer lifespans we have, as well as the ability to move reasonably freely across the world, we in fact could spend elongated periods of our lives with different people, rather than this idealized "one." Further, if we consider the rapid developments in creating robots for friends/partnership/sex (e.g. Kanda et al., 2004; Breazeal et al., 2004; Levy, 2009; Stenzel et al., 2012), perhaps we should be asking: "do we need offline human companionship if our needs can be fulfilled without it?"

Key Differences Between Online and Offline Dating

Commodification, Swiping, and Commitment

By nature, online dating provides a platform where users are able to view and sift through a vast number of potential partners, which has affected the way in which relationships formulate and develop (Paul, 2014). Paul (2014) suggests that having such a variety of options for partners causes individuals to lack commitment as they are aware of other potential partners should one not work out. He therefore suggests this is why those who are engaged with online dating are more likely to remain in non-marital relationships in comparison to those who meet partners offline. Further, this highlights the idea that people are seemingly more replaceable, and are essentially commoditized, when using online dating (Ceraolo, 2016). With this in mind, the commodification of people in online dating allows other online daters to view each other as objects to "swipe left or right on." The wealth of alternatives could lead to relationships beginning in a state of heightened uncertainty, leading to problems with relationship progression. Technology also provides additional information about other potential partners, which changes the way in which we enter relationships and maintain these relationships. For many relationships, the early stages are now characterized by knowing a relatively large amount of information about each other either through dating profile information or "stalking" of social media profiles. This can occur even before any contact has been made due to enough information being displayed on the individual's dating profiles in order to find their profiles elsewhere. While this may be beneficial in that it will reduce uncertainty, additional but partial (and self-managed) information may also create uncertainty and doubt. Moreover, it may be that by skipping toward deeper understanding without conscious disclosure, we remove the opportunity for people to demonstrate trust and increasing intimacy through self-disclosure.

Inside out online dating?

Finkel and colleagues (2012) conducted focus groups in order to uncover the fundamental differences between online and offline dating. They argue that online dating alters two significant processes:

1. *Compatibility matching process*—traditionally, couples have relied on friends and family to assist with the match-making process, whereas this is now being undertaken by automated systems computed by matching algorithms.
2. *Romantic acquaintance process*—first impressions nowadays are based on a broad range of information before meeting in person, whereas, traditionally, these first impressions were based upon a face-to-face encounter only.

Early studies (e.g. Rosen et al., 2008; Whitty, 2007) have revealed that relationships formed online take a different path from those formed offline. Online dating increases the initial availability of information and removes the initial need for a face-to-face meeting to build impressions. Due to the nature of social media, users are often able to research further about the prospective partner outside of the dating website (e.g. on Facebook) (Hancock & Toma, 2009). Further, some dating sites allow profiles to be linked with the user's social media pages (e.g. Tinder can be linked with Spotify and Instagram). With vast amounts of information instantly available, it is possible to learn a lot about another person without actually interacting with them. The timing of self-disclosure is crucial in offline dating; however, online dating platforms are designed to modify and shape the behavior of users by imposing self-disclosure as soon as possible. Further, the increased availability of information has affected the process of information-seeking and uncertainty reduction (e.g. Afifi & Lucas, 2008; Afifi & Weiner, 2004). Fox (2016) describe the process of scoping out information without the prospective partner's knowledge and without leaving traces as "creeping." Online dating, therefore, accelerates the filtering process during the initial states of relational escalation (e.g. Kerckhoff & Davis, 1962; Duck, 1977).

Romantic relationships might take months to develop in an offline setting; in contrast, it can only take weeks or even days to form a close relationship online (Rosen et al., 2008). The reason for such intimacy and in-depth self-disclosure in early online correspondence is due to a combination of factors, including uncertainty reduction strategies (Tidwell & Walther, 2002), changes in self-focus and concern for self-presentation when typing (Joinson, 2001), and the cycle of hyper-personal interaction (Walther, 1996). This general disinhibition (Joinson, 1998) also extends to sexual disclosure (Yang & Chiou, 2010), which contrasts with offline relationships, where sexual disclosure is only encountered once a certain level of intimacy is developed. This suggests that some online relationships develop almost in reverse to that of offline dating—effectively beginning from the innermost core of Altman's model.

Online Dating Preferences

Typically, online dating begins with the users specifying a small amount of information (e.g. gender, age range, and location) (Diaz et al., 2010), which will return a list of results or matches, where users can explore a profile more fully and decide whether to engage with the other user. Older forms of online dating (e.g. PlentyOfFish, Match.com) place more emphasis on profile biographies, which calls for spending more time to read and examine prospective partners' profiles. However, there has been a shift toward instant gratification and the ability to sift through vast quantities of profiles quickly, as seen on Tinder, for example (Tyson et al., 2016).

In a series of papers, Hitsch and colleagues (2005, 2006, 2010a, 2010b) utilized detailed information on the behaviors of online dating service users (e.g. search behavior, profile views, partner attributes, email logs) in order to infer their preferences for romantic partners. Their work was guided by fundamental questions which have been raised repeatedly in a long history of research on mate preferences, spanning a diverse array of fields including economics, sociology, psychology, anthropology, and evolutionary biology (see, e.g., Buss, 1995; Etcoff, 1999; Finkel & Baumeister, 2010). It is unclear as to whether users are most attracted to those with similar attributes to their own—known as "horizontal" attributes, or whether there is a consensus among people regarding the characteristics that are desirable—vertical attributes (Kalmijn, 1998). Increasingly, it has become difficult to distinguish between horizontal and vertical attributes (Hitsch et al., 2010b). For example, correlations in partners' intelligence levels could be caused by a preference for similar intelligence, or conversely, this could be a result of users seeking a more intelligent partner over a less intelligent one.

Kreager and colleagues (2014) found several gender differences regarding online dating preferences based on their study with ~12,000 online daters. They found that men prefer younger women, and women preferred older men (Kreager et al., 2014; Xia et al., 2014). Further, men prefer short biographies while women preferred longer profiles for men. This aligns with the findings of Tyson and colleagues (2016), on Tinder, where it was found that profiles with biographies do indeed receive more matches for both men and women (however, interestingly, this effect is more pronounced on women's profiles). It was also found that the most desirable men for women are "white, athletic or thin, tall, well educated, drinkers, and nonsmokers" (Kreager et al., 2014, pp. 397). Surprisingly, if men have a postgraduate degree, this is seen as a desirable attribute, however, women with postgraduate degrees are not seen as attractive by men with similar education levels (Kreager et al., 2014). Conversely, a Chinese study (Xia et al., 2014) found that men's selection of women regarding education was similar to that of random selection, whereas, women are more likely to select those with higher education, which implies potential cultural differences relating to what is viewed as desirable in partners.

The Role of Physical Attraction

Offline relationships often begin with attraction based on external attributes (e.g. physical appearance) (Huston & Levinger, 1978), then progress into an attachment based on the compatibility of other attributes (e.g. values and beliefs). In contrast, online dating first impressions are grounded on how people express themselves through their self-constructed descriptions (Ellison et al., 2006). Self-presentation is more malleable and controllable online—people can present themselves freely, without initial stereotypical preconceptions from an immediate face-to-face meeting (Kleck, 1968).

Physical attractiveness is still a key component of online dating, just as with offline dating. Offline, it has been comprehensively shown that attractive people are judged more positively and are seen as socially more competent, powerful, intelligent, and even healthier (e.g. Zebrowitz et al., 2002; Zebrowitz & Rhodes, 2004). Therefore, in theory, it would be logical for physical appearance to be less of the focus online, however, that is not necessarily the case. Whitty (2011) found that physical appearance exceeded many other attributes in terms of importance when selecting whom to contact. Further, she suggests that this unprecedented pool of potential romantic partners changes the dating landscape considerably and results in dating site users feeling that there will be no shortage of more attractive people available to "make a play for."

Perceptions of Photographs Online

Physical attractiveness in online dating profiles is primarily conveyed via photographs, which are usually displayed prominently on the profile. Humans are inherently programmed to recognize visual cues (e.g. faces) (Vuilleumier, 2000; Bar et al., 2006), and therefore the photograph is typically the first thing people notice when visiting profiles. This provides users with the ability to create first impressions about the profile owner's weight, skin color, eyes, and so on (Alley, 1988; Herman et al., 1986; Zebrowitz et al., 2002). Due to the importance that lies on these images, users therefore tend to choose photos in which they appear most attractive (Mikkola et al., 2008). Epstein (2007) states that online daters interpret the absence of photos negatively, and that male profiles without a photo draw 25% the response of those with photos, and women's profiles without photos draw 17% the response of those with photos. In the study of Tyson and colleagues (2016), specifically on Tinder, they found that the number of matches on a female profile increases by 37% when you increase the number of profile photos from one to three, and this effect is even higher on men's profiles. In the Chinese study of Xia and colleagues (2014), it was found that the more photos women have on their profiles, the more likely it is that they will receive messages from interested potential suitors.

Hancock and Toma (2009) investigated accuracy of online dating photographs; it was found that 33% of dating profile photographs were inaccurate from an independent judge's perspective. Photographs posted by women were likely to be less accurate than men's (e.g. the photograph is old, digitally manipulated). Interestingly, many studies (e.g. Ellison et al., 2006; Toma et al., 2008; Hancock &

Toma, 2009) show that online daters experience a tension between boosting attractiveness and presenting a photograph that is not deemed deceptive should they meet face to face. Hancock and Toma (2009) found that less attractive online daters were more likely to enhance photographs in order to increase chances of initial contact.

Fiore and colleagues (2008) discovered that physical attractiveness ratings of profile photographs strongly predicted the overall attractiveness rating of the profile, and therefore the likelihood that a user would initiate contact. The attractiveness ratings of photos outperformed other predictive variables such as measures of extraversion, authenticity, and trustworthiness, based on other parts of the profile. Kocsor and colleagues (2011) found that while photographs of attractive faces were rated highly by both males and females, males showed a preference for photographs of female faces that resembled their own, and the opposite was found for female users. Research shows men ascribe a higher value to physical attractiveness (Buss 1989; Buss & Schmitt, 1993; Eastwick & Finkel, 2008; Fisman et al., 2006; Kurzban & Weeden, 2005; Regan, 2000). This automatic evaluation bias, known as the "halo effect," was only found to be true for men judging women. Essentially this is the notion of "what is beautiful is good" (Mierke et al., 2011). Identical findings have long been present within the offline interpersonal attraction literature (e.g. Kaplan, 1978; Lucker et al., 1981). Mierke and colleagues (2011) further discussed the halo effect, and found that this is particularly linked with physical attractiveness, however, other traits such as intellect also contribute to the halo effect. Further, Mierke and colleagues (2011) noted cultural differences with attributes that are considered "good"; they found individualist cultures saw attributes like assertiveness and dominance as particularly positive, whereas, in collectivist cultures, the most positive traits were linked with friendliness and trust.

Similarities Attract?

Many researchers have tested the "similarity-attraction" hypothesis suggesting that people are most attracted to individuals who are similar to themselves (e.g. Burleson & Denton, 1992; Byrne et al., 1966; Morry, 2005; Selfhout et al., 2009; McPherson et al., 2001). These studies have consistently shown that similarity characterizes many interpersonal connections, ranging from friendship to romantic involvement (McPherson et al., 2001). These similarities include attitudes (Newcomb, 1958), demographics (e.g. education, ethnicity) (Buss, 1986), socio-economic status (Byrne et al., 1966), and occupation (Bond et al., 1968).

Wetzel and Insko (1982) had introduced a distinction between one's ideal self and one's actual self. They hypothesize that when these components are separated, similarity to the ideal self can be seen to exert a major influence on attraction, and similarity to the actual self only a minor influence. Their series of experiments indicated a consistent main effect for ideal similarity on attraction and no consistent main effect for similarity to the self. A theoretical account of why attraction is driven by similarity to the ideal self is straightforward, in that the ideal self is the valued or desired state of affairs (Herbst et al., 2003). Kreager and colleagues (2014) found similar results, as online daters regarded as desirable would message other desirable users, which implies some support for homophily. Aligning with the actual/ideal self, the study of Kreager and colleagues (2014) supports the notion of online daters seeking to find partners more desirable than themselves. Heine and colleagues (2009) found that there are cultural differences in similarity-attraction, and that these differences are mediated by self-esteem, that is, those who hold positive self-views are more likely to be attracted to similar individuals.

One needs to acknowledge that these studies need to be interpreted with the understanding that they took place in a well-controlled environment with a lack of ecological validity, and therefore, the applicability outside of this environment may not be as straightforward (Luo & Zhang, 2009). Despite this, Fiore and Donath (2005) performed an analysis involving 65,000 users and showed that users sought people like themselves much more often than chance would predict, which provides corroboration of the similarity-attraction principle.

Although there is a popular conception that "opposites attract," Berscheid and Reis (1998) and Felmlee (1998) argue that evidence favors the similarity-attraction principle over the opposite-attraction principle. While dissimilar qualities are often intriguing or appealing to begin with, this does not often lead to long-lasting relationships (Felmlee, 1998).

Role of Technology: Algorithmic Match-Making

Nayak and colleagues (2010) report that the process of finding potential matches online without additional support from the system is largely unsuccessful; this has become an important element of online dating sites (Cai et al., 2011). Recommendation systems are widely used in online environments (e.g. retailers), and these types of algorithms have been applied in online dating (e.g. Brozovsky & Petricek, 2007). However, many have recognized a distinct difference between product recommendation algorithms and online dating algorithms. Within online dating, the match-making operates in both directions, hence the concept of an active user (buyer) and a passive item (product) is inapplicable (Tu et al., 2014).

Approaches to recommendation systems are often either:

1. *Content-based*—past preferences are used to recommend new products/people.
2. *Collaborative filtering methods*—recommendations are based on accumulated preferences from a set of similar users (e.g. user A is similar to B, and user B has liked user Y, therefore, user A might also like Y).

Some work has shown that basing matches on implicit preferences generates better recommendations than explicit preferences (Akehurst et al., 2011), or the use of rule-based recommendations learning from profiles and interactions (Kim et al., 2010). Diaz and colleagues (2010) further developed an approach for learning based on a ranking function that maximizes the number of positive interactions between online daters. In their research, Tu and colleagues (2014) found significant improvements when utilizing a two-side matching market framework, as this considers both sides' preferences in regard to partners (unlike traditional recommendation systems of buyer and product). Further, Dai and colleagues (2014) take an entirely different approach and challenge these types of recommendation systems for two reasons:

1. They focus too heavily on "hot" or popular users
2. New users are at a disadvantage due to lack of clout/popularity on the website

Dai and colleagues (2014), therefore, proposed a hybrid recommendation system, which addresses the issues with older types of recommendation systems (e.g. content-based or collaborative filtering) by giving higher priority to fresh users.

To Message or Not to Message?

In terms of initial contact, 77% of initial contacts came from men in comparison to only 23% starting from women (Fiore et al., 2010). These findings align with previous conclusions from the offline dating literature, that men take a more active approach, whereas women tend to take a more passive and reactive role (Clark et al., 1999). Interestingly, men of all ages are equally contacted, however, younger women are contacted more frequently than older females (Fiore et al., 2010). Further, users contacted those of the same ethnicity more frequently than chance would predict.

Fiore and colleagues (2010) found correlations between personality traits, such as neuroticism and caution, and the frequency at which people initiate contact with others. Their findings suggest that those most concerned about who they date may use frequent contact initiation as a strategy for evaluating a larger pool of prospective partners before progressing a relationship further. Perhaps unsurprisingly, popular men and women tended not to initiate contact as frequently as less popular people, since potential partners frequently presented themselves to them, which aligns with the findings of Kreager and colleagues (2014). Self-presentation strategies are just as important online as they are offline, as this information is used to decide whether to pursue a relationship or not (Derlega et al., 1987). When interacting with strangers, people tend to exaggerate positive attributes (Schlenker & Pontari, 2000), and online daters might consider this necessary if they perceive other users do the same in order to maintain equal footing with competitors. Hancock and colleagues (2007) found that minor exaggerations (e.g. height, weight, and age) are common on online profiles.

Deceptive Messaging

Offline deception has been shown to carry significant cognitive burden due to the need to fabricate believable information (Toma et al., 2008). However, online dating has arguably mitigated this cognitive burden of deception as there is the added luxury of time to construct a believable self-presentation. Research has shown that lies and deception online can be detected through changes in the way in which users write (Hancock & Toma, 2009). This suggests that users may seek "warranted" information that is difficult to fake. For instance, Tyson and colleagues (2016) found that due to women being more concerned about deception online, the more profile photos the male's profile has, the more comfortable she will be pursuing them should she choose to. People are aware of the need to present one's true self to others, especially when pursuing significant relationships, since being understood by a partner is key to feelings of intimacy (Reis & Shaver, 1988). This tension between legitimacy and impression management is inherent in many aspects of self-disclosure and indeed social interaction generally. In making decisions about what and when to self-disclose, individuals often struggle to reconcile opposing needs such as openness and autonomy (Greene et al., 2006).

Content of First Messages

Schöndienst and Dang-Xuan (2011) studied the linguistic content of 167,276 initial contact messages, and concluded that the linguistic properties of an initial message influence a recipient's decision to respond. These effects are most likely due to subconscious evaluation processes by the recipient, rather than a systematic linguistic analysis. Their findings suggest that the most successful initial contacts are those which contain a significant amount of self-disclosure and avoid showing negative attributes (e.g. depressive symptoms), and instead focus attention on the recipient. Further, the data science team at OKCupid conducted a similar study and found there was a decreased response when "netspeak" (e.g. "ur") or physical compliments (e.g. "sexy," "hot") were used. The chances of a response were increased when a compliment was directed toward profile content, or via the use of a non-conventional greeting (e.g. "how's it going?"). There is some evidence (e.g. Frisby et al., 2011) that women can "afford" to be more flirtatious in their conversations with potential partners without decreasing their chances of a response. Men are, in fact, more likely to respond to initial messages that contain words referring to sexual processes. However, this would jeopardize the likelihood of a women replying if this is referred to in any response they send (Schöndienst & Dang-Xuan, 2011).

Initial Contact Response Patterns

Online dating users vary widely in how often their first contact messages are responded to. Fiore and colleagues (2010) reported an average response rate of 26% from men when women initiated contact, compared to a 16% response rate when a man sent a first contact message to a woman. It has been shown that women are more selective in their communications (e.g. Hitsch et al., 2010b), however, older women are more likely to reply to initiating emails, possibly to compensate for being contacted less often. Kreager and colleagues (2014) found that individuals who receive a high number of incoming messages are more selective in their response patterns, perhaps because they have more choice in the first place. Conversely, those who send a high number of outgoing messages have much less choice in terms of incoming contacts, which implies that they are lowering their standards of desirability in order to maximize response rates. For men contacting women, the interaction between his popularity and her popularity was associated with a higher chance of receiving a reply; implying that a reply is more likely when the two people have similar levels of popularity (Fiore, 2004). Surprisingly, the more specific criteria a person has for an ideal partner on their profile, the more likely they were to respond—perhaps because users not fitting the requirements had already been discouraged from contacting them (Fiore, 2004).

Physical attractiveness plays a significant role in influencing whom online daters choose to contact. Unsurprisingly, it plays an equally significant role in a recipient's decision to reply to an initial message (Schöndienst and Dang-Xuan, 2011). Schöndienst and Dang-Xuan (2011) found that more attractive women are less likely to respond to messages, and more attractive men are more likely to respond. This leads to a slightly counter-intuitive conclusion that women have better chances with more attractive men. They hypothesize the likely reason for this is that these men receive fewer messages overall, as women may not dare to contact them for fear of rejection.

Transitions from Online to Offline Relationships

Regarding the progression of most online relationships, Whitty (2007) found that over half (approximately 57%) of online dating site users who had arranged to meet face to face with a prospective partner had done so within one or two weeks of their initial contact with one another. A further 10% of users met their date offline within one month. Ramirez and colleagues (2016) and Ramirez and Zhang (2007) suggest that online daters could benefit from meeting sooner rather than later, as they believe the longer communication remains online, the harder it would be for prospective partners to accept discrepancies from the actual and idealized construct of one another. This aligns with previous work (e.g. Walther et al., 2001), showing computer-mediated communication can increase intimacy and social attraction, however, this can result in the idealization of prospective partners, which can have detrimental effects on the relationship (Ramirez & Zhang, 2007). However, online daters report that a fear of rejection often acts as a barrier to transitions from online to offline contexts, because of users' acute awareness that they may not live up to expectations (Lawson & Leck, 2006).

At the first face-to-face meeting, Whitty (2007) reports that online daters are most concerned with what their date looks like and how they behave. Over 66% of surveyed daters reported that they had used an initial offline meeting as a further filtering mechanism, weighing up how closely an individual matches their online profile and using this assessment to make decisions about whether to pursue a relationship further. Whitty (2011) reveals that, for safety reasons, a first face-to-face meeting often takes place in a public space and is scheduled for a restricted amount of time (so that individuals feel less vulnerable and have an opportunity to terminate the date if the interaction does not go according to their expectations). Whitty (2011) also reports that some internet daters report that their first offline interactions often feel less comfortable than conventional first dates, where there has already been some offline interaction, because of the increased need to verify a person's resemblance to their online self, rather than to discover new information about them.

Ongoing Relationships and Technology

While prolonged technologically mediated communication may pose a threat to new relationships, there is some evidence that integrating technology into an existing relationship may be beneficial. For instance, Jiang and Hancock (2013) compared the communication strategies of people in long distance and those in geographically close relationships. Jiang and Hancock (2013) found evidence that long distance partners engage in more self-disclosure, and increased idealization of their partner, compared to those geographically close. Interestingly, there was a relationship between long distance partners' use of cue-reduced communication channels and increased intimacy (self-disclosure), which in turn led to increased idealization (when using an asynchronous channel). At the same time, there is also evidence that *some* partially synchronous communication modes (e.g. Snapchat) are being used as playful methods to enhance bonding amongst people who have existing face-to-face connections (Piwek & Joinson, 2016).

However, there are dangers to the introduction of technology into existing relationships that need to be balanced against potential gains in intimacy. Heightened idealization might lead to the raising up of existing partners, but that also means that people are more likely to be disappointed by reality. Joinson and colleagues (2011) discuss the dangers of "digital crowding" and "too much information" in relationships, arguing that, "non-disclosure, secrecy and deceit are also key components of successful relationships . . . over-disclosure can be as detrimental . . . as unwillingness to disclose" (p. 38). Similarly, Norton and colleagues (2007) report that although knowing more about a partner met via online dating led to an increased *expectation* of liking them, this rarely translated to *actually* liking them when the partners met for the first time. Increasingly technology is also reducing the scope to create space for face-saving stories within relationships. For instance, read receipts in phone-based messages (e.g. iMessage, WhatsApp) remove the ability for a recipient to claim that they did not "see" a message, leading to an increased pressure to respond immediately. Otherwise, the sender is left in a position where they are aware that a message has been seen, but not responded to. This has led to a range of coping strategies amongst users—for instance, setting a default high level of preview so that the jist of the message can be understood without needing to open it immediately.

Furthermore, Gernsbacher (1990) discusses how word use will stimulate the activation of multiple meanings as soon as they are heard or read, and this process is normal to the comprehension of language exchange. This can be applied to the context of partners speaking to one another. Should someone misinterpret information, in person this can be easily discussed/rectified immediately, something that might be interrupted once technological mediation is introduced.

Human–Robot Relationships, Escapism and Fantasy

It is natural to assume that when meeting someone online and things were going seemingly well, that the partners would want to meet offline. However, there is scope to ask whether this is always necessary. With the ways in which relationships and technology are progressing, is it reasonable to pose the question: "do we need offline relationships?" If we consider that humans by nature are dreamers, people use books, TV, film and even online gaming worlds as a form of escapism and fantasy (e.g. Li et al., 2011; Beranuy et al., 2013). While within an online game there is the ability to create your own persona and character as opposed to books and films where the scripts are laid out for the audience, these are both forms of escapism and indulgence into another world or life. A key issue mentioned previously is the fear that online daters over-idealize other users, and therefore, meeting offline can lead to disappointment, and therefore we can ask—is it necessary to create an offline relationship? With the development of augmented reality (AR) and virtual reality (VR), it is also reasonable to consider how AR/VR will affect human relationships, and whether there will be a lesser necessity for offline relationships due to the ability to create and develop idealized partners online, which have the potential to be highly realistic. This could be an initial middle-ground between human–robot relationships and traditional human–human relationships as it currently stands.

Further, with an offline relationship, the relationship is likely to develop to the point where partners integrate into each other's lives, which may not be appealing to some users for a variety of reasons (e.g. heavy work–life balance). Hence, we question the necessity of meeting offline, as the internet allows users to mask themselves and build their persona, which comes back to the concept of using forms of online dating or networking online as a means of escapism and fantasy chasing.

If there is a sustainable relationship/companionship online, the offline component may not be necessary with certain types of online relationship. There are websites designed for specific needs; for example, "Mukbang," which is a stream of users eating for the community to watch, and its focus was on the companionship as opposed to the consumption of food (Cheng, 2016). This could be an example of the types of companionship that do not require an offline relationship. Further, there are websites that can allow people to play to personas or indulge in fantasies, which may not translate offline. This is an example of where an offline relationship would not be necessary as this play to a fantasy is enough for the individual's satisfaction. Further, as the potential of venturing toward AR/VR being integrated into everyday lives continues to reiterate, there is potential that offline components of relationships could become less necessary. This highlights the progression and integration of technology within human life, and research developing AI and humanoid robots as friends and romantic partners (e.g. Kanda et al., 2004; Breazeal et al., 2004; Levy, 2009; Stenzel et al., 2012; Lee, 2017) is potentially an example where an online companionship is sustainable without the offline relationship due to the offline physicality of relationships being dealt with already. This views the physical and psychological/emotional needs as separate components of a relationship. However, this poses the question of whether, and when, AI and robotics will be advanced enough to the point where human–human interaction is not strictly necessary, which implies that the physical and psychology/emotional components of relationships can be viewed together again as human–robot relationships could fulfil all needs like traditional human–human relationships.

Relationship Endings

Recalling Knapp's RDM, we understand the ending of a relationship as not just a single event; it is a process that includes a variety of emotions and changes in behavior and communication. Baxter (1982) performed a cluster analysis and found there are four distinct groups of relationship disengagement:

1. *Withdrawal and avoidance*—an individual cuts off all contact.
2. *Manipulation*—for example, a third party expressing the news.
3. *Positive tone*—an individual attempting to avoid hard feelings by offering a positive spin.
4. *Open expression*—an individual being open and honest regarding breaking up.

Rosenfeld and Thomas (2012) found that couples meeting online are just as likely to have success in their relationship as those who meet offline (in terms of marriage and break-up rates). However, interestingly, Paul (2014) found the opposite effect, where those who met online were more likely to remain in non-marital relationships, and were more likely to break-up in comparison to those who met their significant other offline. Online dating has impacted the ways in which people disengage from relationships (e.g. Sprecher et al., 2010). Those who engage in online communication, particularly for online daters yet to meet offline, or those who rely on online platforms for distant communication, tend to use online platforms to communicate the end of a relationship. Madden and Lenhart (2006) reported that approximately 10% of all single adults have broken up with a partner using online communication, and teenagers are even more likely to terminate relationships online (Lenhart et al., 2001). Hardey (2002) found that withdrawal without explanation from email exchange is also common amongst online daters, and is neither considered rude nor inappropriate in this context—a phenomenon now termed "ghosting" in the era of online dating. Further, while technology can be used to maintain a relationship (e.g. offering closer contact if people are in a long-distance relationship), conversely, technology and computer-mediated communication can also be used to increase distance via the use of "socially facilitated lies" (e.g. an individual losing contact details/number), as a justification for the "withdrawal and avoidance" strategy for relationship disengagement.

Some strategies for breaking up are considered more compassionate or sympathetic than others, Sprecher and colleagues (2010) collected survey participants' subjective ratings for how compassionate they perceived different disengagement strategies to be, including the use of online communication. They found that the strategy of breaking up online (e.g. email or instant messaging) was tantamount to adopting an "avoidance strategy," and was considered to be very low in terms of its compassion rating, particularly when compared to more "open" and "positive tone" approaches. However, Merkle and Richardson (2000) contend that where relationships have yet to transition to offline, email notices are less painful, because such relationships have not necessitated considerable investments from those involved, and because opportunities to find another relationship are still prominent.

Geser (2007) suggests that email is frequently used in the abrupt ending of *online* dating relationships because it allows the sender to avoid witnessing the uncomfortable reactions of the recipient. Interestingly, the indirectness of online rejections acts as a motivating force for many people to engage in online dating in the first place, as it avoids the significant feelings of anxiety associated with offline, face-to-face rejections (Valkenburg & Peter, 2007; Blackhart et al., 2014). Blackhart and colleagues (2014) reported that the more sensitive someone is to rejection, the more likely they were to be an online dating website user. It has been suggested that this is due to rejection sensitivity's positive correlation to neuroticism, where those with higher levels of neuroticism are more likely to engage with chatrooms and other social services online as this allows users to express their authentic self.

However, when a relationship has been longer established, Cody (1982) found that the intimacy level of a relationship was linked to strategy selection. More "positive tone" strategies were employed when partners have been in a longer-term intimate relationship with significant integration of social lives (e.g. overlaps in social networks) (Banks et al., 1987; Krahl & Wheeless, 1997). The other option for certain couples would be for the relationship to regress into friendship, and therefore, partners have a motivation to behave compassionately when ending the relationship (Lee & Bruckman, 2007).

Conclusion

Throughout this chapter, we have argued that there are several ways in which technology has impacted, shaped, and augmented the ways in which relationships start, progress, are maintained and end. While technology has vastly increased the volume of potential partners available to an individual, it has also transformed the pace and order in which a relationship develops, and, potentially, the way in which humans go about choosing a suitable partner. The increased integration of technology into the maintenance of existing relationships also poses new questions about whether or not geographically close partners should use technology to communicate. Additionally, there may be scope for new technologies to be developed that are specifically designed to improve existing relationships—rather than requiring that people appropriate technologies designed for the workplace to connect with a wider network—or for one-to-many communication. We have also raised the possibility that the increasing development of technology may begin to change our existing attitudes both to monogamy and to human–robot relations. Certainly, relationships (and love) are typically human in that they are messy, difficult, and sometimes require hard work—and increasing intimacy requires that we make ourselves vulnerable to others. We perhaps should not be surprised if some people use technology to "opt out" of some of that.

In terms of the networked self, the ways in which the individual is connected online, whether that is via dating websites, or just social media in general, these technologies are changing, and continue to change and adapt the ways we connect with one another. We can understand that the way we increase intimacy and progress romantic relationships has reversed from before we had these platforms available. The online environment allows for easier faceting of identity online, as individuals can find websites dedicated to specific interests (e.g. Mukbang profiles), which reconfirms this networked self and faceted identity online. This feeds heavily into our romantic relationships, and the ways we find others, as this increased openness from systems shaping behavior allow us to connect deeply even before we meet offline—if we ever do.

Acknowledgments

This work was part funded by the Centre for Research and Evidence on Security Threats (ESRC ES/N009614/1).

References

Afifi, W. A., & Lucas, A. A. (2008). Information seeking in initial stages of relational development. In S. Sprecher, A. Wenzel, & J. Harvey (Eds.), *Handbook of relationship initiation* (pp. 197–215). Abingdon: Routledge.

Afifi, W. A., & Weiner, J. L. (2004). Toward a theory of motivated information management. *Communication Theory*, 14(2), 167–190.

Akehurst, J., Koprinska, I., Yacef, K., Pizzato, L., Kay, J., & Rej, T. (2011). CCR: A content-collaborative reciprocal recommender for online dating. *Proceedings of the twenty-second international joint conference on artificial intelligence*. Vol. 3 (pp. 2199–2204). Palo Alto, CA: AAAI Press.

Alley, T. R. (Ed.). (1988). *Social and applied aspects of perceiving faces*. Hillsdale, NJ: Erlbaum.

Altman, I., & Taylor, D. (1973). *Social penetration: The development of interpersonal relationships*. New York: Holt.

Banks, S. P., Altendorf, D. M., Greene, J. O., & Cody, M. J. (1987). An examination of relationship disengagement: Perceptions, breakup strategies and outcomes. *Western Journal of Communication* (includes Communication Reports), 51(1), 19–41.

Bar, M., Neta, M., & Linz, H. (2006). Very first impressions. *Emotion*, 6(2), 269.

Baxter, L. A. (1982). Strategies for ending relationships: Two studies. *Western Journal of Communication* (includes Communication Reports), 46(3), 223–241.

Baxter, L. A., & Wilmot, W. W. (1984). Secret tests. *Human Communication Research*, 11(2), 171–201.

Beranuy, M., Carbonell, X., & Griffiths, M. D. (2013). A qualitative analysis of online gaming addicts in treatment. *International Journal of Mental Health and Addiction*, 11(2), 149–161.

Berscheid, E., & Reis, H. T. (1998). Attraction and close relationships. In D. T. Gilbert, S. T. Fiske, & G. Lindzey (Eds.), *The handbook of social psychology*, vol. 2 (pp. 193–281). Boston: McGraw-Hill.

Blackhart, G. C., Fitzpatrick, J., & Williamson, J. (2014). Dispositional factors predicting use of online dating sites and behaviours related to online dating. *Computer in Human Behaviour*, 33, 113–118.

Bond, M., Byrne, D., & Diamond, M. J. (1968). Effect of occupational prestige and attitude similarity on attraction as a function of assumed similarity of attitude. *Psychological Reports*, 23(3f), 1167–1172.

Breazeal, C., Brooks, A., Gray, J., Hoffman, G., Kidd, C., Lee, H., . . ., & Mulanda, D. (2004). Humanoid robots as cooperative partners for people. *Int. Journal of Humanoid Robots*, 1(2), 1–34.

Brozovsky, L., & Petricek, V. (2007). Recommender system for online dating service. arXiv preprint cs/07030

Burleson, B. R., & Denton, W. H. (1992). A new look at similarity and attraction in marriage: Similarities in social-cognitive and communication skills as predictors of attraction and satisfaction. *Communications Monographs*, 59(3), 268–287.

Buss, D. (1989). Sex differences in human mate preferences: Evolutionary hypotheses tested in 37 cultures. *Behavioral and Brain Sciences*, 12, 1–49.

Buss, D. M. (1995). Evolutionary psychology: A new paradigm for psychological science. *Psychological Inquiry*, 6, 1–30.

Buss, D. M., & Barnes, M. (1986). Preferences in human mate selection. *Journal of Personality and Social Psychology*, 50(3), 559.

Buss, D. M., & Schmitt, D. P. (1993). Sexual strategies theory: An evolutionary perspective on human mating. *Psychological Review*, 100(2), 204.

Byrne, D., Clore Jr, G. L., & Worchel, P. (1966). Effect of economic similarity-dissimilarity on interpersonal attraction. *Journal of Personality and Social Psychology*, 4(2), 220.

Cai, X., Bain, M., Krzywicki, A., Wobcke, W., Kim, Y. S., Compton, P., & Mahidadia, A. (2011). Collaborative filtering for people to people recommendation in social networks. In P. Compton & A. Mahidadia (Eds.), *AI 2010: Advances in artificial intelligence* (pp. 476–485). Berlin: Springer.

Ceraolo, M. (2016). It's a match: How society's dependence on efficient technology affects the ways we date. *Scholar Commons*. https://scholarcommons.scu.edu/engl_176/12/

Cheng, E. (2016). Mukbang: The alternative manifestations of pleasure. http://mukbang socialeating.me/mukbang_through_psychoanalysis.

Christopher, F. S., & Cate, R. M. (1985). Premarital sexual pathways and relationship development. *Journal of Social and Personal Relationships*, 2(3), 271–288.

Clark, C. L., Shaver, P. R., & Abrahams, M. F. (1999). Strategic behaviors in romantic relationship initiation. *Personality and Social Psychology Bulletin*, 25(6), 709–722.

Cody, M. J. (1982). A typology of disengagement strategies and an examination of the role intimacy, reactions to inequity and relational problems play in strategy selection. *Communication Monographs*, 49(3), 148–170.

Dai, C., Jiang, W., Wang, Z., & Wu, Z. (2014) Personalized recommendation system for NetEase dating site. *Proceedings of the VLD Endowment* (pp. 1760–1765). www.vldb.org/pvldb/vol7/p1760-netease.pdf

Derlega, V., Winstead, B. A., Wong, P., & Greenspan, M. (1987). Self-disclosure and relationship development: An attributional analysis. In M. E. Roloff & G. R. Miller (Eds.), *Interpersonal Processes: New Directions in Communication Research* (pp. 172–187). Thousand Oaks, CA: Sage.

Diaz, F., Metzler, D., & Amer-Yahia, S. (2010). Relevance and ranking in online dating systems. *Proceeding of the 33rd SIGIR* (pp. 66–73). New York: ACM.

Duck, S. W. (1977). *Study of acquaintance*. Lanham, MD: Lexington Books.

Eastwick, P. W., & Finkel, E. J. (2008). Sex differences in mate preferences revisited: Do people know what they initially desire in a romantic partner? *Journal of Personality and Social Psychology*, 94(2), 245.

eHarmony (2017). 10 online dating statistics you should know. www.eharmony.com/online-dating-statistics/%0D

Ellison, N., Heino, R., & Gibbs, J. (2006). Managing impressions online: Self-presentation processes in the online dating environment. *Journal of Computer-Mediated Communication*, 11(2), 415–441.

Etcoff, N. (1999). *Survival of the prettiest: The science of beauty*. New York: Anchor/Doubleday.

Epstein, R. (2007). The truth about online dating. *Scientific American Mind*, 18(1), 28–35.

Felmlee, D. H. (1998). "Be careful what you wish for . . .": A quantitative and qualitative investigation of "fatal" attractions. *Personal Relationships*, 5(3), 235–253.

Finkel, E. J., & Baumeister, R. F. (2010). Attraction and rejection. In R. F. Baumeister & E. J. Finkel (Eds.), *Advanced social psychology: The state of the science* (pp. 419–459). New York: Oxford University Press.

Finkel, E. J., Eastwick, P. W., Karney, B. R., Reis, H. T., & Sprecher, S. (2012). Online dating a critical analysis from the perspective of psychological science. *Psychological Science in the Public Interest*, 13(1), 3–66.

Fiore, A. R. T. (2004). Romantic regressions: An analysis of behavior in online dating systems. Doctoral dissertation, Massachusetts Institute of Technology.

Fiore, A. T., & Donath, J. S. (2005). Homophily in online dating: When do you like someone like yourself? *CHI'05 extended abstracts on human factors in computing systems* (pp. 1371–1374). New York: ACM.

Fiore, A. T., Taylor, L. S., Mendelsohn, G. A., & Hearst, M. (2008). Assessing attractiveness in online dating profiles. *Proceedings of the SIGCHI conference on human factors in computing systems* (pp. 797–806). New York: ACM.

Fiore, A. T., Taylor, L. S., Zhong, X., Mendelsohn, G. A., & Cheshire, C. (2010). Who's right and who writes: People, profiles, contacts, and replies in online dating. *Proceedings of the 43rd Hawaii International Conference on System Sciences* (pp. 1–10). Los Alamitos, CA: IEEE.

Fisman, R., Iyengar, S. S., Kamenica, E., & Simonson, I. (2006). Gender differences in mate selection: Evidence from a speed dating experiment. *The Quarterly Journal of Economics*, 121(2), 673–697.

Fox, J. (2016). The dark side of social networking sites in romantic relationships. In G. Riva, B. K. Widerhold, & P. Cipresso (Eds.), *The psychology of social networking: Communication, presence, identity, and relationships in online communities* (pp. 78–89). Berlin: Versita.

Frisby, B. N., Dillow, M. R., Gaughan, S., & Nordlund, J. (2011). Flirtatious communication: An experimental examination of perceptions of social-sexual communication motivated by evolutionary forces. *Sex Roles*, 64(9–10), 682–694.

Gernsbacher, M. A. (1990). Language comprehension as structure building. *Psycoloquy*, 3(69). www.cogsci.ecs.soton.ac.uk/cgi/psyc/newpsy?3.69

Geser, H. (2007). Online search for offline partners. Matching platforms as tools of empowerment and retraditionalization. *SSOAR*. https://core.ac.uk/download/pdf/143790695.pdf

Greene, K., Derlega, V. J., & Mathews, A. (2006). Self-disclosure in personal relationships. In A. L. Vangelisti & D. Perlman (Eds), *The Cambridge handbook of personal relationships* (pp. 409–427). New York: Cambridge University Press.

Hancock, J. T., & Toma, C. L. (2009). Putting your best face forward: The accuracy of online dating photographs. *Journal of Communication*, 59(2), 367–386.

Hancock, J. T., Toma, C., & Ellison, N. (2007, April). The truth about lying in online dating profiles. *Proceedings of the SIGCHI conference on human factors in computing systems* (pp. 449–452). New York: ACM.

Hardey, M. (2002). Life beyond the screen: Embodiment and identity through the Internet. *The Sociological Review*, 50(4), 570–585.

Hatfield, E., Utne, M. K., & Traupmann, J. (1979). Equity theory and intimate relationships. In R. L. Burgess & T. L. Huston (Eds.), *Social exchange in developing relationships* (pp. 99–133). San Diego, CA: Academic Press.

Heine, S. J., Foster, J. A. B., & Spina, R. (2009). Do birds of a feather universally flock together? Cultural variation in the similarity-attraction effect. *Asian Journal of Social Psychology*, 12(4), 247–258.

Herbst, K. C., Gaertner, L., & Insko, C. A. (2003). My head says yes but my heart says no: Cognitive and affective attraction as a function of similarity to the ideal self. *Journal of Personality and Social Psychology*, 84(6), 1206.

Herman, C. P., Zanna, M. P., & Higgins, E. T. (1986). Physical appearance, stigma, and social behavior. *The Ontario symposium on personality and social psychology*, vol. 3 (pp. 7–21). Hillsdale, NJ: Lawrence Erlbaum.

Hitsch, G. J., Hortacsu, A., & Ariely, D. (2005). What makes you click: An empirical analysis of online dating. 2005 Meeting Papers, Vol. 207. Society for Economic Dynamics.

Hitsch, G., Hortaçsu, A., & Ariely, D. (2006). What makes you click? Mate preferences and matching outcomes in online dating. MIT Sloan Research Paper No. 4603–06. https://ssrn.com/abstract=895442 and http://dx.doi.org/10.2139/ssrn.895442

Hitsch, G. J., Hortaçsu, A., & Ariely, D. (2010a). Matching and sorting in online dating. *The American Economic Review*, 100(1), 130–163.

Hitsch, G. J., Hortaçsu, A., & Ariely, D. (2010b). What makes you click?—Mate preferences in online dating. *Quantitative Marketing and Economics*, 8(4), 393–427.

Huston, T. L., & Levinger, G. (1978). Interpersonal attraction and relationships. *Annual Review of Psychology*, 29(1), 115–156.

Jiang, L., & Hancock, J. T. (2013). Absence makes the communication grow fonder: Geographic separation, interpersonal media, and intimacy in dating relationships. *Journal of Communication*, 63(3), 556–577.

Joinson, A. (1998). Causes and implications of disinhibited behavior on the Internet. In J. Gackenbach (Ed.), *Psychology and the Internet: Intrapersonal, interpersonal, and transpersonal implications* (pp. 43–60). San Diego, CA: Academic Press.

Joinson, A. N. (2001). Self-disclosure in computer-mediated communication: The role of self-awareness and visual anonymity. *European Journal of Social Psychology*, 31(2), 177–192.

Joinson, A. N., Houghton, D. J., Vasalou, A., & Marder, B. L. (2011). Digital crowding: Privacy, self-disclosure, and technology. In S. Trepte & L. Reinecke (Eds.), *Privacy online* (pp. 33–45). Berlin: Springer.

Kalmijn, M. (1998). Intermarriage and homogamy: Causes, patterns, trends. *Annual Review of Sociology*, 24, 395–421.

Kanda, T., Hirano, T., Eaton, D., & Ishiguro, H. (2004). Interactive robots as social partners and peer tutors for children: A field trial. *Human-Computer Interaction*, 19(1), 61–84.

Kaplan, R. M. (1978). Is beauty talent? Sex interaction in the attractiveness halo effect. *Sex Roles*, 4(2), 195–204.

Kerckhoff, A. C., & Davis, K. E. (1962). Value consensus and need complementarity in mate selection. *American Sociological Review*, 27(3), 295–303.

Kim, Y. S., Mahidadia, A., Compton, P., Cai, X., Bain, M., Krzywicki, A., Wobcke, W. (2010). People recommendation based on aggregated bidirectional intentions in social network site. In B. H. Kang & D. Richards (Eds.), *Knowledge management and acquisition for smart systems and services*. LNCS, vol. 6232/2010, (pp. 247–260). Berlin: Springer.

Kleck, R. (1968). Physical stigma and non-verbal cues emitted in face-to-face interaction. *Human Relations*, 21, 119–128.

Knapp, M. L. (1978). *Social intercourse: From greeting to goodbye*. Boston: Allyn & Bacon.

Knapp, M. L., & Vangelisti, A. L. (2005). *Interpersonal communication and human relationships*. Boston: Allyn & Bacon.

Knapp, M. L., & Vangelisti, A. L. (2009). *Interpersonal communication and human relationships*, 6th ed. Boston: Pearson Education.

Knobloch, L. (2009). Stage theories of relationship development. In H. Reis & S. Sprecher (Eds.), *Encyclopedia of human relationships* (pp. 1590–1593). Thousand Oaks, CA: Sage.

Kocsor, F., Rezneki, R., Juhász, S., & Bereczkei, T. (2011). Preference for facial self-resemblance and attractiveness in human mate choice. *Archives of Sexual Behavior*, 40(6), 1263–1270.

Krahl, J. R., & Wheeless, L. R. (1997). Retrospective analysis of previous relationship disengagement and current and current attachment style. *Communication Quarterly*, 45(3), 167–187.

Kreager, D. A., Cavanagh, S. E., Yen, J., & Yu, M. (2014) "Where have all the good men gone?" Gendered interactions in online dating. *Journal of Marriage and Family*, 76(2), 387–410.

Kurzban, R., & Weeden, J. (2005). HurryDate: Mate preferences in action. *Evolution and Human Behavior*, 26(3), 227–244.

Lawson, H. M., & Leck, K. (2006). Dynamics of internet dating. *Social Science Computer Review*, 24(2), 189–208.

Lee, J. (2017). Robot culture. In *Sex robots* (pp. 19–31). Berlin: Springer International.

Lee, A. Y., & Bruckman, A. S. (2007). Judging you by the company you keep: Dating on social networking sites. *Proceedings of the 2007 international ACM conference on supporting group work* (pp. 371–378). New York: ACM.

Lenhart, A., Rainie, L., & Lewis, O. (2001). *Teenage life online: The rise of the instant-message generation and the Internet's impact on friendships and family relationships*. Washington, DC: Pew Internet & American Life Project.

Levinger, G. (1983). Development and change. In H. H. Kelley et al. (Eds.), *Close relationships*. San Francisco: Freeman.

Levy, D. (2009). *Love and sex with robots: The evolution of human-robot relationships*. New York: Harper Perennial.

Li, D., Liau, A., & Khoo, A. (2011). Examining the influence of actual-ideal self-discrepancies, depression, and escapism, on pathological gaming among massively multiplayer online adolescent gamers. *Cyberpsychology, Behavior, and Social Networking*, 14(9), 535–539.

Lucker, G. W., Beane, W. E., & Helmreich, R. L. (1981). The strength of the halo effect in physical attractiveness research. *The Journal of Psychology*, 107(1), 69–75.

Luo, S., & Zhang, G. (2009). What leads to romantic attraction: Similarity, reciprocity, security, or beauty? Evidence from a speed-dating study. *Journal of Personality*, 77(4), 933–964.

Madden, M., & Lenhart, A. (2006). Online dating. *Pew Internet & American Life Project*. www.pewinternet.org/pdfs/PIP_Online_Dating.pdf

McPherson, M., Smith-Lovin, L., & Cook, J. M. (2001). Birds of a feather: Homophily in social networks. *Annual Review of Sociology*, 27, 415–444.

Merkle, E. R., & Richardson, R. A. (2000). Digital dating and virtual relating: Conceptualizing computer mediated romantic relationships. *Family Relations*, 49(2), 187–192.

Mierke, K., Aretz, W., Nowack, A., Wilmsen, R., & Heinemann, T. (2011). Impression formation in online-dating-situations: effects of media richness and physical attractiveness information. *Journal of Business and Media Psychology*, 2, 49–56.

Mikkola, H., Oinas, M. M., & Kumpulainen, K. (2008, March). Net-based identity and body image among young IRC-gallery users. In *Society for Information Technology & Teacher Education International Conference* (pp. 3080–3085). Association for the Advancement of Computing in Education (AACE).

Morry, M. M. (2005). Relationship satisfaction as a predictor of similarity ratings: A test of the attraction-similarity hypothesis. *Journal of Social and Personal Relationships*, 22(4), 561–584.

Murstein, B. I. (1970). Stimulus-value-role: A theory of marital choice. *Journal of Marriage and the Family*, 32(3), 465–481.

Murstein, B. I. (1977). The stimulus-value-role (SVR) theory of dyadic relationships. In S. Duck (Ed.) *Theory and practice in interpersonal attraction* (pp. 105–127). New York: Academic Press.

Nayak, R., Zhang, M., & Chen, L. (2010). A social matching system for an online dating network: A preliminary study. *Proceeding of the 2010 IEEE International Conference on Data Mining Workshops* (pp. 352–357). IEEE.

Newcomb, T. M. (1958). Attitude development as a function of reference groups: The Bennington study. In E. Maccoby, T. Newcomb & E. Hartley (eds.), *Readings in social psychology* (pp. 265–275). New York: Holt, Rinehart and Winston.

Norton, M. I., Frost, J. H., & Ariely, D. (2007). Less is more: The lure of ambiguity, or why familiarity breeds contempt. *Journal of Personality and Social Psychology*, 92(1), 97–105.

Paul, A. (2014). Is online better than offline for meeting partners? Depends: Are you looking to marry or to date? *Cyberpsychology, Behaviour, and Social Networking*, 17(10), 664–667.

Pew Internet. (2016). Fact tank: News in the numbers. www.pewresearch.org/fact-tank/2016/02/29/5-facts-about-online-dating/

Piwek, L., & Joinson, A. (2016). "What do they snapchat about?" Patterns of use in time-limited instant messaging service. *Computers in Human Behavior*, 54, 358–367.

Ramirez Jr, A., & Zhang, S. (2007). When online meets offline: The effect of modality switching on relational communication. *Communication Monographs*, 74(3), 287–310.

Ramirez, A., Summer, E. M., Fleuriet, C., & Cole, M. (2016). When online dating partners meet offline: The effect of modality switching on relational communication between online daters. *Journal of Computer-Mediated Communication*, 20, 99–114

Regan, P. C. (2000). The role of sexual desire and sexual activity in dating relationships. *Social Behavior and Personality: An International Journal*, 28(1), 51–59.

Regan, P. C. (2008). *The mating game: A primer on love, sex, and marriage*. Thousand Oaks, CA: Sage.

Reis, H. T., & Shaver, P. (1988). Intimacy as an interpersonal process. In S. Duck, D. F. Hay, S. E. Hobfoll, W. Ickes, & B. M. Montgomery (Eds.), *Handbook of personal relationships: Theory, research and interventions* (pp. 367–389). Oxford: John Wiley.

Rosen, L. D., Cheever, N. A., Cummings, C., & Felt, J. (2008). The impact of emotionality and self-disclosure on online dating versus traditional dating. *Computers in Human Behavior*, 24(5), 2124–2157.

Rosenfeld, M. J., & Thomas, R. J. (2012). Searching for a mate: The rise of the Internet as a social intermediary. *American Sociological Review*, 77(4), 523–547.

Schlenker, B. R., & Pontari, B. A. (2000). The strategic control of information: Impression management and self-presentation in daily life. In A. Tesser, R. Felson, & J. Suls (Eds.), *Perspectives on self and identity* (pp. 199–232). Washington, DC: American Psychological Association.

Schöndienst, V., & Dang-Xuan, L. (2011). The role of linguistic properties in online dating communication – A large-scale study of contact initiation messages. *PACIS 2011 Proceedings*. https://aisle.aisnet.org/pacis2011/169

Selfhout, M., Denissen, J., Branje, S., & Meeus, W. (2009). In the eye of the beholder: Perceived, actual, and peer-rated similarity in personality, communication, and friendship intensity during the acquaintanceship process. *Journal of Personality and Social Psychology*, 96(6), 1152.

Shea, B. C., & Pearson, J. C. (1986). The effects of relationship type, partner intent, and gender on the selection of relationship maintenance strategies. *Communication Monographs*, 53, 352–364.

Sprecher, S., & Metts, S. (1999). Romantic beliefs: Their influence on relationships and patterns of change over time. *Journal of Social and Personal Relationships*, 16(6), 834–851.

Sprecher, S., Zimmerman, C., & Abrahams, E. M. (2010). Choosing compassionate strategies to end a relationship. *Social Psychology*, 41(2), 66–75.

Sritharan, R., Heilpern, K., Wilbur, C. J., & Gawronski, B. (2010). I think I like you: Spontaneous and deliberate evaluations of potential romantic partners in an online dating context. *European Journal of Social Psychology*, 40(6), 1062–1077.

Stenzel, A., Chinellato, E., Bou, M. A. T., del Pobil, Á. P., Lappe, M., & Liepelt, R. (2012). When humanoid robots become human-like interaction partners: corepresentation of robotic actions. *Journal of Experimental Psychology: Human Perception and Performance*, 38(5), 1073–1077.

Tidwell, L. C., & Walther, J. B. (2002). Computer-mediated communication effects on disclosure, impressions, and interpersonal evaluations: Getting to know one another a bit at a time. *Human Communication Research*, 28(3), 317–348.

Toma, C. L., Hancock, J. T., & Ellison, N. B. (2008). Separating fact from fiction: An examination of deceptive self-presentation in online dating profiles. *Personality and Social Psychology Bulletin*, 34(8), 1023–1036.

Tu, K., Ribeiro, B., Jiang, H., Wang, X., Jensen, D., Liu, B., & Towsley, D. (2014) Online Dating Recommendations: Matching Markets and Learning Preferences. *Proceedings of the 23rd international conference on World Wide Web* (pp. 787–792). New York: ACM.

Tyson, G., Perta, V. C., Haddadi, H., & Seto, M. C. (2016) A first look at user activity on Tinder. *Proceedings of the IEEE/ACM International Conference on Advances in Social Networks Analysis and Mining* (pp. 461–466). IEEE.

Valkenburg, P. M., & Peter, J. (2007). Who visits online dating sites? Exploring some characteristics of online daters. *CyberPsychology & Behavior*, 10(6), 849–852.

Vuilleumier, P. (2000). Faces call for attention: Evidence from patients with visual extinction. *Neuropsychologia*, 38(5), 693–700.

Walster, E., Walster, G. W., & Berscheid, E.(1978) *Equity: Theory and research*. Boston: Allyn and Bacon.

Walther, J. B. (1996). Computer-mediated communication: Impersonal, interpersonal, and hyperpersonal interaction. *Communication Research*, 23(1), 3–43.

Walther, J. B., Slovacek, C., & Tidwell, L. (2001). Is a picture worth a thousand words? Photographic images in long-term and short-term computer-mediated communication. *Communication Research*, 28, 105–134.

Wetzel, C. G., & Insko, C. A. (1982). The similarity-attraction relationship: Is there an ideal one? *Journal of Experimental Social Psychology*, 18(3), 253–276.

Whitty, M. T. (2007). The art of selling one's self on an online dating site: The BAR approach. In M. T. Whitty, A. J. Baker, & J. A. Inman (Eds.), *Online matchmaking* (pp. 57–69). Houndmills: Palgrave Macmillan.

Whitty, M. T. (2011). E-Dating: The five phases on online dating. In C. R. Livermore (Ed.), *Gender and social computing: Interactions, differences and relationships* (pp. 222–233). Hershey, PA: Global.

Xia, P., Tu, K., Ribeiro, B., Jiang, H., Wang, X., Chen, C., . . ., & Towsley, D. (2014). Who is dating whom: Characterizing user behaviors of a large online dating site. arXiv preprint arXiv:1401.5710.

Yang, M. L., & Chiou, W. B. (2010). Looking online for the best romantic partner reduces decision quality: The moderating role of choice-making strategies. *Cyberpsychology, Behavior, and Social Networking*, 13(2), 207–210.

Zebrowitz, L. A., & Rhodes, G. (2004). Sensitivity to "bad genes" and the anomalous face overgeneralization effect: Cue validity, cue utilization, and accuracy in judging intelligence and health. *Journal of Non-verbal Behavior*, 28(3), 167–185.

Zebrowitz, L. A., Hall, J. A., Murphy, N. A., & Rhodes, G. (2002). Looking smart and looking good: Facial cues to intelligence and their origins. *Personality and Social Psychology Bulletin*, 28(2), 238–249.

9

MOBILIZING THE BIOPOLITICAL CATEGORY

Problems, Devices, and Designs in the Construction of the Gay Sexual Marketplace

Kane Race

This chapter explores the reflexive activity of participants in the gay sexual marketplace with a focus on the websites and apps designed specifically for sexual and intimate networking. I want to suggest that a pragmatist approach to markets and market devices has the potential to move us beyond the critical impasse of sexual commodification—so often levelled at digital sex—to enable a more constructive engagement with the design of sexual networking services on the part of sex researchers and service-users. Online hookup apps and websites are producing new sexual subjectivities, cultures, and practices among the growing number of men around the world who use them to seek connections with other men. Now operating as the most common way men search for and meet intimate partners in many locations, these devices have become part of the infrastructure of sex and intimacy for many men who have sex with men around the world (Race, 2015, 2018). As a result, gay cruising is taking new forms, assuming new genres and proceeding through new avenues—practices that are largely mediated by the design and affordances of gay sexual networking services. Following Callon and colleagues (2002), this article explores the sense in which the digital sexual marketplace "evolves, and . . . becomes differentiated and diversified" because actors in the digital economy (including tech developers and service users) "are caught in a reflexive activity: the actors concerned explicitly question their organization and, based on an analysis of their functioning, try to conceive and establish new rules for the game" (Callon et al., 2002, p. 194). In other words, these market actors are engaged in activities of "problematization" (Foucault, 1985)—a concept I will elaborate in further detail below. My suggestion is that the reflexive and experimental character of these activities provides some basis for constructive collaboration between sex researchers, tech developers, and consumers on how best to design, organize, and enact the sexual marketplace.

Problems play a constitutive role in some of the most celebrated accounts of gay sexual networking devices and their development. Joel Simkhai, the founder of the most successful geo-sexual smartphone app Grindr, gives the following account of the app's origin:

> It came out [of] necessity in my own life. I was like, "How do I meet all these guys?" So as soon as the second generation iPhone was announced, I said this is the technology I've been waiting for. So, I turned to Scott (Lewallen) and I said, "I want to create an app that lets you meet the guys around you," and he's like "Cool, I love it. Let's do it!"
>
> (Ramos, 2012)

Simkhai's account situates Grindr as a practical solution to a problem that has long confronted same-sex attracted men historically; namely, the problem of finding sexual and/or intimate partners in a heteronormative world. (Indeed, it is no coincidence that the name given to one of the most popular early gay cruising websites in the Web 2.0 environment was Gaydar—a vernacular term that refers to a supposed radar-like ability to work out whether someone is gay.) Grindr started off as a home-grown company: its founders had "very little money" and "very little knowledge in terms of technology" at the time of its conception. On Simkhai's account, the GPS capabilities of the second generation of smartphones enabled a couple of gay guys to develop a technological solution to this problem that drew on vernacular desires and situated creativity. Reflecting on this experience, Simkhai has claimed "successful apps are often ones that not only solve a particular problem, but solve it for a large number of people . . . The bigger the problem, the better the business potentially will be . . . You can't convince people that they [have a] problem" (Smiley, 2016). At a 2016 business conference he expanded on this point:

> Whatever problem that you've identified, I guarantee you thousands of other people have already identified that problem also. And many people have also identified the solution. The key is to get it out to market . . . The importance of this is you want to get feedback from the market as quickly as possible. Users are the ones who will tell you whether your idea is good or not. Instead of getting caught up in venture capital, it's better to just release the app and start learning from users about what's working and what isn't. Once you get that information, you want to iterate quickly. You want to make those changes as quickly as possible. You release it, you get data back and you change. Nobody ever launched a perfect product on day one.
>
> (Smiley, 2016)

This passage offers a much more nuanced account of how specific market arrangements inform the design of the product at various stages in the life of its development than popular discourses that cast sexual networking devices as the overdetermined outcome of the inexorable logic of consumer capitalism. Indeed, Simkhai cautions against "getting caught up in venture capital" in the initial phases of the design process in favor of attending closely to user experience. In this respect, Simkhai's remarks resonate with Callon and colleagues' emphasis in their important essay "The economy of qualities" (Callon et al., 2002). If "goods" are market objects whose qualities and characteristics have been stabilized, these researchers use the term "product" to denote an ongoing process of adjustment, customization, calibration, and tinkering—a "bringing forward" of hitherto unrealized qualities in a good or service they refer to as *qualification*. Through the process of qualification, developers seek to distinguish their product from its competitors and establish consumer attachments in their bid to position their product advantageously within the market.

One of the benefits of Callon's team's approach is the attention they direct toward the technical arrangements that constitute these feedback mechanisms between providers and consumers: the specific analytic techniques and procedures; metrics of market research; and ways of tabulating user experience and customer feedback that inform the ongoing development of the product. In this regard, Callon and colleagues observe the "favourable position" that digital providers are in "to monitor users, observe their preferences and, based on these observations, singularize the products offered to them" (2002, p. 210). But while backend data offer a significant window onto patterns of user experience, in this chapter I wish to explore the sense in which tech developers are responsive to external discourses and concerns in their design and development practices. In this respect, since the problem-solution structure features centrally within narratives of tech development, it might emerge as a prime candidate for expanded intervention.

Foucault coined the term "problematization" to refer to the discursive and non-discursive practices through which a matter of concern enters into the play of true and false: of knowledge, determination, and action. How problems are grasped has material effects, since this process anticipates and circumscribes the range and scope of possible responses. But formulating problems always rests on certain contingencies that should dispel the sense that any one solution could ever be definitive or exhaustive. As Foucault insisted, there are always several possible ways of responding to "the same ensemble of difficulties" (Rabinow, 1995, p. 43). As an analytic approach, problematization entails taking certain situations as at once problematic and contingent, with a view to querying and reformulating the terms through which the "problem" is conceived and acted upon. This can serve to multiply the possibilities of transformative intervention—of thinking and doing things otherwise—by countering the idea that any one way of defining or solving a problem is inevitable, fixed, or essential.

There is little doubt that sexual networking services are connecting questions of sex, intimacy, community, friendship, and romance "to other aspects of our lives and identities in new ways" (Albury et al., 2017). If technology is society made durable, as Latour famously claimed (1990), then problematization may constitute a particularly significant intervention, since the shape that problems and solutions take in digitally enabled social networking effectively routinizes certain ways of doing things, while interfering with, destabilizing, undermining, or supplanting other alternatives, rendering them fragile, redundant, or unimaginable (Race, 2015, 2018; Hawkins et al., 2015). In this sense, problematization engages with the situation of tech developers while expanding the range of concerns and possibilities they take on board, which might in turn enable us to envisage more constructive forms of participation in the design and development of sexual and social networking devices on the part of a range of actors beyond the tech company itself.

Configuring the Gay Sexual Marketplace

In the digital context, gay sexual culture takes the shape of a sexual economy in at least two respects. First, the language of marketing, consumption, and economics has become pervasive as a conceptual repertoire for understanding how users experience and get positioned by sexual networking services. As one man who uses the internet to meet sexual partners put it in interview:

> It's great in terms of accessibility 24/7. I can organise my sex around my work schedule. It's also like a shopping cart. You can go, "Okay, I'm interested in Caucasian men", or whatever, down to sexual preference. It's about being able to access an immediate selection of people you might be interested in. I think that is a bonus.
>
> *(Race 2018, p. 53)*

Meanwhile, numerous commentators employ market concepts to make sense of the logics of self-presentation and participation within hookup apps and dating websites. As Ela Illouz puts it:

> The Internet structures the search for a partner as a market, or more exactly, formalizes the search for a partner in the form of an economic transaction: it transforms the self into a packaged product competing with others on an open-ended market regulated by the law of supply and demand; it makes the encounter the outcome of a more or less stable set of preferences; it makes the process of searching constrained by the problem of efficiency; it structures encounters as market niches; it attaches a (more or less) fixed economic value to profiles (that is, persons) and makes people anxious about their value in such a structured market and eager to improve their position in that market.
>
> *(2007, p. 88)*

Thus, even when no money changes hands (as is generally the case on mainstream—or "gay-stream"—apps and websites), we can see how discourses of marketing and consumption offer suggestive rubrics for making sense of social participation in these networking systems. This process is bi-directional, as Mowlabocus has observed: "Gaydar profiles simultaneously display the user as an object to be 'browsed' . . . *and* construct him as the discerning consumer. This consumer/consumed dichotomy is integral to the structure of the profile" (2016, pp. 90–91). In other words, it applies not only to how consumer-participants are configured by these technologies, but also how they are led to conceive fellow participants when engaging in digital practices of sexual networking.

Of course, this is not the first time that parallels between commodification and gay sexual culture have occurred.[1] What is new is that the commodity-frame now features as the template—indeed the infrastructure—mediating sexual communication, social interaction, and the prospect of accessing other people using these services. And if relations among online cruisers are structured and formatted much like a market, the websites and apps men turn to for these purposes are commercial enterprises whose products have emerged as lucrative market objects in their own right. For example, in 2008 the operators of Gaydar (one of the most popular early gay cruising websites from the UK) reported that their website consistently received more traffic than leading retailers such as Marks & Spencer and Ryanair (Light et al., 2008).[2] In 2015, Online Buddies (the U.S.-based parent company of the cruising website Manhunt, the hookup app Jack'd, and a number of other gay sexual networking and dating apps) reported serving over 17 million users worldwide, with 1 million unique visits every day (White, 2015). In 2014, the revenue of Grindr (the first geo-locative gay smartphone app) was disclosed at US$32 million—up 29% from $25 million the previous year (Isaac, 2016). Reported to host 2 million regular visitors every day who spend an average of about an hour on the app, the business has attracted the interest of venture capitalists, with a Chinese online gaming firm, Beijing Kunlun Tech Company, buying a 60% stake in the business in 2016—a purchase that valued the start-up at US$155 million (Isaac, 2016). Meanwhile Hornet (Grindr's chief competitor in the gay app market), recently entered into a mutually beneficial cooperation with Blued, the largest gay social network in China. The revenue raised will enable Hornet to expand upon the impressive growth rates it has been experiencing in several markets around the world, enabling Hornet and Blued to work together with the express aim of bringing gay apps "outside of the first-generation hookup model, and into digital homes for the gay community" (Blued CEO Geng Le, quoted in Umbach, 2016).

The primary revenue stream for gay geo-social networking apps is generally member subscriptions, while advertising revenue contributes the remainder of income—between a quarter and a third of total income, according to recent reports from Grindr and Hornet (Hall, 2013; Mallard, 2016). Measures such as user volume and time-on-device secure sales from advertising networks, while direct sales to local businesses account for a significant proportion of advertising revenue. According to one recent puff piece (Sigee, 2016), Grindr's "staggering 1 million users per minute worldwide" is what makes the app so appealing as an advertising platform. Despite the race to turn gay hookup apps and websites into lifestyle-based platforms, this suggests that the search for sexual and intimate partners is generally regarded as "the beating heart of the brand" (Sigee, 2016), or the bread-and-butter of this market: the primary factor behind the remarkable figures on visitors and length of user engagement on these devices.

Using Profiles, Profiling Users

In terms of functionality, the personal profile operates as the central mechanism of sexual networking, and this makes it a key mediator of user experience. Indeed, if sexual networking and dating sites produce the self as "a packaged product competing with others on an open-ended market" (Ilouz, 2007, p. 90), the personal profile functions much like a product label. On the profile, members market themselves using the categories available to them: generally a combination of public and private pictures, drop-down menus, tick boxes, and some free text, with various pro-forma categories of self-definition available, ranging from age, location, ethnicity, build, physical attributes, sexual and non-sexual interests, subcultural "tribe" or look, and preferences in a partner. With few exceptions, intimate networking services catering to the gay market prioritize questions of physical attraction and sexual compatibility. This is not necessarily the place to "get to know" someone or round out a personality: unlike the dating services of the heterosexual market, there are no complex personality algorithms to establish romantic compatibility here. Indeed, a common response to the job/profession prompt on gay hookup apps and websites is the rather trivializing "I have one"—a quip indicating the irrelevance of this question for the purposes at hand. Meanwhile, when prompted at all, "personality" questions (e.g. hobbies, favorite movies, leisure pursuits) are generally subordinated to questions of physical appearance and sexual attributes and interests. This emphasis is especially evident on geo-sexual networking apps, the profiles of which are populated more sparsely with thumbnail selfies and a few brief descriptors—age, ethnicity, physical stats, preferred sexual practices, and current location are typical. Indeed, given the fast-paced temporality of geo-locative sexual networking, scrolling down or digging deeper into the more detailed, open-ended expositions of individual character and personality that appear at the bottom of app profiles are produced as ancillary activities; distractions from the more central business of locating nearby partners, signaling interest, and clinching a convenient hookup. In this respect, the criteria and categories that are incorporated most prominently into the designs of these social networking services are of some practical consequence.

Of course, from the green carnation of Oscar Wilde's day to the handkerchief code of the 1970s, urban gay subcultures have long made use of certain signifiers, codes, and categories to signal sexual preferences and interests to strangers "in the know." But the database-driven environment of online cruising requires participants to broadcast personal (and often quite sensitive) information to a world of unknown others using pro-forma categories of self-identification (such as ethnicity, erotic fetishes, or HIV status) for the first time. The determination of these categories is largely in the hands of tech developers and designers, rather than an outcome of collective, subcultural elaboration. Meanwhile these categories end up functioning as *preconditions* or *prerequisites* of sociosexual participation, with more than a mere signifying function: members conduct searches according to various categories and have the option of filtering out other members (or "blocking" them) according to age range, ethnicity, look, and various other fixed categories that vary from site to site and app to app. These categories serve to structure users' access to each other, and thus acquire a particularly rigid, performative effect on the criteria of value that become mobilized within these sexual markets. In other words, profile categories operate as structuring devices that situate members within the sexual marketplace, provide a basis for ranking and evaluating other members, and ultimately determine the spheres of exchange to which users gain access and in which their profile-identity will circulate. Moreover, since profile categories are presented as key criteria for evaluating desirability, that is, to sort between the various "goods" on offer, the digital environment has changed the conditions through which abstractions such as age, race, and so on come to matter in gay sexual culture. What were once mere sexual preferences achieve explicit, public, textual expression within the templates of digital cruising, not to mention a structuring function, because they constrain the terms of social and sexual access among participants.

"Prejudice" is the habit of assessing persons using reductive categories prior to any actual experience of them—and this is precisely what digital networking categories make possible. Indeed, certain functions and features of these devices are premised upon this habit and technically institute and consolidate it. Thus, however liberal a perspective one may want to adopt on questions of sexual preference, it is clear these networking media translocate expressions of sexual preference from the private realm into the more public issue of prejudice and its exclusionary effects. Because they tend to promote and cater to certain types of users better than others, it is not surprising that the format of the profile has emerged as an object of contestation and problematization in customer feedback and gay community discourse on user experience. In this sense, the online profile format can be situated as a "matter of concern" (Latour, 2004), a "political object" (Hawkins et al., 2015), as well as a key mechanism for the creation and maintenance of "consumer attachments" (Callon et al., 2002; McFall, 2009).

Caught between desires to maximize one's pool of prospective partners and wishing to confine interactions to other users who meet certain criteria—between seeking to disclose enough information to attract the interest of other users, but not wanting to disclose too much incriminating, identifying, or sensitive information—users of sexual networking apps and websites thus find themselves situated on a precipice in which the "private" (and indeed one's privates) threaten to tumble over into the "public" domain at any moment. Users adopt various tactics to negotiate these tensions and minimize the risks and dangers of unwanted exposure, as numerous researchers have documented (Albury & Byron, 2016; Brubaker et al., 2016; Race, 2018). But in this chapter, my focus lies elsewhere. I want to explore how the formats and design of sexual networking services are made available to more expansive forms of problematization and modification. A related question is how the concerns of a diverse range of actors, beyond the merely commercial (e.g. social, ethical, material, communal, health-related) become involved in, and come to inform, these design and development processes.

The crystallization of sexual preferences into categorical imperatives that structure the terms of sociosexual access between users engenders new affective complications for differently situated participants within these media, installing new modes of intimate object[ificat]ion. This may help to explain the growth of community concern around "sexual racism"—a discourse of communal criticism that has proliferated in tandem with the growing uptake and popularization of these mechanisms in which accounts of digital cruising feature prominently (Mansfield & Quan, 2006).[3] It also explains the intense bitterness pervading much communal and expert discourse on sexual networking devices. Key terms and tropes of some of the most common critiques are neatly encapsulated in a widely shared blogpost authored by a Sydney gay man in 2012, entitled "The iGays are way too sick":

> Here I sit, not twenty years later, and the community has been decimated by the Internet. Completely, utterly decimated. As a whole, gays everywhere have become a sick group of animals who have completely lost their ability to interact on any authentic level, who have fearfully squashed themselves into simplified categories of drop-down boxes, and who banish entire groups of their own kind based purely on unwanted physical characteristics that do not fit the Gay-For-Pay Porn Model Image.
>
> *(endracismandhomophobia, 2012)*

Despite the unpopularity of online cruising in lay and specialist discourses, the rapidly growing uptake and use of these devices around the world shows no signs of abating any time soon. Rather than hanker after some nostalgic, authentic community, presumed to exist before the injuries of commodification and technologization, I believe the first step in addressing the present conjuncture involves taking the subjects and problems these devices propose to us seriously: to inhabit and affirm them in their present complexity, with a view to reframing how such problems and subjects are assembled and formulated. Consumers and producers of sexual networking devices can be grasped as reflexive actors in market situations, as I proposed at the outset of this chapter. One might conceive these market actors as participants in an "economy of qualities" (Callon et al., 2002); which is to say, their participation in this environment involves diverse practices of problematization, reflexivity, and experimentation. While such activities are commercially oriented to some extent (they can serve to generate new market objects, carve out market niches, and create consumer attachments), they cannot be confined to any one domain of social praxis (be it "economic," "social," "political," "ethical," "technological," "biopolitical," and so on): they are diversely and dynamically constituted (Rabinow, 1995; Callon, 2009). In other words, economic concerns are not the only concerns that inform the construction of markets or market-problems, as the following example indicates.

Bareback Realtime

The signaling of HIV risk is a matter that the different gay cruising websites that emerged in the Web 2.0 environment handled in various ways. On the UK-based site Gaydar, founded in 1999, users could indicate their preference for "safer sex" (using a condom) according to the following options: "Always," "Sometimes," "Never," "Needs Discussion," and the rather British "Rather Not Say." By comparison, when the U.S.-based website Manhunt appeared in 2001 it required users to specify their HIV status directly using the following response options: "Ask me," "Negative," "Positive," "Unknown," and "No Answer." There was no mechanism for users to hide this item on their profile. Thus, selecting "No Answer" would appear on the user's profile as "HIV STATUS: [blank]." This was perhaps the first gay sexual environment that required participants to indicate their HIV status as a *design feature of participation*.

Users of these sites deployed and read these indications in various ways.[4] What is clear is that the growing popularity of these websites positioned HIV-positive men quite differently in the sexual marketplace. Where the condom code had originally made the question of HIV status somewhat irrelevant in gay casual sex environments, giving rise to the working presumption "assume all your partners may be HIV-positive and always use a condom," the popularization of websites for gay sexual networking made the category of HIV status matter in new ways. Australian behavioral data suggests that the new digital interfaces of gay cruising were bound up in the popularization of "serosorting"—in which people search for partners of the same serostatus, usually with the intention of dispensing with condoms—as a problematic new HIV prevention ethic within gay sexual culture (Race, 2010, 2018).[5] The increasing pressure on HIV-positive participants to disclose their status also complicated their participation in gay sexual culture, giving rise to new experiences of social exclusion and rejection as well as new pressures around self-representation. Since HIV-negative status was by far the most common indication on personal profiles on these "gaystream" websites, online cruising led to a new state of "seronormativity" within these spaces, creating significant new affective complications for HIV-positive participants (Race, 2010, 2018).

Individuals dealt with the problems that the new interfaces of digital cruising were creating for them in various ways. But one noteworthy response was the creation of a new website, Bareback Realtime, by HIV-positive gay men in Arizona in 2004. Today Bareback Realtime (or "BBRT") bills itself as "the world's largest hookup site for men looking for other barebackers" (Pigmaster, 2008). In a rare interview with its founder, it emerges that the website was established in response to the sort of problems HIV-positive participants were experiencing in the "gaystream" sexual marketplace. As Pigmaster (the pseudonymous founder of BBRT) explains in this interview:

> I started the site out of frustration that when dealing with other websites when you filled in your status as HIV, people were freaked out, even the people who were HIV-positive. People who were HIV positive still wouldn't talk to you because they didn't want you to know their status. It just got very frustrating ... [BBRT] was mainly for positive people to meet other positive people.
>
> *(Leahy, 2014)*

While barebacking is sometimes taken to refer to the eroticization of acts of HIV infection, it is clear from these remarks, and from the design and formatting of this website, that the term is being deployed here to construct a safe space for HIV-positive serosorting. Pigmaster confirms in this interview that his primary aim in founding BBRT was to establish a "poz-friendly" cruising site in which HIV-positive men could safely sort for casual partners. Here, we can see how the *problematization* of a certain experience of sexual networking led to the development of a new sexual networking service, branded in such a way as to attract a different segment of the gay market (HIV-positive men and "barebackers"). However, the founder brackets commercial considerations when accounting for the formation of this website:

> When you started was your motive an altruistic thing, like a move to reduce stigma, or was it a commercial opportunity you saw, or a combination of both?
>
> [Pigmaster] It didn't start out as anything commercial. We don't do outside advertising to this day. Like I said I just started the website out of frustration with other websites where there was a lot of rejection happening
>
> *(Leahy, 2014)*[6]

Certainly, motivations and priorities will vary among the companies that run gay social networking services. But this example suggests that commercial considerations are not the only concerns that inform the design of such services. Rather, in qualifying their products, gay sexual networking companies can incorporate the concerns of a wide array of actors, each with "their own expectations, conceptions, projects and interests, on the basis of which they promote different modes of structuring and organization" (Callon, 2009, p. 540).

The emergence of BBRT is an especially interesting example of networking innovation because it demonstrates how biomedical indicators can emerge as criteria for discriminating between prospective partners, populating personal profiles and qualifying the self in the pursuit of sexual encounters. Indeed, as a website explicitly dedicated to the arrangement of sex without condoms, BBRT has become a key space in which new biomedical designations have been incorporated into the routines of sexual searching. Pigmaster explains:

> [T]here are negative people too though who do come to the website . . . They would like to meet people who are undetectable . . . There has been data out for years that suggests that positive guys with undetectable status are a lot safer to bareback with than a supposedly negative person who may have no idea that they have HIV but have a high viral load through not being on medication.
>
> *(Leahy, 2014)*

This passage refers to the use of antiretroviral medications on the part of HIV-positive individuals to suppress the virus to undetectable levels, a practice that has been found to minimize the risk of passing on the virus. Another new prevention strategy is the use of certain antiretroviral medications on the part of HIV-negative individuals as a form of pre-exposure prophylaxis ("PREP"), the efficacy of which has been demonstrated in a raft of clinical trials recently (Baeten et al., 2013). Because of the attachment of its user base to sex without condoms, BBRT has been at the forefront of efforts to incorporate this information into digital practices of sexual networking. By 2014, the prompt for HIV status on BBRT members' profiles offered no fewer than ten response options, including "Undetectable" and "Neg + PREP." These profile specifications enable members to arrange sex without condoms while reducing the risk of HIV transmission, furnishing users with a form of "calculative agency" (Callon, 1998) that is sensitive to the differences that different clinical and pharmaceutical strategies make for HIV prevention. In this respect, BBRT represents a fascinating convergence of digital and biomedical categories that has the effect of instituting and formalizing new risk reduction practices among its users.[7] It also stages the categories according to which members are required to present themselves online as provisional, historically situated, and available to transformation.

Biopolitical Devices

The emergence of new tools and knowledge around HIV prevention in recent years (including PREP and the knowledge that undetectable viral load dramatically reduces the risk of HIV transmission) has led to the emergence of a new paradigm of HIV prevention, termed "biomedical prevention," which entails a new set of priorities for HIV prevention globally. These include collective efforts to increase rates of HIV testing among affected populations around the world, and the promotion of early, ongoing use of antiretroviral therapy on the part of those infected, not only for clinical purposes, but also in the interests of viral suppression at the population level. In tandem with the emergence of "biomedical prevention," there have been growing efforts on the part of community-based HIV agencies around the world to work out ways of harnessing the capacities of new ICTs (including sexual networking devices) for the purposes of HIV prevention. Since 2012, international health agencies such as the United States Centers for Disease Control, the European CDC, and the Asia-Pacific Coalition on Male Sexual Health have convened high-level symposia bringing various stakeholders (government, scientists, community-based health practitioners, and tech company representatives) together to address this issue. The result has been to constitute HIV prevention as a matter of concern within this market, a sphere of problematization and source of value that has gone on to inform practices of product development and qualification. In the process, gay sexual networking apps are emerging as significant new players in the sphere of HIV prevention, biopolitical devices whose technical affordances are valued and repurposed to reveal new capacities for HIV prevention.

Significantly, the way in which HIV prevention objectives are addressed varies from company to company and product to product. Unlike some of their internet predecessors, gay hookup apps have generally not prompted HIV disclosure until relatively recently, and the way they have sought to do so reveals this terrain to be a site of ongoing controversy and problematization. For example, the hookup app Scruff has declined to offer prompts around HIV status, but instead allows users to select "Poz" as one of several "communities" with which they identify (other options range from "Bear" to "Muscle" to "Jock" to "Transgender" to "Bisexual"). In accounting for this design decision, the app's founder, Jason Marchant, writes:

> This allows guys to be welcoming to Poz members, whether or not they are Poz themselves. Allowing Poz members to disclose their status in this way reinforces the fact that they are not alone in their HIV-positivity, and gives them a community of other Poz guys to connect with. Additionally, those who prefer to discuss status privately are spared the fraught choice that old designs imposed. And by not presenting "Negative" status information, we avoid facilitating risky assumptions, or fostering an environment conducive to HIV stigma.
>
> *(Marchant, 2016)*

This passage reflects many of the concerns and problems that an earlier generation of users experienced on websites such as Manhunt, discussed earlier. By contrast, one of the most popular "gaystream" apps, Hornet, not only prompts HIV status directly, but offers users response options such as "Negative, on PrEP" and "Positive, Undetectable." Moreover, if a user indicates they are HIV-negative, they "receive a friendly testing engagement reminder" every six months as part of Hornet's *Know Your Status* ("KYS") program, with those in the United States being directed to their nearest clinic.

This last example reveals how the geo-locative capabilities of smartphone apps are being adapted in the interests of HIV prevention. In 2012, Hornet teamed up with a Philippine non-profit organization to deliver HIV testing promotion messages to 94,000 users, with links for online registration, reportedly prompting 4300 users to take the test. The app Jack'd ran a similar campaign in Taiwan, reporting that 30,000 users clicked through to their HIV message (Staley, 2013). As these examples suggest, these devices are more than a simple platform for health communication; they can get people to *do* things (in this case, undertake testing for a serious, stigmatized disease). The *performative potential* of these devices makes them available for biopolitical investment: their ability to connect members of at-risk populations with diagnostic services and clinical care proposes to improve the prospects of HIV prevention in the biomedical era through specific new technological affordances.

Conclusion: Bio-Politicising the Gay Sexual Marketplace

> We have 4 million users worldwide who are at highest risk for HIV and we have their attention.

These remarks were made by Sean Howell, creator of the gay geo-sexual networking app Hornet, in a discussion of the initiatives gay digital networking companies are devising to address persistently high rates of HIV transmission among the diverse populations that constitute their principal user base around the world: gay, bisexual, and other men who have sex with men (Staley, 2013). Howell's comments position Hornet as a communicative platform with remarkable reach, scope, and potential. "Having the attention" of millions of users signals the device's potential to contribute to HIV education and prevention in material ways—not only by delivering health messages to a calculable number of individuals around the world, but also by instituting valued health conducts among populations officially regarded as both "hard to reach" and disproportionately at risk of HIV infection. As I have mentioned, these devices are more than a simple platform for health communication; they can get people to *do* things, revealing specific performative capabilities that become available for different sorts of investment on the part of differently situated actors. It is no coincidence, for example, that the term "attention" features here as a key index of the device's value and strategic potential. In the contemporary digital economy, social media companies rely upon the commodification and monetization of "attention" to attract investment and court revenue from second and third party sources such as marketers and advertisers. Thus, however casually the term is invoked, "attention" serves as a buzzword that dog-whistles to a wide array of actors whose interests extend well beyond the parameters of public health.

The polysemous signification of "attention" in these remarks demonstrates the complex, inextricable entanglement of various domains of practical concern in the digital economy: commercial, social, ethical, political, personal, governmental, and regulatory among them. But in highlighting the entanglement of these domains—how "having people's attention" serves to magnetize the interest and investment of a wide range of commercial, social, and governmental actors—my intention is not to suggest that these expressed commitments to HIV prevention are some sort of corporate ploy: a form of "pink-washing" peculiar to the age of digital networking. Nor do I mean to diminish the idea these devices have something new and potentially groundbreaking to contribute to international efforts to reduce rates of HIV transmission around the world. I only mean to flag the diverse range of priorities that tech developers juggle in their day-to-day work: the pursuit of economic profit; the facilitation of sexual and social networking; reducing harms associated with sexual networking such as HIV transmission; and social and political advocacy on behalf of their user base, to list some of the most pertinent. Rather than lamenting the contamination of social and ethical objectives with commercial objectives, or hankering after some pure separation of powers that might extract moral concerns from the corrupting logics of instrumental rationality, capitalization, politics, and regulatory surveillance, in this chapter I have argued for the need to understand how these disparate objectives and concerns get reconciled and enacted in given objects and technological initiatives.

I have argued that problematization (Foucault, 1985) is a useful analytic for conceiving the design of online dating and cruising devices, since tech developers tend to rely on some problematization of the existing sexual marketplace, as it is being enacted, in their efforts to improve the prospects of specific groups of participants, qualify their products and secure a niche in the digital marketplace. The examples I have considered are especially interesting because they demonstrate how biomedical indicators, among other personal and technical specifications, can emerge as criteria for discriminating between prospective partners, populating personal profiles and qualifying the self in the pursuit of sexual encounters. In this respect, they stand as fascinating examples of how innovations in digital culture can eventuate from convergences between digital and clinical media and how such convergences can produce differences in the sexual marketplace and, indeed, beyond it. As I have shown, gay sexual networking apps are now emerging as significant new biopolitical players. But these examples also stage the categories according to which members are required to present themselves online as provisional, historically situated, and available to experimentation, contestation, and critical transformation—including through what I have framed here as practices of problematization.

Notes

1 The depiction of the Manhattan gay scene in Larry Kramer's 1978 novel *Faggots*—with its obsessive focus on quantification, mass production, competition, and display—is replete with allusions to the commodity-form, and with a few changed references, could just as easily stand as an account of logging onto Grindr:

> Anthony Montano stepped out of his cab . . . and faced the gauntlet of Christopher Street, overrun this late afternoon with thousands, bodies on the prowl, pieces of meat, exhibitionists all, things, faceless faces, all in uniform . . . Ah, the streets, the Streets, the streets, let us pause for an Ode to The Streets, Gay Ghetto, homo away from home, the hierarchy and ritual of The Streets, incessant, insinuating, impossible Streets, addictive, the herb superb, can't keep away from you, always drawn to you, STREETS, speak of them singularly in the plural, like Sheep, Kleenex, Jell-o, blending, coalescing, oozing, all into one, all for us, how dramatic, how important, how depressing, fucking loneliness of walking alone and looking, displaying, on the streets—where so much time is spent, summer and winter, cold and HOT, You Can't Go Home Again, anyway you can't go home, who wants to go home, no cock suckers at home, dreary home, how many nights, hours, days, weeks, months, years, who's counting, do these fellows, not me!, walk The Streets: Christopher Washington Greenwich Hudson West and Sheridan Square, such a parade, *everyone dressed alike!*
> (Kramer, 1978, pp. 81–82)

2 For a good discussion of how QSoft, the company that operated Gaydar, constituted the gay community as a largely untapped media consumer market, see Light et al., 2008.
3 The growing immersion in online cruising on the part of gay men generated a sharp critique of "sexual racism" within gay community discourse. While modern gay discourses of sexual desirability have long taken racialized overtones, rarely had such characteristics been so explicit and routinely visible as they became within discourses of online cruising. The selective and exclusionary character of people's sexual preferences took on a new materiality in this context.
4 For example, Mark Davis and colleagues documented some reluctance on the part of the British HIV-positive men they interviewed to list their HIV status explicitly: this was seen as embarrassing, tactless, and a detail that would most likely jar with the affective flows and dynamics of cruising (Davis et al., 2006). Their sample of gay men tended to deal with concerns around HIV prevention primarily by indicating their preferences around safe sex. Thus, some HIV-positive Gaydar users in London reported signaling their HIV status by selecting options other than "Safer sex: Always"—the most common specification on Gaydar profiles at the time. In addition, HIV-negative participants tended to read this as an indication of HIV-positive status—or at least a risky proposition.
5 When operating as a basis for dispensing with condoms during casual sex, the disclosure of HIV-*negative* status can be viewed as problematic on a number of grounds—not least, the possibility that sexual partners may not know (or may lie) about their status. The problem is further complicated by the technical limitations perceived in the standard tests used to detect HIV infection in clinical practice—specifically, their ability to detect the presence of the HIV virus *in vivo*. It is possible to be infected with HIV but show up as "HIV negative" according to these antibody tests, because the development of antibodies in the bodies of infected individuals takes place some time after infection with

the virus ("the window period"). Given what is also known about the immune system response and the dynamics of viral replication in the context of initial infection, this stage is widely thought to be when a body is most infectious. Thus, an HIV-negative test result is not necessarily a reliable guide to whether a body is infected (or, for that matter, infectious).

6 Elsewhere in the interview, it is revealed that the operation has a relatively small staff of fifteen employees.

7 Indeed, this characteristic of the website leads HIV prevention advocate Marc André LeBlanc to criticize the organized HIV sector in Canada for its comparative lack of specificity when it comes to calculating the risk of different sexual practices: "Let's be honest," he says, "[BBRT's response options are] considerably more nuanced than what we see in most prevention messages and HIV-related studies . . . Will the HIV prevention field find more nuanced ways to discuss serostatus and the range of risk reduction options that are now available?" (LeBlanc, 2014).

References

Albury, K., & Byron, P. (2016). Safe on my phone? Same-sex attracted young people's negotiations of intimacy, visibility, and risk on digital hook-up apps. *Social Media & Society*, 2(4). doi: 10.1177/2056305116672887

Albury, K., Burgess, J., Light, B., Race, K., & Wilken, R. (2017). Data cultures of mobile dating and hook-up apps: Emerging issues for critical social science research. *Big Data & Society*, 4(2). doi: 10.1177/2053951717720950.

Baeten, J. M., Haberer, J. E., Liu, A. Y., & Sista, N. (2013). Pre-exposure prophylaxis for HIV prevention: Where have we been and where are we going? *Journal of Acquired Immune Deficiency Syndromes*, 63(02), S122–129.

Brubaker, J. R., Kaye, J., Schoenebeck, S., & Vertesi, J. (2016). Visibility in digital space: Controlling personal information online. *Proceedings of the 19th ACM conference on computer supported cooperative work and social computing companion* (pp. 184–187). New York: ACM.

Callon, M. (Ed.). (1998). *The laws of the markets*. Oxford: Blackwell.

Callon, M. (2009). Civilizing markets: Carbon trading between in vitro and in vivo experiments. *Accounting, Organizations and Society*, 34(3), 535–548.

Callon, M., Méadel, C., & Rabeharisoa, V. (2002). The economy of qualities. *Economy and Society*, 31(2), 194–217.

Davis, M., Hart, G., Bolding, G., Sherr, L., & Elford, J. (2006). E-dating, identity and HIV prevention: Theorising sexualities, risk and network society. *Sociology of Health & Illness*, 28(4), 457–478.

Endracismandhomophobia. 2012. The iGays are way too sick. Weblog. https://stopracis mandhomophobiaongrindr.wordpress.com/2012/07/20/the-igays-are-way-too-sick-turn-off-the-life-support/.

Foucault, M. (1985). *The use of pleasure: The history of sexuality vol. II*. New York: Vintage.

Hall, M. (2013). Up close and personal: Q & A with Grindr founder Joel Simkhai. *PCMag.com*. www.pcmag.com/article2/0,2817,2421918,00.asp.

Hawkins, G., Potter, E., & Race, K. (2015). *Plastic water: The social and material life of bottled water*. Cambridge, MA: MIT Press.

Illouz, E. (2007). *Cold intimacies: The making of emotional capitalism*. London: Polity.

Isaac, M. (2016). Grindr sells stake to Chinese company. *New York Times*. https://nyti.ms/1UKrOCQ.

Kramer, L. (1978). *Faggots*. New York: Random House.

Latour, B. (1990). Technology is society made durable. *The Sociological Review*, 38(1 suppl), 103–131.
Latour, B. (2004). Why has critique run out of steam? From matters of fact to matters of concern. *Critical Inquiry*, 30(2), 225–248.
Leahy, B. 2014. BarebackRT.com—the interview. *PositiveLite.com*. www.positivelite.com/component/zoo/item/barebackrtcom-the-interview.
LeBlanc, M. (2014). PREP pops up on cruising sites. *PositiveLite.com*. www.positivelite.com/component/zoo/item/prep-pops-up-on-cruising-sites.
Light, B., Fletcher, G., & Adam, A. (2008). Gay men, Gaydar and the commodification of difference. *Information Technology & People*, 21(3), 300–314.
Mallard, M. (2016). $700k MRR, 100,000 pay $7/mo for gay dating app Hornet, will beat Grindr? *Nathan Latka*. Weblog. http://nathanlatka.com/thetop440/.
Mansfield, T., & Quan, A. (2006). Sexual racism sux. https://sexualracismsux.com.
Marchant, J. (2016). Beyond 'HIV status': Interface design is personal at Scruff. *Huffington Post*. www.huffingtonpost.com/jason-marchant/beyond-hiv-status-interfa_b_6227964.html.
McFall, L. (2009). Devices and desires: How useful is the "new" new economic sociology for understanding market attachment? *Sociology Compass*, 3(2), 267–282.
Mowlabocus, S. (2016). *Gaydar culture: Gay men, technology and embodiment in the digital age.* London: Routledge.
Pigmaster. 2008. BarebackRT.com Facebook Fan Page. www.facebook.com/pg/bbrts/about/?ref=page_internal.
Rabinow, P. (1995). Midst anthropology's problems. In A. Ong & S. Collier (Eds.), *Global assemblages: Technology, politics, and ethics as anthropological problems* (pp. 40–54). Oxford: Blackwell.
Race, K. (2010). Click here for HIV status: Shifting templates of sexual negotiation. *Emotion, Space and Society*, 3(1), 7–14.
Race, K. (2015). Speculative pragmatism and intimate arrangements: Online hook-up devices in gay life. *Culture, Health & Sexuality*, 17(4), 496–511.
Race, K. (2018). *The gay science: Intimate experiments with the problem of HIV*. London: Routledge.
Ramos, D. (2012). Interview: Grindr CEO Joel Simkhai on how the gay social app is taking over the world. *NewNowNext*. www.newnownext.com/interview-grindr-ceo-joel-simkhai-on-how-the-gay-social-app-is-taking-over-the-world/03/2012/.
Sigee, R. (2016). Grindr is growing up: How the gay dating app became a major digital player. *The Standard UK*. www.standard.co.uk/lifestyle/london-life/grindr-is-growing-up-how-the-gay-dating-app-became-a-major-digital-player-a3178076.html.
Smiley, M. (2016). Grindr CEO Joel Simkhai explains how he turned his idea for the app into a reality. *The Drum*. www.thedrum.com/news/2016/05/25/grindr-ceo-joel-simkhai-explains-how-he-turned-his-idea-app-reality.
Staley, O. (2013). Gay dating apps become messengers for warnings on HIV. *Bloomberg*. www.bloomberg.com/news/articles/2015-02-13/gay-dating-apps-become-messengers-for-warnings-on-hiv-health.
Umbach, M. (2016). Hornet and Blued enter into first global cooperation. *Hornet App Blog*. http://love.hornetapp.com/blog/2016/12/16/gay-social-networks-hornet-and-china-based-blued-enter-into-first-global-cooperation.
White, D. (2015). Online buddies appoints new CEO following departure of president. *Global Dating Insights*. https://globaldatinginsights.com/2015/11/25/25112015-online-buddies-appoints-new-ceo-following-departure-of-president/.

10
"HOW ANGELS ARE MADE"
Ashley Madison and the Social Bot Affair

Tero Karppi

Social media may bring people together but the relationships we have on these platforms are not only human relationships. During the recent years, we have witnessed the rise of social bots. These bots are actors with which the human users interact and communicate. Focusing on the dating site Ashley Madison, this chapter explores how social bots are discussed as networked modes of being, and as such have their own identity and agency and can form particular relations with the human users.

Ashley Madison, a social media site founded in 2002, is one of the biggest online dating services and social networking sites marketed to people who are married or in a committed relationship. In 2015 the site made headlines after a data breach where the site was hacked and portions of its user data made available for the public; on July 15 a group calling itself "The Impact Team" hacked into the Ashley Madison dating site platform and stole the site's user data. Soon a link appeared on a dark web site, which leads into a package containing several gigabytes of data shared on a file sharing site. While the owners of Ashley Madison did not confirm this breach, a number of security experts who analyzed the data and matched, for example, people with credit card numbers argued that the data was, in fact, real and taken from the site's archives (Gibbs, 2015). According to the news, these data revelations led not only to lawsuits but also to personal tragedies of, for example, someone taking their life after being publicly exposed as a user of the site (Brown, 2015).

What the hack illustrated was how our networked selves are becoming intrinsically and intimately connected with social media platforms. These connections do not take place merely between other human users of the platform, but as Ben Light (2016) notes, social media sites such as Ashley Madison are also occupied with "non-human actors, such as bots (software applications that run automated tasks) and hook-up site user profiles." By analyzing the leaked Ashley Madison data, Annalee Newitz (2015a), an editor-in-chief of Gizmodo technology blog, argued that "Ashley Madison created more than 70,000 female bots to send male users millions of fake messages, hoping to create the illusion of a vast playland of available women." In fact, Newitz's (2015a) data analysis suggested that "Out of 70,572 hosts, 70,529 were female and only 43 were male. So we can say for sure that roughly zero percent of bots on Ashley Madison are male."[1] These claims pushed Avid Life Media, the company owning and running Ashley Madison, to conduct a review of "past business practices around bots and the ratio of male and female US members who were active on the site" (Avid Life Media, 2016). According to an official statement, the investigation confirmed that bots were no longer in use and that the female members of the site were authentic. James Millership, the new president of Avid Life Media, stated that "My understanding is that bots are widespread in the industry, but they are no longer being used, and will not be used, at Avid Life Media and Ashley Madison" (ibid.).

Even if the social bots, some of which were called "Ashley's Angels," no longer exist on the platform, the discussions analyzed in this chapter suggest that they once had a significant role. Authors like Newitz maintain that the data show that the platform had generated tens of thousands of social bots to interact with human users. What is essential here is that this case should not be regarded an anomaly, but as Newitz, reminds us, it is an event of the prehistory of artificial intelligence, which will shape the ways in which we respond to and live with "[t]omorrow's sentient bots" (Newitz, 2015b).

In this chapter, I argue that rather than contextualizing the social bots through the negative (fake, scam, and not-real) we should pay attention to how the social bots have become actors on social media sites. I am not engaging with the leaked data per se but instead I am examining the discourses that surrounded the data leak. Hence, the material for this chapter is a combination of second-hand sources that discuss and make interpretations based on the alleged data leak; these discussions were published in technology blogs and online news sites. I am also exploring documents related to the operations of Ashley Madison, such as their terms and conditions. While some of the speculations presented in these writings about Ashley Madison's use of social bots may be inaccurate, in this chapter they are used as an indication of how the use of social bots and the relations we form with them are seen, understood and in this case also criticized in public discourse. As Gina Neff and Peter Nagy argue, these discourses with their perceptions and misperceptions in the context of social bots and AI are important because they have the power to reshape technologies and our understandings of technology (Neff & Nagy, 2016).

Furthermore, on social media sites humans are always in an intimate relation to technology. Thus, if the human users enter Ashley Madison to find love or have an affair, it is important to ask how the relations with the social bots fit into these purposes. Hence, this chapter begins to contextualize some of the implicated relations by looking at how social bots can be seen to bridge communication between the online and offline worlds. To be more specific, I argue that the distinction between online and offline is produced and brought together in synthetic situations (Knorr Cetina, 2009, 2014), which are not neutral but politicized and also programmed in themselves. In these situations, I argue, our relations are not only interactions between humans and social bots, but also intra-actions (Barad, 1996) where humans and bots form inseparable assemblages, and infra-actions where our sociality is being programmed before and beyond rational inputs (Sampson, 2017). This means that social bots do not only build boundaries between what is human and what is not but also help us to define what is a platform and who or what is a user on that platform.

Synthetic Situations

According to the critics, the social bots on Ashley Madison do not paint a very bright picture of the future of social media connectivity:

> Instead of looking at Ashley Madison as a dating site, I think it's more accurate to call it an anti-community—a hugely popular social site where it's impossible to be social, because the men can't talk to each other, most of the women are fake, and the only interaction available is with credit card payments. It is one of the purest representations of dystopia I've ever seen.
> (*Newitz, 2015c*)

Dystopias aside, on a more general level, social bots are operators in what Karin Knorr Cetina (2009; 2014) calls a "synthetic situation." Synthetic situation is a concept coined to describe how we have shifted from "the face-to-face situation—which is so foundational for how we conceive of the emergence of sociality and effects like trust" (Knorr Cetina 2014, p. 45) into situations of augmented and temporalized environments with "fully or partially scoped components—in which we find ourselves in one another's and the scopic components' response presence, without needing to be in one another's physical presence" (Knorr Cetina, 2014, p. 47). Knorr Cetina's examples of synthetic situations include the trading floor of the stock market, the living room with TV sets, surgery rooms with monitors to assist operations, and videoconference meetings with physical and virtual participants. Monitors and screens in these settings are scopic media, which project and orient reality and people's responses to them (ibid., p. 42). With the integration of scopic media, these situations can be local and translocal, and with different degrees, human interaction becomes technologically mediated and the need for face-to-face communication dissipates (Knorr Cetina, 2009, p. 69).

While synthetic situations for Knorr Cetina are human-centric, one of its most notable effects is that the need for "embodied presence" disappears (Knorr Cetina, 2014, p. 47). The critics of Ashley Madison's use of social bots found specifically this potential for the disappearance of embodied presence as a potential for cheating:

> Ashley Madison, the dating website for cheaters, has admitted that some women on its site were virtual computer programs instead of real women. . . . It means that lots of men who paid for the dating website's features—such as sending messages to supposed ladies—were actually spending cash to speak to fembots. They thought they were cheating, but they were actually all alone.
>
> *(Pagliery, 2016)*

In these commentaries, it is the physicality of the relations that is missing from the site, and thus what is implied is that the authenticity of the relationships cannot be guaranteed:

> Using the site as a man is a little bit like playing Farmville, except instead of blowing your money on fake cow upgrades, you're blowing it on messages to fake women. At least Farmville is up front about the fact that you're burning money for a dumb fantasy.
>
> *(Newitz, 2015c)*

In these discussions, the understanding of the possible interactions with the bots is quite limited. This limitation can be defined by the lack of offline body, the other human being behind the screen. Since the human users are not interacting with other humans but artificial actors the authenticity and value of these relations becomes questioned.

If Ashley Madison's social bots are an indication of the future, I suggest that they need to be contextualized as what Raymond Williams (1977) defines as "structures of feeling." Social bots are the culture of the particular historical moment, which emerges in the contexts where user participation on social media is no longer limited to human-to-human interaction and algorithmic selves are automated. It is a moment where non-human actors of social media platforms are tied into the ways of digital capitalism and the practices of monetizing different engagements. As structures of feeling, social bots become indicative of the multifarious connections users searching for digital love are subjected to when they enter these platforms and want to take part in the services offered by these sites. More specifically, they explicate how the non-human has agency in building, mediating, and engaging users into different relations with each other and the sociotechnical platform. From this perspective there is indeed value and authenticity in social bots and the relations they establish. This value just differs from the value often given to human-to-human communication.

In fact, in its terms and conditions, Ashley Madison makes clear that social bots are not humans and they are "not intended to mimic or resemble any actual persons" in these synthetic situations; they are "fictitious" and should not be mixed with human references (Avid Dating Life Inc., 2013).[2] When Ashley Madison defines social bots as Ashley's Angels, one could easily associate "angels" with a number of feminized instances of fantasy in popular culture such as Charlie's Angels or the Angels of Victoria's Secret, but angels can also be seen as particular non-human actors. What I want to say is that we should not seek the definition of social bots in opposition to human users, but as specific sociotechnical systems that form assemblages with humans. To rephrase, in my analysis, I am deliberately trying to problematize the comparison of social bots with humans in order to understand their agential features. This is to say that social bots have their own material configurations and they also become social entities through these material configurations, which form affective assemblages (often together with humans), where different dynamics become produced and activated (Gemeinboeck, 2017).

Ashley's Angels

According to Newitz (2015b) "How angels are made" is a title for a long email thread where the developers and owners of the Ashley Madison site allegedly discuss the role and functions of social bots on the site; she (Newitz, 2015b) gives us a brief description of what bots in these discussions are:

> When men signed up for a free account, they would immediately be shown profiles of what internal documents call "Angels," or fake women whose details and photos had been batch-generated using specially designed software.

For Newitz, Ashley Madison's social bots are "fake women." This anthropocentric comparison seems typical of the different discussions that try to explain Ashley's Angels to a general readership. These comparisons are also not absent from scholarship discussing social bots. Robert Gehl and Maria Bakardjieva trace the first definition of social bots in their stealthiness and capability of mimicking human beings (Gehl & Bakardjieva, 2017). In specific, Gehl and Bakardijeva quote Boshmaf and colleagues who argue that "What makes a social bot different from self-declared bots . . . and spambots is that it is designed to be stealthy, that is, it is designed to pass itself off as a human being." If the notion that 70,000 of bots were gendered as female and under 100 were gendered as male is true, then what is also clear is that the platform produces a gendered distinction where the offline is predominantly seen as the regime of male users and the algorithmic self of the social bot is that of a female.

According to Gehl and Bakardjieva (2017, p. 2), from the cultural and social perspective it is highly significant that these bots are not just performing tasks or emulating human conversation but trying to present a self and be someone with whom users build social relationships. By their definition, the so-called humanness of these bots is achieved by mimicking other social media users or building an artificial intelligence that simulates human users on the site (ibid.). The "passing itself off as a human being" is about appearances and performances that take place on the site. Possible appearances and performance relate to things like how the company profiles their users for marketing purposes, who they are targeting as a particular user group, and where their investments are. Here the gendered division of Ashley's Angeles matters. But appearances and performance also relate to how the human is turned into a profile and performs their identity through a ready-made set of operations: such as liking, sharing, and commenting. These, as also Grant Bollmer and Chris Rodley (2017, p. 148) note, are the same actions the social bots can perform. The platform conditions the possibilities for both humans and bots making them look alike.

Importantly, it is also possible to argue that the stealthiness—which according to previous definitions is seen as essential to social bots—is not a quality we can associate with Ashley's Angels. For users who signed up in 2013, and read Ashley Madison's terms and conditions when they signed up for the site, the presence of the bots was no surprise. The terms and conditions state:

> You acknowledge and agree that some of the profiles posted on the Site are associated with our "Ashley's Angels™" and may be fictitious.
> (*Avid Dating Life Inc., 2013*)

The fact that social bots are called angels is also not a revelatory finding, since the site's terms of service from 2013 indicate the trademarked use of Ashley's Angels. Ashley's Angels are first and foremost non-human actors, which should not be mixed with any real human user. To re-iterate, when the users sign up for an account, they also subject themselves to interactions with the bots, with the non-human, which does not resemble a human user. Again we can refer to the terms and conditions:

> [A]ny interaction or messaging with Ashley's Angels™ is independent of, and separate from, our general database of Members seeking personal or physical or other kinds of encounters or introductions.
> (*Ibid.*)

The terms of service quite clearly make the point that social bots used by the site are not mimicking human beings or trying to pass themselves off as human beings. Rather they are very specific social media users which operate together with the human. This is also highlighted in the terms of service document, which explicitly states "you cannot meet any of our Ashley's Angels in person" and Ashley's Angels are not based on any user or member of our Service. A single Ashley's Angel™ may have more than one profile on our Service.

(*Ibid.*)

While the terms and conditions do not exclusively write off the possibility that Ashley's Angels are appearing as human users to the extent that descriptions, pictures, and information included in the profiles of Ashley's Angels are based on the appearance of human users, they ask the user to acknowledge and agree that these features are not associated with real persons.

The denial of association with human users is important because it challenges the ideas of representation and mimicry. To rephrase, if human users are divided between online and offline identities, Ashley's Angels exist only at the level of the online platform. They do not have a body outside the communicative acts undertaken on the platform. Symptomatically, this is not only an understanding of social bots derived from our research materials but also how, according to John Durham Peters, angels have been described in Scholastic angelology (Peters, 1999, p. 76). Indeed, the name "Ashley's Angels" could also be used as indicative of the nature of these bots. According to Peters (ibid., pp. 74–75), angels provide us with "a lasting vision of the ideal speech situation, one without distortion or interference." This is because angels do not have a body, which would obstruct the message (ibid., p. 76). The body is the place where human communication is differentiated from communication with angels. Following Saint Thomas Aquinas, Peters notes that the flesh always limits human communication, which is divided into inner and outer speech. Inner speech happens within the limits of our bodies, and outer speech tries to express what is hidden and concealed in the body. Since angels have no bodies, their communication is clear and never concealed (ibid., pp. 76–77).

Since Ashley's Angels do not have a body in the offline world, they embody the logics and affordances of the social media platform. This is to say that Ashley's Angels cannot be discussed only as fake human users. Rather they are agential communication of the platform. The platforms speak with the voice of these angels. To rephrase, instead of representational analysis, we should consider how social bots work as themselves in the context of the sociotechnical platform.

Conceal and Congeal

Ben Light (2016) points out that the social bots of Ashley Madison are defined as helpers and entertainers. According to him, bots help the users to navigate and learn about the site and the communications, and monitoring that everyone complies with the rules of the platform is an example of the former. When bots act as entertainers, according to Light they send Ashley's Gifts, winks, private keys to additional content, and are inscribed "with a language of sexually charged playfulness" (Light, 2016). The terms and conditions state that the purpose of our Ashley's Angels™ is to provide entertainment, to allow you to explore our Services and to promote greater participation in our Services.

(Avid Dating Life Inc., 2013)

What the terms and conditions implicate with entertainment, promotion of greater participation, and exploration of services is a simulation of "communication with real members" which is said, "to encourage more conversation and interaction with users." Newitz gives an example, and simultaneously criticizes the depth of some of these simulations of communication:

[I]nstead of talking to real women, men were mostly fielding robo-mails from the system that say things like, "Sexicindi has indicated she is interested in someone just like you. You should send her a custom message to connect."

(Newitz, 2015c)

This quote indicates a process where the user logs on to the Ashley Madison site and is then suggested a person named Sexicindi to connect with.

Light (2016) points out that users may enjoy the "erotic" chat with a social bot even if they are aware of the fact that they are chatting with a social bot and even if they acknowledge that they can never meet that bot offline. This reminds us of Peters's angels whose body does not matter in communication but who still can have meaningful agency.

Many of the Ashley Madison critics, however, note that in the context of Ashley's Angels the online body (as in the appearance) indeed matters. They argue that Ashley's Angels try to appear as female and thus are completely fake, and their identity as bots is concealed. Instead of leaning one way or the other, what is important is the way these social bots mediate; Ashley's Angels are the "intervening substance through which impressions are conveyed to the senses or a force acts on objects at a distance" (Grusin, 2015).

Now Peters is not the only media theorist who has discussed angels as media. In fact, the operation of Sexicindi resembles the way Sybille Krämer (Krämer, 2015, pp. 60–61) describes the operation of angels as communicative entities. For Krämer, what is important is the relation of exchange between the two worlds the angels mediate. According to Krämer there is a fundamental distinction between heaven and earth, and communication between humans and the transcendental is only possible if the angel embodies the human form (Krämer, 2015, pp. 60–61, 88, 91). Here angels become intermediaries between two worlds (ibid., 87). And like angels, we can think of social bots as "hybrid entities" (ibid., p. 91). What is of the essence here is how the social bot establishes connections between users and the platform. To exemplify, in the context of Ashley Madison the online presents one world and the offline the other. Ashley's Angels are software programs programmed to transmit messages from the online platform to the screens and interfaces of the human user, and establish new relationships between the two. Like angels according to Krämer (ibid., p. 60), also social bots hide their own nature; the meaning of the message is more important than the mechanism of its delivery. For Krämer, the nature or the meaning of the messenger actually has to disappear in order for the message to be successfully transmitted (Krämer, 2015, p. 60). If the user pays too much attention to the fact that they are communicating with the bots, the actual communication will disappear behind the techno-social conditions that establish it in the first place.

The message, "Sexicindi has indicated she is interested in someone just like you. You should send her a custom message to connect," matters as much as the medium of its transmission (social bot). While it is very difficult to separate the portrayed gender of Sexicindi as being also part of the message, and rather than stating that the medium is the message, I want to point to another line of thinking; we are operating here with "the ethics of mediality" (Krämer, 2015, p. 61), which do not begin from what users do or can do on social media but what social media does to its users. In other words, the ethics of social media contest the idea that social media are neutral platforms where users operate freely.

Robert W. Gehl (2014, p. 21) notes that "social bots are built to be *social,* to interact with us while we are using Facebook and Twitter. They also work to subtly alter how social media users interact with and link to one another." Ashley Madison is a typical social media site in the sense that it is also actively programming sociality. Programming sociality or "programmed sociality" is a concept used by Taina Bucher (2013) in describing the artificiality of our social media relations. This is not the only term coined to mean the same thing; for example, Van Dijck speaks of "engineering sociality" (2013) and in the context of social bots Gehl and Bakardjieva discuss "social architecting" (2017, p. 8). Bucher's (2013) example of programmed sociality is Facebook's People You May Know function, which actively seeks connections between Facebook users based on for example their smartphone contacts, locational data, or friends of friends. Indeed, there is a similar implication that Sexicindi is not suggested for the user only by a random choice, but because there is a match in interests. Whether the user is actually matched with the preferences of the user named Sexicindi is an open question, but the rhetoric used here resembles the social media's capability to search and analyze patterns and make meaningful connections among human users and thus is appealing as such.

How does this programming of sociality take place? According to Light (2016) "In Ashley Madison, bots appear to be used to chat with human users to keep them engaged, and they use fake profiles, created by Ashley Madison employees, as a 'face' for the interaction." Light finds different "interaction possibilities" from Ashley Madison's terms and conditions, these include: collecting messages, instant chat, and/or replies from individuals or programs. Furthermore "the profiles may offer, initiate or send winks, private keys, and virtual gifts" building direct interactions with the user (ibid.).

Interaction, for Peters (1999, p. 59), is an important part of communication. He divides communication into the processes of "individuated interaction" and "generalized access." Paraphrasing Peters, in moments of individuated interaction—such as in dialogue with one's friends—one is treated as a unique individual, and in moments of generalized access—such as in court—one is treated as any other human (ibid.). This framework can also be used to describe how social bots and humans are encountering each other and having effects upon each other. They form relations of individuation and generalization.

Furthermore, interaction assumes that there are two bodies or objects, which have effects upon each other: the human user and the social bot. The Turing test is a famous example of these interactions, where individuated interaction is deliberately tried to separate from generalized access. As the popularized version of the Turing test goes, the bots try to conceal their identity and the human tries to decide whether they are chatting with a bot or another human user based on questions and answers. The test is proven positive when the bot after answering a set of questions has become indistinguishable from a human. Interaction here is based on a feedback loop; success is then evaluated in the human terms.

Newitz (2015a), by interpreting the source code of Ashley Madison, gives us another example of these interactions of concealing one's identity. By analyzing the columns on the source code titled "bc_email_last_time," "bc_chat_last_time," and "email_reply_last_time," Newtiz argues that Ashley Madison was tracking and controlling how and when social bots called "engagers" were interacting with human users. According to her, the interactions were rather simple starting with "Hi," "hows it going?" "chat?" "how r u?" or "anybody home? Lol," and then if the user replied, the social bot would say things like "Hmmmm, when I was younger I used to sleep with my friend's boyfriends. I guess old habits die hard although I could never sleep with their husbands" (Newitz, 2015a). Especially the last line could be interpreted as a line that conceals the bot's algorithmic self and leads the human user into thinking that they are chatting with an actual person. As Newitz (2015b) points out: "What you see on social media isn't always what it seems. Your friends may be bots, and you could be sharing your most intimate fantasies with hundreds of lines of PHP code." The interactivist interpretation of this discussion indeed suggests that there is a categorical need for the subject (human user) to be able to distinguish the object (the bot); being a social media user is partaking in an endless Turing test. If the Turing test fails, the user will be scammed, lured into a paying customer and being manipulated by fake beings (cf. ibid.).

For this understanding of social bots, it is fundamental that we can make a clear Cartesian cut between humans and social bots and that the boundaries of these two entities are transparent. There is also a strong assumption that social bots, if their identity is concealed, as the definition of the stealthiness of social bots passing off as human beings suggests, are ethically questionable and the interactions we have with them are not real and cannot form real experience.

However, the dissolving of social bots and human users, the disappearance of their boundaries, to the extent that we no longer know what is real and what is fake, should not be taken only as a negative feature of our culture of connectivity. For me it signifies the importance of non-human actors on social media and agential qualities that cannot be reduced to human users or social bots. Barad (1996, p. 179) speaks about agential realism, where knowledge is situated, boundaries are in flux, and objectivity is embodied. Barad's example, of course, does not come from angelogy but quantum physics. What Barad wants to argue is that what we can know of things like physics is related to the measurement apparatuses (1996, pp. 169–171).

To rephrase, Barad's agential realism turns our attention to how instead of concealing their identities social bots congeal our experiences on social media platforms. Hence, the phenomenon of being a human Ashley Madison user is inseparable from the operation of the social bots on the platform. For example, the social bots are tools for seeking for information or assisting the human users in navigating the site. The users are either aware that they are not chatting with a real person, or the algorithmic self of the other does not matter. Arguably here social bots provide a generalized access rather than an individual experience; they are agencies of information, observation, and navigation and they are not separable from the relation they generate (Barad, 1996, pp. 181–182).

In these cases, users do not merely interact with social bots but rather generate relations of intra-action with them where there is no need to separate one entity from the other. As Barad (1996, p. 183) notes, an agency "is matter of intra-acting, that is, agency is enactment, it is not something someone has." Instead of positioning interaction between the binary of human user and the social bot, intra-action shifts the focus to the context of the relation in which these two components are made up. Gina Neff and Peter Nagy (2016) describe this co-dependent relation as symbiotic agency. To rephrase, it is easy to take the subject-object, human-social bot dualism as inherent and fixed. However, neither the social bots nor the human users are entities separate from the platform where they appear. The relations they generate are situated and so are the knowledges, experiences, and encounters produced in those relations.

Programming the sociality as intra-action is to give the online body a capability to do something it could not without the other entities that are joined with it in the relation. Intra-action establishes the conditions for the formed body to act. In other words, it conditions the actions possible. The social bots, in other words, do not lead their own lives on Ashley Madison but become actualized only in the moments when users are engaging with them. In these moments they lead users to certain directions, give them information, and open the platform for the user and user for the platform.

Guaranteed Affair

The economic logic of Ashley Madison, as explained by Light (2016) is tied to turning guests into members by acquiring paid users through a "guaranteed affair" function, which promises authentic interactions with other human users. He explains that the platform has a specific membership fee and credit system, where users' different actions cost credits (ibid.). Also, the texts focusing on Ashley Madison's use of social bots note that the use of bots has strong ties with the economic logic of the platform. As one of the commentaries notes:

> Men can even pay a premium rate for a "guaranteed affair." To email women, men have to pay extra, and then they have to pay more still if they want to send a "gift" of a silly gif or picture.
>
> (Newitz, 2015c)

On Ashley Madison, all users can create accounts, chat and reply to messages, send and receive photos, add members to favorites lists and perform a search but, for example, the initiation of chat session and sending custom mail-messages is limited to paid users only (Light, 2016).

Returning to Peters's individuated interaction and generalized access, to understand the guaranteed affair we need to distinguish two experiences created by the social bot: personal and social. Indeed, paying for the membership guarantees more individualized experience in the form of chat session or sending custom messages. But while these interactions and intra-actions on Ashley Madison operate on a personal and individuated level, they are also part of a larger social experience of forming and not-forming relationships with social bots.

To be more specific, for the members sociality is limited exclusively to human to human interaction. Light (2016) quotes the platform's terms and conditions: "Our profiles message with Guest users, but not with Members. Members interact only with profiles of actual persons." In 2013, this was phrased as "Ashley's Angels™ message with Guest users, but not with Members" (Avid Dating Life Inc., 2013). Here the platform itself defines the use of social bots through the negative: social bots can be interpreted as fakes/profiles/impersonators and their communication is seen as inferior to an actual human-to-human communication. The promise of a guaranteed affair is also a promise that the synthetic situation is exclusively human: bots may engage these affairs, but they disappear when money is paid. There is an affective pull, where the human and human relations are lifted to the pedestal. The exclusiveness of human-to-human communication turns into a privilege one needs to pay for.

It is perhaps indicative that while on their terms and conditions Ashley Madison defines the use of social bots through the positive, they are defined as helpers or entertainers, the member/guest binary makes a more negative distinction, highlighting the authenticity of human-to-human communication at the expense of social bots. But these binaries are only the surface of how social bots have a meaningful role on social media platforms. To explicate the third way of understanding social bots we need to go beyond the negative and positive and think of them not as classified categories but as general structures of feeling.

Williams's structures of feeling operate beyond classification, rationalization, or exact definition; they are "pre-emergent or emergent" and "exert palpable pressures and set effective limits on experience and on action" (1977, p. 132). Social bots understood as structures of feeling are infra-structures in the sense that they operate below the level of the individual intensifying experiences and affecting the users of the platform.

Social bots intensify, what Tony Sampson (2017, p. 112) describes as "vulnerabilities to persuasive suggestibility in the sensory environments." Sampson, following the nineteenth-century criminologist Gabriel Tarde, defines human subjectivity as being always in the making. Humans are always divided between desire and affect, belief and cognition, conscious and unconscious, volition and mechanical habit (ibid., p. 113). A figure of such subjectivity is the somnambulist, who "unconsciously and involuntarily reflects the opinion of others, or allows an action of others to be suggested to him" (Tarde, quoted in ibid.). According to Sampson (ibid.), the "sleepwalker is caught in an intersection between a culture of attraction and a biologically hardwired inclination to imitate."

If we take this idea of human subjectivity, what follows is that humans are suggestible to bots and their actions outside the regimes of direct interaction or intra-action. Here programming sociality no longer denotes the direct process of a social bot recommending the human user to connect with another user such as "Sexicindi." Programming sociality in synthetic situations means, for example, that "embodied presence" gives way to "response presence," where the parties communicating with each other do not need to be physically present but still need to respond to the incoming cues in a timely manner (Knorr Cetina, 2014, p. 47). What then guarantees an affair are the processes that subject humans to parts of a feedback loop mechanism responding to cues just like bots, in a timely manner. This could be an example of what Bollmer and Rodley (2017, p. 160) call "machinic sociality" developed by social bots. What is implied is that as social media users we become programmed on an infra-structural level where our possibilities are conditioned by the platform and actions reduced to actions on the level of response presence. In other words, here social bots are no longer imitating humans but quite the contrary, the human user has become the imitation of a social bot (see also Bollmer & Rodley 2017, p. 157). This is what guarantees an affair with the platform.

Conclusion

If we really want to embrace the non-human perspectives on social media, we have to give up the belief that relationships we have on social media are essentially human relationships and the networked modes of being are always human-like. The two views examined in this chapter, that Ashley's Angels were fake female and designed to lure (male) users of the site, and that Ashley's Angels need to be understood as non-human entities, give us two views of the algorithmic self of the social bots. Neither of the views denies that the bots can have agency, but the ways in which agency is understood are in the former based on ethical valuations, and on the practical interactions in the second. However, what my analysis points out is that regardless of which perspective we choose, the agential realism of social bots cannot be limited only to moments of interaction. To understand how sociality is programmed, or the way in which the platform speaks and manifests itself through the bots, we need the distinctions of interaction, intra-action, and infra-action.

In synthetic situations, interaction describes the social bot as somebody. The social bot is an individual or self, an entity the human user encounters and interacts with on a given social media platform. In these cases, the social bot is often described to be somebody that tries to pass itself off as someone else. Specifically, both historically (i.e. the Turing test) and empirically (criticism toward Ashley's Angels) the bot is seen to imitate the human user. Intra-action describes the social bot as nobody. The social bot is given an identity only when it forms affective assemblages with the human user. The social bot here resonates with the human user. It does not try to fake or mimic the human user but merely co-operates with them by helping or providing entertainment. Infra-action defines the social bot as anybody. Social bots are here seen to structure our experiences of the synthetic situation on levels that cannot be reduced to specific interactions or intra-actions between human and non-human users. Rather they set up a field of affective intensities which engage the user with the platform.

It is perhaps ironic that a social media platform dedicated to cheating in a relationship was itself accused of cheating in the exact relationships it established. If we follow this irony in predicting our future with social bots, we can conclude by arguing that not only our situations will be synthetic but also our relationships. What is important here, and what my analysis has tried to do, is to argue that we need to stop thinking that synthetic is somehow fake and not real. When synthetic is seen as real, and algorithmic selves, social bots, and social media platforms all form symbiotic relations, the human perspective is only one among many.

Notes

1 These numbers are interpretations not confirmed by Ashley Madison.
2 I have accessed the terms and conditions of May 15, 2013 with the Wayback Machine. A method also used by Ben Light (2016). https://web.archive.org/web/20130515121746/https://www.ashleymadison.com/app/public/tandc.p?c=1

References

Avid Dating Life Inc. (2013). Terms and conditions. *Ashley Madison*, May 15. www.ashleymadison.com/app/public/tandc.p?c=1

Avid Life Media. (2016). New leadership and vision set to transform Ashley Madison. *Ashley Madison Media*, July 4. http://media.ashleymadison.com/avid-life-media-breaks-its-silence/

Barad, K. (1996). Meeting the universe halfway: Realism and social constructivism without contradiction. In L. H. Nelson (Ed.), *Feminism, science, and the philosophy of science* (pp. 161–194). Dordrecht, Netherlands: Kluwer Academic.

Bollmer, G. & Rodley, C (2017). Speculations on the sociality of social bots. In R.W. Gehl & M. Bakardjieva (Eds.), *Social bots and their friends: Digital media and the automation of sociality* (pp. 147–163). New York and London: Routledge.

Brown, K. V. (2015). Recapping the aftermath of the Ashley Madison hack: Suicide, fembots, cracked passwords and more. *Fusion*, September 10. http://fusion.net/story/195787/whats-going-on-with-ashley-madison/

Bucher, T. (2013). The friendship assemblage. Investigating programmed sociality on Facebook. *Television & New Media*, 14(6), 479–493.

Dijck, J. Van. (2013). *The culture of connectivity: A critical history of social media*. Oxford: Oxford Univeristy Press.

Gehl, R. W. (2014). *Reverse engineering social media. Software, culture, and political economy in new media capitalism*. Philadelphia: Temple University Press.

Gehl, R. W., & Bakardjieva, M. (2017). Social bots and their friends. In R. W. Gehl (Ed.), *Social bots and their friends: Digital media and the automation of sociality* (pp. 1–16). New York and London: Routledge.

Gemeinboeck, P. (2017). Introduction. *Fibreculture Journal* (28). http://twentyeight.fibreculturejournal.org/.

Gibbs, S. (2015). Ashley Madison condemns attack as experts say hacked database is real. *The Guardian*, August 19. www.theguardian.com/technology/2015/aug/19/ashley-madisons-hacked-customer-files-posted-online-as-threatened-say-reports

Grusin, R. (2015). Radical mediation. *Critical Inquiry*, 42(1), 124–148.

Knorr Cetina, K. (2009). The synthetic situation: Interactionism for a global world. *Symbolic Interaction*, 32(1), 61–87.

Knorr Cetina, K. (2014). Scopic media and global coordination: The mediatization of face-to-face encounters. In K. Lundby (Ed.), *Mediatization of communication* (pp. 39–62). Berlin/Boston: De Gruyter.

Krämer, S. (2015). *Medium, messenger, transmission: An approach to media philosophy*. Amsterdam: Amsterdam University Press.

Light, B. (2016). The rise of speculative devices: Hooking up with the bots of Ashley Madison. *First Monday*, 21(6). doi: http://dx.doi.org/10.5210/fm.v21i6.6426

Neff, G., & Nagy, P. (2016). Talking to bots: Symbiotic agency and the case of Tay. *International Journal of Communication*, 10, 4915–4931.

Newitz, A. (2015a). Ashley Madison code shows more women, and more bots. *Gizmodo*, August 31. http://gizmodo.com/ashley-madson-code-shows-more-women-and-more-bots-1727613924

Newitz, A. (2015b). How Ashley Madison hid its fembot con from users and investigators. *Gizmodo*, August 9. http://gizmodo.com/how-ashley-madison-hid-its-fembot-con-from-users-and-in-1728410265

Newitz, A. (2015c). The fembots of Ashley Madison (updated). *Gizmodo*, August 27. http://gizmodo.com/the-fembots-of-ashley-madison-1726670394

Pagliery, J. (2016). Some Ashley Madison women were actually computer "fembots." *CNN Money*, July 5: http://money.cnn.com/2016/07/05/technology/ashley-madison-fembots/

Peters, J. D. (1999). *Speaking into the air: A history of the idea of communication*. Chicago and London: University of Chicago Press.

Sampson, T. D. (2017). *The assemblage brain. Sense making in neuroculture*. Minneapolis, London: University of Minnesota Press.

Williams, R. (1977). *Marxism and literature*. Oxford: Oxford University Press.

11

DISRUPTIVE JOY

#BlackOutDay's Affirmative Resonances

Alexander Cho

If you were on Twitter or Tumblr on March 6, 2015, you might have noticed something unusual. Scores and scores of black Twitter and Tumblr users were taking, uploading, and circulating selfies, intentionally flooding the system with black faces. According to one report, by noon there were over 58,000 tweets with the hashtag #BlackOutDay (Tan, 2015). In my own experience, given the queer-of-color networks I am involved in on Tumblr, the saturation was much higher; some selfies that came across my dashboard eventually received over 250,000 notes each.[1]

I had been participating in queer-of-color Tumblr networks for five years at this point as a user-ethnographer and I hadn't seen anything like this—this massive, this guttural, and this affirmative. Many people read the selfie as the consummate act of vanity, and the "millennial" generation has been dismissively referred to as the "selfie generation" (Blow, 2014). However, this practice, on this day, had a different tilt. According to one widely read Tumblr, TheBlackout. org, the original impetus for #BlackOutDay was:

> In a show of community and solidarity, for those 24 hours, we are exclusively posting and reblogging pics, gifs, videos, selfies, etc. of Black people. We want to show that Black History is happening today, right now. That we are all Black History.
>
> *(#TheBlackout, 2017)*

This practice was also proposed as an exercise in affirmation, a flooding of blackness in what is normally a popular cultural understanding of beauty being equated with only white bodies. A person widely credited to be one of the inventors of #BlackOutDay, Tumblr user T'von, wrote this after the fact:

> I got inspired to propose Blackout day after thinking "Damn, I'm not seeing enough Black people on my dash." Of course I see a constant amount

of Black celebrities but what about the regular people? Where is their shine? When I proposed it, I thought people would think it was a good idea, but not actually go through with implementing it. Luckily people wanted to get behind the idea, and @recklessthottie created the #Blackout tag . . . I'm really sick and tired of seeing the "European standard of beauty" prevail. It's past time for the beauty of Black people to be showcased. I love all people of color, but this here is for *us*.

(Twitter users celebrate, 2015)

#BlackOutDay got major media attention, including stories by ABC News (Tan, 2015) and *Washington Post* (Izadi, 2015). But more than that: #BlackOutDay was *intense*. I don't think people were expecting it to be as emotional as it was. I remember seeing posts pop up on my Tumblr feed a few minutes before midnight on March 5; people couldn't wait. As it happened—as it really started to materialize before your eyes—it became an emotional thing. Emotional because there were really so many beautiful people out there, emotional because we all knew how white-dominated our image regimes are, but it was still jarring and freeing to see, for once, an alternative. It was emotional for the sheer intensity and amount of participation that happened, emotional to see the range of blackness that came through, and to realize how flattened "black" is allowed to be when it does emerge in mainstream representations. It was emotional because, as many people on Tumblr pointed out, we are often only presented with black bodies in mainstream media as corpses.

People were excited. People couldn't contain themselves. People posted a few minutes before midnight, calling what they posted "pre-BlackOutDay" selfies. There were #BlackOutDay parties. Many people on my feed wrote that they were moved to tears. I think people half expected it wasn't going to happen. Then the power of the collective began to overwhelm them.

The goal of this chapter is threefold. First, it is to try to honor and document the spirit of the moment, as much as it is possible for a non-black observer to do. As a user and researcher of Tumblr, as a critical race theorist interested in the politics of feeling, and as an activist academic and queer multiracial person, I felt that there was something very important happening right before my eyes. I initially did not want to write about it because I have white-passing privilege in the United States, and that was the whole point. Yet as the years went by I grew anxious, as I did not see academic literature on it, and I did not want to see its traces erased from official record, as ephemeral as Tumblr is, as it is bought and sold by corporation after corporation. It should go without saying, but I welcome any black-identified writer, or anyone else for that matter, to flatten or refine everything I assert here; it is only my take.

Second, this chapter attempts to argue for the radical potential of collective affirmation, theorizing a middle way in the face of a recent critical literature that is (rightly) dubious of dutiful "happiness" or other good feelings. Third, this chapter calls upon an interpretation of affect theory that advocates for close attention to the play of emergence and variation of the event-in-motion as an analytic heuristic to try to understand the viscerally powerful—and indeed, radical—heft of a collective act such as this one. In other words, #BlackOutDay would be easy to dismiss as an ephemeral millennial "clicktivist" moment (White, n.d.), lacking conventional badges of political significance, centered around the most mundane and self-serving act of digital participation (the selfie). This chapter argues that these reasons are precisely why it mattered.

Ultimately, holding these three lines of comment together, this chapter explores the "networked self"—one in which users marshal the tools at their disposal on social network sites to perform selfhood in a way that both echoes and updates long-standing theories of identity performance to include multiple simultaneous and collapsed contexts, accelerated network connections especially involving weak ties, and "a variety of multimedia tools that enable the possibility for more controlled and imaginative performances of identity online" (Papacharissi, 2011, p. 307). The selfie, here, is one of those tools, and this chapter pays close attention to the "patterns of sociality that emerge" (ibid., p. 309) via the agentic taking and circulating of the selfie over the network. It also hints at pushing "the networked self" even further: that perhaps, in this oddly collective moment of affective networked sharing, the feeling of "self" itself ceases to be pure singularity, that the networked self can, for a brief moment, retain a real political bodily specificity while at the same time transcend strict Cartesian bounds of individual subjectivity via a sense-in-common.

Selfie Politics

Can the act of taking and/or circulating selfies ever be a political, or even counter-hegemonic, one? This is a tricky question, especially since the selfie is perceived by the legacy press and other commentators as an eye-rollingly trite act of self-indulgent millennial vanity. There is, however, academic research that points to the fact that the answer is "yes," especially when selfies are part of a network or collective. Theresa Senft and Nancy Baym tackled this question (in addition to many others) in editing a substantial collection of original scholarship on selfies in a special section of the *International Journal of Communication* in 2015 (Senft & Baym, 2015).

One of the special section's articles, an examination of the power of the taking and circulation of the selfie in the context of Brazilian slums, concludes:

> [F]or marginalized users who are suffering in a relatively severe living environment, selfies are not a shallow way to show narcissism, fashion, and self-promotion and seek attention; selfies, rather, empower the users to exercise free speech, practice self-reflection, express spiritual purity, improve literacy skills, and form strong interpersonal connections.
> *(Nemer & Freeman, 2015)*

Elsewhere, Katrin Tiidenberg, in an examination of Tumblr users who exchange NSFW ("not safe for work") selfies, explains that her interview participants "have reclaimed the body-aesthetic from the regime of shame (Koskela, 2004) of the body-normative consumer society, thus redefining, what sexy or beautiful is" (Tiidenberg, 2014). Tiidenburg argues that her interviewees have successfully used the agentic potential of participatory media (in this case, Tumblr), to challenge hegemonic regimes of beauty and shame.

If critical selfie scholarship has disrupted any simple read of selfies as throwaway "narcissism," it has also disrupted the idea that a selfie is an isolated, solipsistic act at all. Aaron Hess (2015) asks us to think of the selfie as an always-in-flux component of a Deleuze and Guattari-inspired assemblage—or perhaps multiple assemblages—on a number of simultaneous registers. He writes, "While the easy explanation is that selfies exist as emblems of a narcissistic contemporary culture, a deeper reading of selfies instead provides insight into the relationships between technology, the self, materiality, and networks" (Hess, 2015, p. 1630), expanding, "Selfies are, on face, about the self, yet they long for—require, even—sharing to be considered 'true' selfies" (p. 1631). For Hess, the selfie always implicates not just the picture-taker, but also the physical space, the device, and the network upon which it is shared (p. 1632), including its viewers, real, or, I'll add, anticipated. This observation undergirds a crucial point in my argument to follow: one must look at the play of the selfie across the network, in this case, the specifically timed emergence of visible blackness in a digital space otherwise dominated by ex-nominated white beauty ideals, as an agentic and hegemonically resistant act.

In one powerful #BlackOutDay selfie, which received over 12,500 notes by the time I saw it (my timestamp indicates it was early am on March 7, 2015, just over twenty-four hours after #BlackOutDay started), a smiling father who appears to be in his late twenties poses with his young son, also smiling broadly at the camera. The post reads:

> My 4 year old son asked me this afternoon why God made us black. He didn't understand why he was black when all the other kids in his preschool class are white. It was amazing I could get on tumblr today and show him all the black people who were proud of their dark skin and how black people come in different shades, sizes, and backgrounds. I love my black skin and I will make damn sure he loves his too.[2]

As of this writing, the post has over 32,000 notes. In another widely circulated selfie, a young man has tears in his eyes, arms outstretched, mouth slightly open in a hint of a smile. He writes:

> Sorry I'm crying. As someone in my position; Bisexual, disabled (hearing impaired), not confident in my appearance, and struggling. I tend to avoid posting pictures for a movement. Even if it is one meant to motivate,

inspire, and more. However, after seeing some pictures of other African-Americans in similar positions as myself . . . after some thought I built up the courage. Thanks you all so much for #blackout.

This post and selfie were also featured in an article on Buzzfeed (Adewunmi, 2015); by that point, at 11:52 am on March 6, it had garnered over 285,000 notes. Lest there be any doubt that this flooding and sharing of black selfies was political, one user succinctly literalized one of #BlackOutDay's ongoing emotional undercurrents:

> These aren't just selfies, they should remind you that #BlackLivesMatter.

The testimony kept going. Scrolling after scrolling. One text post read:

> Man I am seriously about to cry right now this is the most beautiful I've ever really felt to be honest with you guys. Our BLACK IS BEAUTIFUL THROUGH OUT THE NATION.

One Tumblr user I follow reblogged an image of multiple Tumblr text posts compiled from different black Tumblr users:

> I'm honestly getting so emotional going through my dash. Thinking about how I used to hate my skin and how I wanted to be white cause I thought then maybe I could be loved. I even got fooled into being hateful towards my own people.

Another:

> But honestly I feel so beautiful right now. I'm not the most confident person in the world but today I've gained so much confidence. Like to see so many people with my complexion stand in solidarity and positivity is so beautiful. It's so dope that we came together and shared our beauty and to hear people's stories about how they weren't confident either brought tears to my eyes. Like please you guys are so beautiful don't let anyone tell you any different. I don't know I'm just so happy and emotional lol.

And another:

> Blackout is such an amazing thing. Seeing my lil sis confident in her hair, nose, curves, makes me want to cry.

It is hard to capture the strange rawness of feeling that people on my dash were literalizing as #BlackOutDay started in its early hours. It was a flood, a rush. So many pictures of faces you never see. People literally crying. Smiling. Partying. Over the years, I have learned to actively avoid following gay Tumblrs that post what one might call normatively "sexy" images of scruffy artsy/hunky hipster white guys in service of my own self-esteem in the face of a racialized hegemonic mirroring in which I am erased or distorted, and it was still a flood for me, too.

True to Tumblr's tradition of critical discourse, #BlackOutDay had its own correctives. Some Tumblr users observed that, even within the critical mass of black selfies flooding social media, there were rhythms of old-time stratifications: colorism, ableism, certain types of normalized hair styles. According to one Tumblr user, "We still need to be critical about it and DO BETTER. . . . Some people didn't feel safe or attractive enough to even take selfies because they were triggered by the huge number of 'tumblr aesthetic' light skinned/loose 3a curls/ neurotypical kinds of people reaching thousands of notes on their selfies."

But this was part of the whole energy of the thing, the multiple lines of variation in perspective and discourse that shot out of the moment, all underpinned by a wildly resonant affective energetics located squarely in the affirmative. Hess's assertion that, paradoxically, selfies depend on circulation and only have meaning in community—the selfie as a communal moment—is quite appropriate here, and was the genesis of, I argue, something full of radical potential.

Happiness and the Affirmative

It is very hard to argue *for* happiness in the critical left tradition of cultural studies. A wave of critical (un)happiness studies has sprung up in recent years (Berlant, 2011; Ahmed, 2010; Cvetkovich, 2012), and genealogically-related key works in queer theory are very preoccupied with feeling bad (Edelman, 2004; Love, 2009; Halperin & Traub, 2010; Halberstam, 2011). I want to recognize that this work is valuable in highlighting the lived experience of oppression and how our emotional orientations are themselves structured by rigid, internalized schemes of colony and family; I wrote about the radical potential of bad feelings, borrowing Heather Love's phrase "stubborn negativity" to describe other kinds of queerly felt dynamics on Tumblr (Cho, 2015). Yet I think there is more nuance to be teased in this area.

What about the tendrils of potential reaching out from a moment of cathartic joy under a weight of systemic oppression? What about the shock of being moved to smiling tears? What about the power of an event that is not an appeal for distant utopia, not a productive duty toward blithe and dumb happiness, but rather a realization of a resistant solidarity engendered by unexpected feelings of kinship (Eng, 2010)? In other words, #BlackOutDay: can we skeptically regard late capital's machinic operation, massaging our feelings for profit across the network, and at the same time understand that these messages can be radical—and can be radically *felt*?

Tumblr was surely happy that #BlackOutDay happened; it drove people to post and participate on its platform and it generated major press coverage. It would be easy to levy a simple political-economic critique here and claim that it was all in the service of profit at the end; roll credits. After all, social media companies are hungrily churning out new tactics to capture and monetize feelings (McNeal, 2014; Machkovech, 2017). But, as an observer of the moment, it is difficult for me to ignore the radical charge of the affirmative. In addition to the rightful political-economic critique, I also view this as a moment of resistant politics—in this case, a politics that accumulates from a shared affective register, an affirmation that is highly charged, a disruption of psychic structures that are so ingrained that we don't even realize how it can affect something as fundamental as attraction, or how we regard beauty. We all *know* there is a white standard of beauty, and we all *know better* than that. But when do we ever get the chance to *feel* better than that? We know that #BlackLivesMatter matters, at least in terms of shifting discourse and making it newsworthy to talk about the systematic state murder of black people. I view #BlackOutDay as an emotionally chiral companion.

Lauren Berlant's *Cruel Optimism* (2011) is a signpost here, suggesting that our current neoliberal situation is defined by retreating opportunity and increasing fantasy for the "good life." Is our happiness, or striving for it, a ruse, a carrot, a cruel sleight of hand? Berlant describes cruel optimism as the relation that exists "when something you desire is actually an obstacle to your flourishing" (p. 1). Berlant cautions us to not get too attached to optimism as object or guiding orientation; she even warns us not to get too attached to normative political attachments at all (pp. 2, 224). But, as we will see later, she offers a way out in terms of noise and silence—a register on which #BlackOutDay seems much more resonant than that of "normative speech" (p. 230).

Likewise, Sara Ahmed interrogates positive psychology's fascination with "happiness"—especially happiness as "what you reach at the end of an 'unmarked path,'" quoting Darrin McMahon (2010, p. 199). Ultimately, Ahmed argues for breathing room outside of dutiful happiness, its own powerful tautology, for an exit from its totalizing ethics, and to regard happiness simply "as a possibility that does not exhaust what is possible" (p. 219). She adds, "We can value happiness for its precariousness, as something that comes and goes, as life does. When I think of what makes happiness 'happy,' I think of moments . . . a sense of lightness in possibility" (p. 219). This is precisely how I would describe the affective mechanics of #BlackOutDay: a moment, a lightness. I'd also wager that many of the participants in #BlackOutDay are very much aware of the precariousness of happiness and the corollary coming-and-going of life, especially in terms of state-sanctioned murder.

So I ask: Is #BlackOutDay a moment of terrible fantasy of the good life? Is #BlackOutDay simply "slow death" with a smile? Is it a directive toward dutiful happiness? I think it is very tempting to say yes, to write it off in a flourish of critical-academic bravado. But, there is something there that won't let me do it.

I don't want to throw the affirmative out the window. Affirmation and even joy are not the same as happiness or optimism. I would like to train my ear toward a more sympathetic understanding of "affirmation." Again, Ahmed takes pains to clarify these terms: "[Not] calling for an affirmative approach to life, or calling for affirmation as an ethics" (p. 222), but rather an affirmative that is simply an opening up of other possibilities, instantiations, ones that are not over-determined, small events, precarities, and even, using the language we've often seen used to describe selfies: "all those forms of happiness which are deemed superficial" (p. 222).

Deborah Gould's work on the political potential of the feel-good, affirmative erotics of the ACT UP movement at the height of the Western AIDS crisis also opens up the possibilities made possible by affirmation (2009). Quoting one former ACT UP member, Gould writes: "Ferd Eggan described ACT UP meetings as filled with 'a lot of sexual feeling and validation'" (p. 192). The ACT UP meeting: a legendarily precarious, erotic, affirmative, contentious, charged affective sociality in the midst of death (Hilderbrand, 2006). Greg Bordowitz, quoted in Gould's account, invokes the radical possibility of joy in the political atmosphere of ACT UP: "'I had heard about revolutionary joy . . . I just loved it . . . It was life-saving" (2009, p. 184). "Revolutionary joy." A life-saving act taught to us by those inhabiting dying bodies. The utter opposite of the blithe happiness duty. How can we further nuance *that*?

A Dynamic Unity

It was actually happening. Even before midnight, it was actually happening. People were doing it. It was real.

It would be a disservice to the affective energies of #BlackOutDay to speak about it in shards and pieces, absent the vector of time (as I have done thus far). This is hard to escape, since the critical apparatus of much humanistic or social-scientific scholarly analysis is largely predicated on isolating discrete pieces of static evidence, pinning them to the page, and dissecting. Our instruments are built to interpret the static; they are clumsy at best, and crumple at worst, when dealing with the fluid or processes in motion.[3] Yet, I want to spend some time here thinking about the event as it existed in motion because I believe that this was part of what made #BlackOutDay so *moving*. We may even be able to extrapolate from here to think about how the affective dynamics of the event can be harnessed for a radical politics in other arenas. Brian Massumi (2002) offers a challenging but compelling humanistic vocabulary to think about the affective properties of the event-in-process. In general, he implores a "fluidifying" (p. 7) of our usually static ways of dissecting, arguing for attention to processes of "passing into" and "emergence" as vital zones of activity that are usually glossed in critical study and that perish under our knee-jerk tendency toward binary thinking: "The kinds of distinction suggested here pertain to continuities under qualitative transformation. They are directly processual . . . They can only be approached by a logic that is abstract enough to grasp the self-disjunctive coincidence of a thing's immediacy to its own variation" (p. 8).

As I understand it, Massumi is advocating for an "abstract logic" that is capacious enough to reject binarisms—or, rather, hold them together—in favor of an appreciation of the thing and its potential to transform in-motion as a "dynamic unity" (p. 8). It is neither here nor there, but becoming.[4]

The thing in motion, a dynamic unity, holding together its immediacy and variation—to me, this is a far more satisfactory way of thinking about #BlackOutDay as it gathered and played out in the early hours of March 6 than filing it away in stasis. I argue that part of the reason why #BlackOutDay was so powerful, why it moved participants and onlookers to tears, why it cut through the usual layers of Tumblr and other short-form internet snark to something bare and visceral was that, in addition to the ideological register of its content (positive and multiple representations of blackness), its *form* was affective incipience, birthed of collectivity, honed by suspense. I want to add a spin to Massumi's own words: the thing, the event and its variances, was a processual dynamic unity indeed—but it also gave us the visceral resonance of what it felt like to be part of a dynamic unity of users. Users simply didn't know what to expect; perhaps no one really thought it was going to happen, and at the stroke of midnight, as the incipience held forth as immanence, its variances unfolding in front of us like a gorgeous peony in time-lapse, as it moved, so we were moved.

As time progressed, variations calcified. In the early hours, it was "#BlackOut" or even "#TheBlackOut"; as it garnered more major media coverage and discourse amplified, users and the press seemed to home in on #BlackOutDay as the tag-of-record. There was critical discourse on what to do as a non-black Tumblr user, and the general consensus among the people I follow and interact with on Tumblr was that this was a great opportunity for non-black Tumblr users to excuse themselves in a show of support, to purposefully abstain from posting any selfies for the next twenty-four hours in an act of silent allegiance. There were detractors as well. A selfie of a young bearded white man holding up a small bottle of Wite-Out to the camera with the headline "Race and Nationality Transcend Skin Color You Pretentious Fucks" appeared on my feed with a short caption vilifying the "SJWs of Tumblr who think they can claim a tag or own the right to free speech. MLK is rolling in his grave."[5] It appeared on my feed because a black user I follow reblogged it, imploring that the original poster "do us all a favor and drink that bottle of your blood." It only had 595 notes by the time I saw it twenty-four hours after #BlackOutDay had officially started; it seems that #BlackOutDay participants mostly stuck to the affirmative energetics of the moment. Another rhythm of the event: people seemed to sway back and forth between boosting everyone who appeared on their dash and, as the correctives mentions above, people who appeared to be hegemonically "hot." Was this turning into a notes accumulation and sexiness popularity contest before our eyes? Some posts I saw expressed dismay at this trend, the fact that one could post a selfie on #BlackOutDay and receive barely any notes and therefore feel doubly rejected; these bloggers pledged to reblog every single black selfie that they came across, regardless of number of notes or perceived sexiness.

As I interpret Massumi, these variations and encrustings of the event's affective energy are to be expected, they are the flow of the affective dynamics as played out over the vector of time and through the tidal spillage of the affective charge into discourse, into management, into territory, and back again. They fold and shift and appear and disappear as part of the fluidity of the event, the "immanance" of the thing as well as its "indeterminate variation" (2002, p. 9). The thing, the event, as it moves in weird and coiled ways, is a whole unto itself, while simultaneously filled with potential.

Disruptive Joy

The journalist who wrote about #BlackOutDay for ABC News kept calling it a "campaign": "A highlight of the diverse faces of people from the social media campaign #BlackOutDay . . . [I]s a social media campaign today celebrating Black beauty and fighting against negative images and stereotypes perpetuated in the media" (Tan, 2015). Yet, "campaign" seems like the wrong word. "Campaign" rings false, like it's propaganda or advertising, masterminded in a small executive conference room and deployed from the top down, with a defined lifespan and quantifiable objectives. That doesn't capture the feeling of #BlackOutDay.

If it wasn't a "campaign," what was it? We are at a loss for words to understand and describe these passionate acts of connection across social media. Not quite a "movement," not a "campaign," and not quite a "subculture," it was something more organic and amorphous, something that came into being, or emerged, folding outward exponentially, by process of refrain. Was it a meme? Something viral? Both of those terms could apply, but seem to hint at something, an artifact, that is distributed or replicated. "Meme" also seems like a huge disservice, a flattening of the affective heft catalyzed in #BlackOutDay's political project.

As *Cruel Optimism* closes, Berlant offers us sonic metaphors, of noise and its companion, silence—an affective training toward the political that can possibly be levied to interfere with, and not reproduce, normative political speech acts. In her words, "noise" is equal to affect (2011, p. 230); she refers to Charles Hirschkind's understanding of noise as "the social circulation of affective building" (p. 224). To be clear, Berlant is dubious, observing that most political attachment is made of noise, only. But, also, noise and silence are adjudicated in and through movement (p. 230); silence and noise are companions and interrupt intelligible speech, "Noise interferes, makes interference. Interference made loud within political communication makes time for adjustment and counter-thought" (p. 232).

I would call #BlackOutDay a highly visible moment of sensuous participation, a synchronizing of networks of passion. If Tumblr, as I've argued elsewhere, can operate on "queer reverb," then #BlackOutDay was an alignment, a harmonic resonance that registered off the charts. I choose to understand these resonant affirmations as produced by the overwhelming multiplication of black faces across Tumblr emphatically *not* as a pining for the "good life." Rather, I want to ultimately be quiet, observe, and absorb the resonant quality of affirmation across the network, reblogged hundreds upon hundreds of thousands of times, flooding the system. I want to disentangle affirmation in this sense from its connotation as a superficial platitude and understand that, on a register of visual, collective interference, it can be joyous, disruptive, and militant. Berlant finds a noisy bedfellow in Massumi on this topic, writing on intensity's non-linearity, doing a bit of wordplay with the term "static." Rather than a linear progression, "intensity is qualifiable as an emotional state, and that state is static—temporal and narrative noise. It is a state of suspense, potentially of disruption" (2002, p. 26).

#BlackOutDay was intense, affective noise on an affirmative register—a register of joy that also welcomed in bittersweetness and ache—clogging out, for a moment, more "normative speech" acts such as discursive argument. In this sense, it was an example of Massumi's potential to disrupt: of the privileging of normative speech, of the profound reality that normative speech itself is usually crafted by and in service of whiteness, of the guttural settler colonies of desire and beauty we all carry around with us, and of simply feeling angry or ugly all the time. Tracking this affective noise over the vector of time—the intensity of suspense—is another way of putting the goal of this chapter, and Berlant's suggestion that this sort of noise "makes time for adjustment and counter-thought" (2011, p. 232) within a regime of normative political speech can be pushed further: I'd suggest "counter-*feel*" as well. In other words, as Albert-László Barabási states in the introduction to the volume *A Networked Self* (2011), "Networks exist for a reason. They spread ideas; they spread knowledge; they spread influence" (p. 12). I want to add: they spread *affective, guttural sense-knowledge*, and when this gut-in-common hits a resonance, they spread the boundaries of the networked "self," too.

Notes

1 On Tumblr, a "note" is something akin to a registered interaction with a post: "notes" are generated if someone "likes" or "reblogs" a post to their own Tumblr. The actual number of simple views of a post may be much higher.
2 Though this post is widely shared and publicly viewable to anyone on the Internet and has been circulated tens of thousands of times, I have altered several minor words in this quotation. This is in keeping with Markham's entreaty for internet researchers to adopt, where appropriate, "ethical fabrication" (2012) of internet artifacts to make them un-searchable in order to preserve the original poster's privacy and image. As it appears here, it is no longer searchable on Google or Tumblr. This same method has been used in various quotations of high-profile public Tumblr posts in this chapter.

3 Massumi elaborates: "The concept of field, to mention but one, is a useful logical tool for expressing continuity of self-relation and heterogeneity in the same breath. Embarrassingly for the humanities, the handiest concepts in this connection are almost without exception products of mathematics and the sciences" (2002, p. 8). Elsewhere, Kathleen Stewart explains, "Affect studies forms part of a renewed search for modes of ethnographic theory and critique divested from the distanced, sheerly evaluative plane of academic conversation based on the stability of academic terms" (2017).
4 This use of "becoming" is my own invocation of Deleuze and Guattari (1987). To be very clear, Massumi does not use this term in his explanation and I do not want to imply that he does, lest I force a misread of his careful argument and his highly specific choice of words.
5 "SJW" is Tumblr slang for "social justice warrior," a pejorative term used to indicate outspoken advocates of social justice, often used by Tumblr's more conservative elements to imply a frustration with what they consider an unthinking adherence to "political correctness."

References

#TheBlackout. (2017). Official #BlackoutDay masterpost. *#TheBlackout – home of #BlackoutDay*. http://tumblr.theblackout.org/post/114966275331/official-blackoutday-masterpost-created-march

Adewunmi, B. (2015) Today is the first #BlackOutDay, and it is wonderful. *BuzzFeed*, March 6. www.buzzfeed.com/bimadewunmi/blackoutday-is-blackity-black-yall?utm_term=.fa15AmXvR#.qbqqyQVOZ

Ahmed, S. (2010). *The promise of happiness*. Durham, NC: Duke University Press.

Barabási, A.-L. (2011). Introduction and keynote to a networked self. In Z. Papacharissi (Ed.), *A networked self: Identity, community, and culture on social network sites* (pp. 1–14). New York: Routledge.

Berlant, L. (2011). *Cruel optimism*. Durham, NC: Duke University Press.

Blow, C. M. (2014). The self(ie) generation. *New York Times*, March 7. www.nytimes.com/2014/03/08/opinion/blow-the-self-ie-generation.html

Cho, A. (2015). Queer reverb: Tumblr, affect, time. In K. Hillis, S. Paasonen, & M. Petit (Eds.), *Networked affect* (pp. 43–57). Cambridge, MA: MIT Press.

Cvetkovich, A. (2012). *Depression: A public feeling*. Durham, NC: Duke University Press.

Deleuze, G., & Guattari. F. (1987). *A thousand plateaus: Capitalism and schizophrenia*, trans. B. Massumi. Minneapolis: University of Minnesota Press.

Edelman, L. (2004). *No future: Queer theory and the death drive*. Durham, NC: Duke University Press.

Eng, D. L. (2010). *The feeling of kinship: Queer liberalism and the racialization of intimacy*. Durham, NC: Duke University Press.

Gould, D. B. (2009). *Moving politics: Emotion and ACT UP's fight against AIDS*. Chicago: University of Chicago Press.

Halberstam, J. (2011). *The queer art of failure*. Durham, NC: Duke University Press.

Halperin, D. M., & Traub, V. (2010). *Gay shame*. Chicago: University of Chicago Press.

Hess, A. (2015). Selfies | the selfie assemblage. *International Journal of Communication*, 9, 1629–1646.

Hilderbrand, L. (2006). Retroactivism. *GLQ: A Journal of Lesbian and Gay Studies*, 12(2), 303–317.

Izadi, E. (2015). Why #BlackOutDay took over social media. *Washington Post*, March 6. www.washingtonpost.com/news/inspired-life/wp/2015/03/06/why-blackoutday-took-over-social-media/?utm_term=.1b13c3531306

Koskela, H. (2004). Webcams, TV shows and mobile phones: Empowering exhibitionism. *Surveillance and Society*, 2, 199–215.

Love, H. (2009). *Feeling backward: Loss and the politics of queer history*. Cambridge, MA: Harvard University Press.

Machkovech, S. (2017). Report: Facebook helped advertisers target teens who feel "worthless" [updated]. *Ars Technica*, May 1. https://arstechnica.com/information-technology/2017/05/facebook-helped-advertisers-target-teens-who-feel-worthless/

Markham, A. (2012). Fabrication as ethical practice. *Information, Communication & Society*, 15(3), 334–353.

Massumi, B. (2002). *Parables for the virtual: Movement, affect, sensation*. Durham, NC: Duke University Press.

McNeal, G. S. (2014). Facebook manipulated user news feeds to create emotional responses. *Forbes*, June 28. www.forbes.com/sites/gregorymcneal/2014/06/28/facebook-manipulated-user-news-feeds-to-create-emotional-contagion/#aaf657b39dc7

Nemer, D., & Freeman, G. (2015). Empowering the marginalized: Rethinking selfies in the slums of Brazil. *International Journal of Communication*, 9, 1832–1847.

Papacharissi, Z. (Ed.). (2011). *A networked self: Identity, community, and culture on social network sites*. New York: Routledge.

Senft, T. M., & Baym, N. (2015). Selfies introduction ~ What does the selfie say? Investigating a global phenomenon. *International Journal of Communication*, 9, 1588–1606.

Stewart, K. (2017). In the world that affect proposed. *Cultural Anthropology*, 32(2), 195.

Tan, A. (2015). #BlackOutDay: Trending Twitter hashtag celebrates black people, fights negative stereotypes. *ABC News*, March 6.

Tiidenberg, K. (2014). Bringing sexy back: Reclaiming the body aesthetic via self-shooting. *Cyberpsychology: Journal of Psychosocial Research on Cyberspace*, 8(1).

Twitter users celebrate #BlackOutDay to promote black beauty and pride. (2015). *MyPraise 102.5, Atlanta's Inspiration Station*, March 8. https://mypraiseatl.com/1559665/twitter-users-celebrate-blackoutday-to-promote-black-beauty-and-pride/

White, M. (n.d.). The definition of clicktivism. Original Essay. *michmwhite.com*. www.micahmwhite.com/clicktivism/

12

AM I WHY I CAN'T HAVE NICE THINGS? A REFLECTION ON PERSONAL TRAUMA, NETWORKED PLAY, AND ETHICAL SIGHT

Whitney Phillips

In 2015, I published a book titled *This is Why We Can't Have Nice Things: Mapping the Relationship between Online Trolling and Mainstream Culture*. Pulling from ethnographic research conducted between 2008 and 2014, the book—which was based on my 2012 PhD dissertation—explores the rise and evolution of subcultural trolls on and around 4chan's infamous /b/ (or "random") board. The book's title is a nod to the prevalent assumption that trolls are the primary stumbling block to a kinder, gentler internet. Trolls certainly are *a* stumbling block, I argue. But rather than being wholly aberrational, trolling is in fact born of and fueled by culturally sanctioned ideals, from media sensationalism to colonialist ideology to the androcentric privileging of rationality over emotion. The embeddedness of trolling within mainstream culture thus raises the question: exactly what are people criticizing, when they criticize trolls?

The book is also a survivor narrative, not that average readers would have any way of knowing that. I was raped, is the quickest way to explain it, at the outset of the research project. The assault was committed by a man I loved, a fellow PhD student at the University of Oregon. It occurred on May 1, 2010, the night I returned home from that year's ROFLcon internet culture conference. The dirty kitchen floor where it happened had a direct line of sight to his living room, where I collected the majority of my dissertation research. And while that was, of course, bad, things would only get worse from there; the following few months were a blur of attacks and recriminations, emotional and sexual humiliations, and countless attempts to gaslight.

What my abuser did to me is the cruelest, most painful, most humiliating experience of my life. It also helped me write my book. It also stripped me of my sight. It also gave me sharper eyes, in that order.

In exploring how and why, three main points emerge. First is the deep interconnection between how people see and experience the world in embodied spaces, and how this embodiment influences what is seen, really what *can* be seen, on the internet. Second is the ambivalence of connection; the fact that our networks, however they might be mediated, are equally as capable of harming as they are of supporting. Third is the reciprocity of care, and the ways empathy directed externally cultivates empathy directed internally, and vice versa.

While I will be connecting each of these points to my own experiences, the story I am sharing isn't just about a traumatic thing that happened to me. It's also a story about the affirming things that can happen to us all, when we look beyond our own screens and open ourselves up to the lives of others.

Seeing Clearly

> I'm thinking back to when you were first working on trolls, and how you were kinda unwilling to really address how violent some of their actions were . . . perhaps, this is making more sense.

So went the email from my former professor and dissertation committee member Lisa Gilman, in response to an article I'd written following the 2016 presidential election. The article focused on Trump's victory, and talked about what it felt like, as a survivor, to know that the president-elect was a professed sexual predator and multiply-accused abuser, not to mention a man who could not seem to stop himself from dehumanizing women. This was the first time I'd told my story publicly, and I'd wanted to share with Lisa in particular. I did this, at one level, because I respect Lisa and value her opinion; she's one of the many people I thank in my book's acknowledgments section (in her case, for pushing me to think more self-reflexively about the politics of trolling), and had been a great source of support as I navigated a department that wasn't exactly thrilled with my dissertation project.

More than that, however, I shared the link because it spoke to something that had happened while I was a graduate student in her spring 2011 Gender and Folklore class. We'd been assigned a reading about sexual assault narratives, and the empowerment that can result when survivors choose to share their stories. At the time, I was only beginning to understand what had happened to me. It wasn't just the assault I was struggling to process, it was the months of incessant, baffling abuse that followed. It was all the times I'd been punched in the bruises—the very bruises he'd given me, for laughs—and then been told by him, often in the presence of friends, that punching was just part of our dynamic. It was all the times I was made to feel malicious and paranoid as I sat next to him, red-faced, as he giddily sexted with god knows who on Facebook messages, a pointed reminder that he'd grown tired of sexting with me. It was all the times he reprimanded me for being a bad, selfish friend (my abuser never described me as anything more than a friend, sometimes with the gold star of *best* friend) because I didn't want to listen to him coo lovingly on the phone to his long-distance fiancé—typically just before or just after he would start Facebook message flirting with other women. It was all the times I was told through his words and through his actions that who I was—the way I spoke, how I saw the world, the things I cared about the most—was why he treated me this way.

And then there were the individual incidents, more acute, even, than his workaday tauntings. The time my sister was graduating from the police academy and I asked him, please, not to give me any fresh bruises so I could wear a sleeveless dress to her ceremony, to which he responded by giving me a series of fresh bruises up and down my arms. The time I planned to take a road trip with my abuser and my younger brother, and asked him, please, to be nice to me while we were in the car, and felt great when he was on his best behavior—only to find out that my typically easygoing, non-confrontational brother had been so horrified by how my abuser talked to me, even when he was being "nice," that he had spent the entire car ride texting with my mother, needing to be talked down from reaching forward and strangling him from the back seat. Another time I can't bring myself to describe, although I've spent the last hour trying; I still can't believe the things I agreed to do for him, or thought I was agreeing to do for him, it's difficult to know for sure. (I feel compelled, here, to clarify that I never had consensual sex with this man; the relationship was much stranger than that.)

I'd only recently worked up the courage to tell my therapist any of this, although I'd been seeing her regularly throughout the whole ordeal, in a kind of denial-induced trance. I would even mention my abuser in those early sessions. These conversations were related to the more banal aspects of my life, including the fact that I was in love with him (he's so talented and funny, I gushed, and we have so much fun exploring the divey parts of Eugene), and that I was struggling to accept the fact that he'd just proposed to his girlfriend. I'd also only recently told some of the story to a few close friends, one of whom sat next to me in Lisa's Gender and Folklore class.

Needless to say, I didn't have the strongest handle on my own mental health. And when I raised my hand to speak that day in class, just how tenuous the handle had become came like a blow to the stomach. I said something about the reading. Paused. Felt myself turn crimson. Then in front of Lisa, in front of my friend, in front of a lecture hall full of graduates and undergraduates, I burst into tears. I never would have spoken if I knew what speaking would unleash. But I did, and there it was. When class ended I bolted, sweaty, still violently crimson, without saying a word to Lisa.

This was why that happened, I told her in my post-election email. Her response, quoted in part above, sent me reeling.

To help illustrate what she was talking about, and why she was absolutely correct in her assessment, here is a deeply embarrassing—and given the recent ascendency in the United States of the white nationalist far right, deeply prescient—story from 2010. A 94-year-old emeritus professor at the University of Oregon, whose title carries a lifetime privilege of booking rooms on campus, had been hosting meetings for the Pacifica Forum, a white nationalist discussion group. At their most recent meetings, forum members and speakers (one of whom had recently claimed that the feminist Andrea Dworkin was "too ugly to rape") had repeatedly given the Nazi salute, harangued protesting students, and generally been terrible. Even more students would be protesting the next meeting.

I decided to attend with one of my trollishly inclined male friends, as well as the man I would soon know as my abuser (this protest took place in early 2010, I believe in February, a few months before the assault—though by that point, our relationship had already taken a very dark turn). When we arrived, the meeting space was thronged, and it took several claustrophobic minutes to get to our seats in the back row. The emeritus professor was sitting up front in a wheelchair, already half asleep. His invited speaker sat beside him, wearing a kilt. The speaker began his talk by asserting that the swastika wasn't a hate symbol because Buddhists used it before the Nazis, and that everyone needed to stop being so sensitive. People started screaming. His white skinhead bouncer, who was wearing an all-white Adidas track suit, started screaming back in apparently sincere Black Vernacular English. He capped this performance off by giving a Nazi salute and bellowing "Hail Hitler," as in, frozen water from the sky, on repeat, as the crowd revolted.

Sitting there, I knew that everything about the speaker's presentation and the forum generally and of course that ridiculous, accidentally transcultural bouncer was a disgrace. I knew exactly that I should have been offended, and knew exactly why. Still, I found myself slipping into precisely the trollish mode I had learned to identify, and when needed, learned to replicate, while conducting my research. My friends were right there with me. One of us—one of them? me?—scribbled a note that read, "I did it for the lulz," and we chuckled.

It would be better—certainly less mortifying for me to recount, all these years later—if this reaction didn't characterize my early work. Painful in some ways, at least. In other highly ambivalent ways, my ability to immerse myself so thoroughly in trolling subculture—to affect the posture of a troll, when it served me—was, undoubtedly, an asset to the overall project. As I say in the book, and stand behind even now, as I cringe, if I hadn't been able to fully immerse myself in the subculture, I wouldn't have been able to write about it as well. But Lisa's post-election point speaks to the highly sharpened side of that double-edged sword: that there was a lot back then—about trolling itself, about my relationship to all that trolling, about my own mental health—I was, as she noted in her email, "kinda unwilling to really address." Or at least, that I was kinda un*able* to really address.

The reason I wasn't can be traced to a theory I forwarded in my own dissertation: that of the fetish. Fetish in the way I was using it builds on Marx's commodity fetish, and refers to myopic focus on decontextualized content (just as capitalism, according to Marx, obscures the material and ethical conditions that result in you being able to buy, say, a $15 plastic chair at Target, and not have to think about how exactly it got there). This ability to pick and choose, to only deal with what someone wants to see when they want to see it, means that the full historical, political, and emotional circumstance of a given narrative isn't just lost to participants, it might as well not exist (to them, anyway).

I connected this sense of the fetish to another theory first floated in my dissertation, the mask of trolling. This metaphorical mask describes the process of emotionally dissociating from a story, and reducing entire media narratives, mitigating circumstances, or instances of emotional fallout to a pinhole aperture. The trolling mask and its fetishized gaze, I argued, helped explain the origins of and subcultural emphasis on *lulz*, trolling parlance for amusement derived from other people's distress, particularly their anger, which was the trolls' favorite. It also helped explain why trolls were so quick to argue that what they'd done was "just" a joke, that they were "just" trolling on "just" the internet. For the trolls I studied, all they saw—all they had to see—was that cordoned-off "just."

It is worth noting that I began to theorize the mask of trolling after attending that Pacifica Forum. It is also worth noting that I never wrote a word about the forum itself, or that I'd based my emerging theory on the fact that I felt myself put the mask on. I was somewhat aware that I had "become a site of that which I seek to explain, and most importantly, that which I seek to critique" (Phillips, 2012, p. 19), as I awkwardly put it in my dissertation. But I had no idea, even upon depositing the dissertation, just how deep the connection was between my research and my life.

With seven years of hindsight, this connection isn't just neon lights-flashing conspicuous, its source is painfully clear. I had been convinced by a person I loved that I myself was also "just"—just a punchline, just a punching bag, literally just some thing for him to punch, all vaguely bracketed by "our dynamic." That was his exact message when he told me one night, eyes smiling as he sipped on the beer I'd bought him, that I was like a piece of furniture—an inanimate object you take your aggressions out on when you've had a bad day. Once my project was a bit more established, he would even borrow language from my research and say he was—of course!—just trolling, and that he was, that *we* were, just doing it for the lulz. The slightest glimmer that I was a body and heart worth protecting, and yet was not being protected by anyone, would have been too much for me to bear. So I didn't bear it. I was just a piece of furniture. Lulz made perfect sense to me.

And so, every evening, I would drive, summoned, to his apartment, unload the groceries I paid for, do his dishes and cleaning, and trudge to the recliner, holding my laptop. Then, sitting just a few feet from where I'd been assaulted, sitting just a few feet from the man who had assaulted me, who was more often than not exchanging furtive sexts with a stable of women (one of whom, I found out later, he ended up moving in with), I would wade through the sewage drain of 4chan/b/. There I'd be assailed by a shit parade of cut up bodies and absurdist photoshops, murdered children and sleeping kittens, violent pornography and 90s nostalgia. Every disgusting thing you could do to a woman. After hours of this I would drive back home—I never stayed the night—only to see that my abuser would still be logged into his Facebook messages, still flirting with whomever, because conversation with me, who had been right there, was never enough for him. Because I was never enough for him. I would fall asleep sick to my stomach, alone.

Just like that, day in, day out, all I saw were things that couldn't be unseen, to borrow a common trolling phrase. And yet, during that time, I saw almost nothing. I had identified the fetish, yes, but my framing was that of an apologist. It's not so bad, they're actually sidestepping the emotional impact of their own behaviors. It's not so bad, they're actually the engine powering meme culture forward. It's not so bad, they're actually all just trolling, as what was happening to me offline reinforced my blind spots online, and my blind spots online reinforced what was happening to me offline. It wasn't that my experiences pushed onto the internet, in other words. It was that the internet pushed right back.

Eventually I stopped sitting on that recliner. Eventually I stopped apologizing. The catalyst came over Thanksgiving of 2010. A few weeks earlier, my abuser had harangued me for making an offhand comment about how we needed to figure out our Thanksgiving dinner plans. Why would I assume we'd do Thanksgiving together, he sneered, why would I assume *anything* about his holidays? Or anything he did? I wasn't his *girlfriend*. I apologized, and later made plans to have dinner with my advisor and her family. Then a few days before the break, he made an offhand comment about how we needed to figure out our Thanksgiving dinner plans. Confused, I told him about dinner at my advisor's, and he harangued me for not inviting him along. Hadn't we agreed to have dinner together? Weren't we best friends? I apologized, and suggested we could go to my advisor's that afternoon for appetizers, then back to his place for dinner with his roommate and his roommate's new boyfriend. He was still hurt, but agreed.

Appetizers at my advisor's was fine, memorable only because I'd worn a new dress—an emerald sheath paired with textured black leggings—and had wanted him to say something nice about how I looked. But I couldn't even get him to look directly at me. I started drinking as soon as we got back to his house, and by the time dinner was on the table, I was shitfaced. We went around the table and said what we were thankful for. When it was my turn, I raised my glass and thanked everyone for their friendship and for their support and for opening up their home to me. My eyes welled up; I loved them so much. And then I was being attacked by him, accused of being annoying, accused of being myself. The rest of the dinner fades into a brownout, until sometime later that night when I was standing at the sink doing dishes, two feet from where I'd lain six months earlier, frozen and confused, on that dirty floor. I was scrubbing the meat pan when my abuser came up from behind me and gave me a bear hug, his signal that I was forgiven. I was so relieved. Without saying a word, he bent down and ripped a six inch gash in the fabric of my leggings, first on the back of my left leg, followed by the back of my right. Then he walked away.

I don't remember if I finished doing the dishes. I don't remember when I left that night. I do know that afterwards, I didn't see him for the rest of the year. I do know that he came to my office sometime on the other side of winter break, and got choked up when I was stony-faced and wouldn't tell him about my New Year. I do know that we would go on to have one conversation over drinks the following summer, at Rennie's, the grad student bar. He put his hand on mine and in the low amber light had told me, hushed, that he had violated me. He then admitted that the nicer I was to him, back then, the more he wanted to hurt me, and I realized that this was supposed to be a justification, and felt myself shrinking to the same old size until I thought I could have fit into my glass. I imagined crawling into it, and throwing myself out the window. I do know that several weeks after that, he called me because word was getting around that he'd raped me (I'd confided in a mutual male friend, another grad student, who proceeded to tell everyone we knew) and while he would admit to the sexual assault, the word rape really bothered him, and could I help him do damage control. I do know that I paused, and for the first and only time, told him that he was a bastard. I do know that I never spoke to him again.

A person doesn't just snap out of something like this. There was no triumphant moment of redemption, no psychological switch flipped. I wasn't suddenly safe or ok. But as I began crawling out of the wreckage of my life, inch by inch, day by day, I was able to start seeing things I couldn't see before. Or wasn't willing to see before, it doesn't matter.

It began with the realization, opaque at first, that I had been harmed. I was fully aware that I had been *hurting*, but for the longest time had blamed myself. If I hadn't been so tedious, or so paranoid, or so selfish, he wouldn't have needed to treat me that way. I have no idea when I started to believe this. I have no idea when he started to tell me. Whenever it happened, I convinced myself that I didn't deserve better. But of course I did, and the more I came to accept that fact, the less I came to identify with a piece of fucking furniture.

As that happened, slowly, over months, I was able to recognize—literally re-cognize—the violence done to my heart and body. This, in turn, compelled me to look up, and I became increasingly aware of, and increasingly sensitive to, all the other wounded hearts and bodies I was encountering in my research. Particularly in cases when trolls were actively, maliciously targeting vulnerable people—when their play *hurt*, and was designed to hurt—the idea that they were "just" trolling, that it was "just" the Internet, and that the pursuit of lulz could ever be employed as a legitimate excuse for harming another person, was suddenly as untenable as my abuser's claim that his violence against me had "just" been part of our dynamic. He was right, it had been part of our dynamic. The problem was, that "just" obscured the fact that the dynamic was one of abuse.

Even in examples when the trolls' behaviors were more mischievous than malicious, the underlying ethical issues I hadn't much thought about before became increasingly difficult to ignore. The most significant—and most vexing—of these related to consent, and whether or not trolls' amusement, even if the amusement didn't cause any lasting or obvious harm, could ever supersede someone else's preference not to be roped into a game they hadn't asked to play. By the time I deposited my dissertation in 2012, I was beginning to articulate these stakes in earnest. By the time I submitted my final manuscript to MIT Press, they were baked into my argument.

Again, it would have been so much better if my sight hadn't been limited to begin with. I wish it hadn't been, more than anything. But what I've come to understand is that it's not the eyes we start out with that matter the most. It's where we choose to look, once we know what we're seeing.

Once mine had some time to adjust, it was fetishized sight that became the unseeable thing. Ryan M. Milner and I developed this point in subsequent work, culminating in our book *The Ambivalent Internet* (2017). As we argue, myopic, decontextualized vision—precisely the sort of vision characteristic of trolling—isn't a *bug* of online spaces, it is, instead, a basic feature. For this we can thank four overlapping affordances of digital media: modularity, the ability to recombine components of a digital text without destroying the totality of that text; modifiability, the ability to alter those components; archivability, the ability to store digital texts for later use; and accessibility, the ability to search for and easily find these texts through search indexing and tagging. As we note, every GIF, every photoshop, every meme, every retweet, owes its existence to these four affordances.

Consequently, examples of broader narratives overshadowed by resonant detail abound online. "Classic" cases include 2011's Bed Intruder meme, in which local news footage featuring a queer man of color condemning the attempted rape of his sister was remixed into a jaunty pop song, spinning off several well-known memetic catch phrases ("Hide your kids, hide your wife"; "They're raping everybody out here"). Another is 2012's Ermahgerd meme, which features a picture of a young woman dressed in a girl scouts uniform. Clearly ecstatic about her haul, she's fanning out a set of Goosebump books, and is captioned with the phrase "Gersberms Mah Fravrit Berks"; the image was adopted by countless online participants as the go-to signal for excessive nerdiness ("Ermagerd," i.e. "oh my god" said through orthodontia and/or a speech impediment, was adopted in later iterations of the meme). More contemporary examples include 2017's United Man meme, which was precipitated by footage of an older Asian man being violently dragged off a United Airlines flight, which untold thousands of individuals used to create, share, and remix fun and playful images of the man alongside United's corporate logo and other PR materials.

In cases like these, where the GIFs, jokes, and memes de jour ricocheting across social media aren't obviously malicious, or at least aren't directly targeted attacks, the ethical stakes might not seem especially high. Certainly nothing compared to the most destructive forms of trolling. But as Milner and I argue, even when participants share GIFs and jokes and memes de jour for benign, or even explicitly pro-social reasons (to make their friends laugh, to bolster a sense of collective identity), the act of sharing without fully seeing, and playing without fully knowing what's being played with, risks precisely the same outcome as the trolling mask; broader vistas narrowed to a tiny pinprick. In the above cases, a man whose sister was almost raped. A woman who didn't ask to be plastered across the internet, certainly not as the poster child for teenage awkwardness. A man who was publicly assaulted, and whose children were then forced to relive his trauma again and again. None were approached holistically, as situated individuals with unique stories, needs, and fears (to say nothing of the unique stories, needs, and fears of those closest to them). They were approached, instead, as flattened pieces of content. As *memes*. Not as bad as pieces of furniture, perhaps, but fetishized objects nevertheless.

Though initially catalyzed by my own highly specific, highly personal experiences, this argument—that the tools of digital media lend themselves to decontextualization, which lends itself to fetishized sight, which lends itself to ethical myopia—provides an entrypoint to a variety of conversations about online civility. Most fundamentally, it challenges the notion that bad behavior online sits squarely at the feet of those who seek to cause harm. Yes bad actors do bad things. Simultaneously, we all have the potential—through our play, our commenting, our laughter, our connection—to make the internet a little less safe and a little less hospitable to those who share our networked spaces.

While it may not be possible for all of us to fully contextualize every single thing we encounter on the internet, what is possible, and what is necessary, is to remember that the people we encounter on the internet *are never things*. A person is never just a meme, or just a picture, or just a tweet. A person, regardless of their relative degree of mediation, regardless of how little of your time you might spend thinking about them, is a body and heart worth protecting. Always. As we careen into an era in which offline identity is so easily warped through online sharing, in which the lives of others are so easily flattened into memetic fodder, we must actively resist efforts both large and small, online and offline, institutional and interpersonal, to see only surfaces, and beyond that, only the parts of those surfaces we choose. This is particularly critical given the cacophony of targeted, deliberate, unrepentant antagonisms that characterize the Trump-era internet. There is already too much harm swirling around, already too many bodies at risk. We should do what we can not to add to that pile.

Such an outcome is worth pursuing in and of itself. It is better to approach others empathetically. It is better to situate them in their broader interpersonal context. It is better to try and be better. But the benefits of care go far beyond the external. In my case, learning to see others as worthy of love proved to be reciprocal.

It took years to approach myself with anything even close to love, of course. At the height of the abuse, I hated myself because he hated me, and because he'd isolated me from everyone who could have challenged that hatred. After I untangled myself, I had a few significant breakthroughs, notably the realization that I wasn't a couch. That was progress, but it hardly bounced me back to where I'd been before. In fact, the further I got away from him, the more cracked down the middle I felt. Suddenly, everything made me jump. Suddenly, the entirely justified paranoia I experienced while under his thrall was thrown into hyperdrive. My ability to trust—people's motives, words, and especially their love—was decimated. I developed a variety of phobias, including an abiding fear of (suspicion about? disgust toward?) sitting next to people as they text or type on their laptops. This has been a particular point of tension in subsequent romantic relationships, but has proven equally vexing in other contexts; my hackles even go up when I'm watching television with my utterly trustworthy, utterly devoted father and he pulls out his phone (*Who are you talking to? What disgusting thing are you doing? What lies have you been telling?*). This is the PTSD brain; everything is a threat, so you'd better start fighting or flighting.

For so long, I resisted these experiences, and resented myself for continuing to have them. As my eyes adjusted from fetish to context, however, and I came to see others in their full, imperfect totality, a more loving sense of self also came into focus. I began to understand how, to paraphrase Leonard Cohen, light shines through the broken places. More than that, the habit of empathetically looking at others helped me understand that I can't be reduced to my light, and can't be reduced to my cracks, and can't be reduced to my overburdened endocrine and neurotransmitter pathways. I am all of it; every gentle word, every bitter thought, every triumph, every heartbreak, just like everyone else. And just like everyone else, I'm doing my best. As this newfound sense of inward care grew, it fed directly into my external channels of empathy, which fed directly into the inward ones, back out, back in.

This, at the end of it all, is why I am sharing my story. What is directed inward, goes outward. And what is directed outward, goes inward—across media, across networks, across time and geography. We may not be able to control how others direct themselves to us. But we can control how we direct ourselves to them. Fetishized sight has had its run. Disconnection has had its run. Let's try love instead.

References

Phillips, W. (2012). This is why we can't have nice things: The emergence, evolution, and cultural embeddedness of online trolling. PhD diss., University of Oregon.

Phillips, W. (2015). *This is why we can't have nice things: Mapping the relationship between online trolling and mainstream culture*. Cambridge, MA: MIT Press.

Phillips, W., & Milner, R. M. (2017). *The ambivalent Internet: Mischief, humor, and antagonism online*. Cambridge: Polity Press.

13

ON LOVE AND TOUCH

The Radical Haptics of Gestational Surrogacy

Margaret Schwartz

In this chapter, I will explore the possibilities of *touch*. Touch can be understood as a practice of love, where love implies a network of physical connections. Touch is often cast as an archetype of the irreducibly human, but I will argue that it by no means precludes an interface with technical objects. Touch is a metonym for intimacy and immediacy. It traffics in the metaphysics of presence, yet resists representation. Touch has long been the sense championed by luddites lamenting a world "out of touch," screened off from intimate immediacy. Yet technology offers us new kinds of touch, from the haptics of virtual reality to the manipulation of touch screens, to the opportunities for far-flung, distant bodies to come in contact with one another. After all, the undersea diver enjoys a kind of touch unavailable without technology; so does the surrogate who feels the stirrings of a baby inside that is not "hers."

Touch is a mode of understanding the relationship between media and corporeality. Touch is a material practice both crucial to and disavowed by global capital, so excavating and honoring its work exposes contradictions and valorizes those bodies, practices, and contexts that are overlooked or oppressed under these contradictions.

Practices of touch are the essence of caring labor. Bathing, feeding, soothing, and even the act of sexual love are life-sustaining labors that produce no consumable "product" except for other human bodies. Without this skin-to-skin contact, no babies would be born, let alone survive to maturity. The grind of living is a matter of touch. Nevertheless, caring labor is inextricable from the use of technologies. These technologies may be as simple as a wooden bowl, or a pitcher, Heidegger's example (Heidegger, 2009)—or they may be as complex as the medical technologies involved in a high-risk pregnancy and childbirth. Therefore, touch also connects caring labor to the question of technology: its role in human society, its historical specificity, and its ontological status. Is technology culturally determined, or is it rather a determining factor in human society? Is that true now, in the so-called digital age, more than it was a century or more ago? All of these questions may be meaningfully explored by looking at the role of touch in caring labor.

The question of the role of technology in touch and caring labor brings us inevitably to the value such labor commands. More precisely, it brings us to the disparity between the usefulness of that labor and its exchange value in the market. On the one hand, this labor is invaluable—as I pointed out, without it human life simply could not continue. On the other hand, caring labor is economically undervalued in an advanced capitalist society. Nancy Folbre demonstrates in *The Invisible Heart*, that caring labor is unpaid or underpaid, and it is not counted as "wealth"—it is, for example, invisible when calculating GNP (Folbre, 2002). We are living in an era of austerity where putatively unavoidable measures are taken to reduce the money states spend on caring labor, with the result that the most vulnerable—the elderly and sick, the disabled, children, and colonized populations, who as we know are overrepresented among the poor and needy—are made even more so by the withdrawal of state support for caring labor. This neoliberal privatization of care means that very real choices are being made on a structural level about who deserves to enjoy the life-giving benefits of caring labor, and who does not. Touch is no less a question, then, of what Mbembe calls necropolitics: who deserves to be cared for (given life), and who is left to die (Mbembe, 2003).

This is the global outline of what's at stake in the issue of touch—both for an intersectional, anticapitalist feminism and for media theory. In what follows, I will explore an example—a high profile embryo custody case—as a way of getting at the specifics of these stakes. In particular, I am interested in the kinds of touch that are effaced in the account of parenthood, love, and care that the court cases take as axiomatic. The touching, caring relationship between surrogate and baby, between medical caregivers and their patients, and between nannies and the children they care for are all effaced in problematic ways in the discourse surrounding the case. I will argue that the implications of this effacement are to restrict and police the borders of a network of care and love that overspills the boundaries of traditional selfhood within the nuclear family. Thus the notion of "family" appears only at the cost of exploiting or erasing the laboring, caring bodies of women and other caregivers, most of whom are drawn from the ranks of society's most vulnerable. I will then move to suggest some theoretical pivots that are aimed toward redressing this disparity between the use-value of caring labor and its exchange value. If we are able to see touch as the nexus of an ethical relation, I argue, then it becomes legible in a different discourse, one that meaningfully engages with the embodied self as distributed across both affective and technological networks.

A Contested Network of Care

My central example foregrounds the ugly side of love: a custody battle. The actress Sofia Vergara (best known in the United States for portraying Gloria on the sitcom *Modern Family*) and her ex-partner Nick Loeb are in a protracted court battle over the fate of two embryos they made during their relationship (Staff, 2016a). To clarify, the embryo is a fertilized egg, and thus contains genetic material from both parties. In this case, the embryos were created outside of the confines of the body in a process called "in vitro fertilization"—literally, egg and sperm were combined "in glass." (This is what is sometimes uncritically referred to as a "test tube baby.") Rather than immediately implant them, the couple chose to freeze the embryos, with the intention to use a surrogate to gestate them at a later time. So it was that when the couple fell out of love, the embryos remained as a question to be decided.

In the state of California, where the in vitro fertilization (IVF) took place, both partners' consent is required before any action is taken regarding an embryo, whether to destroy it, keep it frozen, or implant it. Neither Loeb nor Vergara wants to destroy the embryos. Vergara wants to keep them indefinitely frozen, and does not consent to release them to Loeb's custody even if she had no responsibility, fiscal or otherwise, for the resultant children. She did not elaborate further on her reason for this, except to say she did not want to destroy them and, because of the status of her relationship with Loeb (and her subsequent marriage to another man), she did not want them to be implanted in a gestational surrogate (Olya, 2015). Meanwhile, Loeb wants "sole custody," as it were, so that he can implant them in a surrogate and raise the children separate from Vergara, with the latter not required to play any role in the children's lives.

There were two separate lawsuits attempting to adjudicate the parties' right to decide the embryos' fate. In the first, Loeb himself was the plaintiff. He sought permission to implant the embryos with the rationale that he had always wanted to be a father and that he had a right to his children, regardless of Vergara's wishes (Loeb, 2015). When this lawsuit was decided against him, Loeb transferred the case from California to Louisiana and adopted a more explicitly political, pro-life argument. The embryos were now the sole plaintiffs in the lawsuit, even given names—Emma and Isabella—and they were suing Vergara for their right to live so as to inherit the trusts established in their names when they were created (Staff, 2016b). That lawsuit has since been dismissed, and it is unclear whether or not Loeb will refile; meanwhile Vergara filed court documents in February of 2017 to end the case.

No other public custody battle has taken such dramatic turns into the ontological questions raised by current advances in reproductive technology. The case foregrounds how the self may be distributed across a range of fields, from the physical (the literal bodies of the parents and the surrogate) to the technological (the various technological media that make up IVF, embryo storage, and surrogacy), to the discursive (the embryos as legal plaintiffs with names, a rhetorical assignation of personhood). Two lovers, now separated, are fighting to decide custodianship of something or someone that is bound to them in intimate, physical ways, but which has, through technologies of reproduction, been separated from both of their bodies. This something or someone is frozen, both literally and metaphorically: freezing arrests the embryos in their "natural" process, either toward development or denaturation. Emma and Isabella wait on life's threshold but behind glass, while those on the other side argue about their fate, all in the name of love.

The ontological nuances of this case are deeply imbricated in the technological, discursive and political structures of our historical moment. This conflict would not be possible without IVF and other alternative reproductive technologies (ART). A more repressively patriarchal legal system might deny a woman the legal right to her children, thus obviating the conflict staged here—which nevertheless relies upon certain gendered assumptions about the rights and roles of men and women as fathers and mothers. Vergara's relative curtness on the topic in her public statements contrasts sharply with Loeb's emotionally florid statements—he even published an op-ed in the *New York Times* writing openly about the difficulties of his own childhood, his desire to be a father, about the nanny who raised him, whose Catholic faith instilled in him a conviction that life begins at conception (Loeb, 2015). Our discursive constructions of personhood allow for this virtual projection of the embryos into the future, as people, selves, with names and interests and rights as heirs. This case makes it painfully obvious how selfhood is, in the most existential sense, truly inextricable from the technological, political, and discursive patterns articulated to the structure of network.

Why Love Matters

What kind of project does it advance to ask the question of love? Why invoke love in the apparent absence of any such thing?

Because one of the deepest consequences of global capitalism is its toll on the human heart. The world we live in drives ever more single-mindedly toward profit and accumulation, in the process seeking to assign value to ever more aspects of human everydayness, including intimacy. Yet this telos also depends upon a disavowal of the caring human activities that produce society itself. To repeat a simple but crucial observation, if there were no more children, or if they could not be cared for and socialized to become (laboring) adults, all of the other questions would be moot. Love thus entails the question of *care*.

Who will care for these embryos? Who will care for the children they may someday become? There are caretakers all along the way, and in part (though not entirely—more on that below) because of the technology involved, they are not just mommy and daddy. *How* should they best be cared for? What are the practices of care that are demanded in this situation? Do some of those practices count more than others, and if so, why?

The question of care is distributed among a network of relationships of touch and intimacy. Even if Loeb and Vergara had stayed a couple, they planned to use a surrogate to gestate the embryos. Now that they are no longer a couple, there would be an additional branching of the network into the new family that Loeb and a partner might share by bringing these embryos into the world—again, via a surrogate. And, there would be the legalities of the relationship Vergara had to the children, as their biological mother, even if those legalities existed to assert that she had no connection to them. Vergara is now married, and she may choose to have children in this new relationship, either through surrogacy or adoption. If so, these children would also have some relationship to their half-siblings, again even if that were simply a legal matter of asserting that there was no relationship (or no requirement for one). As adults, the children might decide they want to have contact with their half-siblings; it would be potentially irresponsible and likely impossible to deny them any knowledge of them. All of this to say that the use of IVF, surrogates, and the time-delay inherent in the use of ART means that the question of "who cares for the children" is distributed among a large network of people, family constellations, and state institutions.

However, ART are not the only factor distributing the responsibility of care over a network. As Julie A. Wilson and Emily Chivers Yochim point out in their ethnography *Mothering Through Precarity* (2017), family autonomy is a stubborn myth of late neoliberalism. It truly does "take a village," but the seeming triteness of this phrase glosses over the deep ambivalence about distributions of care outside of the nuclear family.

With love comes the ethical question of care, and its emergence as a practice of touch among the various bodies at stake in the case. These include not only those of the couple and their embryos (if those can indeed be considered bodies), but those of the surrogate or surrogates that would carry them to term, of the partner or partners who might also feel a loving connection to the children. Caregivers are necessary at every single stage of this reproductive endeavor: the nurses and doctors who assist in the IVF; those who will attend to the surrogate(s) during pregnancy, and immediately postpartum; the nannies and tutors and housekeepers who will surround children raised in privilege. And, in every instance of caregiving I have just listed, there are both profound practices of touch and complex technological imbrications.

Elemental Media and Container Technologies: Reimagining the Touch/Tech Divide

Technology and touch are not mutually exclusive categories, despite the common dichotomy between the warmth of skin-to-skin touch and the coldness of machine interface. I define technology as relational ordering practices that may or may not involve machines, logic boards, bodies, tools, information or electricity. John Durham Peters characterizes media as historically situated, taken-for-granted "agencies of order" inextricable from the human strategies of meaning-making that claim them as mere tools. Peters's model is one of interdetermination, wherein so-called "elemental" phenomena such as clouds or fire play crucial roles in human invention. Thus the car becomes a kind of holder and director of the fire of combustion, the clouds become a scrying glass through which people try to forecast the weather and better manipulate their plantings and harvests. In this model, then, touch is not a separate sense only attributed to the body, but one of many extensions of both humanity and the world around us. Peters writes extensively about dolphins, and their use of senses not available to humans. The dolphin may not use technology, but it has recourse to a mode of communication, sonar, that is only available to humans via technology. Moreover, that built-in sonar equips the dolphin to inhabit a world that humans may only penetrate through the use of machines to help us dive and breathe underwater. This example thus undermines the clear definition of a "natural" or "bodily" sense against a tool or a technology: sonar is neither natural nor technological, the undersea world neither a welcoming nor an alien environment (Peters, 2015).

Networks of all kinds play a big part in *The Marvelous Clouds*, both as infrastructure and as structures of feeling. Media are ordering technologies, rather than static objects or historical innovations. As such, media create relations between different entities, properties, bodies, and surfaces. Peters cites, the feminist media scholar Zoë Sofia, who asserts the importance of *containment* as a technological relation. Containment is a relationship of holding, or of creating space to be filled with something whose properties require that holding. Thus the liquidity of water and the hardness and impermeability of ceramic form a relationship expressed in the pitcher.

In their putative passivity, containment technologies are also associated with the feminine. Indeed, many containment technologies are in evidence in the home, from bowls and baskets and spoons to washtubs and bedsheets. Their holding, enveloping qualities are central to the practice of caring labor. Sofia cites Lewis Mumford's sociology of technology, noting the use of containers in labor like tanning, dying, cooking, brewing, gardening, milking, and so on. For Mumford, these activities all have to do with the vital processes of birth and decay, and are thus historically and sociologically feminine. In her critique of Mumford, Sofia moves past the feminist objection to this devaluation or effacement of women's traditional labor, and asserts merely that the container is a "structurally necessary but frequently unacknowledgeable precondition of becoming" (Sofia, 2000, p. 188). For Sofia, containment technologies create and maintain space, and are thus deliberately unobservable—though of course, take the bowl away, and the oatmeal spills on the table. "The analyst of container technologies," she writes, "must constantly work against the grain of the objects and spaces themselves—not to mention the ingrained social habit of taking for granted mum's space-maintaining labors—to bring to the foreground that which is designed to be in the background" (ibid.).

The womb is included in Sofia's survey of container technologies, in a move that complicates our understanding of the term "technology." Indeed, the uterus or womb is often rhetorically positioned as irreducibly embodied—as in pro-choice slogans that assert a woman's right to decide what to do with her own womb over and against claims to legislate its access to reproductive technologies such as contraception or abortion. Both sides of this question take for granted that the womb itself is a non-technological space: that it either should or should not have recourse to outside technologies to control its "natural" function. As Sofia points out, however, the womb is precisely equipped to make space and to hold—it is a relation of care, a "facilitating environment" that seamlessly provides nourishment and shelter. Yet she is quick to mention that both men and women's bodies have container technologies, from bladders and blood vessels to skin, mouth, and stomach. So the usefulness of choosing the womb as an exemplar of a container technology points to a feminist politics explicitly grounded in the material practice of care, as opposed to a purely discursive critique of gender and embodiment as cultural constructions.

I don't mean to suggest that there isn't a common sense way to distinguish between a crafted technological object and a natural body—a computer is not a baby, a giraffe is not a telephone—but that the closer and more carefully one looks, the more one sees technology in bodies and bodies in technology. This point is crucial for what we're talking about here, because reproductive technologies have such a dramatic impact on practices surrounding reproduction and childbirth. At the same time, I refuse to relinquish the assertion that this seemingly seismic shift in what it means to conceive and bear a child only highlights the crucial role technology has played in reproduction. Before the cesarean there was the birthing stool; before IVF there was the mistress, the second wife, the wife who secretly took a lover to conceive the child she knew her husband could not. Social practice and technologies are all inextricable from reproduction, and the dramatic innovations in ART only make it more obvious that childbirth was never only "natural."

Just as technology is not merely a matter of machines, so touch is not only a matter of skin-to-skin contact. Alison Kafer illustrates this point in her detailed return to Donna Haraway's cyborg in *Feminist Queer Crip*. Kafer shows that dismissing the cyborg as dated (usually in the sense of tritely postmodern) belies a certain ableist privilege. For Kafer, an adequately cripped[1] feminism must theorize the interactions between, for example, bodies and cochlear implants or prostheses or wheel chairs as something more nuanced than neutral support or prosthetic recuperation of a lack. Further, the "corrective" to this rhetoric of supplementarity all too often results in an image of disabled bodies as superhuman, both in their persistence and in their machine retoolings—the bionic woman is not a real person with legitimate claims to accessibility and accommodation. The feminist, queer, crip futures Kafer imagines understand technology as an integrated partner in the everydayness of negotiating certain bodies in certain spaces. Moreover, their affordances are not the only ones: helpers, partners, interpreters, and other allied bodies also co-create a feminist, queer, and crip futurity. For example, she discusses the ways that crip sexuality may often involve non-partner helpers such as aides in lifting, holding, and moving, thus exploding the construction of intimacy in touch as exclusive to the sexual partners. Crip bodies may also touch elements of the natural world in specific ways that require theorization and better accommodation. In her chapter subtitled "The environmental politics of disability," Kafer illustrates the ways in which the wilderness is often constructed as a no-access space to those whose bodies require technological supports. Moreover, pollution, climate change, and the destruction of habitat play an enormous role in the rise of chronic illness, cancer, autoimmune disorders, and chemical sensitivities, proving how interconnected human bodies are to the earth. Touch in this context becomes a multi-layered interaction between flesh and metals or plastics, flesh and built and lived environments, as well as the contact of flesh with flesh (Kafer, 2013).

Finally, to conclude this section laying out my definition of technology, I write toward a concept of media that is practice based. This means attending to the series of practices, processes, and articulations by means of which life is ordered. Therefore, when I ask about how touch fits into the context of media studies, I am actually asking about how practices of care articulate to technological processes. This conceptualization of media offers a way out of the common bind between media as technological objects and culture as a discursive practice that may or may not be determined by those objects (and their histories). Instead, we have a series of practices that may be discursive but may also involve tactile, material vectors such as touch. This inclusion of the material is crucial to a feminist media studies, because it allows for a body that is not *solely* discursively constructed while still attending to the ways in which discourse and ideology determine the affordances, significations, and legibility of different bodies (for more on the feminist problems of postmodernism see Chanter, 2001). In the next section of analysis, I turn to the radical feminist, ethical potentiality of touch as a crucial component in care labor.

Touch Matters: The Politics of Care

Attending to touch, particularly in its material role in care labor, undermines the patriarchal, white supremacist, capitalist hierarchies that relegate care to invisibility and undervaluation.

I start from the premise that in its current configuration, the social depends for its very existence on the exploitation and disavowal of care. Silvia Federici illustrates in *Caliban and the Witch* (2004) that primitive accumulation—the amassing of capital necessary to fund capitalism's continuing expansion—happens by means of the exploitation of women's work. This work, which she follows Marx in calling social reproduction (though her project explicitly critiques Marx's failure to adequately theorize the importance of social reproduction), includes everything from sex work to literal reproduction, to housework and the labors necessary to maintain, support, and shelter human life. Before the laborer can sell his labor power to the capitalist in exchange for a wage that barely supports him, he must be born, cared for, raised and socialized. And, someone must continue to care for the worker's body by preparing its food, keeping its living space clean and livable, and so on (Federici, 2004).

All of this is traditional "women's work," even if not exclusively done by women—and all of it is largely unpaid or underpaid. Hannah Arendt calls this kind of work *labor*, rather than *work*, so as to preserve the ancient Greek distinction between activities that maintain human life (labor), and activities that create lasting and tangible results in the world (work). For the Greeks, labor was linked to enslavement, such that the role of the enslaved person was to support the biological needs of the free man so that he could go into the world and make things (Arendt, 1998). It is consistent with this ancient but buried distinction that the people who do this kind of labor, worldwide, are overwhelmingly women and colonized populations—those enslaved by global capitalism's patterns of scarcity, value, and want.

So, for example, Rae Lessor Blumberg (1984) estimated that women produce about 50% of the world's subsistence food. Subsistence farming is labor, it produces no surplus, it only contributes to the biological sustenance of the household. Commercial farming, in that it produces surpluses and profits, would be work. In parts of the world—from India to Flint, Michigan—where potable water is a scarce resource, water fetching is women's work, or labor, to conserve Arendt's distinction. All of the daily, sustaining labors require water, from cooking to bathing to cleaning to animal care. Caring for the sick is labor in that it produces no monumental result except vitality—thus the overwhelming majority of hospital care workers in the United States are women, often immigrant women of color. Child care workers, hospice workers, nursing home workers, and adult daycare providers are all majority women of color engaged in the labor of keeping different bodies alive, clean, sheltered, and fed.

Sometimes the burden of oppression merely shifts to a different group made newly available by the pressures of globalization. In *Revolution at Point Zero*, Federici (2012) observes that the so-called liberation of white Western women depends upon the exploitation of immigrant women of color—the nannies and day care workers and house cleaners hired to perform the labor the working woman is not available to do. Surrogacy, too, falls into this category as a small but growing number of professional women freeze their eggs for future implantation in a surrogate, just as Vergara did. In this way, a woman may safely and indefinitely put off children in favor of career, as the egg once extracted retains its "youth" and the surrogate would be chosen based almost solely on her physical ableness. Because the surrogate bears no genetic relationship to the child she bears, immigrant women of color are often surrogates for the children of wealthy white couples—hetero or queer.

This shifting of burden also has an emotional vector because it involves the intimacies of touch and care. Ehrenreich and Hochschild's collection *Global*

Women documents the displaced care and affection that the children of these liberated Western women receive from their caregivers, who are often separated from their own children and, in their absence, lavish their charges with the kind of "as if they were her own" affection that anxious parents want—so long as it does not overstep the bounds of parental authority (Ehrenreich & Hochschild, 2004). Nannies and other household workers are thus ghostlike figures in the homes they work in, with intimate, tactile relationships that must be kept invisible so as not to disrupt the autonomy of the family as a biological and economic unit.

This ideological work is all the more difficult because of the contradiction between the devaluation of care labor and its absolutely irreducible necessity. No matter how crucial care is to the persistence of the human condition, in our historical moment (and indeed much of Western modernity), it is assigned little or no monetary value. It is not incentivized, to use the language of neoliberal economics. It does not count when gross national products are calculated, does not factor as a security or an asset, provides no collateral for a loan. Touch, then, emerges as a site of ideological resistance, a tactile, emotional, and ethical practice that defies the circuits of value invented to restrain it.

Any theoretical effort to excavate and re-inscribe the value of care labor is therefore an intersectionally feminist, anti-capitalist endeavor. I am exposing this contradiction by asking about what happens to touch in a networked society, under new technological and cultural conditions that, if anything, exacerbate the contradiction I describe.

Redrawing the Boundaries of Love: How the Surrogate Disrupts Family Autonomy

The nuclear family is the site of powerful contradictions between ideology and lived experiences. The ideology of the family coalesces around its *autonomy* as an economic unit and as a refuge from the outside world. In reality, families are not autonomous units but distributed networks of care labor, touch, and affective relationships. Effacement of certain kinds of touch and labor glosses over this contradiction (Wilson & Yochim, 2017). I will return to some specifics of the Loeb/Vergara embryo custody case to illustrate these points where they relate to caring touch. The previous sections have worked to excavate the mutual imbrications of the technological and the biological or elemental. In this section, I will run this theory through the example of the gestational surrogate, who plays a crucial yet complexly ideological role in the Loeb/Vergara embryo custody case. The entire question of the fate of the embryos relies on a surrogate, for if Loeb wants to bring them to term he will need one and Vergara is in essence denying him access to one by withdrawing her consent to gestate the embryos. At the same time, the legal discourse of the case constructs the surrogate as passive and nearly invisible, despite her deeply intimate, technologically complex relationship to the embryos. In focusing on the surrogate, then, I excavate a complex network of relations of touch, contact, technological couplings and legal definitions. Thus touch emerges as a hybrid site where caring practices are assembled out of a variety of materials, including skin, container technologies, legal discourse, and social construction of parenthood.

Gestational Surrogacy: Legal and Rhetorical Discourses Versus Practices of Touch

The best critical literature on the paid surrogacy market is Daisy Deomampo's ethnography on surrogacy in India, France Winddance Twine's sociology of surrogacy, *Outsourcing the Womb*, and Heather Jacobson's ethnography of surrogacy in the United States, *Labor of Love* (Deomampo, 2016; Twine, 2015; Jacobson, 2016). Generalizing from this literature, many surrogates are women of color, often but not always from the global South, who are paid a one-time fee to gestate other people's embryos. They are usually paid between $30,000 and $50,000 for their services, but there is no regulation of the market and practices vary widely. The standard contract does not usually contain a provision for life-long medical care, for example—only for care during the pregnancy, despite the fact that most women incur life-long consequences to their bodies from pregnancy.[2] The literature is clear that many of these women are horribly exploited—and that whatever care they get is dependent altogether on their role as the means of production for this most valuable commodity, human life. In the surrogate, then, we find the most literal example of *labor* in Arendt's sense: a punishing physical hardship undergone with no other result than a human life.

A standard gestational surrogacy contract binds three figures: the Surrogate, the Genetic Father, and the Intended Mother. The Surrogate is never referred to as the mother, so as to distinguish between her incubating role and a mother's role as caregiver. In this contract, the Intended Mother is the caregiver, if not the incubator. The surrogate's obligations of care relate solely to her gestational role, and thus interestingly challenge boundaries between self and other. In caring for herself, she cares for the child—yet the contract is written to construct the confines of the surrogate's body as neutral container.

Under "Duties of Surrogate," the contract stipulates that the Surrogate submit to all medical procedures deemed necessary by her obstetrician, and to amniocentesis if required by the Genetic Father and Intended Mother. She agrees "not to participate in dangerous sports or hazardous activities, and not to knowingly allow herself to be exposed to radiation toxic chemicals or communicable diseases." Further, "[t]he Surrogate agrees not to smoke any type of cigarettes, drink alcoholic beverages or excessive caffeinated beverages, or to use any illegal drugs, prescription or non-prescription drugs without the written consent of her physician and/or obstetrician" (Sample Gestational Surrogacy Agreement, n.d.). In following these requirements, the surrogate's everyday practices are reoriented toward the care of the fetus: though she may normally enjoy cigarettes or caffeine, for example, the surrogate gives these up as part of her contract with the Intended Mother and Genetic Father. Insofar as abstinence from cigarettes or caffeine is consistent with a Western notion of "health," the surrogate may be said to be caring for the child.

Now—as anyone who has been pregnant knows—even with cigarettes and alcohol, individual practice varies widely. Historically speaking, these are not universal practices: they vary, as do any other health norms, over time. There are also countless prohibitions based in folk custom—like, for example, that pregnant women should not go to cemeteries or should not come in contact with cats or should not rub their bellies too much—that while not part of medical discourse form strong behavioral norms for different subcultures that themselves evolve over time and from place to place. These interplays of convention, culture, and personal choice do not apply to the surrogate, who is following the directions given by the contractual Intended Mother and Genetic Father. If they deem consumption of soft cheeses a hazard to the pregnancy, or prefer that she not attend a funeral while carrying their child, she will have to comply with their wishes.[3]

But no one can legislate what happens in her body between her and the baby. In stipulating the terms of this relationship in narrow, medicalized terms, the contract marks its irreducibility. A baby's first sensible movements in utero are, in my experience, a fluttering feeling. It asserts itself to perception because it precisely is *alien*—it is the touch of an *other*, from the inside. It is unnerving, and it is emotionally powerful, no matter what one's relationship to the baby. To be clear: I do not mean to say that this kind of touch creates any particular *kind* of feeling, that it naturally produces a maternal feeling or sense of responsibility. I only mean that it is powerful, and powerfully private in the way that only bodily sensations can be. It resists communication, and it resists commodification (for more on the hard-to-define feeling between mother and child from a critical perspective, see Adrienne Rich, *Of Woman Born* (1995)).

Later on in pregnancy, the baby is even more of a separate presence inside the body. It wakes you at night because it is turning over, or it kicks you in the ribs. These are private moments of touch between two separate beings who inhabit the same skin. This is why an earlier age did not consider a pregnancy viable—"quick"—until movement could be sensed. It is the only haptic, experiential relationship one experiences in pregnancy: one cannot "make" the baby stop kicking at night, or predict when it will move. It is a trace of a separate subjectivity registered in the medium of touch.

Even as I assert the irreducibility of this tactile relationship, this embodied experience of absolute alterity—I want to just as quickly pivot to remind us that this relationship happens via technology as well. Ultrasound imaging, as well as the sound of the heartbeat, are technologically mediated traces that operate independently of the specific touch between the pregnant person and the child growing inside. Moreover, touch is an integral part of the deployment of these technologies: a technician smears conductive jelly on the pregnant belly and uses a rounded wand to press into it, seeking the right angle to capture measurements and anatomical checklists required for standard obstetric care. I remember my ultrasound technician chuckling in frustration at my "busy baby" who would not hold still so we could measure her, or who would not turn over so we could take a look at his face. All the while, she—and it is always, in my experience, a she—is pressing hard on my belly, trying to reach the baby inside but also asking me if I am ok, if she is hurting me. This is a crucial relationship of touch, and it drives right to the kernel of what we are trying to explore here to note that it is neither independent of technology nor reducible to the images produced as the endpoint of the technological intervention.

Moreover, in the case of the surrogate, her pregnancy is the result of complex technological manipulations. There has been an extraction of egg and sperm and an in vitro fertilization; these procedures often must be repeated many times before they "take." There may have been implantation of several embryos, and then a decision, after a successful implantation, to terminate one or more of the embryos because the Intended Mother and Genetic Father do not want multiples, or because bringing multiple embryos to term would entail dangerous complications. These technological relationships also entail their own networks of caring touch, as countless health care providers and technicians have handled, soothed, manipulated, and analyzed the bodies in question. What is interesting here, then, is the way that technology reveals a networked relationship of love and touch, even as the discursive, cultural context in which the surrogacy takes place strives to preserve family autonomy. I am arguing, therefore, that this autonomy of the nuclear family becomes all the more ideologically exigent when the relationships of touch are radically distributed by reproductive technologies. These technologies, in turn, highlight the tenuousness of the reproductive body's claim to pure, unmediated flesh.

The standard surrogacy contract uses language to police the boundaries of a networked self, restricting caring touch, contact, and love to only two parties: the Intended Mother and Genetic Father. The contract starts from the position of the primacy of the nuclear family, prohibiting the possibility that children may be born outside its confines, no matter what their genetic relationship to the birth mother. Some, but not all agencies require the surrogate to be married. Others require only that her spouse or partner undergo a blood/urine test and that he or she be "supportive." In either case, the partnership status of the surrogate becomes important, in part, from a rhetorical standpoint, to emphasize the disconnect between the surrogate's family and the one she is being paid to create.[4] Legal boundaries are drawn around the surrogate's partnership against contagion: literally, to assure that no ailment or condition such as HIV be passed from the surrogate's partner to the surrogate and then the baby, but also to establish the surrogate as belonging elsewhere, to someone else, and to seal the baby inside her body off from that elsewhere. The use of the term "Intended Mother" rhetorically highlights the primacy of intent over nature: the only Mother here is the Intended one, the one who will have a right to intimacy of touch with the child via practices of loving care.[5] In placing intent over incident, the contract places culture over nature: to be a mother requires intentional choice, not an accident of biology. Part of the reason for this hierarchy is that reproductive technologies have separated the person called mother from the person in whose body the fetus grows. Thus technology in this case actually falls on the disavowed, abject side with biology, and by extension with the special relationship of touch that the surrogate will by necessity have with the baby she gestates.

In contrast, the Genetic Father is identified purely by his biological relationship to the child. He does not need to be given the specialness of intent because his relationship to the child is not threatened by the use of reproductive technologies. Indeed, assuming that the Genetic Father is the partner of the Intended Mother, he bears the exact same biological relationship to the child that he would if his partner were bearing it.[6] It is not clear to me why the Genetic Father is not referred to as the Intended Father except to highlight that he has the biological relationship to the child, which has a legal bearing on his status. Indeed, if Vergara and Loeb had created the embryos using a sperm donor, it is doubtful he would have gotten as far as he has in overturning her wishes with regard to their gestation. The contract reifies paternity as a biological relationship, not a relationship of care. Attention to this reification reveals how selectively biological connection matters for the contract, and how carefully it must be negotiated: the Intended Mother's lack of biological connection is unimportant laid against her intent, while the Surrogate's deep physiological imbrication with the fetus is policed by extending that "intent" of care into the Surrogate's own body and behavior. Nevertheless, the *touch* relationship escapes this policing, revealing a site irreducible to either the legal construction of the family or the discursive ideological construction of the family as an autonomous and naturalized unit.

Conclusion

This speculative exploration of the relationship between the surrogate and the baby she cares for—if only briefly—recognizes touch as a primary nexus in the relationship between the body and technology. I have shown that touch falls prey to the general disavowal of women's work—the feminized care labor that creates life, and keeps it safe and thriving. I have also shown that technology, understood as an always-already intertwined relationship between object and practice, element and alloy, enables new forms of touch that present potential challenges to the hierarchy that relegates care labor and touch to mere animal striving. Gestational surrogacy, especially where it is legally contested, is a useful case study because of the complex ways that technological practices, biological functions, and various sorts of caring labor come together to create a distributed network of love.

It is important to recognize that what the surrogate is going through, as a pregnant person, is enormous. It is medically complex, emotionally and physically exhausting, and potentially very dangerous. My analysis has sought to begin the work of enfleshing and thus materially recognizing the surrogate as a part of this network of love, because to efface, ignore, or even legally restrict her role is to reinscribe the structures of oppression that win the happiness and privilege of the few at the cost of the suffering of many.

At the same time, attention to the surrogate complicates the assumed sacred relationship between mother and child. Recent years have seen an explosion of consumer products for expectant mothers, and an attendant explosion in discourse about what pregnant women should do, be, and want. To take the surrogate seriously is to acknowledge that there can be a relationship of touch that is both intimate and not exclusively maternal. To uncover these relationships is to honor and acknowledge the ties that bind queer families and other families of choice, as well as the communal relationships that undergird any family, whether we acknowledge them or not.

In this attempt to flesh out and make sensible the surrogate's relationship to the fetus without resorting to truisms about motherhood or misogynist ideas about a passive vessel, this analysis has highlighted the mutual determinations and articulations among technologies, discourses and rhetorics, and bodies. A further analysis would likely reveal the imbrication of spaces and environments, as well as the particular movements of time. Love emerges as distributed network that is not only technologically enabled but also grounded in material practices of touch. Boundaries between self and other, between mother and baby, between helper and needy one, are all blurred in the surrogacy relationship. It is my belief that attending to the various mediated practices of touch across multiple social spaces will yield similar results: a valorizing of the radically material yet technologically imbricated practices of care that are the literal condition of possibility for our being.

Notes

1 Much as queer theorists and activists have reclaimed the word "queer" from its pejorative context and redeployed it as a symbol of proud identification, so disability activists and scholars use the term "crip" or the verb form, "to crip." To crip, much like to queer, is to look at a textual or social formation that is not necessarily "about" disability and see it in terms of its relevance to disability, embodiment, and access. Not all disability scholars use the term; I use it here because Kafer does, and because I like it. It helps me, as a temporarily able-bodied person, to identify myself as an ally. For more on this issue, see Kafer (2013), and also Robert McRuer's *Crip Theory* (2006).
2 Some examples include: liver and kidney strain or damage, incontinence or fistula, high blood pressure, plantar fasciitis, and heart strain. Not all of these conditions would require treatment immediately postpartum, though some might, but all of them would emerge as problems later on in life. At least in the United States, surrogates are usually

cared for by their own doctors and deliver at their local hospitals, which means that their postnatal care and delivery conditions would likely reflect the socioeconomic inequalities present in non-surrogacy deliveries, with the only difference being that there would be perhaps an even greater pressure to prioritize the baby's health over the surrogate's.
3 It might be interesting to know whether and to what extent surrogates "cheat" on these instructions. I imagine there would be then an added risk wherein the surrogate would become liable for any complications in the pregnancy or health problems in the fetus. I do not know of any cases like this, which of course does not mean they do not exist or that among surrogates there is not a culture that plays with the line between contractual obligation and personal choice/cultural convention.
4 As I mentioned, the fee is about $30,000–50,000 in the United States, so a pretty low hourly wage for a year's work, which assuming the pregnancy took a few months to achieve and counting recovery time and lost wages for time spent at OB appointments or with complications, it could well be.
5 One of the things I have noticed, as a parent, is that one has almost infinite license with the bodies of one's own children, and they with yours. My children and I pat each other's bottoms and stroke each other's hair; I have had my mouth probed with tiny fingers and my nose, too. Part of being a parent is to have that license, and part of being a child is to negotiate it. Until a certain age, parents must clean up after children's toileting, must brush their teeth and hair, examine their skin for rashes or bruises, pry open their mouths to see if they have put something inside that could hurt them. One sign of maturity is being able to do such things for yourself, and thus having the right to prohibit others from this kind of intimate access to one's body. Similarly, I do not stroke my own mother's face and hair as I did as a child; these touches are reserved, if used at all, for special moments of intimacy.
6 If the Genetic Father is not in fact the partner of the Intended Mother, I am assuming that the contract would simply not list Genetic Father as Sperm Donor but could also include Intended Father as a legal entity.

References

Arendt, H. (1998). *The human condition*, 2nd ed. Chicago: University of Chicago Press.
Blumberg, R. L. (1984). A general theory of gender stratification. *Sociological Theory*, 2, 23–101. doi: 10.2307/223343
Chanter, T. (2001). The problematic normative assumptions of Heidegger's ontology. In N. J. Holland & P. Huntington (Eds.), *Feminist interpretations of Martin Heidegger* (pp. 73–108). University Park, PA: Pennsylvania State University Press.
Deomampo, D. (2016). *Transnational reproduction: Race, kinship, and commercial surrogacy in India*, rept ed. New York: NYU Press.
Ehrenreich, B., & Hochschild, A. R. (Eds.). (2004). *Global woman: Nannies, maids, and sex workers in the new economy*. New York: Holt Paperbacks.
Federici, S. (2004). *Caliban and the witch: Women, the body and primitive accumulation*. New York: Autonomedia.
Federici, S. (2012). *Revolution at point zero: Housework, reproduction, and feminist struggle*. Oakland, CA: PM Press.
Folbre, N. (2002). *The invisible heart: Economics and family values*. New York: New Press.

Heidegger, M. (2009). Bremen lectures: Insight into that which is. In G. Figal (Ed.), J. Veith (Trans.), *The Heidegger reader* (pp. 253–283). Bloomington and Indianapolis: University of Indiana Press.

Jacobson, H. (2016). *Labor of love: Gestational surrogacy and the work of making babies*. New Brunswick, NJ: Rutgers University Press.

Kafer, A. (2013). *Feminist, queer, crip*. Bloomington, IN: Indiana University Press.

Loeb, N. (2015). Opinion | Sofia Vergara's ex-fiancé: Our frozen embryos have a right to live. *New York Times*, April 29. www.nytimes.com/2015/04/30/opinion/sofiavergaras-ex-fiance-our-frozen-embryos-have-a-right-to-live.html

Mbembe, A. (2003). Necropolitics. *Public Culture*, 15(1), 11–40.

McRuer, R. (2006). *Crip theory: Cultural signs of queerness and disability*. New York: New York University Press.

Olya, G. (2015). Sofia Vergara responds to Nick Loeb's lawsuit. *People celebrity*, April 17 http://people.com/celebrity/sofia-vergara-responds-to-nick-loebs-lawsuit/

Peters, J. D. (2015). *The marvelous clouds: Toward a philosophy of elemental media*. Chicago: University of Chicago Press.

Rich, A. (1995). *Of woman born: Motherhood as experience and institution*. New York: W. W. Norton & Company.

Sample Gestational Surrogacy Agreement. (n.d.). www.allaboutsurrogacy.com/sample_contracts/GScontract1.htm

Sofia, Z. (2000). Container technologies. *Hypatia*, 15(2), 181–201. https://doi.org/10.1111/j.1527–2001.2000.tb00322.x

Staff, W. (2016a). Sofia Vergara's embryo lawsuit has taken a bitter turn. *Women in the world*, November 15 http://nytlive.nytimes.com/womenintheworld/2016/11/15/sofia-vergaras-embryo-lawsuit-has-taken-a-bitter-turn/

Staff, W. (2016b, December 7). Legal battle over Sofia Vergara's frozen embryos takes a very unusual turn. *Women in the world*, December 7. http://nytlive.nytimes.com/womenintheworld/2016/12/07/legal-battle-over-sofia-vergaras-frozen-embryos-takes-a-very-unusual-turn/

Twine, F. W. (2015). *Outsourcing the womb: Race, class and gestational surrogacy in a global market*, 2nd ed. New York: Routledge.

Wilson, J. A., & Yochim, E. C. (2017). *Mothering through precarity*. Durham and London: Duke University Press.

14

WHAT'S LOVE GOT TO DO WITH IT?

Shaka McGlotten

This chapter is a love letter dedicated to You.

Black Boxy

This love is a black box.

They know the inputs: a first encounter between student and professor, flirting, then the distances of time, then renewed proximity, then more.[1]

"I feel like we skipped a bunch of steps and ended up in a relationship," Sparky texts. The network provides endlessly varied means of communicating, a never-ending streak of texts, emojis, snaps, and early morning video chats. These are some of the sparks the lit the slow, slow burn, that lit up Sparky, that lit up Kit.

And they know the outputs: some kind of netting together, a bonding that sometimes feels like bondage, as when they began to become attached to the pings of social media applications—contact has been made![2] Or when troublesome jealousies arise, like when Sparky sends photos of the fancy apartment that belongs to the guy he was hooking up with. There's a framed photo of yet another beautiful young white man ("Aryan Nation poster child," Kit thinks ungraciously). Kit gets it too, these little pangs, like when they[3] stay mum about visiting G-Skillz, the twunk Sparky's been chasing forever, but who's more into Kit than him, and Sparky sees the date in Kit's calendar.

What's happening in the middle, in the black box (see Figure 14.1)? That's the point. Neither of them know. Maybe it could be named an "algorithmic-affective-somatic-technical-alchemy," at least that's what Kit imagines Paul Preciado might call it. Or maybe there's nothing, no box at all, just a formless void.

They agree on at least one other input, though: the willingness to enjoy transgressions, and the pleasures to be taken in them, like the charge that gathers

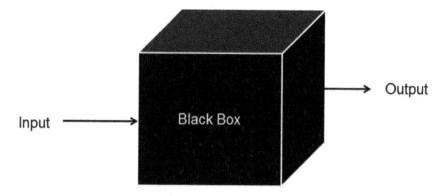

Internal behavior of the code is unknown

FIGURE 14.1 Love as a black box

around intergenerational or student–teacher relations, even though the little push that happened to draw them closer happened well after Sparky was Kit's student. Before the little push (a night in Venice after lessons and successes in cruising at a gay beach), when they still orbited one another as student and teacher, they tried to keep whatever nascent thing that was happening opaque, or at least foggy, to others, but people picked up on it, assumed they were fucking in the black box.[4] They weren't. Still, Kit panicked when one day they kissed Sparky on the lips in the quad.

The two of them agreed on an output too: transgressive inputs "unknown internal algorithms," a pedagogical encounter that made them more porous to one another. This porousness, mediated by love's black box, has, following Alexander Galloway, two expressions: cipher[5] and function. They try to look at the box. It's so mysterious! There's wondering, a wondering like you might have when looking awry at your closed laptop or the black mirror of your seemingly quiescent smartphone screen. *What exactly is happening in there?* And after the little push, when something opens up a little—when they admit to each other that this is love—the black box is "[s]played open, the box begs to be touched, it exists to be manipulated, to be *interfaced*" (Galloway, 2010, p. 239). One interface: when Sparky wakes Kit up in the middle of the night crying to tell them that he loved them. Another when Sparky closes his eyes and begins to kiss Kit with open lips.

Being interfaced is like being inhabited. Kit doesn't have a name for this genre of inhabitation other than love, but pedagogy comes close.

In the Graveyard, in the Wilds

A classic Tantric practice involves sitting in funeral grounds in the woods at night. Dead things all around, live things waiting to eat you. You confront it all, not to transcend it or get over things—Tantra isn't about transcendence—but so you can have a direct encounter with your own fear, the fear of your own impermanence.

A few years ago, Kit arrived at a meditation retreat buzzing with anxiety. Their teacher picked up on it right away, of course, and while part of Kit was pissed that she could see right through them, Kit still wanted her advice.

"So I should lean into my fear?" they tried to clarify over lunch.

"No," she said in her familiar tone, a mix of the gentle and the scolding and loving, "Just feel it."

Later, sitting, their heart pounding, their body trembling, Kit desperately wanted to get up and run out of the room.

These intimacies with students likewise frighten them with the threat of recognition, not just by punitive institutional admonitions, but also by their objects of attachment. Maybe they'll want to run out of the room too.

Thank the Goddess for Lauren Berlant

> Maybe I should say what I always say, which is that I propose love to involve a rhythm of an ambition and an intention to stay in sync, which is a lower bar than staying attuned, but still hard and awkward enough. The anxiety to define—a key feature of being in proximity to all magnetic ideas—especially cleaves to love, and so the conversion of a love into a properly political concept must induce attention to what to do with the freight the term ports with it: in this case, quite a huge dust ball.
>
> *(Berlant, 2011a, p. 683)*

It's a good thing Kit has Lauren because they get lost fast trying to talk about love. And, if you're reading this, sorry, but Kit can't imagine you not appreciating the awkwardness of permanently crushing out on people and wanting to sidle up to them and their ways of thinking through the world.

Love is Kit's melted heart. At the sight of a beloved's face. Or in gratitude for their friends' support when they call them on Skype so messy Kit keeps the light turned off. Or as devotion swells as they chant the names of the goddess and some small few of their tensions start to relax. Or just getting caught up looking at some trees blowing in the wind. Of course reading Rumi at the 4:30 am witching hour.

Kit promises to send Lauren pages from Tantric teacher Sally Kempton's *Awakening Shakti* (2013), comparing them to pages from Lauren Berlant's *Desire/Love* (2012). Expertly parsing Freud and Laplanche, Berlant writes about the ways the infant's loss of a love object, and its desire to "reclaim an impossible attachment," represents a "traumatic loss of continuity with the world [which] is the core motive for the formation of subjectivity" (Berlant, 2012, pp. 28–29). Kit never sent those pages from Kempton, but this is the basic view of suffering shared by most Buddhist and Hindu traditions, namely that painfully felt sense of apartness. "This basic skew toward separation, the veiling of our fundamental oneness, is the work of Shakti as Mahamaya—the great illusion. In that guise, she conceals her presence and the fundamental identity between you and the world" (Kempton, 2013, pp. 48–49).

Maybe thinking these things are connected is a delusion (in terms of Tantra) or fantasy (in terms of psychoanalysis). In either case, however, this thinking is creative. That feeling of separation can burst in ordinary moments as much as in the numinous ones we associate with falling in love.

So Kit deletes quotes from Rumi, and doesn't bother to look up ones they don't really remember from Shakespeare. A lot of song lyrics do come to mind though, like Beyoncé's *Crazy in Love* (the titular Tina Turner song comes later).

> You ready?
> Uh oh, uh oh, uh oh, oh, no, no
> Uh oh, uh oh, uh oh, oh, no, no
> Uh oh, uh oh, uh oh, oh, no, no
> Uh oh, uh oh, uh oh, oh, no, no

Is this love's "cruel optimism"? A worryingly powerful force we intuit might not be good for us even as we can't help getting danced by its rhythms (Berlant, 2011b).

Kit's friend emails them back during the heart-wrenching, heart-opening effort to align themselves again with an object of attachment: "good luck maintaining the aspiration to protect and expand the way you can stay in sync." Only much later does that "good luck" take on more ambivalent tones.

A Very Brief Introduction to Tantra

Kit knows what you're thinking, but it's not really about sex.[6]

Tantra is a technology that helps us to grow, to realize "that the world is filled with divine energy, with Shakti" (Kempton, 2013, p. 25). Shakti refers to dynamic, creative expressivity. In Tantric traditions Shakti is understood as a feminine principle; her masculine counterpoint is Shiva, who while, like Shakti, typically represented as a deity, also describes something that isn't embodied, namely continuous, undifferentiated Awareness. Shakti is the power that activates him, a reversal of many Western notions that understand gendered archetypes the other way around. Here, Shakti is power. Together Shakti and Shiva are Spanda, a pulsating dance of expansion and contraction, lightness and densification. Kit's teachers have also described Spanda as a cosmic game of hide and seek. Peek-a-boo! I see You!

"Another meaning of the word *tantra*," Kempton writes, "is weaving" (ibid., p. 29). Like the mesh of a net, Tantra weaves together consciousness and energy, reminding us that literally everything is divine.

The Intimate Matrix

Kit's spent more time in the intimate matrix than Sparky, but Sparky knows it too: Instagram, Snapchat, Grindr, Tindr, Feeld—Sparky casts a very broad net. So do his expert selfies.

Kit dedicated their earlier work to someone with whom they were deeply committed to staying in sync with. They still believe in the immanence of intimacy part.

During one last effort at reconciliation to that someone, Kit's teacher advised them to drop all expectations and just let Reality show up as it is. She urged them for the hundredth time to drop all the other stories they were telling themselves too, like wondering about their academic chops, or keeping spirituality out of it, or worrying about whether their writing style had calcified into a storytelling shtick about stories.

They thought they'd dropped their expectations, but Kit's still crushed when things don't work out. Again.

It's very likely that Kit doesn't know anything at all about intimacy, and their teacher said as much. They're not sure they agree with her, yet they can't help thinking about it as they grudgingly scroll through the hard-to-follow instructions for filing for a no-fault divorce.

In the not-too-distant past Kit understood intimacy as a structure, an assemblage of ideologies, institutional sites, and material and semiotic practices, as forces operating on, through, and in us.

Kit spends some time in the research for this chapter digging around citations of books that share their interest in affect in the network. In *Networked Affect* they find one—there's "love"! Except it's a reference to Heather Love's *Feeling Backward*, a citation that only reminds them that some failures, some losses, aren't recuperable.[7]

Against Love

Kit nods and chuckles to themselves on the U-Bahn in Berlin on the way to meet friends, the same ones who answer those freaking out calls, and who sit with them via Skype until they regain some composure and, often—gratitude to the Goddess!—a little humor.

They're re-reading Laura Kipnis's acerbic *Against Love* (2004).

Early on Kipnis warns her readers that the book is a polemic, so she's going to overstate her case against love. She's definitely talking to Kit: her point of entry into love is infidelity, "commitment's dark other" (2004, p. 13). Kit's too. Over the years infelicitous opportunities for infidelity multiplied online—chatrooms, cams, or websites devoted entirely to cheating, and then came all those fucking apps. Even their old school cruising during long walks in the woods or trips to the sauna were always mediated by instructions or reviews they found online.

Tapping fingers leading, if they got lucky, to fingering holes. (Kit wants you to know that that's one of Sparky's suggestions. So is the use of emojis.)

Kit first read chunks of Kipnis's book in a book store not long after a different break-up and, reading the book standing up, it was a balm for their grief. Not many weeks earlier Kit had been crying outside the Whole Foods next door with a friend, who didn't know what to do with them—she'd just wanted to show off her new puppy. Unprepared for a public breakdown, she called her brother-in-law and passed the phone to Kit.

Kipnis's efforts, like those of other feminist and queer theorists to whom Kit's thinking is especially indebted, focuses on unpacking love's formal structures. Indeed, Kipnis's polemic begins with this formal claim: "the sequence 'love-couple-marriage' . . . structure[s] prevailing social expectations, regardless of variations in individual practices" (2004, p. 15).

Kipnis admits that love is tied to feeling alive, but only rarely under the conditions of compulsory coupledom, what she calls the "domestic gulag"; one is more likely to find it in the utopian tumescences of adultery or its promise. Anthropologist Charles Lindholm makes a similar point when he outlines a brief history of love across cultures: one loves slaves, prostitutes, the daughters of enemies, but not one's spouse (Lindholm, 2006). Kipnis punctuates her account with *New Yorker* cartoons: "cartoon husband to cartoon wife at marriage counseling. Husband to therapist: 'No heroic measures'" (2004, p. 67).

Kipnis is sneaky though, as she closes her book on less strident note: like "cleave," "against" has two seemingly contradictory meanings. It means to be opposed to, but it also means to be alongside.

Over the years Kit has gotten to know some of these love critics, and not incidentally the ones who have taught them the most were all assigned female at birth. They realize that public declarations about love or intellectual workings through of love don't stop many of these folks from being committed to their own love relationships. And why should they? Kit learns as much through informal discussions with them about their own practices of relating, which are always tinged with wry self-awareness about their capacities for self-delusion and the many ambivalences that attend the couple form, or, for that matter, anarchic polyamory, which demands exponentially more communication, needs meeting, and reassuring.

Kit usually gets caught up by being earnest, or maybe just by getting caught up.

Pedagogies

In Daniel Odier's commentary on Stanza 5 of the *Spandakarika*, a classic Tantric text whose title he translates as the "Song of the Sacred Tremor," he writes about the relationship between teacher and disciple: "Abandon the hope that someone will pour over you the fine ambrosia considered in these texts; taste it as the source of your own heart. Fundamentally, there is neither master nor disciple, although there is sometimes a non-neurotic connection between two people who walk together in space. It can be said that this is love" (2005, p. 15).

Kit and their students aren't there yet. They are, however, learning something about love; their student–teacher relations became increasingly "mobile."

In "Pedagogy of Buddhism," Eve Sedgwick draws on an array of Buddhist texts to teach us about the intimacies of learning: "in this world it is as though relation *could only* be pedagogical—and for *that* reason, radically trans-individual" (2003, p. 160). This porousness is viral, and as with other viruses, Kit and their students sometimes try to immunize themselves against it (those lowered expectations again). At other times they chase it, unable to help themselves. For a while, Kit dispenses PrEP to G-Skillz, who by the way is another former student (imagine another see no evil monkey emoji here if you like). G-Skillz was visiting Kit and had forgotten his own supply. For a week or so both of them pop the little blue pill in the morning, an act made touchy by their attachments to one another. Kit wonders with whom G-Skillz might enjoy the pleasures of this inoculation.

G-Skillz knew that the professor has loved students before—and that they love teaching—but these particular kinds of intimacies, like sleep overs or sex or earnest declarations of non-attached love, were new for them. Those prior forms of love were, after all, still within the realm of reputable pedagogical practices.

Even now, five years after G-Skillz's graduation, it can feel dangerous. They both remember when tongues wagged when he was still a student. They left together after a *RuPaul's Drag Race* screening at another student's off-campus apartment. A few days later another student casually remarked, "I assumed you two went back to yours and fucked." "No, no," G-Skillz protested in vain.

"Yeah, right," came the response, "I'm sure lots of professors do it."

Former student and professor don't know anything about all that.

As a student, G-Skillz had tea and treats at Kit's apartment. He studied there to get away from home or the always too-chatty library. So did other students. Kit can be touchy—pats on the shoulder or light touches on a leg (when G-Skillz recounts this story, Kit makes a short-lived denial).

He always wanted a little more from Kit and confessed much later how brazenly he tried flirting with them. But Kit never made any kind of move. During an earlier visit, this time in Berlin in 2013, G-Skillz asked them to join him for a night out at the Kit Kat Klub, the space made famous by *Cabaret*, and where the late night crowd checks not only their coats but, often, the rest of their clothes at the door. Kit responded to the invitation with a polite, "Maybe later," accompanied with direct eye contact, knowing smile, and curious interest in the stories G-Skillz later told them about that night. G-Skillz had a sense then that his years' long crush might one day turn into something else.

Two years later Kit invited him to an event with lesbian artist and activist Sarah Schulman, who was speaking about her new book *Conflict is Not Abuse*, a challenge to some of those on the left who are increasingly looking to various forms of power to remedy their injuries.

At the reading, Kit introduced G-Skillz as a former student after unselfconsciously kissing him on the lips. In front of everyone! It made G-Skillz feel great, special. Maybe that's why he agreed to drive Schulman back to New York, even though he hates driving in the city. He drove white-knuckled, terrified of killing this important figure in queer art and politics. On the way Schulman sadly observed that some of the students were "really attached to their own victimization."

They finally do something.

During a recent visit to G-Skillz's place in Brooklyn, Kit buries themself in his scent, admitting they'd always been paying attention. "I could always smell you from across the room," they confess. Knowing this now, he's newly attuned to the ways Kit's attention gathers to him: nose first.

All the Feels

Sparky cuddles Kit on the couch. They're a little high. Sparky atypically plays big spoon as Kit, after doing a little "need to connect to myself" yoga, tries to keep their voice from breaking as they try to articulate something thirty-six hours into their chaste date day (holding hands in the park, seeing a movie, and lots of cuddling).

"What is this? What are we doing? I feel like we're in a genre of relating that I don't have a name for." All of this means something to Sparky too, but he feels awkward.

"What should I be feeling?" he wonders.

"Maybe Kit feels things more deeply than I do."

"What should I be doing right now?"

So he lattices his fingers through his former teacher's and just waits, a little embarrassed about all "the feels," but also recognizing in the moment that he can offer comfort to his friend.

Later Sparky texts Kit: "I got a lil upset leaving your place" (see Figure 14.2).

Kit observes in that moment of ambivalence and leakiness that they are both working on their respective projects: this essay and Sparky's new art projects. Sparky talks about what it's all about for him—it's a figuring out, albeit one that is incomplete and subject to revision.

Sparky has spent a lot of time in deep dives into the net looking for some idealized object, as well as for a community of belonging. Something lives underneath too, a hard to express vulnerability and fear of the vulnerable back and forth that comes with feeling connected, with all the tremoring feels.

Tremoring expresses itself as confusion, sadness, and comfort: waking in the night to one another's warmth, hazy memories of brushing lips against the nape of a neck. More tremoring later: morning wood and detached fondling.

> All the feels

(sent with Gentle Effect)

> What do you think of "NUDES; Queerness, Community, Loneliness, and Vulnerability"

That's an awesome title! 🖤🖤🖤

> Thanks you 😊

FIGURE 14.2   All the feels

Blue Heart/Blue Throat

Blue heart emojis mean "love you, thinking of you." Yet it's not that passionate red heart of romantic love. It's stable, though, built in trust. When Kit learned that this is how their husband saw their relationship—in contrast to Kit's "I've never not been in love with you"—another embarrassing public break down ensued. When they asked him later why he didn't say anything, he accused Kit of taking up all of the emotional oxygen.

When Sparky tells Kit nearly the same thing, Kit is a little disappointed, but also pleased. "Sparky loves me!" It was easier for Kit to adjust their expectations for what they might have or what their tremoring together might become than

Humans have long associated the feeling of love with their **heart**. The organ used to pump blood around the body. The symbol for Valentine's Day is a **heart**. A **blue heart** can symbolize a deep and stable love. Trust, harmony, peace and loyalty.

 Blue Heart Emoji (U+1F499/U+E32A) - iEmoji.com
www.iemoji.com/view/emoji/36/symbols/blue-heart

FIGURE 14.3   Blue heart emoji symbolizes a deep and stable love

doing the same for someone with whom Kit thought they were synced up with in red heart and diamond gem emoji love (see Figure 14.3). Plus there was the fact that Kit's own erotic desiring for Sparky has been a little come and go.

In a classic story about Shiva, a story the details of which are just too long to get into here, the Lord of Yoga ingests poison to save the world. In his throat he transmutes the substance into amrita, the nectar of immortality. In many stories, he doesn't do this on his own. His consort Parvati, another manifestation of Shakti, either enters or holds his throat to control the spread of the poison. His throat turns blue, and this is one of Shiva's many names—Neelkanth, the blue-throated one.

Attachments, we've all learned via therapeutic cultures, can be toxic. Transmuting those feels takes time, and often it's not just our throats that stay all kinds of blue. But other attachments can come along and keep the poison from spreading.

I'm Not Just a Node in the Network

In "Networks," Alexander Galloway identifies "two related but incompatible formal structures. On one side, the chain of triumph; on the other the web of ruin" (2010, p. 281). Using examples from the Greek tragedy *Agamemnon* in order to show that networks not only refer to contemporary technical infrastructures, ecologies, and systems of control, among others, he identifies the chain of triumph as "communicative and telepresent": it is made of pure energy (ibid.). It helps constitute rather than destroy reality (ibid.). The web of ruin is something else altogether, imagined as a destructive "swarm, or a pack of animals, unknowable in quantity and innumerable in form" (ibid.). The networked web of ruin dissolves order (Galloway, 2010, p. 282). Galloway's aims are political: networks represent and embody "real world power and control" and these two ways of understanding networks are just that, two glimpses into their diversity and inconsistencies.

Later in the essay he reproduces a famous image produced by Paul Baran at the Rand Corporation in 1964 visualizing three different kinds of networks: centralized, decentralized, and distributed (see Figure 14.4).

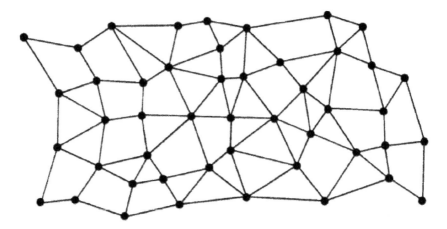

FIGURE 14.4 Distributed network

Kit teaches this essay to their students every year, spending a considerable amount of time unpacking the implications of each model. They follow Galloway's lead and talk about them in terms of power and control, their diverse expressions, and like many others, Kit favors the distributed network, continuing to imagine it is preferable, more democratic than the other models, even as they understand that it isn't. The distributed model is increasingly favored by every actor engaged in networks, high-tech industries, attention engineers, the military industrial complex, as well as hacktivist cells. This is Deleuze's "control society" (1992).

There is no network, however, without protocols, "the systems of material organization [that] structure relationships of bits and atoms in which they are embedded" (Galloway, 2010, p. 289).

Networks and the protocols that shape infrastructures, like formal accounts of love, are increasingly unsatisfying to Kit. They don't feel like a node in the network, and they aren't the only one. In "Contra-Internet" artist-theorist Zach Blas outlines ways of thinking against techniques of "protocological control and management" that flow in and through the net (2016, p. 4). Blas proposes to "transform 'the internet' in order to locate the potentialities of a militant alternative or outside to the totality the internet has become" (Blas, 2016, p. 4). One way to do this is to begin to think beyond the network, or at least the "nodocentrism" that dominates its conceptualization. Drawing on Ulises Ali Mejias's "paranode," Blas points to the limits of nodal thinking: lines connect dots, but what of the spaces between, "the negative space of networks, the noise between nodes and edges" (p. 6)? What's in there? An infinite number of other, invisible nodes? Where exactly are the insides and outsides of a network?

Rather than a node in the network, Kit feels more like a mess of tangled yarn. And with Sparky they fight against various protocols, like those that would seek to structure their relating.

Kit is wound up, fraying, and they can be knotted up to others (and vice versa). Beyond that they don't know much more about the protocols of yarn, just as they remain uncertain about the protocols for the hard-to-talk-about genres of relating—of love and pedagogy and spirituality—they are trying to stitch together here. The RAQS media collective offers some useful thoughts, although they are mostly talking about coding: "Fabrics, and stories, are made from yarn. A yarn is a snatch of reality that travels by word of mouth. Or it is shipped along with lots of html cargo. It is said that each fragment of code contains rumors and gossip, or yarns about the makers of the code" (2003, p. 365).

And Tim Ingold, in his book *Lines*, offers the "meshwork" as an alternative to the ways we understand the network "as a complex of interwoven points" (2007, p. 80). A meshwork, instead, is made up of the entangled lines of a life lived, of trails, threads, traces, rather than lines connecting points abstractly mapped onto the world.

The deep code of Kit's yarning is the desire to remember that they are never not connected.

Streaking

> Sitting in each other's fields, they feel a mutual tug in each other's direction.
> *(Barad, 2015, p. 395)*

In Karen Barad's stunning essay "Transmaterialities," she ties lightning and other queer science experiments to experiments in queer political imaginings. Like Mel Chen and Jane Bennet, among others; (Bennet, 2010; Chen, 2012), she is interested in matter's curious liveness, its "agential wanderings" (Barad, 2015, p. 387). Love, and everything that attends it, might, like all other mattering energies, possess its own agencies, lured toward us and moving in us according to its own curiosity, just like computational intelligences that seem increasingly attracted to human experience. This tugging goes both ways.

Sparky has a kind of breakthrough watching the new *Ghost in the Shell*. It's pretty, and the whitewashing doesn't bother Kit as much as it does others, but it definitely doesn't hold up to the original 1995 anime. Sparky realizes that, like cyborg heroine Major Kusanagi, his ghost is in the network. Here he is sitting in the theater holding hands with Kit, but he's also, simultaneously, elsewhere, his attention, his image, his identity spread out (like an unraveling ball of yarn, or to add another image, a mist—but not a node!). There he goes: bits of data, light(ning) bouncing off the walls of fiber optic cables, bits dis- and re-assembled between servers, algorithms scraping and repurposing his online activities. For all of their seeming intangibility, these energies are real: he's putting something out there, and it has an impact. Guys are saving his snaps or fapping to the videos he posted to the same secret Facebook group Kit used to belong to.

Later, Kit's attention piques after Sparky shares his reflections on the film, especially a comment he makes about how he understands differently the ways he's "putting energy in the network." Kit jumps in right away, commenting on the ways energy is a virtual mattering, simultaneously material and immaterial. They get wound up, like they used to do in class: bright eyes, fast talking. Kit lays it out. It goes something like this:

> There is a whole material chain of events that result in the devices we caress and disappear into: economic and political wrangling over resources, the extraction of those resources, the labor exploited to obtain them, and all of the violences that attend these processes, human and ecological alike.
>
> Chinese workers are jumping to their deaths literally sick to death of polishing iPads; Amazon employees are crawling on the floor to find the synthskin dildo you ordered, backs fucked from hustling miles back and forth in giant warehouses; global catastrophic climate change, just so we can get a meal or a trick delivered, or so I can snap my friends after walking into a glass door at that too-rare academic party that gets gloriously wild.
>
> Then there are all of these affective investments, like we wait for a text or write one, or all the shows we've binged: *Broad City*, *Luke Cage*, *AbFab*, Vogue Femme battles on YouTube; porn. Down the rabbithole we go!

Sparky waits patiently until they're spun out.
"Um, I don't think that's what I meant."
"Oh."
Kit has misrecognized the direction of this queer pedagogy again. It's Sparky's turn:
"It's more like I feel indebted. One, there's the day-to-day social media stuff that takes time. Two, there's the energy of sex and romance. It's like a build up of energy. You can try to get a community from afar, or look at it or join it. It's about how intimacy overlaps between these two things. There's something that pulls me in, something deeper. Like with Snapchat and Grindr, I have this need to check in even when I'm not responding or posting. I care what other people think" (see Figure 14.5).
"Does this feel like work?" Kit asks.
"People snap, and I feel like I need to participate, chat, read, go back," Sparky responds. He does this in spite of the fact that he knows about Stanford University's Persuasive Technology Lab which is devoted to using technology to change human behavior, which despite their efforts to positively spin their efforts, is also committed to finding means by which Sparky and Kit and everyone reading this essay and everyone else who's plugged in to keep coming back for more.
Sparky is invested in what is known in Snapchat lingo as "streaking." Streaking describes a process by which users of Snapchat seek to achieve an unbroken series of snaps—you post and reply daily for as long as you can. You can streak

FIGURE 14.5 The indebtedness of notifications

with your friends or sociable strangers. These posts can be relatively banal—you ate a burger, you walked into a glass wall, you jerked off again—and they can also be quite creative.[8] They can also lead to creepiness—to digging around the backend of things to find out more (too much) about these strangers, or to being too selfishly pushy: "send more nudes!"

Streaking is an ongoing burst of gamified relationality, one that solicits your attention and that you feel compelled to want to keep up with. "Don't break the streak! Show that your friendship is worth it" (WNYC, 2017). Our desires have never wholly been our own, but, like our attention, they are increasingly being engineered. #FOMO! "Habit formation is built into the design of the tool . . . They've maximized FOMO by design" (WNYC, 2017).

Recently Kit notices that the meditation app Headspace they unnecessarily downloaded after eight years of steady, app-free meditation practice is admonishing them to keep their streak going and to share their unbroken chain of practice with their friends on Facebook. They get gold stars if they do.

These are the moments of mutual tugging that Barad uses to describe fields of matter/energy, or the experiments lightning makes with itself. And they are the way machine zones attract us, put us in a flow that isn't going to go anywhere, just looping. We don't know what we're after, but we still want to continue (Schull, 2012).

Sparky and Kit have the conversation about *Ghost in the Shell* with the notifications on their phones turned off, one of the rules Kit lays down early on in their friendship—let's tug together as much as we can.

Sparky is animated while talking about his realization. Kit feels all the feels again as virtual traces of connections snap into the briefest incandescent flash. Kit is energy and light, and Sparky is luminous.

Self/Selfie

> Well, darling, just try to be little bit less Western in your thinking, if you can, please. I mean, you realize, of course, that in Zen terms everything in the universe is just molecules, don't you? Ying and yong, ping and pong . . . Mmm? You know that, darling? These are my molecules and that's your little clump of molecules over there, sweetie. I mean, in real terms, there's no difference between me and the coffee, me and the table, me and a tree, me and Madonna, for God's sake!
>
> (Edina Monsoon, "Fashion," *Absolutely Fabulous, 1992*)

In Tantra, Reality, the big "S" Self, is engaged in a cosmic dance of hide and seek, another way of understanding the pulsations of Spanda, the movements of Shakti and Shiva and, perhaps, the hide and seek of networked intimacies. This Self, your own Self, forgets itself. But even forgetting can also offer a kind of delight, just like the sublime ecstasies of heartbreak, or the building tension and release and repetition that takes shape as addiction. Forgetting's immanence is remembering your own innate goodness, your inherent divinity.

You know those times when you look in the mirror? Regardless of your age, shape, gender, race, you think you look really fine—that's not vanity, it's Reality delighting in itself, in the play of surfaces because after all there's you, your mirrored reflection, your feelings, and that fine ass, and all of it is made of the same stuff. It's more enjoyable than a night hugging the toilet after overindulging, but it's the same thing really.

Somehow though, in spite of knowing all this, and having moments of recognition (smiling in the mirror, hugging the toilet), Kit can't take a decent Selfie. So they turn to another differentiated expression of themself, Sparky, their new tech guru, to instruct them.

"How," Kit asks, exasperated, "do you hold the camera to get the right bits of your body in the frame and look so good?" Kit thinks Sparky's selfies are divine, though they do want to tell him that he doesn't always need the duck face sneer. "Relax your face," Kit wants to say, the same thing they say when they teach Sparky some basic meditation techniques to help him with his anxiety. "Don't stare, just smile." Kit lives for Sparky's unaffected, spontaneous, and very goofy grin. He doesn't need the pursed lips. Not with cheekbones that could cut glass.

Sparky promises to teach Kit some of his tricks, and eventually he does. And they joke about other kinds of tricks, like a fleshy human one they might share. It's the way they end up in a sexual scene together, and that's just fine.

On Not Ghosting

One way Sparky begins to demonstrate his love is by learning to be responsible to their friendship. After a year or so of texting and sexting, but never meeting for more than a cuddle, there was a conversation after dinner at a Mexican place when Kit did some needs expressing. They'd had enough with being haunted by emotional disappearing acts.

"If you want to be a friend, then be a friend. That means not ghosting me."

Present absences resonate with a key paradox in "non-dual" Tantra. Sure, non-dual, but compared to what? The non-dualisms' dualistic other itself establishes a duality. So later Tantrikas teased this out. Their upgrade was quantum: *bheda/abheda*, dual/non-dual. This means that we have real experiences of duality—it's not just something we're making up—even as there is an underlying sameness. It's like waves arising in expressions of differentiation from an endless expanse of water. They're different, yet made of the same stuff.

Sparky and Kit settle into new rhythms, but they never quite escape the in/determinacies of wanting/not wanting. Sure, they're always ready to get naked together, but they don't have sex (spoiler alert: eventually they do). Sparky knows Kit's still hurt by the absent presence of their ex. So he's afraid his own lack of lustiness might hurt them. Expectations rise and fall like waves. When Kit makes it clear that they've adjusted their expectations about the kind of relationship they might have, Sparky is disappointed in spite of his own ambivalence. Or maybe its ambivalence all the way down? After all, their jealousies, about that Aryan Nation poster child or that twunk, also somehow prove the existence of some other kind of non-Platonic feeling.

And what to make of their cuddle sessions? Kit rubs against him, Sparky pulls down his pants and opens his legs, Kit's hard cock finds its way between his thighs. It softens as they drift off together.

Remembering, making an effort, communicating are the everyday sorts of netting together that are usually framed as the "work" of relationships. Thankfully there's playfulness as well; there are other ways of netting together that don't feel laborious, like when Kit needed models to practice his Shibari, Japanese rope bondage. Sparky volunteered by sending a raised hand emoji (Figure 14.6).

FIGURE 14.6 Me please!

For a few weeks Sparky comes over for a few hours on afternoons when he's free, and while Kit watches the instructional videos he's downloaded from the course they took, Sparky's tied up (Figure 14.7). He remembers the dry gliding touch of fingers, the warmth of Kit's breathing body, and the hiss of the rope. It was meditative, as well as awkward, for both of them, except when Sparky

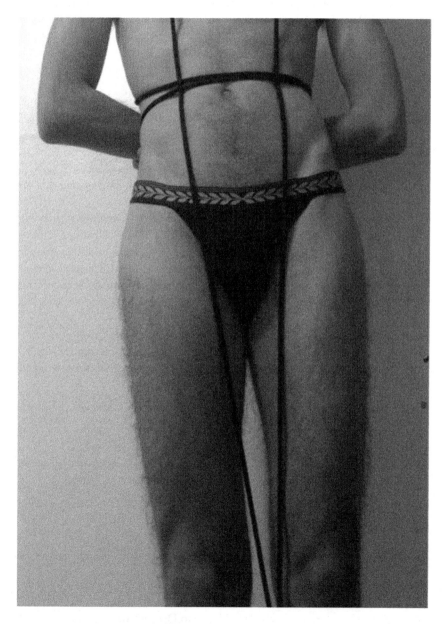

FIGURE 14.7 Not very good Shibari

caught on that Kit wasn't tying the knot correctly. Being sassy, he told Kit so, only to be met with raised eyebrow, pursed lips, and firm gaze.

After he's untied and the rope put away, they move to the couch and watch *Steven Universe*, a show about a boy with a rose quartz gem in his belly, inherited from his mother, who is, because her essence was in the gem, therefore also quite literally Steven (another way to say this is that Steven is an avatar of his mother, Rose Quartz). Steven lives with a group of female-shaped beings of light called the Crystal Gems, a group of renegade refuseniks. Together, Steven and the Crystal Gems protect their local town, Beach City, and by extension the Earth, from colonization by the leaders of the Gem's homeworld. Steven, Garnet, Amethyst, and Pearl form a queer family and dwell in the Obsidian temple, which is in the shape of a four-armed female deity. Kit says it's obviously a Hindu reference. This association is multiplied when gems fuse with one another, which they achieve by syncing up their differences through dance. When they come together, they form assemblages of their personalities into new beings. They are goddesses, multi-armed giantesses wielding magical weapons like Durga or Kali.

The looping lines of bonding and cuddling between Sparky and Kit are threaded through with other power plays too.

Usually when Sparky comes to Kit's place, he silences his phone. Of course, if Kit's not there, he doesn't bother; he needs his iPhone 7 "banky." Still he knows well enough to follow the other instructions: he takes off his underwear, puts on a jockstrap and a pair of nearly sheer basketball shorts Kit mopped from the laundry room, and does the dishes if there are any. Eventually Sparky brings Kit his banky and changes the privacy settings so that only Sparky can unlock it, a digital chastity belt.

"I need help," he says.

There is something soothing about dropping into subspace. Sparky's enjoyment of these kinky intergenerational games paradoxically diminishes the rough edges of their power dynamics.

"Thanks, Father."[9]

Kit was bossy as a professor too.

What's Love Got to Do With It?

> You must understand though the touch of your hand
> Makes my pulse react
> That it's only the thrill of boy meeting girl
> Opposites attract
> It's physical
> Only logical
> You must try to ignore that it means more than that
> Oooo
>
> *(Tina Turner,* What's Love Got to Do with It?*)*

In the titular "What's Love Got to Do With It?" Tina Turner describes love as a plaintive appeal and presubjective affective force. There's patterning as well: opposites attract, it's only logical.

This could be another title for this chapter, though one likely more difficult to sing: "There is no cure for ambivalence" (Berlant, 2011, p. 685). Turner wants her beloved to know what this love is doing to her, where she's been, and the fear she might go there again.

(Yeah, Kit's seen *Little Miss Sunshine*, and they have been thinking of their own protection.)

Who needs a heart when a heart can be broken? There's hope there, then, the hope that things might be otherwise.

Yet hope, Daniel Odier writes in his Introduction to the *Spandakarika*, is just another form of fear. He warns spiritual aspirants, that is, love aspirants, to "Rid yourself of all beliefs; leave metaphysics to the sectarians of the absurd; understand that hope is fear gone bad; confront reality directly" (Odier, 2005, p. xv).

For Sparky and Kit confronting reality directly means figuring out what part of their yarned out selves they can gather together. What kinds of energies need to be mobilized to confront their differences? There are differences between these two queers. Yet they're made of the same stuff too, and not just because they have resonant histories of traumatic daddy issues, expansive desirings, and inhabiting the net. Or investments in stitching some uncertain thing together. What do they dare hope for? Will they aim for being in sync or being attuned?

Confronting reality directly means that deconstructing the structural patterns of love—whether those of feminists, or by the common sense ones that view pedagogical or intergenerational intimacies skeptically (to say the least)—isn't sufficient. Abandoning hope means confronting the in/determinant fear of what might happen. Maybe their "patchwork [will] not be a sewing together of individual bits and pieces but a phenomenon that always already holds together, whose pattern of differentiating—entangling may not be recognized but is indeed re-membered" (Barad, 2015, p. 406). For Sparky he begins to commit to their weaving together a love, a life after seeing a photograph of Kit "innocent, hurt, vulnerable, young, beautiful."

In another classic Tantric text, the *Vijñāna Bhairava Tantra*, Bhairava (another name for Shiva) engages in a dialogue with his beloved counterpart, Bhairavi (his Shakti). Bhairavi already knows the answer to her questions, but still she asks her partner, who is her own self, what techniques to use to directly encounter him, that is his Heart, that is Reality. In the end a lot of it is about letting go.

The practice of Mahamudra, the Great Seal, is a letting go into emptiness, it's flow in free fall form, a relaxed experiencing of whatever is happening. Their efforts to knit a meshwork of some kind of co-present life together, one shaped in no small part by networked communication and the motilities of pedagogy, feels like free fall too.

In the video, Tina walks (a little jerkily, but those legs!) through the streets of 1980s New York City, coming across people, some of whom she draws in before pushing them away, others with whom she shares a brief groove. But she ends up walking on her own, longing, aggression, and joy pulsing in her song.

Oooo!

This is a love letter dedicated to You, my very own Heart.

Notes

1 Disavowals always risk evoking precisely the thing being denied. Bill Clinton's "I did not have sex with that woman" comes to mind. But here's one anyway. The intimacies described here are composites drawn from experiences that have taken place over many years, and they include real events and feelings, as well as fantasies and fictions. G-Skillz and Sparky provided their consent in allowing them to re-imagine these experiences and actively participated in the construction of this text. Hence Kit is not its sole author. Signing the essay anonymously gestures toward the multiplicities associated with the loosely knit group of the same name. It is also necessary given the contemporary climate of sexual paranoia in institutions of higher learning although these waves of paranoia are also a regular feature of American culture writ large. Again, just to be explicit (Anonymous is talking to you, Title IX officers, administrators, promotion committees, concerned parents, social justice warriors), Kit has never had sex with any student enrolled in any of his classes ever. That does not mean they think it is inherently wrong either.
2 Jodi Dean (2015, p. 90) makes the ways social media bind us explicit: applications "produce and circulate affect as a binding technique."
3 Yes, the pronouns are confusing! Here's how it works: Kit uses they/them pronouns and Sparky uses he/him. Confusions can be productive, so keep that in mind?
4 Galloway isn't talking about love, but politics. Drawing on an essay by the anarchist collective Tiqqun, he writes "Yet there is always a strategic obscurantism in their proscriptions, what Tiqqun calls here 'invisible revolt.' 'It is invisible because it is unpredictable to the eyes of the imperial system,' they write, lauding the virtues of mist and haze: 'Fog is the privileged vector of revolt . . . Fog makes revolt possible'" (2011, pp. 238–239). Given their many antecedents, the intimacies I describe here are not necessarily revolutionary—that would be a little melodramatic—but like the use of the Down Low by black and brown men, they do lead to worldings that are in and for these publics even as they may resist others.
5 Sparky wants readers to know that he's the one to teach Kit good digital security practices. Kit protests.
6 But isn't not about sex either. Tantra is often delineated into two major strands, the "right-handed" and "left-handed" paths. The former concerns itself largely with working toward Realization through a variety of techniques like visualization and mantra, while the latter works with various transgressive practices like eating meat, drinking alcohol, or sleeping with someone who isn't your spouse. In both strands, however, one is likely to find that sustained practice eventually loosens, or disorganizes, our

attachments to our identities, objects of desire, as well as our feelings of separateness. Sally Kempton (2013, pp. 25–54).
7 In her book Love "resist[s] the affirmative turn in queer studies to dwell on 'dark side' of modern queer representation" (2009, p. 4). She's interested in backward feelings, especially queer refusals to "get over it," as in melancholic attachment to one's losses.
8 A note to those over thirty-five: snaps are distinguished from media in other platforms because they disappear after a predetermined amount of time, although other users can screenshot an image—you'll receive a notification if they do. You can also save videos, though you have to be a bit savvier to do that. Increasingly, other social media applications like Instagram are also borrowing Snapchat's approach to drawing you in. Instagram stories, like those on Snapchat, disappear after twenty-four hours, thereby encouraging you to check your friends' posts more frequently.
9 They stop using "Daddy" after learning about how the artist Mark Bradford views the term as tinged with elements of sad exploitation. "Father" might sound creepier at first, or too patriarchal, but it also expresses elements of responsibility and respect. Anyway, who doesn't have Daddy, or Father, issues?

References

Barad, K. (2015). Transmaterialities: Trans*/matter/realities and queer political imaginings. *GLQ: A Journal of Lesbian and Gay Studies*, 21(2–3), 387–422. doi: 10.1215/10642684-2843239
Bennet, J. (2010). *Vibrant matter: A political ecology of things*. Durham, NC: Duke University Press.
Berlant, L. (2011a). A properly political concept of love. *Cultural Anthropology*, 26(4), 683–691.
Berlant, L. (2011b). *Cruel optimism*. Durham, NC: Duke University Press.
Berlant, L. (2012). *Desire/Love*. Brooklyn, NY: Punctum Books.
Blas, Z. (2016). Contra-Internet. *e-flux* 74. www.eflux.com/journal/74/59816/contra-internet/
Chen, M. (2012). *Animacies: Biopolitics, racial mattering, and queer affect*. Durham, NC: Duke University Press.
Dean, J. (2015). Affect and drive. In K. Hillis, S. Paasonen, & M. Petit (Eds.), *Networked affect* (pp. 89–100). Cambridge, MA: MIT Press.
Deleuze, G. (1992). Postscript on the societies of control. *October*, 59, 3–7.
Galloway, A. (2011). Black box, black bloc. In B. Noys (Ed.), *Communization and its discontents* (pp. 239–249). Wivenhoe: Autonomedia.
Galloway, A. (2010). Networks. In W. J. T. Mitchell, & M. Hansen (Eds.), *Critical terms for media studies* (pp. 280–296). Chicago: University of Chicago Press.
Ingold, T. (2007). *Lines: A brief history*. New York: Routledge.
Kempton, S. (2013). *Awakening Shakti: The transformative power of the goddesses of yoga*. Louisville, CO: Sound True.
Kipnis, L. (2004). *Against love: A polemic*. New York: Pantheon Books.
Lindholm, C. (2006). Romantic love and anthropology. *Etnofoor*, 10, 1–12.
Love, H. (2009). *Feeling backward*. Cambridge, MA: Harvard University Press.
Odier, D. (2005). *Yoga Spandakarika: The sacred texts at the origins of tantra*, trans. C. Frock. Rochester, VT: Inner Traditions.

RAQS Media Collective (2003). A concise lexicon of/for the digital commons. In J. Bagschi et al. (Eds.), *Sarai Reader 03: Shaping Technologies.* http://sarai.net/sarai-reader-03-shaping-technologies/
Schull, N. (2012). *Addiction by design.* Princeton: Princeton University Press.
Sedgwick, E. K. (2003). *Pedagogy of Buddhism: Touching feeling.* Durham, NC: Duke University Press.
WNYC (2017). Will you do a snapchat streak with me? *Note to Self*, March 8. www.wnyc.org/story/snapchat-ipo/

INDEX

Note: index entries in the form 200n3 refer to page and endnote numbers.

ABC model (acquaintance, build-up, continuation) 132, 133
ableism 194, 219
abuse 202–4, 206–7, 209, 211
accessibility 24, 26, 209
active communication 89
Actor–Partner Interdependence Model 102
actual/ideal self 138, 139
ACT UP movement 196
addiction 20–3, 245
advertising 113, 115, 120, 125, 160–1
affairs 174, 184–5
affect 1, 88, 198, 200n3
affirmation 194–6, 199
affordances approach 6, 37, 41, 95, 101, 209
Against Love (Kipnis) 234
agency 95, 115, 176, 180, 183, 186, 241
agential realism 183, 186
Ahmed, Sara 195, 196
AI *see* artificial intelligence
AIDS (acquired immune deficiency syndrome) 196
Ainsworth, M. D. S. 97
Albury, K. 159
algorithms: Ashley Madison bots 176, 186; attention capital 41; break-ups 113, 120, 125; love and connection 4, 7; online dating 6, 53–5, 58, 135, 139–40

alternative reproductive technologies (ART) 216, 217, 219
Altman, I. 129, 132, 135
The Ambivalent Internet (Milner) 209
American Academy of Pediatrics 86
angels 177, 178, 179, 180, 181
anonymity 37
antiretroviral therapy 166–7
anxiety 12, 69, 70, 100, 245
anxious attachment 69, 70, 74, 77, 79, 97, 98
Appignanesi, L. 118
Apple iMessage 122
apps 7, 156, 157, 160, 234
AR *see* augmented reality
archivability 209
Arendt, Hannah 4, 221, 223
ART *see* alternative reproductive technologies
artificial intelligence (AI) 145, 174, 178
Ashley Madison: "Ashley's Angels" 174, 177–9, 184, 186; guaranteed affair function 184–5; identity concealment 179–83; overview 7–8, 173–5, 185–6; synthetic situations 175–7
Asia-Pacific Coalition on Male Sexual Health 167
Ask.fm 37
assault 202, 203, 207, 208
assemblage 192

assessment signals 42
asynchronicity 68, 73–4, 75
attachment: anxiety 69, 70, 74, 77, 79, 97, 98; avoidance 67, 69–70, 79, 97–8; Berlant 232, 233; break-ups 118; relationship management 67, 69–70, 74, 79–80; subjective well-being 6, 90–1, 96, 97–9, 102; toxicity 239
attention 23, 40–2, 44, 120, 168–9, 244
attraction 136–9, 142, 161, 195
attractiveness 56, 138, 142
augmented reality (AR) 144, 145
authenticity 13, 42, 46, 176
authorship 14–15
autonomy 2–4, 80, 88, 217, 222–3
Avid Life Media 174, 180
avoidant attachment 67, 69–70, 79, 97–8
Awakening Shakti (Kempton) 232

backstalking 43, 44
Backstrom, L. 120
Bakardjieva, M. 181
Barabási, Albert-László 199
Barad, Karen 183, 241, 244
Baran, Paul 239
Bareback Realtime (BBRT) 165, 166, 171n7
Barkadjieva, Maria 177
Bauman, Z. 2, 3
Baumer, E. P. 35
Baxter, L. A. 145
Baym, Nancy 66, 191
Bazarova, N. N. 37, 94
/b/ board (4chan) 202, 207
BBRT *see* Bareback Realtime
beauty 192, 193, 195, 199
Bed Intruder meme 209
behavioral trace data 32, 33
Beijing Kunlun Tech Company 160
Bell, Alexander Graham 27
Benjamin, W. 123
Bennet, Jane 241
Berlant, Lauren 195, 198, 199, 232, 249
Berscheid, E. 139
Beyoncé 233
Bhairava 249
big data 125
biopolitical devices 7, 166–8, 169
Birnholtz, J. 37, 38
black box systems 54, 230–1
Blackhart, G. C. 146
#BlackLivesMatter 193
Black Mirror (TV show) 121, 122

#BlackOutDay: disruptive joy 198–9; dynamic unity 196–8; happiness and the affirmative 194–6; overview 8, 189–91; selfie politics 191–4
Blackwell, C. 51
Blas, Zach 240
blocking 114, 121, 162
Blued network 160
Blumberg, Rae Lessor 221
bodies 192, 213, 217, 218–20, 226–7, 228n5
Bollmer, Grant 178, 185
bonding 2, 4, 44, 89, 143
Bordowitz, Greg 196
Boshmaf, Y. 177
bots (Ashley Madison): "Ashley's Angels" 174, 177–9, 184, 186; guaranteed affair 184–5; identity concealment 179–83; overview 8, 173–5, 185–6; synthetic situations 175–7
Bowlby, J. 97
boyd, danah 29n3, 115, 123
Bradford, Mark 251n9
Brazil 191
The Breakup 2.0 (Gershon) 114
break-ups 113–25; against love 235; attachment 98; *Black Mirror* and fragmented digital 121–5; exhibited self and exhibited relation 114–16; Facebook 16, 20; love and social media 118–21; neoliberal self 16, 20, 24, 28, 29n5; online dating 145–7; overview 113–14; relationship management 62, 63; relationship models 132; world of networks 116–18
broadband internet 35
broadcast communication 89, 92, 95
broadcast mediated communication 63, 68–70, 79, 80
browsing behaviors 36, 45, 89
Bucher, Taina 181
Buddhism 232, 236
Bumble 54
Burge, J. D. 75
Burgess, J. 115
Burke, M. 45
Butler, Judith 114
Buzzfeed 193

calculative agency 166
Caliban and the Witch (Federici) 220
Callon, M. 156, 158, 166
cameras 121, 123

Canary, D. J. 66, 93
capitalism 27, 194, 214, 216, 220–2
capitalization 100–1
care: contested network of care 214–16; politics of care 220–2; surrogacy 227; touch/tech divide 219, 220; trauma and ethical sight 203, 211; why love matters 216, 217
caring labor 8, 213, 214, 218, 220–2, 226
Castells, M. 3
Castoriadis, C. 2
Caughlin, J. P. 39, 96
cell phones: channel navigation 32, 35, 36; Facebook 16, 19–23; neoliberal self 12, 15, 16, 19–23, 24–8; relationship management 77–8; well-being 96
Centers for Disease Control 167
centralized networks 239
chain of triumph 239
channel navigation 31–46; dyadic communication 33–7; future research directions 37–45; multi-channel approach 32–3; overview 5, 31–2, 45–6; relational media literacy 38–40; signals of relational investment 40–2; social information seeking 42–5
channel switching 34–5, 40, 42, 73
cheating 176, 186, 234
Chen, Mel 241
China 160
choice overload 54, 55
Choi, M. 65
Clark, M. S. 101
"clicktivism" 191
Clinton, Bill 250n1
close relationships: communication in 96–101; healthy social media use 87; interdependence of relationships 101–2; social media and well-being 90–1, 95; subjective well-being 102–3
CMC *see* computer-mediated communication
coding 241
Cody, M. J. 147
collective affirmation 190
collectivist cultures 138
Collins, N. L. 100
comments 32, 33, 41, 42, 43
commitment 70, 79, 80, 93, 134
commodification 134, 160, 224
commodity fetish 206
communication: Ashley Madison and social bots 179, 180, 181–2; in established close relationships 96–101; neoliberal self 15, 23, 24; patterns 88; processes 92–4; relational closeness 95; types 89
communication technologies: channel navigation 31; relationship management 62, 63, 71, 78; subjective well-being 86, 96, 103
communicative interdependence perspective 39, 96
compatibility 53, 135, 137, 161
computer-mediated communication (CMC): channel navigation 32, 33, 34, 35; subjective well-being 93; technologically enhanced dating 142, 146
conflict: channel navigation 34–5, 36, 38, 39; definition 71; dyadic media use 72; media use and conflict resolution 74–6; media use as source of conflict 76–8; relationship management 6, 63, 71–8, 79–80; subjective well-being 94
Conflict is Not Abuse (Schulman) 236–7
connection: break-ups 7, 113, 114, 119, 125; broadcast mediated communication 68–70; channel navigation 5–6, 35; definition 63; happiness 10; and love 4–10; relationship management 6, 63–70, 80; sexting 66–8; subjective well-being 86, 92; synthetic situations 175; trauma and ethical sight 8, 203
connectivity 113, 114, 119, 125, 175
consent 209, 215, 222
consumption 159, 160
contact 22–3, 28, 62
containment technologies 218, 219
contextualization 210–11
"Contra-Internet" (Blas) 240
Corriero, E. F. 57
couples 34–7, 63, 76, 133, 235
Cramer, H. 36
Crazy in Love (Beyoncé song) 233
"creeping" 43, 135
crip bodies 219–20, 227n1
Crip Theory (McRuer) 227n1
Cruel Optimism (Berlant) 195, 198, 233
cruising 156, 160, 162–5, 169, 234
culture 138, 139, 220
cyberstalking 123
cyborgs 219

Dai, C. 140
Dang-Xuan, L. 141
data leaks 173, 174

data traces 32, 33, 41
dating apps/sites: gay sexual marketplace 159, 160, 161; messaging 140–2; neoliberal self 16, 28; "the one" 133–4; online dating preferences 6, 135–40; online vs offline dating 133–5; profiles 6, 50–5, 57–9, 134–8, 141; relational closeness 92; relationship endings 145–7; relationship models and theories 129–33; social bots 173, 175; technologically enhanced dating 7, 140–7; transition from online to offline relationship 142–5; *see also* online dating; technologically enhanced dating
Davis, K. E. 131
Davis, Mark 170n4
deactivating social media 12, 16, 20, 22, 23
Dean, Jodi 250n2
death 115
decay 122, 218
decentralized networks 239
deception: messaging 141; online dating 6, 51–2, 57, 58, 137–8; photographs 137–8; social bots 7
deception consensus effect 57
deletion of content 122
Deleuze, G. 192, 200n4, 240
Deomampo, Daisy 223
depression 44, 45, 86, 100
desire 199, 232
Desire/Love (Berlant) 232
Diaz, F. 140
digital crowding 143
digital footprint 32
digital orality 5
Dijck, J. Van 181
DiMicco, J. 40
directed communication 89, 92, 95
disability 219, 227n1
Discipline and Punish (Foucault) 29n5
disclosure 37 *see also* self-disclosure
disconnection 7, 76, 125, 211
discovery phase of dating 50–1, 55–7, 58, 59
disengagement strategies 146
displaced persons 2–4
disruptive joy 8, 199
distributed networks 239, 240
divorce 9, 16
dolphins 218
Donath, J. S. 139
drunk dialing 12, 22
duality 245
Duran, R. L. 77

dutiful happiness 195
Dworkin, Andrea 205
dyadic communication 32, 33–7, 63
dyadic media 72–4, 78, 79
dyadic mediated communication 63, 64–6
dynamic unity 196–8

economy of qualities 164
Edison, Thomas 27
editability 68, 73, 95
education 14, 136
Eggan, Ferd 196
eHarmony 51, 53, 55, 133
Ehrenreich, B. 221–2
Elias, Norbert 113
Ellison, N. B. 41, 42, 44, 45, 123
email: channel navigation 36, 37, 39; dyadic media use 64, 72, 73; neoliberal self 16, 24–5, 26; online dating 56, 142, 146; passwords 24–5; well-being 96
embodied contact 73, 74
embodied presence 175–6, 185
embodied self 214
embodiment 203, 219
embryos 214–17, 222, 225, 226
Emery, L. F. 68
Emirbayer, M. 113
emojis 235, 238–9, 246
emoticons 26, 33
emotional flooding 73
empathy 203, 211
encoding love 119, 120, 122, 123, 124, 125
energy 242, 244
engagement with content 41, 42, 46, 95
engineering sociality 181
The Entire History of You (*Black Mirror* TV episode) 121, 122, 123
envy 45, 89
Epstein, R. 137
Ermahgerd meme 209–10
escapism 144, 145
ethical fabrication 199n2
ethical sight 209, 210
ethics of mediality 181, 183
everyday talk 66, 79
exhibited relation 7, 115, 116
exhibited self 7, 114, 115, 116
eyes 121, 122

Facebook: addiction 21, 22, 23; age of users 15–16; break-ups 116, 118–20, 122, 124–5; cell phones 15–16, 19–20, 21, 23; channel navigation 33, 35, 36, 39, 42, 44, 45, 46n1; deactivating 16, 20, 22;

Index 257

depression 45, 86; envy/jealousy 19, 45, 76–7; ethics 181; judging others 23–6; loneliness 4; mission statements 119; neoliberal and unmanageable self 12–16, 19–21, 23–6, 28; online dating 56, 135; People You May Know 181; relationship management 68, 69–70, 76, 79; stalking 12, 21–2; subjective well-being 89–90, 92–5, 98, 100, 102; Timeline 46n1; trauma and ethical sight 203, 204, 207
Faggots (Kramer) 170n1
false consensus bias 57
false information 51–2
family autonomy 217, 222–3, 225, 226
family relationships: love and touch 214, 217, 222–3, 225–7; roles and statuses 117; subjective well-being 90, 96
fantasy 144, 145, 177, 195, 233
farming 221
fear of missing out (FOMO) 45, 244
Federici, Silvia 220, 221
Feeling Backward (Love) 234
Feeney, B. C. 100
Felmlee, D. H. 139
feminism 214, 218, 219, 220, 222
Feminist Queer Crip (Kafer) 219
fetish 206, 207, 209, 210, 211
fetishized sight 210, 211
Filter Theory 131
Finkel, E. J. 53, 134
Fiore, A. T. 138, 139, 140, 142
first impressions 135, 137
flirting 6, 20, 23, 24, 77, 141, 207
flooding, emotional 73
Folbre, Nancy 214
FOMO (fear of missing out) 45, 244
Foucault, Michel 7, 14, 29n5, 158
4chan 202, 207
Fox, J. 69, 76, 135
Freeman, G. 191
friendships 39–40, 65, 92, 115, 117, 119, 147
Frisby, B. N. 72
Fulk, J. 38

Galloway, Alexander 231, 239, 240, 250n4
gaming 144, 244
Gaydar 157, 160, 164, 170n2, 170n4
gay sexual marketplace 156–71; biopolitical devices 166–8; configuration 159–61; HIV risk 164–6; overview 7, 156–9, 168–9; user profiles 161–4
gaystream apps/sites 160, 164, 165, 168
gaze 123, 206

Gehl, Robert W. 177, 181
gender: Ashley Madison bots 174, 177, 178; containment 219; contested network of care 216; exhibited self 114; online dating 52, 57, 136–8, 140, 142; relationship management 79; Tantra 233
generalized access 182, 183, 184
genetics 88
geolocation data 54, 157, 160, 161, 168
Gergen, Kenneth 2, 3, 4, 10n1
Gergle, D. 35, 36, 38, 39, 75
Germany 14
Gernsbacher, M. A. 144
Gershon, I. 114, 123
Geser, H. 146
gestational surrogacy 215, 222, 223–6
ghosting 114, 146, 245
Ghost in the Shell (film) 241, 244
Gibbs, J. L. 56
Giddens, A. 3
GIFs 209, 210
Gilman, Lisa 203, 204, 205
globalization 221
Global Women (Ehrenreich and Hochschild) 221–2
Goffman, E. 114
Google 56, 121
Gould, Deborah 196
Grindr 51, 57, 157, 160, 161, 170n1, 242
Guattari, F. 192, 200n4

habit formation 5, 36–7, 244
hacking 173
Hall, J. A. 66
halo effect 138
Hancock, J. T. 51, 52, 57, 100, 137, 138, 141, 143
handwriting 14, 15
happiness: #BlackOutDay and disruptive joy 190, 194–6; love and connection 5, 7–9; relationship management 69; subjective well-being 87, 103
haptics 213
Haraway, Donna 219
Hardey, M. 146
Haythornthwaite, C. 36, 96
Hazan, C. 103
Headspace app 244
health outcomes: gay sexual marketplace 168; subjective well-being 87, 96, 99, 100, 102, 103; surrogate pregnancy 224, 225, 227n2, 228n3
Healy, K. 117
Heidegger, M. 213

Heine, S. J. 139
Hess, Aaron 192, 194
Hinduism 232
Hinge app 51
Hirschkind, Charles 198
Hitsch, G. J. 55, 56, 136
HIV (human immunodeficiency virus) 164–7, 168, 169, 170–1, 225
Hochschild, A. R. 221–2
hookup apps/sites 156, 159, 160, 161, 165, 167
hope 249
horizontal attributes 136
Hornet app 160, 168
housework 220
Howell, Sean 168
human–robot relationships 144–5, 147
Hyperpersonal model 65, 79
hyperpersonal projections 65, 79, 123, 135

IBM 40
idealization 143, 144
ideal self 138, 139
identity: Ashley Madison bots 179–83, 186; #BlackOutDay 191; break-ups 114, 124; concealment 179–83; contextualization 210; online dating 50–2, 55, 57, 59, 147; performance 191; relationship models 133; self-reflexivity 3; well-being 87
Illouz, E. 159
IM *see* instant messaging
iMessage 144
"The Impact Team" 173
impression management 57, 58, 94, 116, 120, 135, 141
imprinting 15
impulsive self 23
impulsivity 20–4, 74
India 223
individualism 3, 138
individuated interaction 182, 184
infatuation 119
infidelity 74, 234
information 1, 13, 21–3, 27–8, 143
information-seeking behaviors 21, 42–5, 56–7, 134, 135
infra-action 8, 175, 186
Ingold, Tim 241
Insko, C. A. 138
Instagram 4, 40, 43, 135, 251n8
instant messaging (IM) 16, 72, 75, 100, 144, 146
intellectual property 27

intelligence 136, 138
interaction 181–2, 183, 184, 186
interdependence in relationships 101–2
International Journal of Communication 191
internet 35, 209, 210–11, 240
internet-enhanced self-disclosure hypothesis 92, 93, 94
interpersonal communication 31, 34, 38, 79–80
interpersonal dynamics 33, 36, 90, 138
intimacy: channel navigation 37, 42; commodification and commitment 135; connection and conflict 7–9; intimate matrix 234; love and touch 8, 213, 216, 220; online dating 135, 141, 143, 147; subjective well-being 87, 90, 95, 100
Intimacy Theory 131
intra-action 8, 183, 184, 185, 186
The Invisible Heart (Folbre) 214
in vitro fertilization (IVF) 215, 216, 217, 219, 225
Isaacs, E. 34

Jack'd app 160, 168
Jacobs, M. L. 36
Jacobson, Heather 223
jealousy 14, 19, 62, 76–9, 98, 230
Jiang, L. 100, 143
Joinson, A. N. 143
jokes 68, 206, 209, 210
joy 8, 194, 196, 199
judging others 23–7

Kafer, Alison 219, 220, 227n1
Keane, Webb 29n2
Kempton, Sally 232, 233, 251n6
Kerckhoff, A. C. 131
Kim, J. 115
Kipnis, Laura 234, 235
Kittler, Frederick 13, 14, 15, 19, 28, 29n1
Kleinberg, J. 120
Knapp, M. L. 132, 133, 145
Knorr Cetina, Karin 175
knowledge 44, 199
Know Your Status (KYS) program 168
Kocsor, F. 138
Kramer, Larry 170n1
Krämer, Sybille 180, 181
Krasnova, H. 78
Kreager, D. A. 136, 139, 140, 142

labor 8, 213, 214, 218, 220–2, 223, 226
Labor of Love (Jacobson) 223

language 141, 144
LaRose, R. 36
latent ties 40
Latour, B. 159
Leahy, B. 165, 166
leaked data 173, 174
learning 235–6
LeBlanc, Marc André 171n7
Ledbetter, A. M. 35, 102
Lee, J. 42
Lenhart, A. 146
Leonardi, P. M. 44, 45, 95
letter writing 14–15
Levinger, G. 132, 133
Lewallen, Scott 157
Lewandowski, G. W. 124
lies *see* lying
life satisfaction 88, 90
Light, Ben 173, 179, 180, 181, 184
lightning 241, 244
"likes" (Facebook) 32, 33, 41, 42, 43
limerence 119, 120
Lindholm, Charles 235
Lines (Ingold) 241
LinkedIn 39, 122
Lin, N. 40
liquid love 2, 4
literacy 14, 46
Little Miss Sunshine (film) 249
LiveJournal 122
Loeb, Nick 215, 216, 222, 226
loneliness 4, 10, 44, 45, 86
long-distance relationships 63, 64, 65, 94, 100, 143
longevity 87
love: against love 234–5; Ashley Madison bots 174; as black box 230–1; break-ups 118–21, 125; and connection 4–10; contested network of care 214–16; contextualization 211; information and sentiment 1–2; intimate matrix 234; judging others 24; liquid love 2, 4; meaning of 10; "the one" 133; online dating 133; politics of care 220–2; practices of touch 223–6; reimagining the touch/tech divide 217–20; relationship management 62; and social media 118–21; subjective well-being 88; and touch 213–28; what's love got to do with it? 230–51; why love matters 216–17
Love, Heather 194, 234, 251n7
lying 6, 52, 57, 58, 141, 146

machinic sociality 185
Madden, M. 146
Mahamudra (the Great Seal) 249
managed self 13
Manhunt 160, 164, 167
Mann, Steve 121
Marchant, Jason 167
marketing 159, 160
Markham, A. 199n2
Markowitz, D. M. 57
marriage 9, 90, 100, 102, 117–18, 133, 146
The Marvelous Clouds (Peters) 218
Marwick, A. E. 115
Marx, Karl 206, 220
mask of trolling 206
Massumi, Brian 196–7, 198, 199, 200n3, 200n4
Match.com 4, 133, 136
matching stage 50, 53–5, 57–8, 59, 135, 139–40
Mazer, J. P. 35
Mbembe, A. 214
McLuhan, M. 5, 46
McMahon, Darrin 195
McRuer, Robert 227n1
media 6, 133, 190, 213, 217, 218, 220
media ecologies 16, 28, 35, 39
media ideologies 15, 16, 18, 19, 26, 28, 38
media literacy 5, 35, 38–40
media multiplexity theory (MMT) 6, 36, 39, 92, 95–6
media richness theory 37
media studies 214, 220
media use 36, 72–8, 79, 80
meditation 244, 245
Mejias, Ulises Ali 240
Melcher, J. M. 124
memes 198, 207, 209–10
memories 46, 123, 124, 125
mental health 204, 205
Merkle, E. R. 146
Merton, R. K. 117
meshwork 241, 249
messaging 55–6, 140–2 *see also* instant messaging; texting
Meyer, S. R. 44, 45
Mierke, K. 138
Millership, James 174
Milner, Ryan M. 209, 210
mixed mode relationships 34
MMT *see* media multiplexity theory
mobile dating 50, 51, 54–5, 57, 58
mobile maintenance 66, 79

mobile media 64
mobile phones *see* cell phones
Mod, G. B. B. A. 68
monetization 168, 176, 195
monogamy 7, 147
Mothering Through Precarity (Wilson and Yochim) 217
movement 198
Mowlabocus, S. 160
Mukbang website 145, 147
multi-channel communication 32–7, 46
Mumford, Lewis 218
mundane communication 66, 93–4, 99
Murstein, B. I. 131
mutable self 3
MySpace 15, 29n3, 115

Nagy, Peter 174, 183
nannies 214, 217, 221, 222
narcissism 191, 192
Nayak, R. 139
Nazism 205
necropolitics 214
Neff, Gina 174, 183
negative emotions 52–3, 73, 78, 88
Nemer, D. 191
neoliberalism 12–13, 27, 195, 214, 217, 222
neoliberal self 12–29; Facebook and cell phones 15, 20; judging others 23–7; Kittler and technology 13–15; overview 5, 27–8; unmanageable self 12, 13
"netspeak" 141
network analysis 116
Networked Affect (Hillis et al.) 234
networked self: Ashley Madison and social bots 173–86; #BlackOutDay and disruptive joy 189–200; break-ups 113–25; channel navigation 31–46; and displaced persons 2–4; gay sexual marketplace 156–71; love and connection 4–10; love and touch 213–28; neoliberal self 12–29; online dating 50–9; overview 1–10; relationship management 62–80; subjective well-being 86–103; technologically enhanced dating 129–47; trauma, play and ethical sight 202–11; what's love got to do with it? 230–51
A Networked Self (Papacharissi) 199
networks 1, 116–18, 199, 218, 239–41
"Networks" (Galloway) 239
network society 114, 116, 117, 120, 121
neuroticism 74, 140, 146–7
Newitz, Annalee 174, 175, 176, 177, 180, 182

news sharing 41
New Yorker 235
niche theory 37
nodes 116, 117, 240, 241
noise 195, 198, 199
non-verbal cues 73, 74, 75, 91
Norton, M. I. 144
notes (Tumblr) 199n1
notifications 243, 244
NSFW ("not safe for work") selfies 192
nuclear family 214, 222, 225

ocular technology 121, 122
Odier, Daniel 235, 249
offline dating 133–7, 142–5, 175
Of Woman Born (Rich) 224
OkCupid 51, 53, 54, 141
"the one" 7, 133–4
Ong, W. J. 5, 46
Onion Model (Social Penetration Theory) 129–31
Online Buddies 160
online dating 50–9; discovery phase 55–7; love and connection 6, 7; matching stage 53–5; messaging 140–2; "the one" 133–4; online dating preferences 135–40; online vs offline dating 133–5; overview 50–1, 59; preferences 139–40; profiles 6, 50–3, 57–9, 134–8, 141; profile stage 51–3; relationship endings 145–7; social bots 173, 175; transition from online to offline relationship 142–5; trends and future directions 57–8; *see also* Ashley Madison; gay sexual marketplace; technologically enhanced dating
online gaming 144
online identity 50, 51, 52, 53, 57, 59
openness 119
opposite-attraction principle 139
oppression 194, 221
optimism 195, 196
organizational communication 38, 44
Outsourcing the Womb (Twine) 223
oversharing 76, 94

Pacifica Forum 205, 206
Pagliery, J. 176
Papp, L. M. 70, 76
paranode 240
paranoia 211, 250n1
parenthood 90, 97, 214, 215, 216
Parks, M. R. 34
participatory media 192

partners: idealization 65; perceived partner responsiveness 91, 96, 99–101, 102; preferences 36–7, 38; selection 54; surveillance 76, 77, 93, 98, 102
passive communication 89, 92, 95
passive SNS behavior 32, 44
passwords 24–5, 26
pastiche personality 3
Paul, A. 134, 146
pedagogies 235–7
"Pedagogy of Buddhism" (Sedgwick) 236
perceived partner responsiveness (PPR) 91, 96, 99–101, 102
performativity 114, 117
performed self 114, 115
personality 15, 39, 55, 58, 140, 161
person-centered messaging 100
personhood 215, 216
Peter, J. 94
Peters, John Durham 179, 180, 182, 184, 217, 218
Philippines 168
phobias 211
phone calls 26, 27, 33, 36, 98 *see also* cell phones
phone messaging *see* instant messaging; texting
phone numbers 20, 22, 36, 39
photographs: break-ups 122, 123; judging others 27; online dating 51, 52, 53, 137–8; relationship management 66–70, 76; sexting 66, 67; Snapchat streaking 241; subjective well-being 94, 98; *see also* selfies
phubbing (phone snubbing) 63, 77–8, 80
physical attraction 136–7, 138, 142, 161
physical health 87, 96
Pigmaster (founder of BBRT) 165, 166
platforms 4, 40, 42, 58, 120, 175
play 3, 7
PlentyofFish 53, 54, 136
political correctness 200n5
politics of care 220–2
polyamory 235
positive affect 88, 90, 101
positive psychology 195
postmodernism 220
PPR *see* perceived partner responsiveness
Preciado, Paul 230
pregnancy 213, 217, 223–5, 227, 228
prejudice 162
PREP (pre-exposure prophylaxis) 166, 168, 236
presence 98, 213

privacy 24–5, 27
privatization of care 214
problematization 7, 156–9, 162–5, 167, 169
processes 113, 117
profiles: cyberstalking 123; dating 57, 135–6; Facebook 19–20, 21; gay sexual marketplace 161–4; matching 50–1, 53–5; online dating 6, 50–5, 57–9, 134–8, 141; photographs 137–8, 141
profit 194, 195, 216
programmed sociality 181, 183, 185, 186
proximity maintenance 97, 98
psychoanalysis 233
psychological well-being 44, 87
PTSD (post-traumatic stress disorder) 211
public commitment theory 70, 80
public self-presentation 76, 78

QSoft 170n2
qualification 158
queer identity 189, 199, 219, 227, 241, 249
queer studies 9, 251n7
queer theory 194

Race, K. 159
Ramirez, A. 34, 43, 142
Ramos, D. 157
rape 202, 205, 208
RAQS media collective 241
RDM *see* Relational Development Model
read receipts 144
reciprocity 40, 41, 42
recommendation systems 139–40
reflexivity 3
Reis, H. T. 100, 101, 139
relational being 4
relational closeness 6, 36, 39, 87, 90, 91–6, 102
relational commitment 79, 93
Relational Development Model (RDM) 132, 133, 145
relational dialectics theory 80
relational maintenance behaviors 66, 92–4, 95, 98
relational media literacy 5, 38–40
relational satisfaction: channel navigation 39; relationship management 65, 67, 69, 77–8; subjective well-being 6, 90, 92, 93, 98, 102
relationship management 62–80; broadcast mediated communication 68–70; conflict 71–8; connection 63–70; dyadic mediated communication 64–6; overview 6, 62–3, 78–80; sexting 66–8

relationships: break-ups 7, 113, 115, 117, 118, 122; broadcasting 94; channel navigation 33–6, 39, 40–2, 46; endings 145–7; human-robot relationships 144–5; information and sentiment 1; interdependence 101–2; models and theories 129–33; neoliberal self 16–18, 19, 23, 28; online dating 50–9; quality 65, 67; relational being 4; subjective well-being 90–4; technologically enhanced dating 129, 144–7
relationshopping 53
representation 51, 52, 179
reproductive technology 215–17, 219, 225, 226
response presence 175, 185
responsiveness 91, 96, 99–101, 102
Revolution at Point Zero (Federici) 221
Rheingold, H. 41
Rich, Adrienne 224
Richardson, R. A. 146
risk 117, 166
robots 134, 144–5
Rodley, Chris 178, 185
roles 117, 118, 131
romantic love 6, 9, 62
romantic relationships 36–7, 62, 94, 97
Rosenfeld, M. J. 146
Rumi 232, 233

safe haven 97, 98, 99
Sampson, Tony 185
The Saturated Self (Gergen) 2
Schöendienst, V. 141
Schoenebeck, S. 44
Schooler, J. W. 124
Schulman, Sarah 236–7
Scissors, L. E. 35, 36, 38, 39, 72, 75
scopic media 175
scrolling 44, 89, 161, 193
Scruff app 167
search engines 43
Second Life 16
secure base 97, 98
security breaches 173
Sedgwick, Eve 236
see-and-screen format 53
selective self-presentation framework 68, 69, 79
self: contested network of care 215; exhibited self 7, 114, 115, 116; Facebook 19, 21; fragmented digital 124; gay sexual marketplace 161; impulsive self 21; managed self 13; neoliberal self 5, 12–29; noise and silence 199; online dating 59, 138; overview 2–5; performed self 114, 115; relationship models and theories 130; self as business 13; and selfies 191, 244, 245; unmanageable self 12–13, 23; *see also* networked self
self-actualization 2, 5
self-concept 124
self-control 23, 36
self-disclosure 65, 92–4, 100, 134–5, 141, 143
self-esteem 44, 69, 75, 139
self-fulfillment 2, 4, 5
selfhood 216
selfies: #BlackOutDay 8, 189, 190, 191–4, 196–8; intimate matrix 234; and self 191, 244, 245
self-monitoring 3, 39
self-presentation: gay sexual marketplace 159; online dating 50, 51–3, 57, 135, 137; relationship management 68, 69, 70, 76; self-reflexivity 3; technologically enhanced dating 137, 140, 141
self-references 52
self-reflexivity 3
self-representation 52, 115, 164
semiotics 29n2, 234
Senft, Theresa 191
senses 8, 218
sentiment 1, 10
separation 233
serosorting 164, 165, 171n7
sex 7, 161–3, 204, 233, 250n6
"Sexicindi" (bot) 180, 181, 185
sexting: attachment 98; relationship management 62, 63, 66–8, 79, 80; trauma and ethical sight 203, 207
sexual assault 203, 208
sexual disclosure 135
sexuality 37, 196, 219–20
sexual love 8, 213
sexual marketplace 7, 159
sexual networking 156–9, 160, 161–6, 167, 169
sexual paranoia 250n1
"sexual racism" 163, 170n3
sex work 220
Shakti 233, 239, 244, 249
Sharabi, L. L. 39, 96
shared media ecology 35
sharing: information 1; mundane moments 41, 93, 99; news 41; oversharing 76, 94;

passwords 24–5; photos 37, 41, 192, 193; positive emotions 100–1
Shaver, P. 103
Shiva 233, 239, 244, 249
sight 203–11
signals 43, 120, 121
silence 195, 198
similarity-attraction hypothesis 138–9
Simkhai, Joel 157, 158
SIPT *see* social information processing theory
SJWs (social justice warriors) 200n5
Skype 16
sleepwalking 185
Slotter, E. B. 124
smartphones 16, 35, 54, 98, 157
Smiley, M. 157
Snapchat: age of users 16; break-ups 114, 120, 122; channel navigation 37, 39; mundane communication 93; online to offline relationships 143; snaps 251n8; streaking 242, 244
SNSs *see* social network sites
social architecting 181
social bots (Ashley Madison): "Ashley's Angels" 174, 177–9, 184, 186; guaranteed affair 184–5; identity concealment 179–83; overview 8, 173, 175, 185–6; synthetic situations 175–7
social capital 40, 44, 89, 99
social constructionism 38
social information processing theory (SIPT) 38, 91
social information-seeking 42–5
sociality 3, 175, 181, 183–5, 186, 191
social justice warriors (SJWs) 200n5
social media: age of users 15–16; Ashley Madison and social bots 173–5, 181, 182, 185–6; bonding 2, 4; break-ups 114, 118–21, 123, 125; campaigns 198; channel navigation 40, 43, 45; deactivating 12, 16, 20, 22, 23; definition 88; energy 242; ethics of 181; frequency of use 92, 96; healthy social media use 86–7; jokes and memes 210; limiting time 86; monetization of feelings 195; online vs offline dating 134, 135; pathways to subjective well-being 90–101; relational closeness 91–6; self-reflexivity 3; and well-being 6, 88–90, 102–3
social network analysis 116
social networks 21, 116, 119, 159

social network sites (SNSs): attachment 98; break-ups 118, 119, 122, 123; channel navigation 32, 36, 40–2, 44, 45; passive SNS behavior 32, 44; relationship management 33, 62, 63, 68–70, 72, 76, 78, 79; *see also* Facebook; Snapchat; Twitter
Social Penetration Theory (SPT) 129–31, 132
social reproduction 220
social saturation 2–3, 4
social support 42, 87, 88, 99, 120
sociology of technology 218
Sofia, Zoë 218, 219
solidarity 194
somnambulism 185
sonar 218
Sosik, V. S. 94
source code 182
space of flows 3
Spanda 233, 244
Spandakarika 235, 249
speech 179, 198
Spence, Rob 121
Spotify 135
Sprecher, S. 146
SPT *see* Social Penetration Theory
Stafford, L. 66, 93
stage models: ABC model 132, 133; Relational Development Model 132, 133, 145; Social Penetration Theory 129–31, 32
stalking 12, 21–2, 43, 44, 123, 134
Stanford University Persuasive Technology Lab 242
status 117, 118, 124
stereographs 27
Steven Universe (TV show) 247
Stewart, Kathleen 200n3
Stimulus-Value-Role (SVR) theory 131
storytelling 3, 5, 234
strategic communication 93
"streaking" (Snapchat) 242, 244
stress 97, 98, 100
structures of feeling 8, 176, 185
stubborn negativity 194
students 15, 16, 68
subjective well-being (SWB) 86–103; communication in established close relationships 96–101; definition 87–8; interdependence of personal relationships 101–2; overview 6, 86–7, 102–3; pathways to SWB on social

media 90–101; relational closeness 91–6; social media and well-being 88–90
subjectivity 185, 191, 232
subsistence farming 221
suffering 232
support 42, 87, 88, 99, 120
surrogacy 213–17, 221, 222, 223–8
surveillance 45, 76–7, 89, 93, 98, 102
survivor narratives 202, 203
SVR *see* Stimulus-Value-Role theory
SWB *see* subjective well-being
swiping 54–5, 58, 134
symbiotic agency 183
symbolic signaling 37
synthetic situations 175, 184, 185, 186

Taiwan 168
Tandoc, E. C. 45
Tantra 231–2, 233, 235, 244, 245, 249, 250n6
Tarde, Gabriel 185
taste memories 124
Tatar, D. 75
Taylor, D. 129
teaching 235–6
technological affordances 6, 68, 95, 168
technologically enhanced dating 129–47; human–robot relationships, escapism and fantasy 144–5; messaging 140–2; "the one" 133–4; online dating preferences 135–40; online vs offline dating 133–5; overview 129, 147; relationship endings 145–7; relationship models and theories 129–33; transition from online to offline relationship 142–5
technologies of social saturation 2–3, 4
technology: channel navigation 35, 36, 38; definition 217; deletion of content 122; displaced persons 2; gay sexual marketplace 159; love and connection 4–5, 7, 9, 10; neoliberal self 12–15, 20, 22, 27–8; persuasive technology 242; relationship management 71, 72, 73–4; sociology of 218; technological affordances 6, 68, 95, 168; technologically enhanced dating 143–4, 146, 147; and touch 213–14, 217–20, 224, 225, 226
teenagers 102, 146
Telegram 122
telephone calls 26, 27, 33, 36, 98 *see also* cell phones

Tennov, D. 119
"test tube babies" *see* in vitro fertilization
texting: attachment 98; break-ups 16–19, 28, 122; channel navigation 33, 37, 39; judging others 24–6; neoliberal self 12, 16–19, 20, 22, 24–6, 28; relationship management 64, 65–8, 72, 74, 76–8; self-control 24–5; sexting 66–8
theory of the niche 37
This is Why We Can't Have Nice Things (Phillips) 202
Thomas, R. J. 146
Thomas Aquinas, Saint 179
ties 40, 44, 99, 191
Tiidenberg, Katrin 192
timeless time 3
Tinder 4, 37, 51, 54–5, 135, 136–7
Tiqqun collective 250n4
Toma, C. L. 52, 65, 137, 138
tone 26, 39
Tong, S. T. 55, 57, 98
touch 213–28; contested network of care 214–16; legal/rhetorical discourses vs practices of touch 223–6; overview 8–9, 213–14, 226–7; politics of care 220–2; reimagining the touch/tech divide 217–20; surrogacy and family autonomy 222–3; why love matters 216–17
touch screens 213
trace data 32, 33, 41
tracking 62, 182
"Transmaterialities" (Barad) 241
trans persons 115
trauma 210, 211
Treem, J. W. 95
trolling 202, 203, 205–7, 208–9, 210
Trump, Donald 203, 211
trust 25, 134, 138, 211
Tu, K. 140
Tumblr 122, 125, 189, 190, 192–5, 197, 199, 200n5
Turing test 182, 186
Turkle, S. 4
Turner, Tina 248–9, 250
T'von (Tumblr user) 189–90
Twine, France Winddance 223
Twitter 16, 114–15, 120, 122, 181, 189
typewriters 14–15, 29n1
Tyson, G. 136, 137, 141

ultrasound 224, 225
uncertainty 41–3, 57, 74, 102, 134, 135
Uncertainty Reduction Theory 43

unhappiness 194
United Man meme 210
unmanageable self 12, 13, 23
uses and gratifications theory 37

Valkenburg, P. M. 94
value 131, 216, 222
verbal overshadowing 124
Vergara, Sofia 214–15, 216, 217, 221, 222, 226
vertical attributes 136
video calls 35
Vijñāna Bhairava Tantra 249
violence 203, 206, 208, 209
virality 198
virtual reality (VR) 144, 145, 213
visibility 41, 42, 68–70, 95
vision 209
visual memories 124
visual technology 121, 122
Vitak, J. 41, 115
Vivienne, S. 115
voice calls 26, 27, 33, 36, 98
VR *see* virtual reality

Walther, J. B. 34, 98, 123
warrants 56
Washington Post 190
weak ties 40, 44, 99, 191
web-based dating 51, 53–4, 55, 56, 58
web of ruin 239
Wee, J. 42
Weeks, A. 41

well-being 6, 44–5, 86–90 *see also* subjective well-being
Westerman, D. 72
Wetzel, C. G. 138
WhatsApp 122, 144
"What's Love Got to Do with It?" (song) 248–9
White Christmas (*Black Mirror* TV episode) 121, 122
white nationalism 205
Whitty, M. T. 137, 142, 143
Wilde, Oscar 161
wilderness 220
Williams, Raymond 8, 176, 185
Wilson, Julie A. 217
wine tasting 124
withdrawal strategies 145, 146
Wohn, D. Y. 37, 38
womb 218–19
women's labor/work 218, 220–1, 223, 226
women's rights 219
world of networks 116–18
World of Warcraft 16
writing 14–15, 46

Xia, P. 137

yarn 240–1
Yochim, Emily Chivers 217

Zhang, S. 142
Zhao, X. 115